鳥 山 明

The nice, warm spring was just around the corner,
when my kids suddenly asked me to take them skiing.
As I've written before, I really hate the cold, so I've
been dreading those words. I can't believe people go
out of their way to go to cold places...but I like sports,
so I'll give it a try. I'll probably have a cold by the time
this book comes out...

—*Akira Toriyama, 1994*

Widely known all over the world for his playful, innovative
storytelling and humorous, distinctive art style, **Dragon Ball**
creator Akira Toriyama is also known in his native Japan for
the wildly popular **Dr. Slump**, his previous manga series
about the adventures of a mad scientist and his android
"daughter." His hit series **Dragon Ball** ran from 1984 to
1995 in Shueisha's **Weekly Shonen Jump** magazine. He is
also known for his design work on video games such as
Dragon Warrior, **Chrono Trigger** and **Tobal No. 1**. His
recent manga works include **Cowa!**, **Kajika**, **Sand Land**,
Neko Majin, and a children's book, **Toccio the Angel**. He
lives with his family in Japan.

DRAGON BALL Z VOL. 21
SHONEN JUMP Manga Edition

STORY AND ART BY
AKIRA TORIYAMA

English Adaptation/Gerard Jones
Translation/Lillian Olsen
Touch-up Art & Lettering/Wayne Truman
Design/Sean Lee
Editor/Jason Thompson

DRAGON BALL © 1984 by BIRD STUDIO. All rights reserved. First
published in Japan in 1984 by SHUEISHA Inc., Tokyo. English translation
rights arranged by SHUEISHA Inc.

Some art has been modified from the original Japanese edition.

In the original Japanese edition, DRAGON BALL and DRAGON BALL Z
are known collectively as the 42-volume series DRAGON BALL. The
English DRAGON BALL Z was originally volumes 17–42 of the Japanese
DRAGON BALL.

Printed in the U.S.A.

Published by VIZ Media, LLC
P.O. Box 77010
San Francisco, CA 94107

11
First printing, July 2005
Eleventh printing, January 2019

SHONEN JUMP MANGA

DRAGON BALL Z

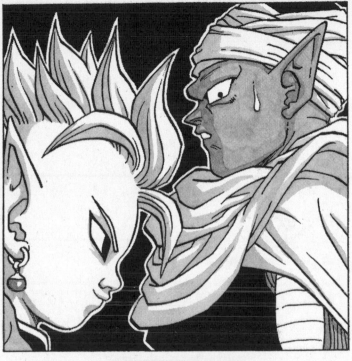

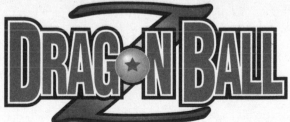

Vol. 21

DB: 37 of 42

STORY AND ART BY
AKIRA TORIYAMA

THE MAIN CHARACTERS

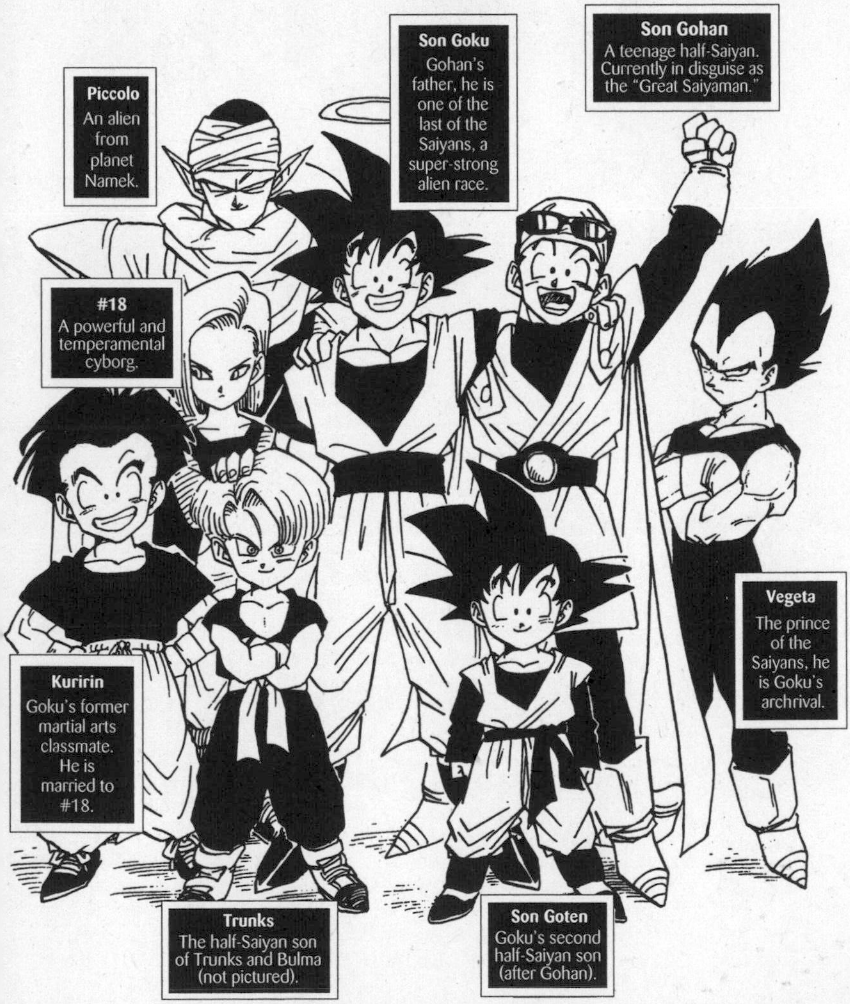
Son Gohan
A teenage half-Saiyan. Currently in disguise as the "Great Saiyaman."
Son Goku
Gohan's father, he is one of the last of the Saiyans, a super-strong alien race.
Piccolo
An alien from planet Namek.
#18
A powerful and temperamental cyborg.
Vegeta
The prince of the Saiyans, he is Goku's archrival.
Kuririn
Goku's former martial arts classmate. He is married to #18.
Son Goten
Goku's second half-Saiyan son (after Gohan).
Trunks
The half-Saiyan son of Trunks and Bulma (not pictured).

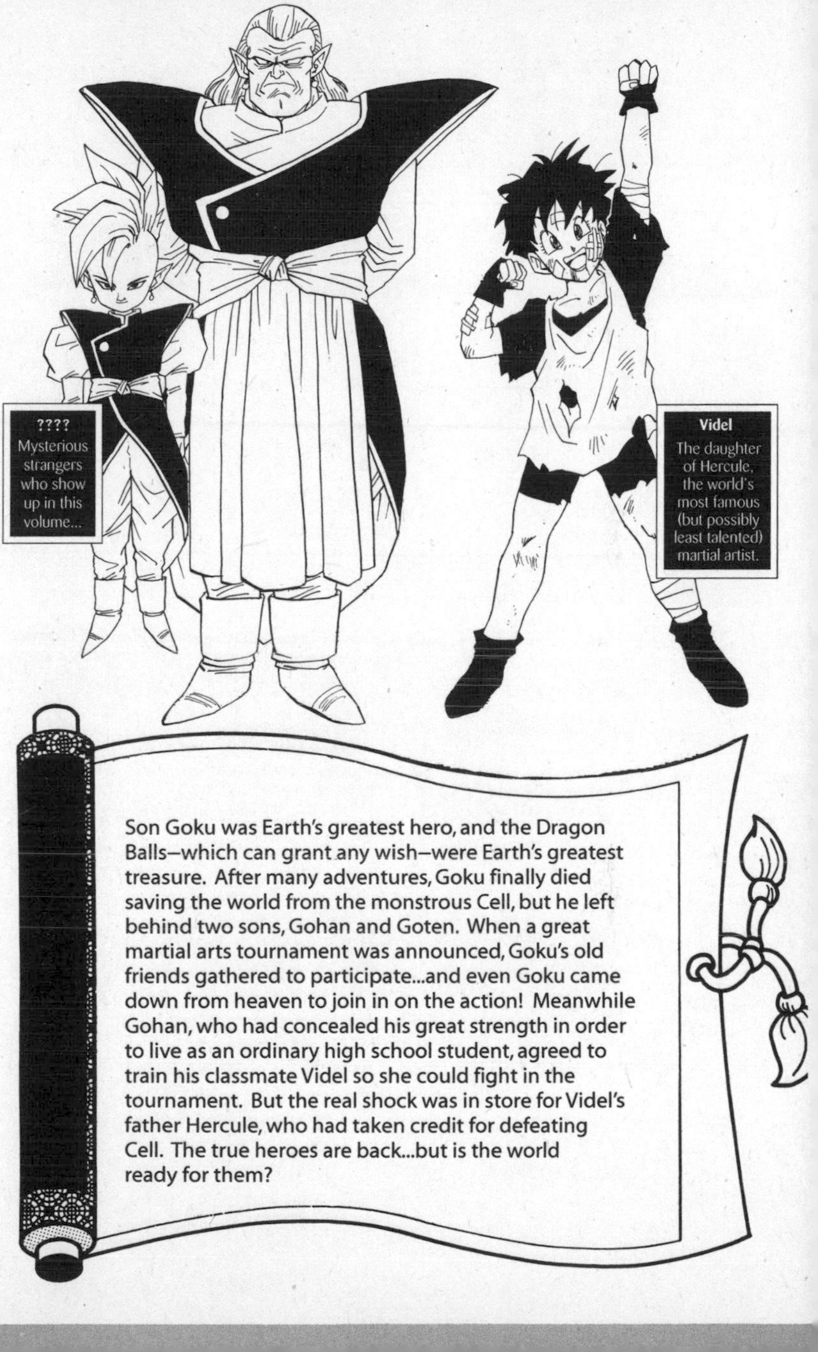
????
Mysterious strangers who show up in this volume...
Videl
The daughter of Hercule, the world's most famous (but possibly least talented) martial artist.

Son Goku was Earth's greatest hero, and the Dragon Balls—which can grant any wish—were Earth's greatest treasure. After many adventures, Goku finally died saving the world from the monstrous Cell, but he left behind two sons, Gohan and Goten. When a great martial arts tournament was announced, Goku's old friends gathered to participate...and even Goku came down from heaven to join in on the action! Meanwhile Gohan, who had concealed his great strength in order to live as an ordinary high school student, agreed to train his classmate Videl so she could fight in the tournament. But the real shock was in store for Videl's father Hercule, who had taken credit for defeating Cell. The true heroes are back...but is the world ready for them?

DRAGON BALL Z 21

CONTENTS

DRAGON BALL ドラゴンボール

DBZ:239 · Trunks vs. Goten

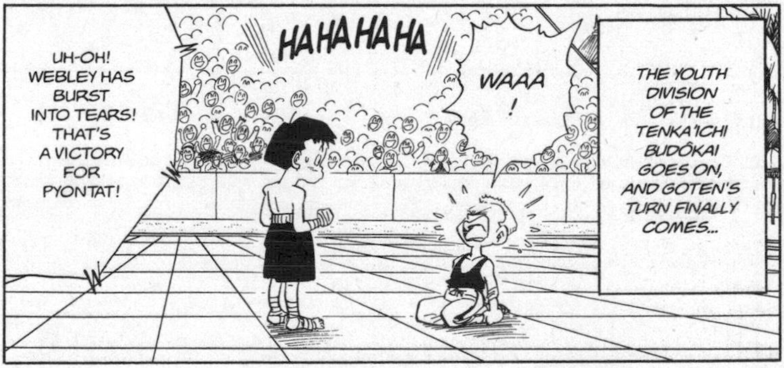
THE YOUTH DIVISION OF THE TENKA'ICHI BUDÔKAI GOES ON, AND GOTEN'S TURN FINALLY COMES...
WAAA!
HAHAHAHA
UH-OH! WEBLEY HAS BURST INTO TEARS! THAT'S A VICTORY FOR PYONTAT!

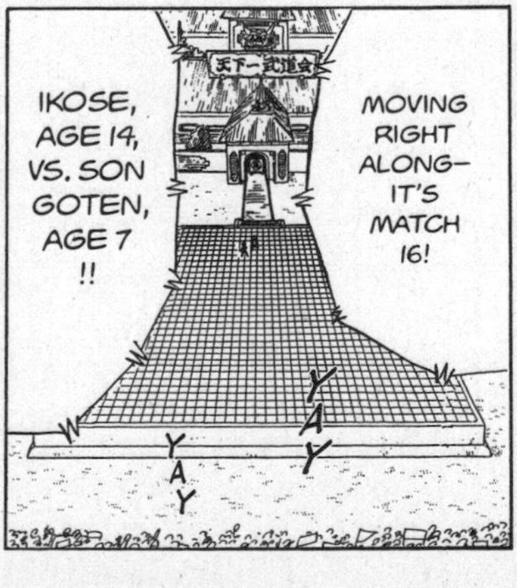
天下一武道会
MOVING RIGHT ALONG— IT'S MATCH 16!
IKOSE, AGE 14, VS. SON GOTEN, AGE 7 !!
YAY
YAY
YAY

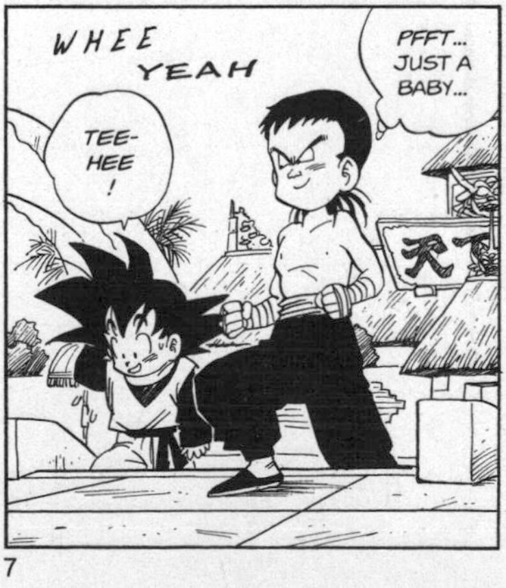
PFFT... JUST A BABY...
WHEE
YEAH
TEE-HEE!
天

READ THIS WAY

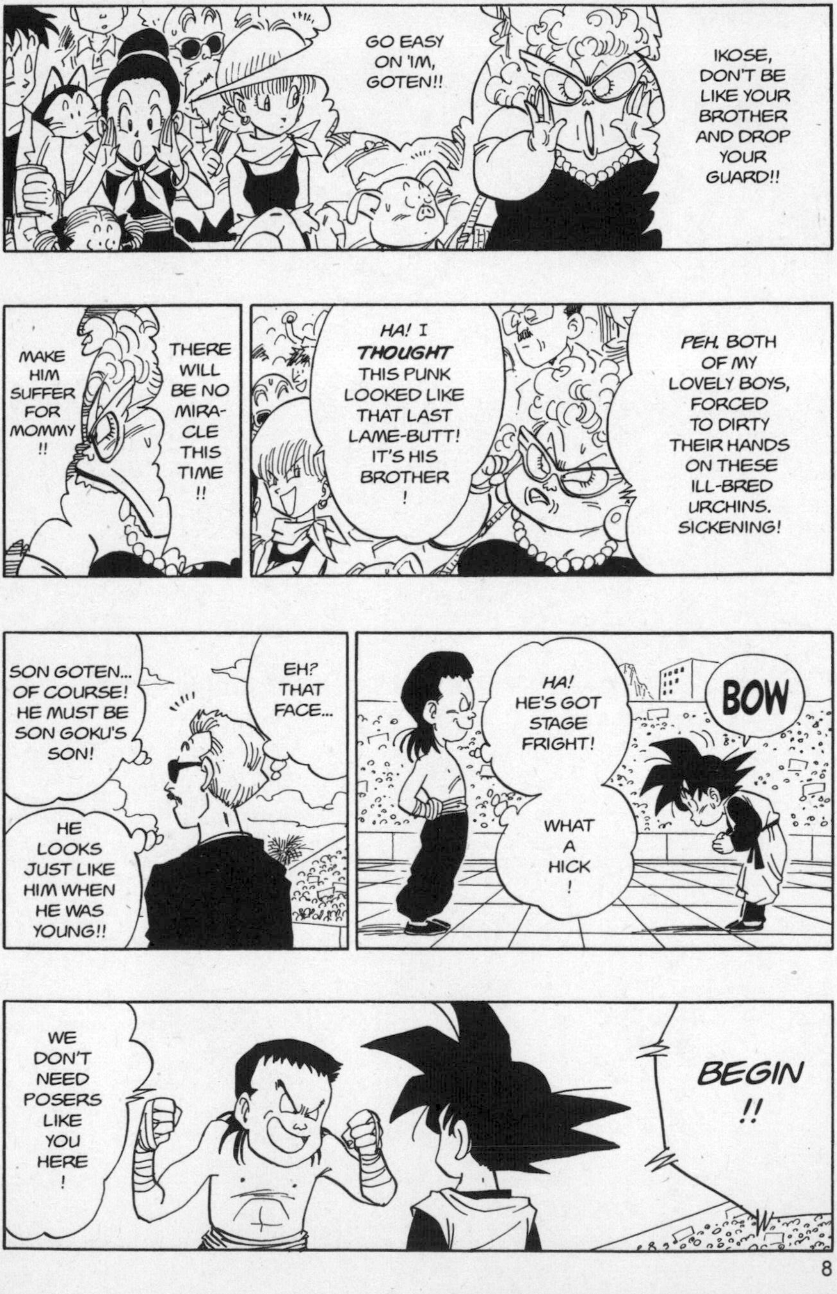
IKOSE, DON'T BE LIKE YOUR BROTHER AND DROP YOUR GUARD!!
GO EASY ON 'IM, GOTEN!!
PEH. BOTH OF MY LOVELY BOYS, FORCED TO DIRTY THEIR HANDS ON THESE ILL-BRED URCHINS. SICKENING!
HA! I **THOUGHT** THIS PUNK LOOKED LIKE THAT LAST LAME-BUTT! IT'S HIS BROTHER!
THERE WILL BE NO MIRACLE THIS TIME!!
MAKE HIM SUFFER FOR MOMMY!!
BOW
HA! HE'S GOT STAGE FRIGHT!
WHAT A HICK!
EH? THAT FACE...
SON GOTEN... OF COURSE! HE MUST BE SON GOKU'S SON!
HE LOOKS JUST LIKE HIM WHEN HE WAS YOUNG!!
BEGIN!!
WE DON'T NEED POSERS LIKE YOU HERE!

READ THIS WAY

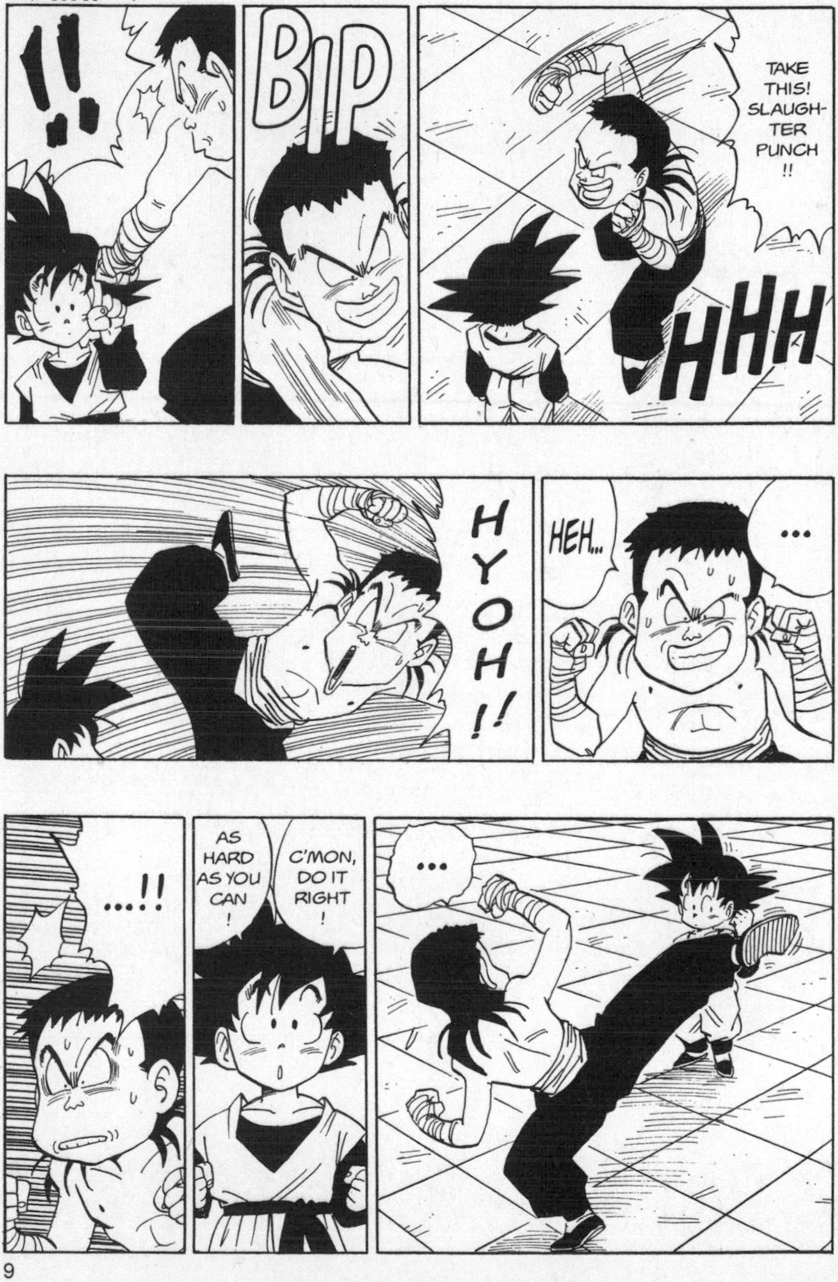

TAKE THIS! SLAUGHTER-TER PUNCH !!
HHH
BIP
!!
...
HEH...
HYOH!!
...
C'MON, DO IT RIGHT !
AS HARD AS YOU CAN !
...!!

READ THIS WAY

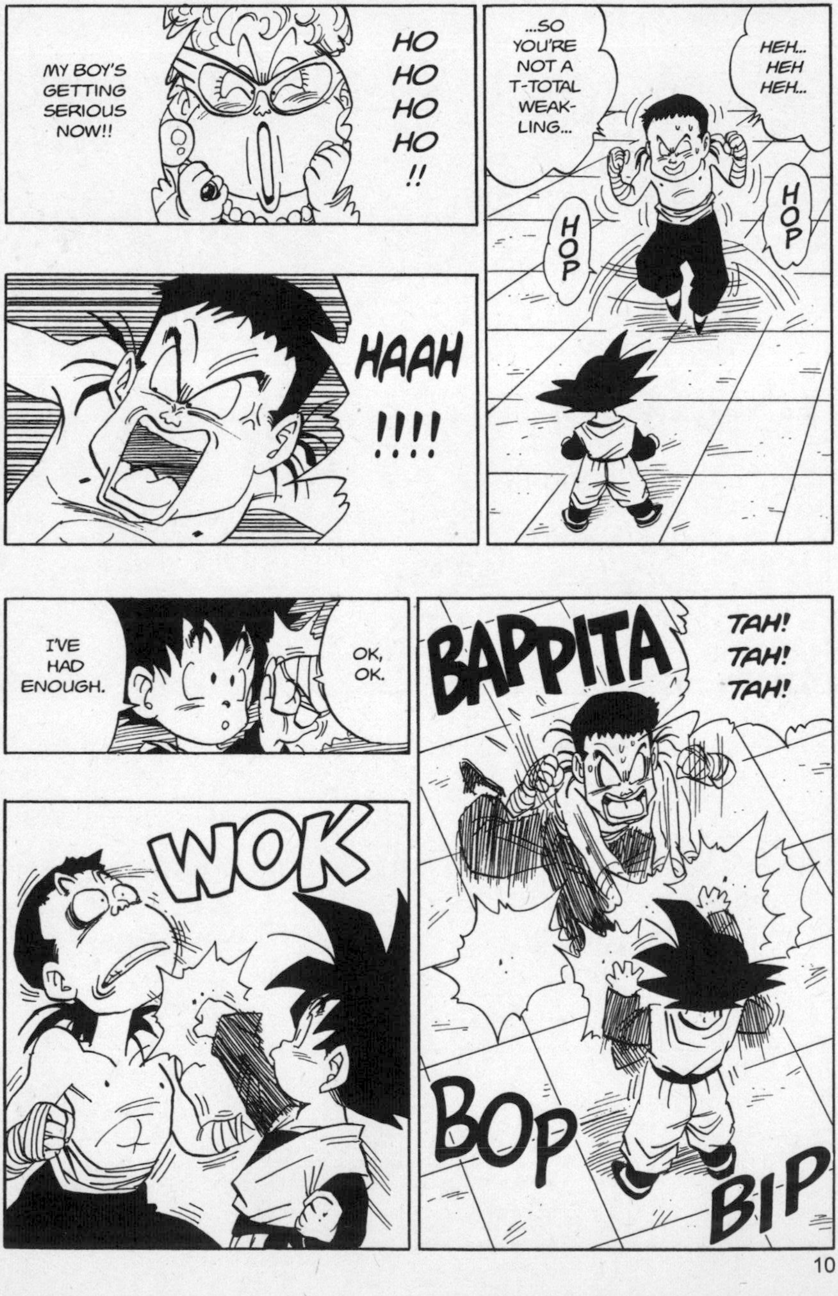
HEH... HEH HEH...
...SO YOU'RE NOT A T-TOTAL WEAK-LING...
HOP
HOP
HO HO HO HO !!
MY BOY'S GETTING SERIOUS NOW!!
HAAH !!!!
TAH! TAH! TAH!
BAPPITA
BIP
BOP
OK, OK.
I'VE HAD ENOUGH.
WOK

READ THIS WAY

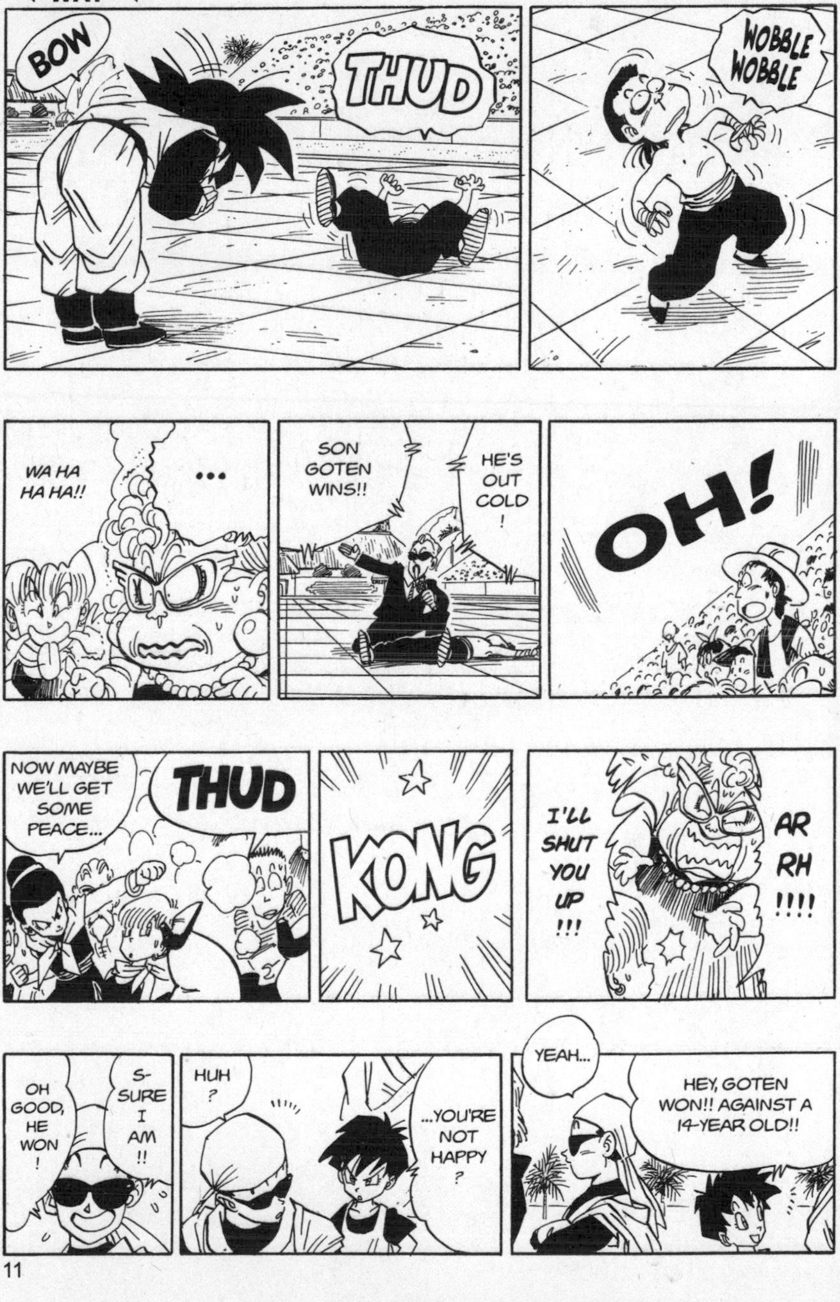

WOBBLE WOBBLE
THUD
BOW
OH!
HE'S OUT COLD!
SON GOTEN WINS!!
...
WA HA HA HA!!
AR RH !!!!
I'LL SHUT YOU UP !!!
KONG
THUD
NOW MAYBE WE'LL GET SOME PEACE...
HEY, GOTEN WON!! AGAINST A 14-YEAR OLD!!
YEAH...
...YOU'RE NOT HAPPY ?
HUH ?
S-SURE I AM !!
OH GOOD, HE WON !

READ THIS WAY

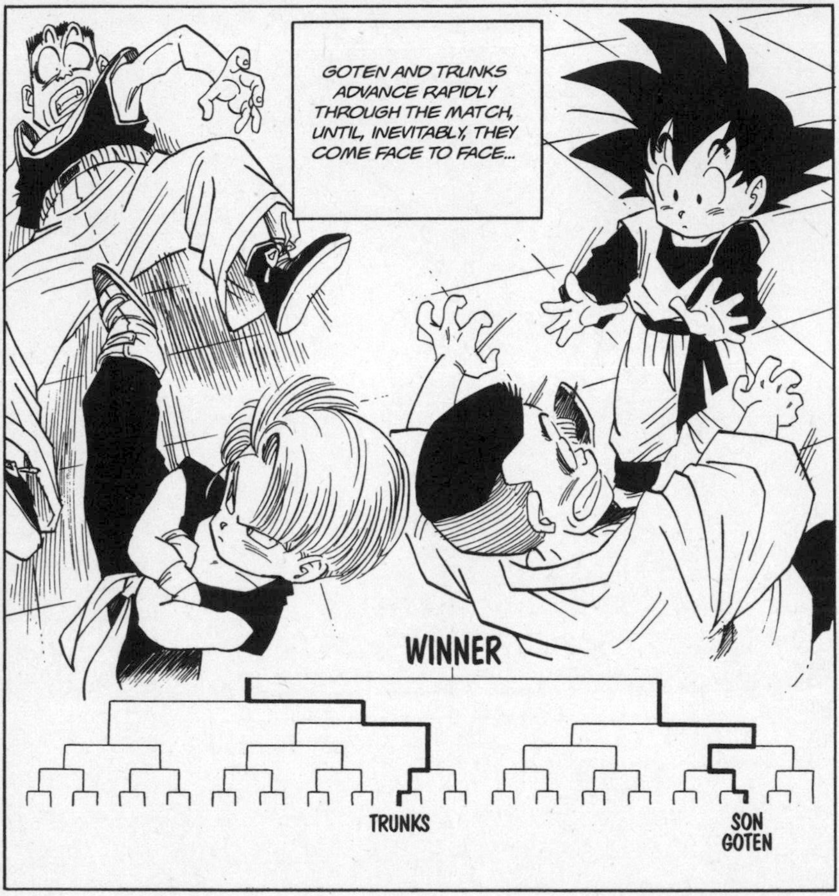
GOTEN AND TRUNKS ADVANCE RAPIDLY THROUGH THE MATCH, UNTIL, INEVITABLY, THEY COME FACE TO FACE...
WINNER
TRUNKS
SON GOTEN

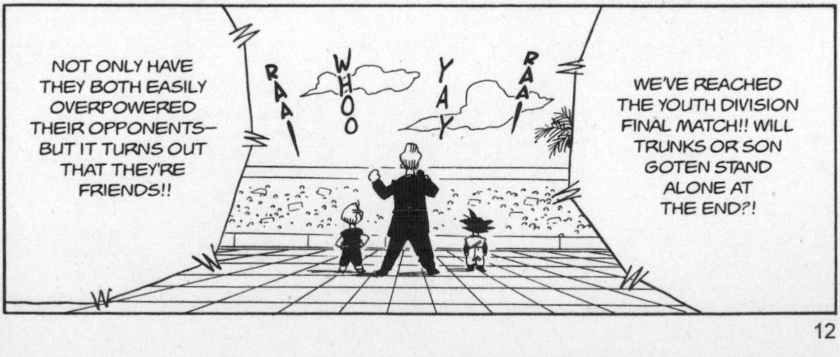
WE'VE REACHED THE YOUTH DIVISION FINAL MATCH!! WILL TRUNKS OR SON GOTEN STAND ALONE AT THE END?!
RAA!
YAY
WHOO
RAA!
NOT ONLY HAVE THEY BOTH EASILY OVERPOWERED THEIR OPPONENTS— BUT IT TURNS OUT THAT THEY'RE FRIENDS!!

READ THIS WAY

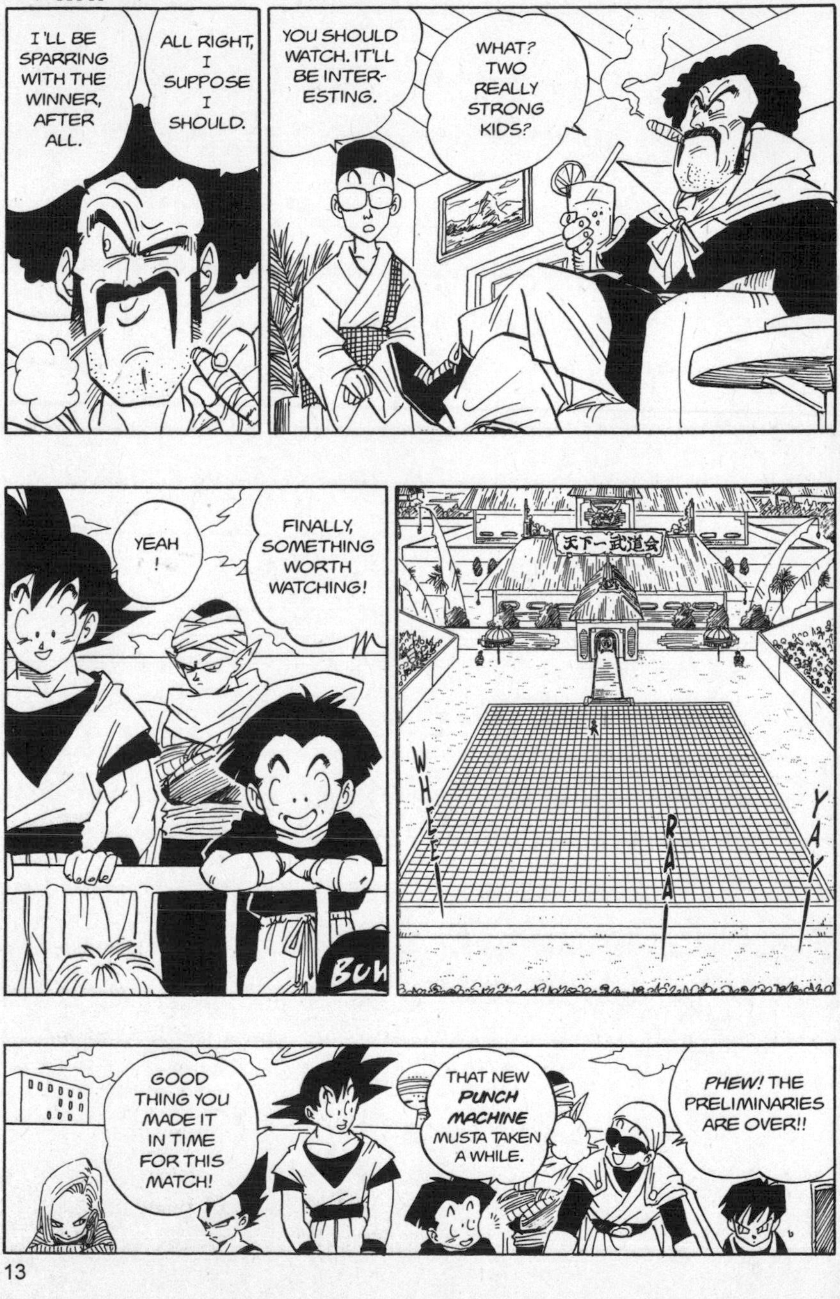
WHAT? TWO REALLY STRONG KIDS?
YOU SHOULD WATCH. IT'LL BE INTERESTING.
ALL RIGHT, I SUPPOSE I SHOULD.
I'LL BE SPARRING WITH THE WINNER, AFTER ALL.
天下一武道会
YAY!
RAA!
WHEE!
FINALLY, SOMETHING WORTH WATCHING!
YEAH!
PHEW! THE PRELIMINARIES ARE OVER!!
THAT NEW PUNCH MACHINE MUSTA TAKEN A WHILE.
GOOD THING YOU MADE IT IN TIME FOR THIS MATCH!

READ THIS WAY

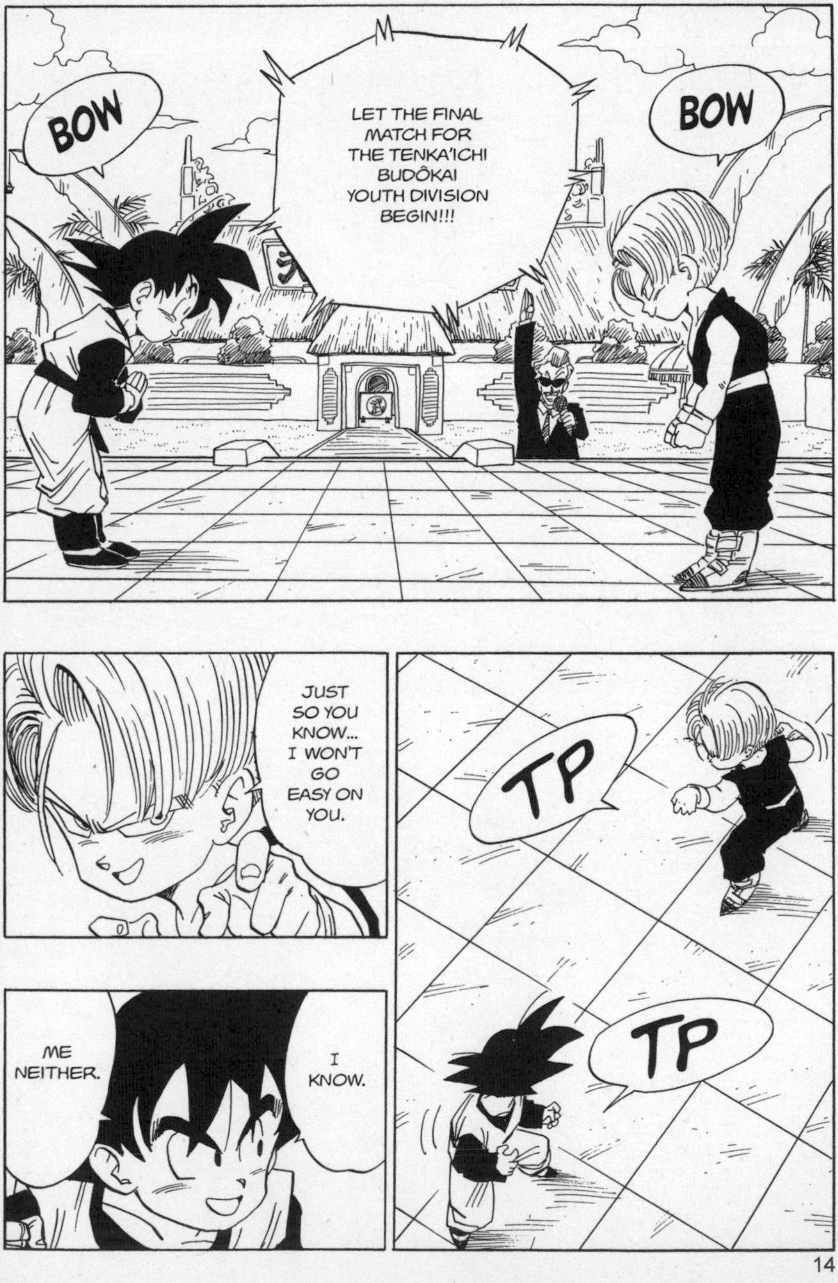

BOW
LET THE FINAL MATCH FOR THE TENKA'ICHI BUDÔKAI YOUTH DIVISION BEGIN!!!
BOW
TP
TP
JUST SO YOU KNOW... I WON'T GO EASY ON YOU.
I KNOW.
ME NEITHER.

READ THIS WAY

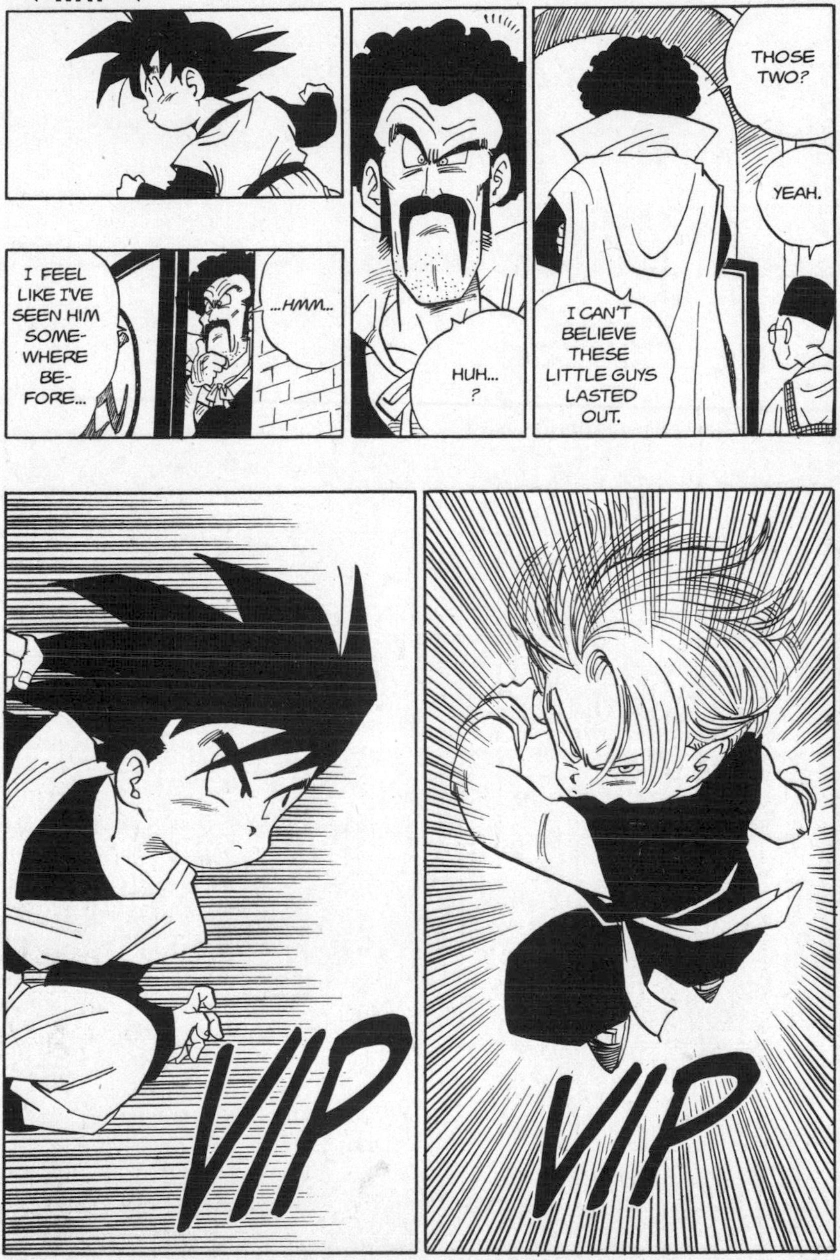
THOSE TWO?
YEAH.
I CAN'T BELIEVE THESE LITTLE GUYS LASTED OUT.
HUH... ?
...HMM...
I FEEL LIKE I'VE SEEN HIM SOME-WHERE BE-FORE...
VIP
VIP

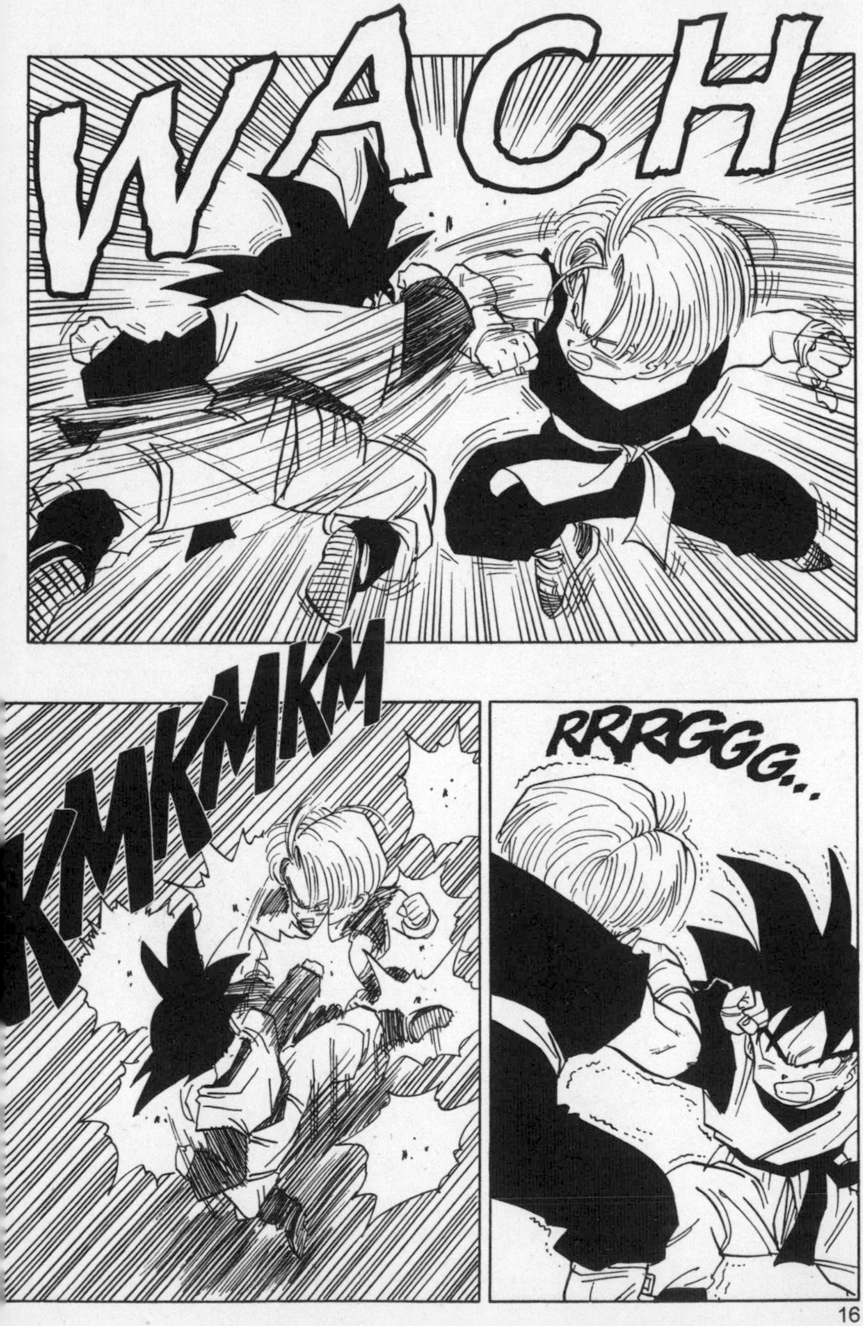
WACH
RRRGGG...
KMKMKMKM

READ THIS WAY

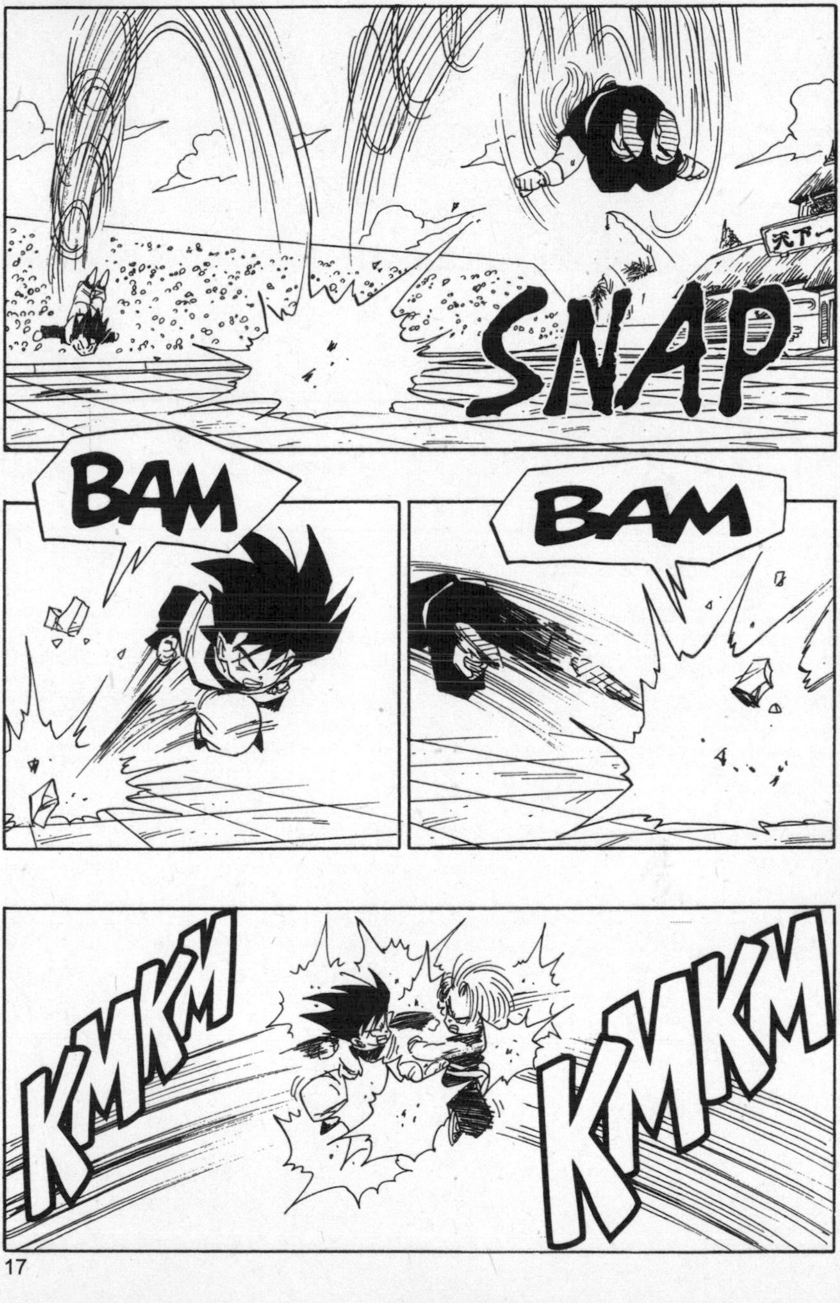
SNAP
天下一
BAM
BAM
KMKM
KMKM

READ THIS WAY

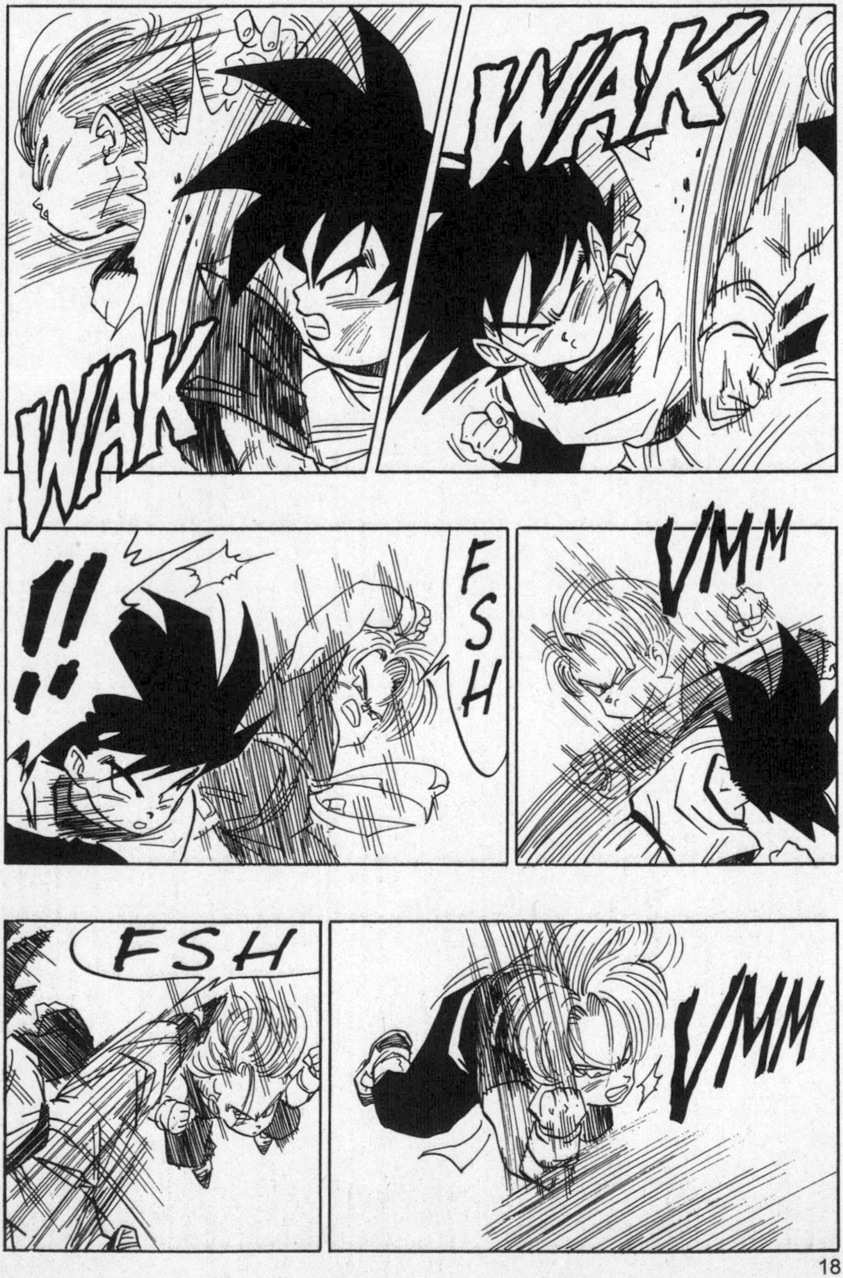

WAK
WAK
VMMM
FSH
!!
VMM
FSH

READ THIS WAY

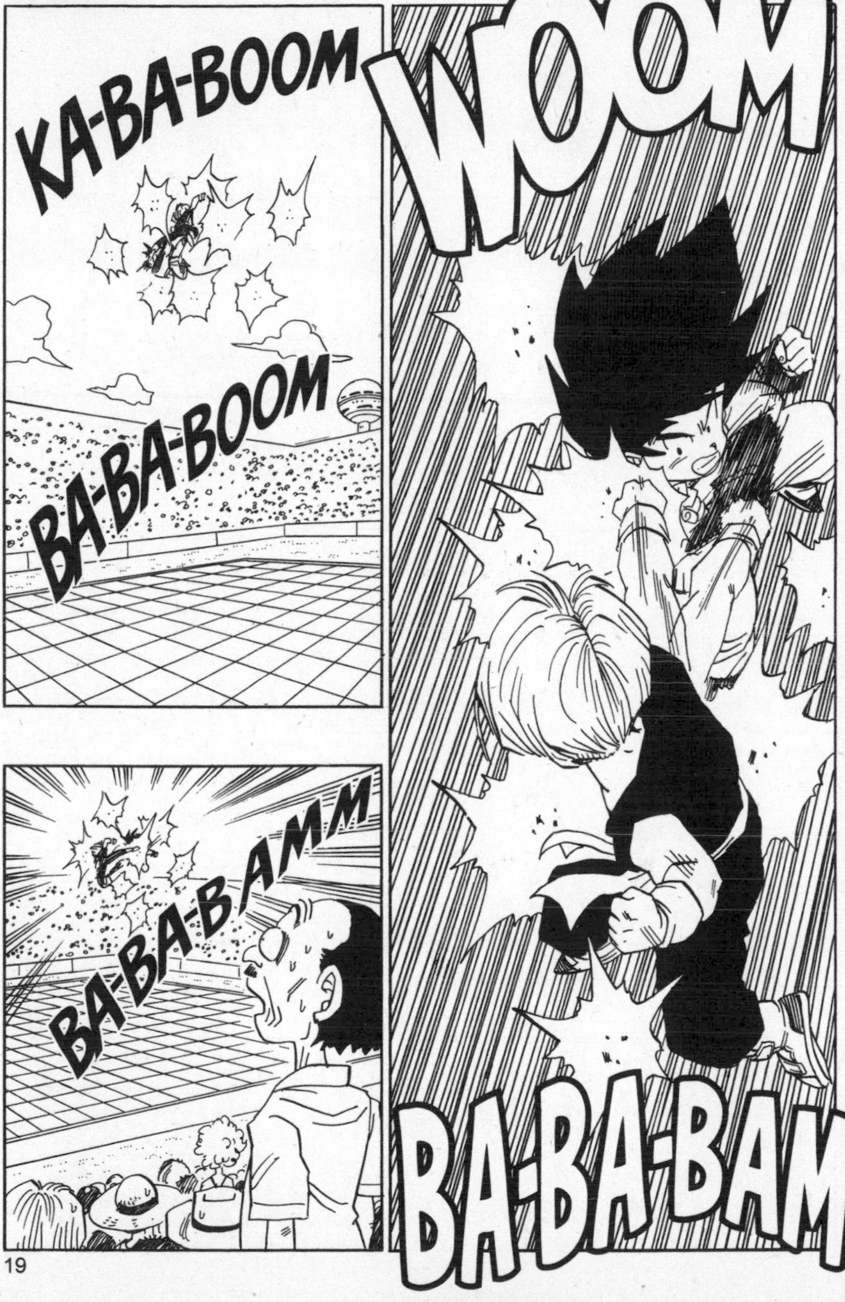
WOOM
BA-BA-BAM
KA-BA-BOOM
BA-BA-BOOM
BA-BA-BAMM

READ THIS WAY

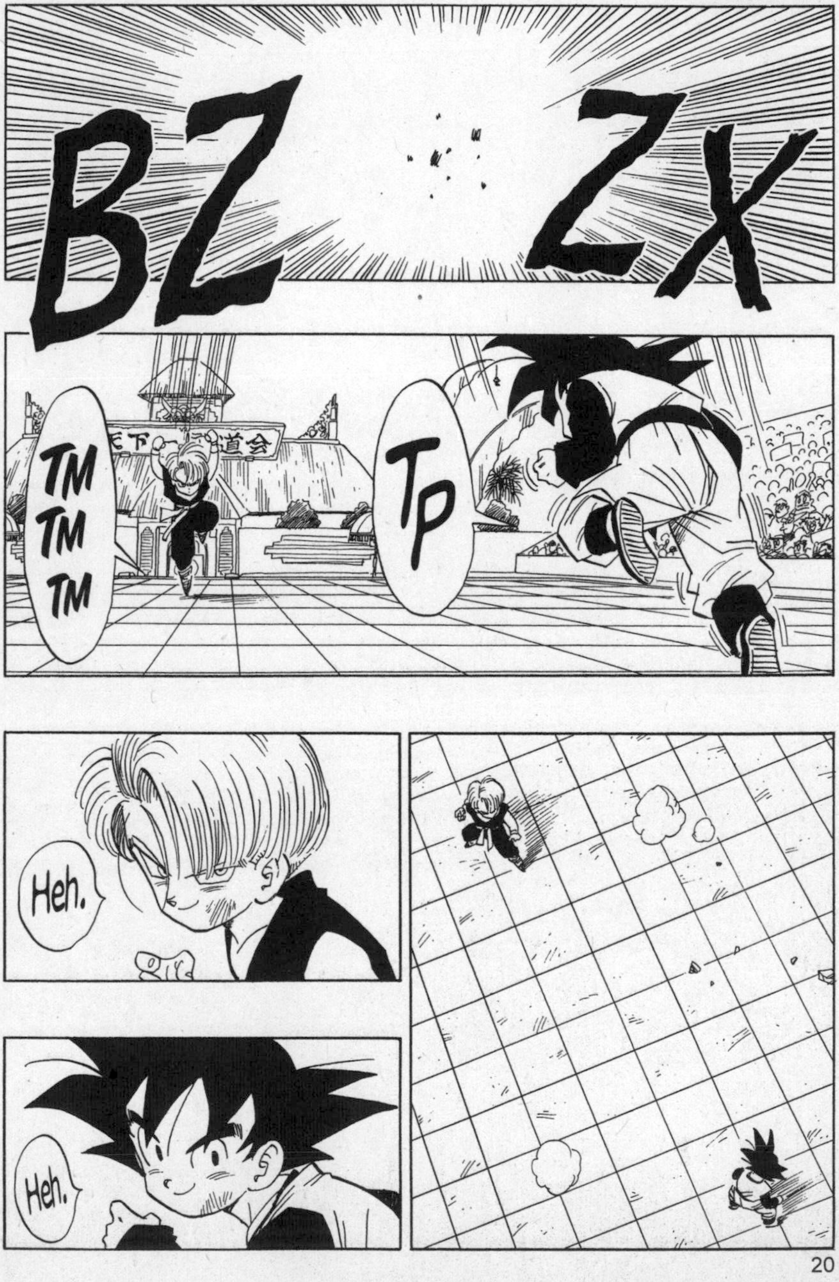
BZZX
TP
TM TM TM
Heh.
Heh.

READ THIS WAY

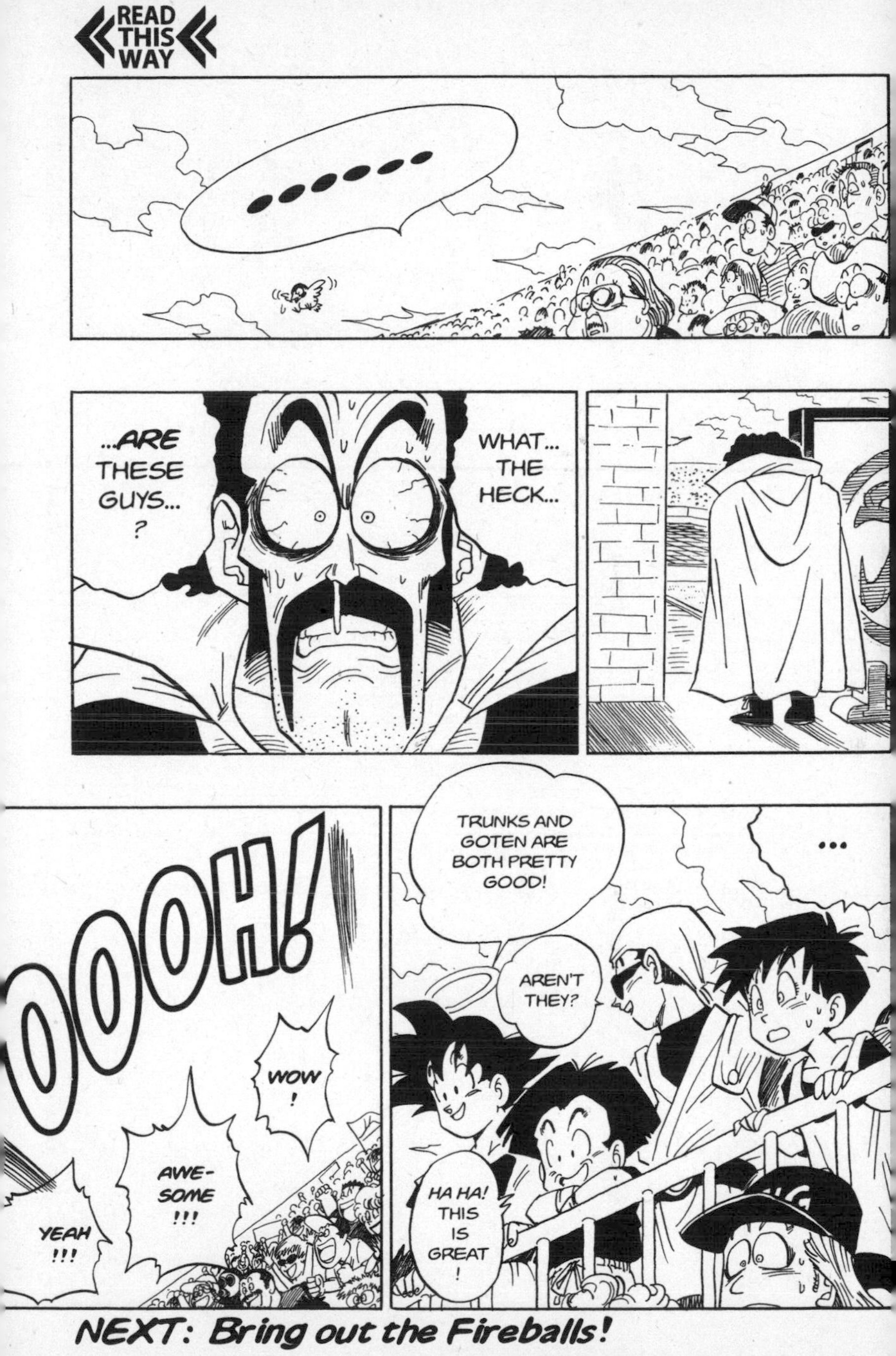
......
WHAT... THE HECK...
...ARE THESE GUYS...?
...
TRUNKS AND GOTEN ARE BOTH PRETTY GOOD!
AREN'T THEY?
HA HA! THIS IS GREAT!
OOOOH!
WOW!
AWE-SOME!!!
YEAH!!!

NEXT: Bring out the Fireballs!

DBZ:240 • Trunks vs. Goten, Part 2

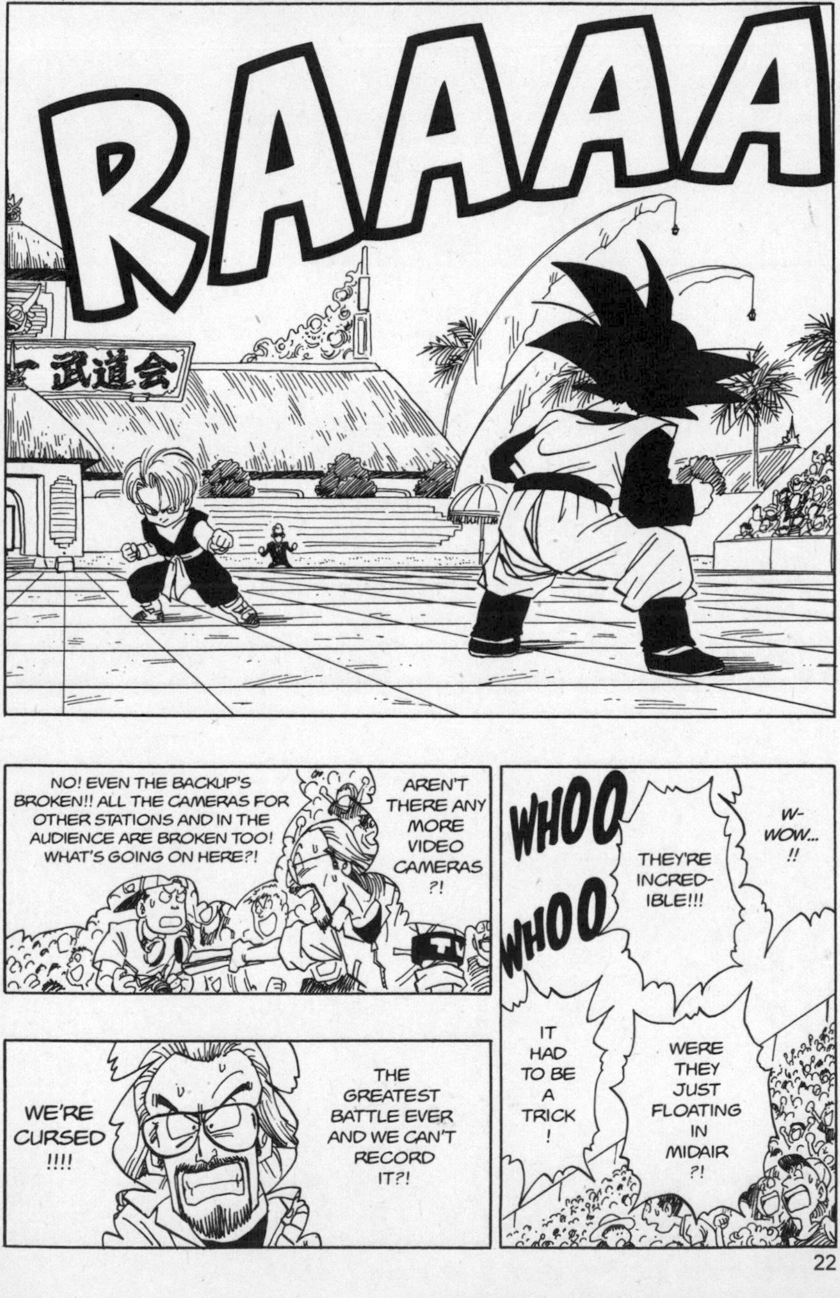

RAAAA
武道会
W-WOW...!!
THEY'RE INCREDIBLE!!!
WHOO
WHOO
WERE THEY JUST FLOATING IN MIDAIR?!
IT HAD TO BE A TRICK!
AREN'T THERE ANY MORE VIDEO CAMERAS?!
NO! EVEN THE BACKUP'S BROKEN!! ALL THE CAMERAS FOR OTHER STATIONS AND IN THE AUDIENCE ARE BROKEN TOO! WHAT'S GOING ON HERE?!
THE GREATEST BATTLE EVER AND WE CAN'T RECORD IT?!
WE'RE CURSED!!!!

READ THIS WAY

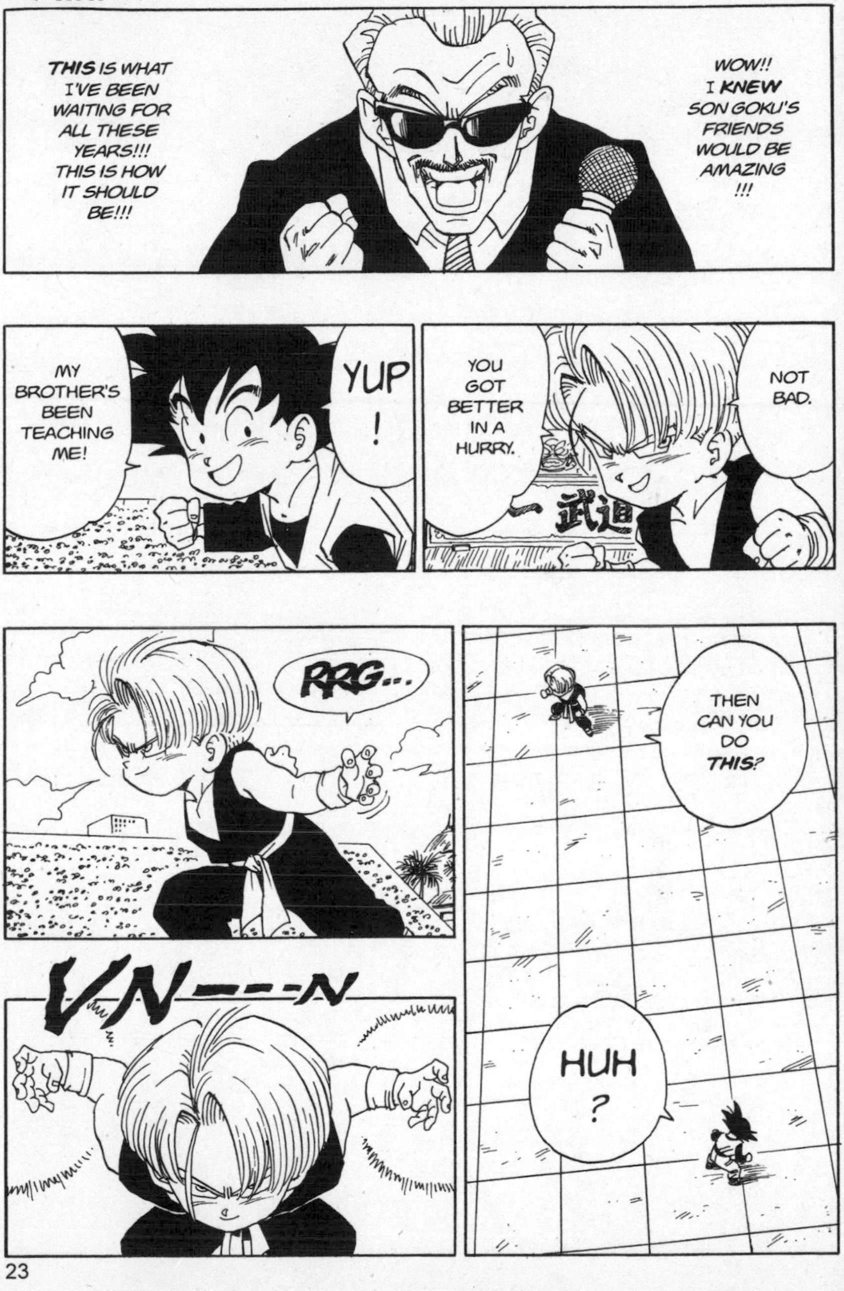

WOW!! I KNEW SON GOKU'S FRIENDS WOULD BE AMAZING !!!
THIS IS WHAT I'VE BEEN WAITING FOR ALL THESE YEARS!!! THIS IS HOW IT SHOULD BE!!!
NOT BAD.
YOU GOT BETTER IN A HURRY.
YUP !
MY BROTHER'S BEEN TEACHING ME!
THEN CAN YOU DO THIS?
HUH ?
RRG...
VN---N

READ THIS WAY

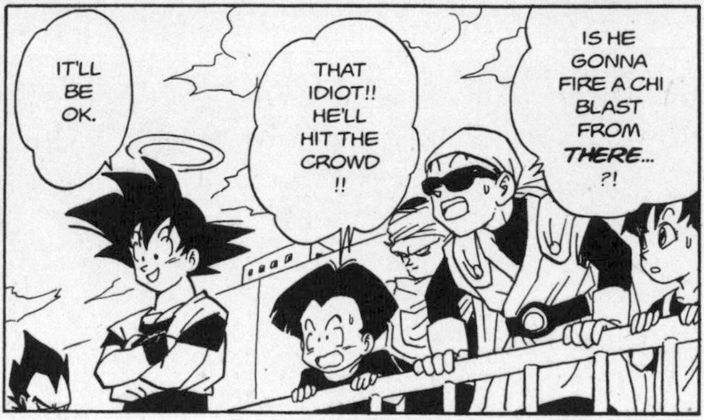
IS HE GONNA FIRE A CHI BLAST FROM *THERE*...?!
THAT IDIOT!! HE'LL HIT THE CROWD!!
IT'LL BE OK.

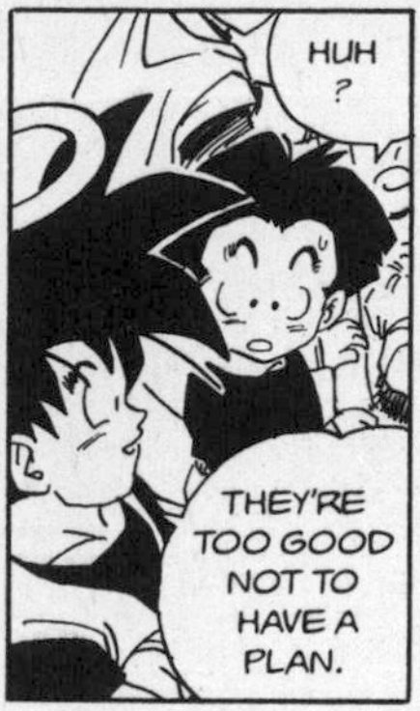
HUH?
THEY'RE TOO GOOD NOT TO HAVE A PLAN.

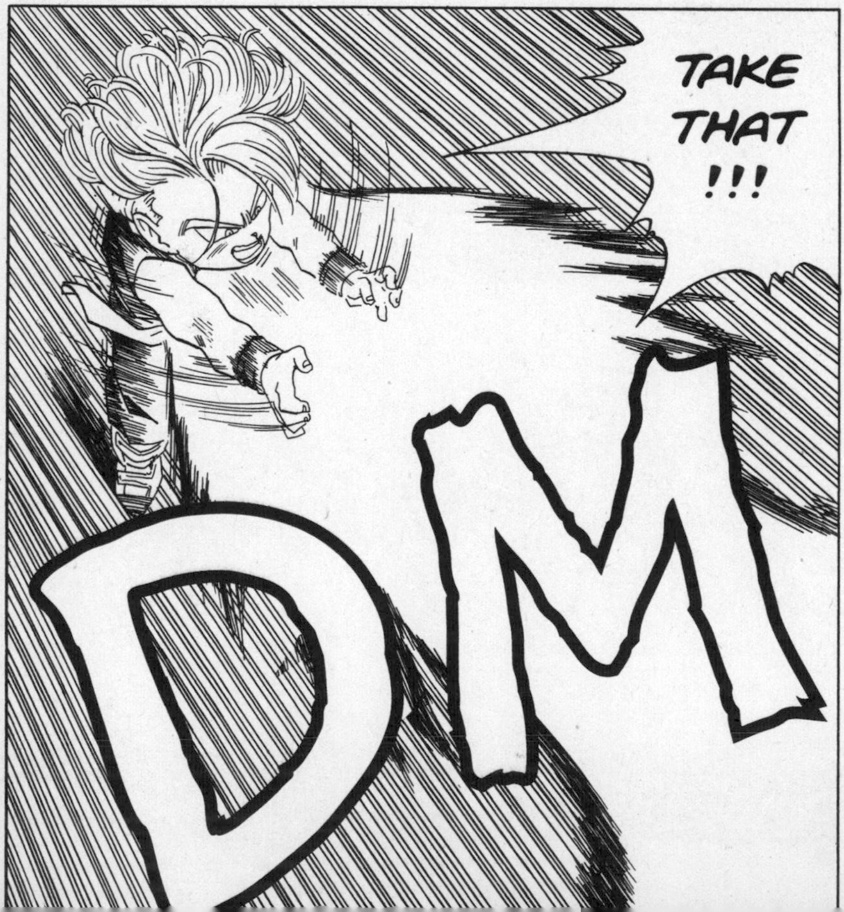
TAKE THAT!!!
DM

READ THIS WAY

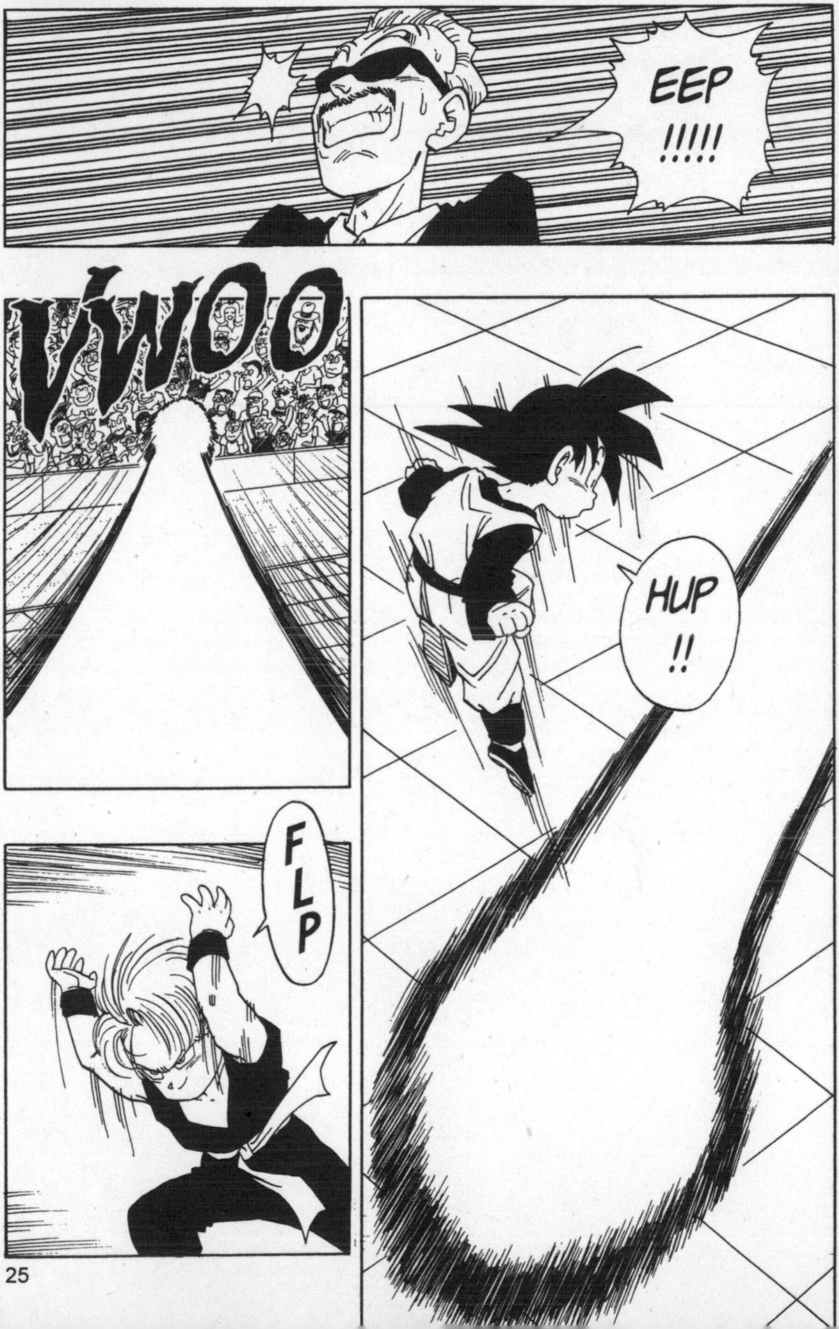
EEP !!!!!
HUP !!
VWOO
FLP

READ THIS WAY

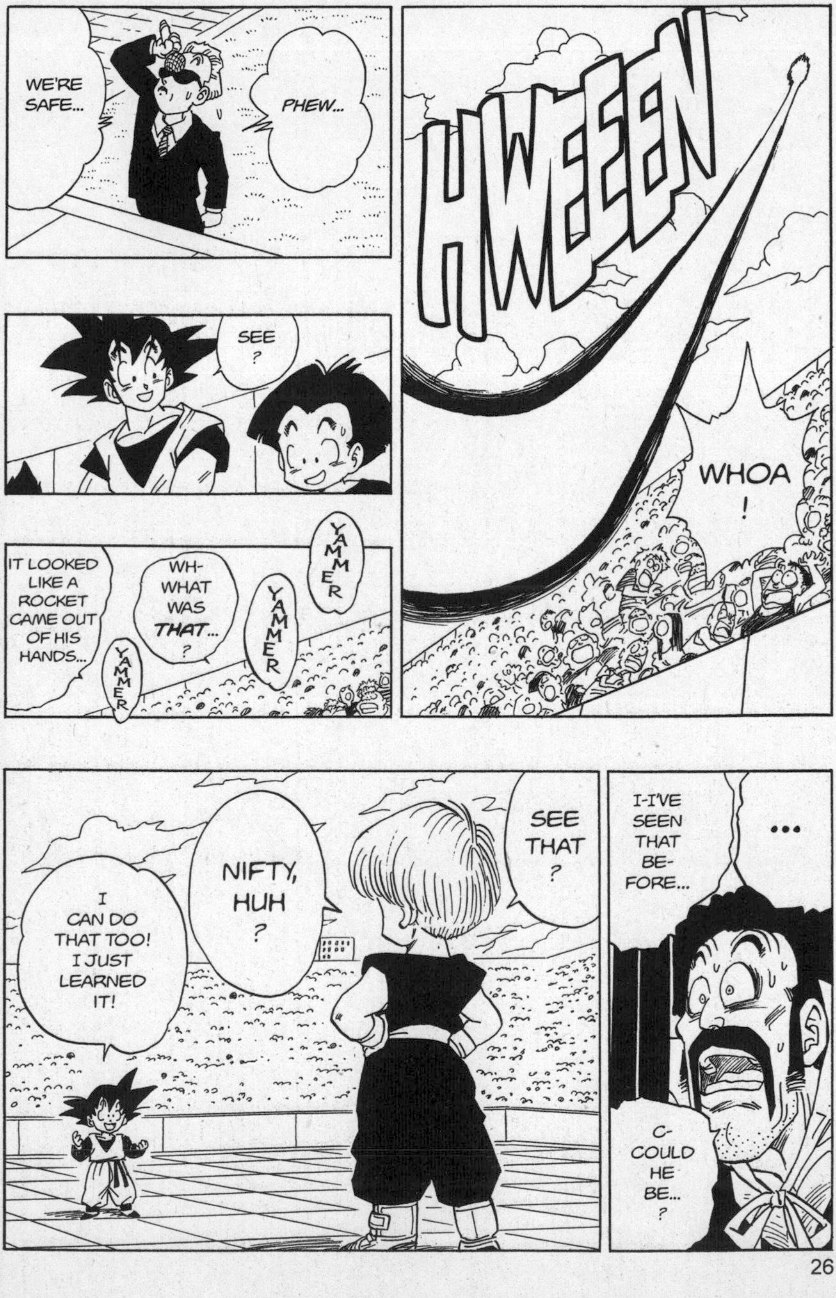
HWEEEN
WHOA !
PHEW...
WE'RE SAFE...
SEE ?
YAMMER
WH- WHAT WAS *THAT*... ?
YAMMER
IT LOOKED LIKE A ROCKET CAME OUT OF HIS HANDS...
YAMMER
...
I-I'VE SEEN THAT BE- FORE...
C- COULD HE BE... ?
SEE THAT ?
NIFTY, HUH ?
I CAN DO THAT TOO! I JUST LEARNED IT!

READ THIS WAY

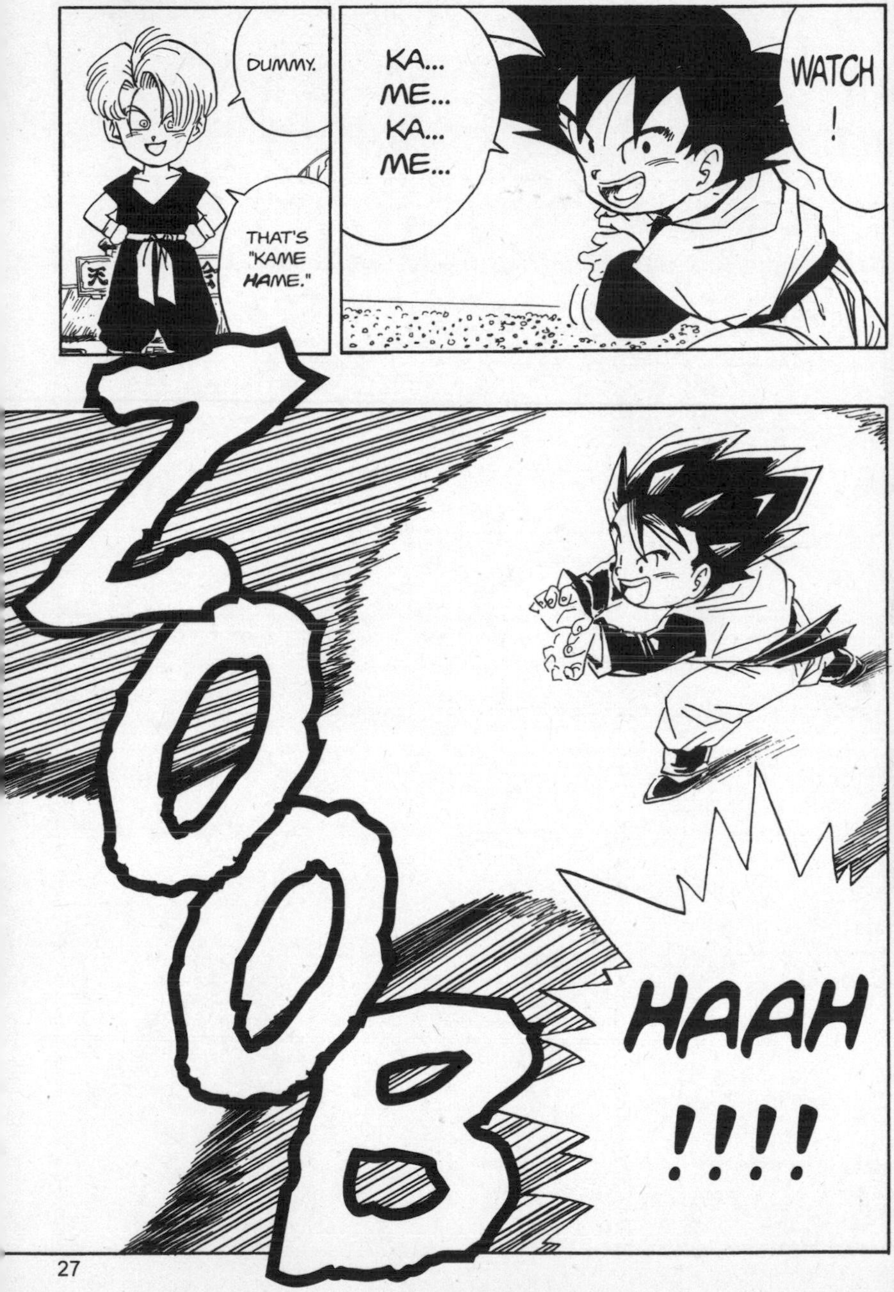

WATCH!
KA... ME... KA... ME...
DUMMY.
THAT'S "KAME HAME."
HAAH!!!!
ZOOB

READ THIS WAY

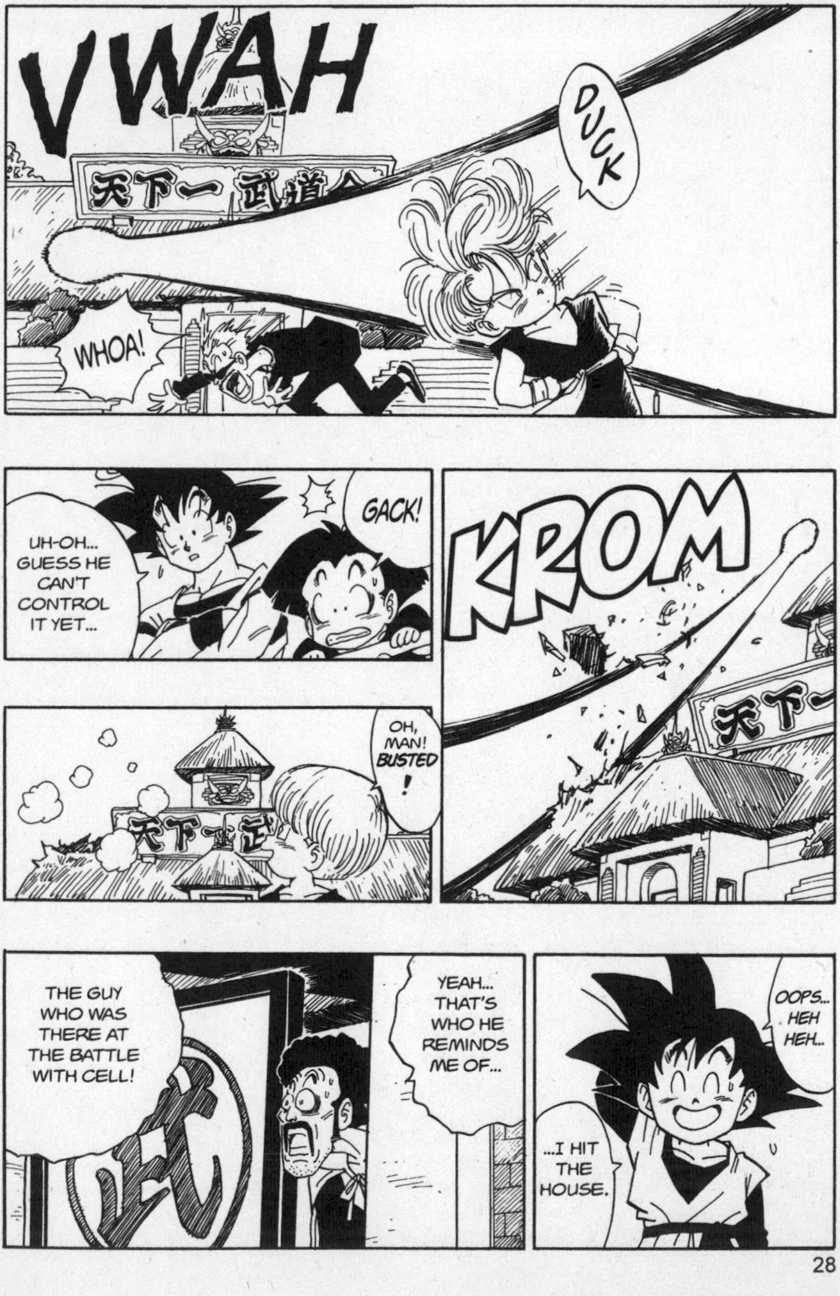

DUCK
VWAH
WHOA!
KROM
GACK!
UH-OH... GUESS HE CAN'T CONTROL IT YET...
OH, MAN! BUSTED!
OOPS... HEH HEH...
...I HIT THE HOUSE.
YEAH... THAT'S WHO HE REMINDS ME OF...
THE GUY WHO WAS THERE AT THE BATTLE WITH CELL!

READ THIS WAY

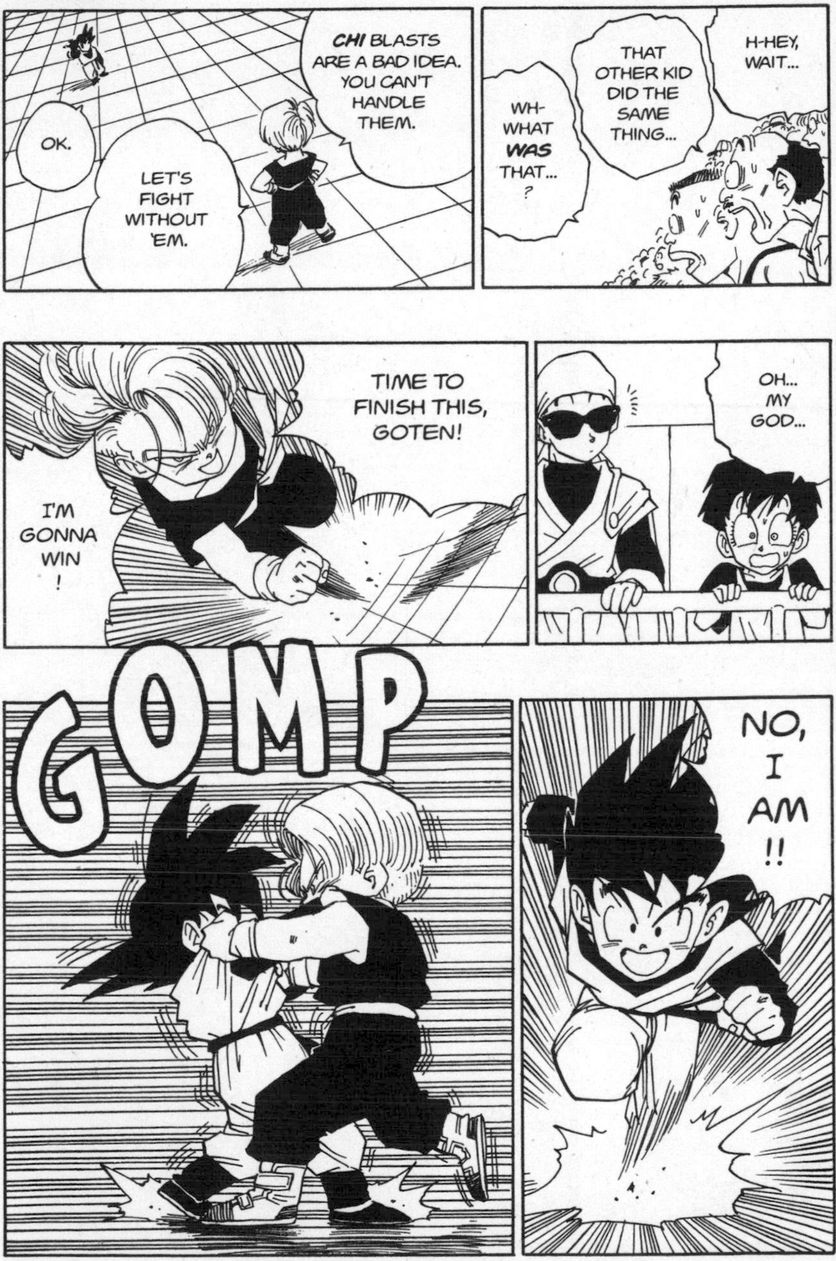

H-HEY, WAIT...
THAT OTHER KID DID THE SAME THING...
WH-WHAT *WAS* THAT...?
CHI BLASTS ARE A BAD IDEA. YOU CAN'T HANDLE THEM.
LET'S FIGHT WITHOUT 'EM.
OK.
OH... MY GOD...
TIME TO FINISH THIS, GOTEN!
I'M GONNA WIN!
NO, I AM!!
GOMP

READ THIS WAY

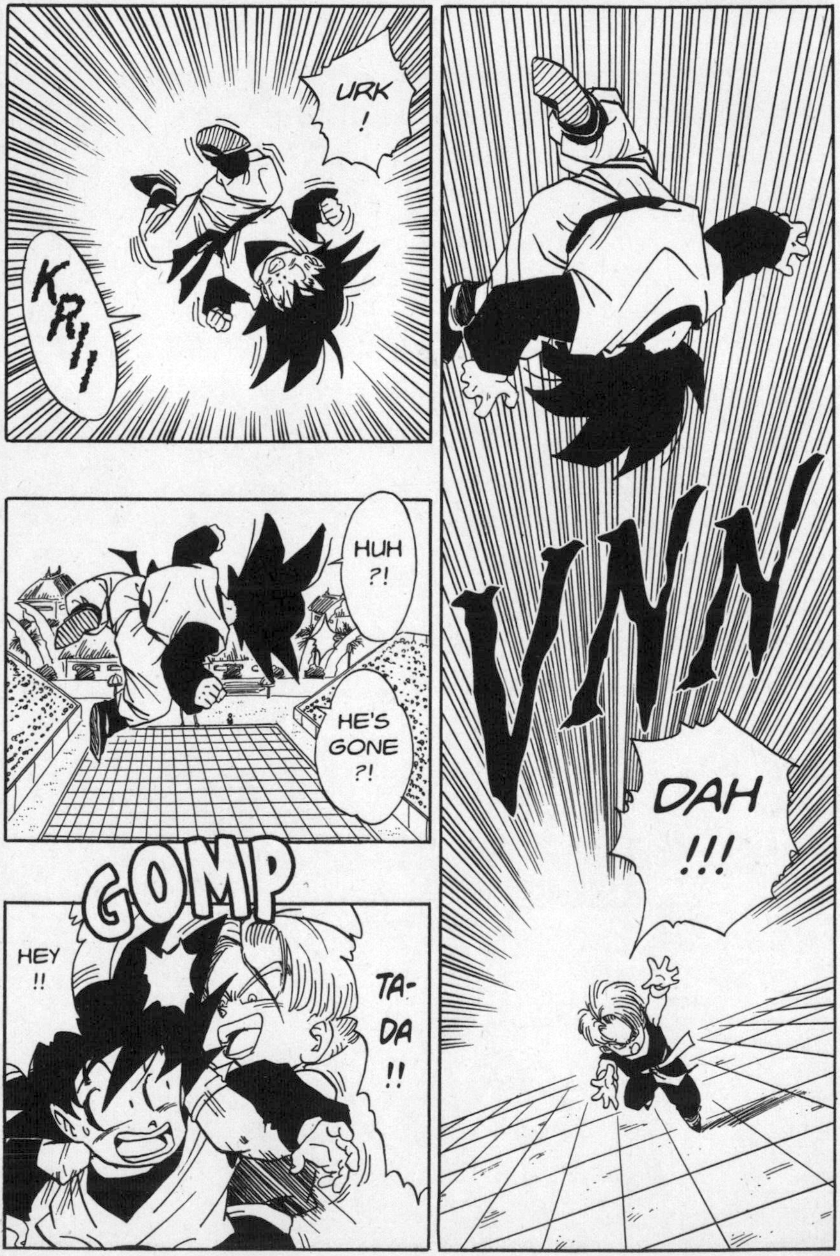
VNN
DAH !!!
URK !
KRII
HUH ?!
HE'S GONE ?!
GOMP
TA-DA !!
HEY !!

READ THIS WAY

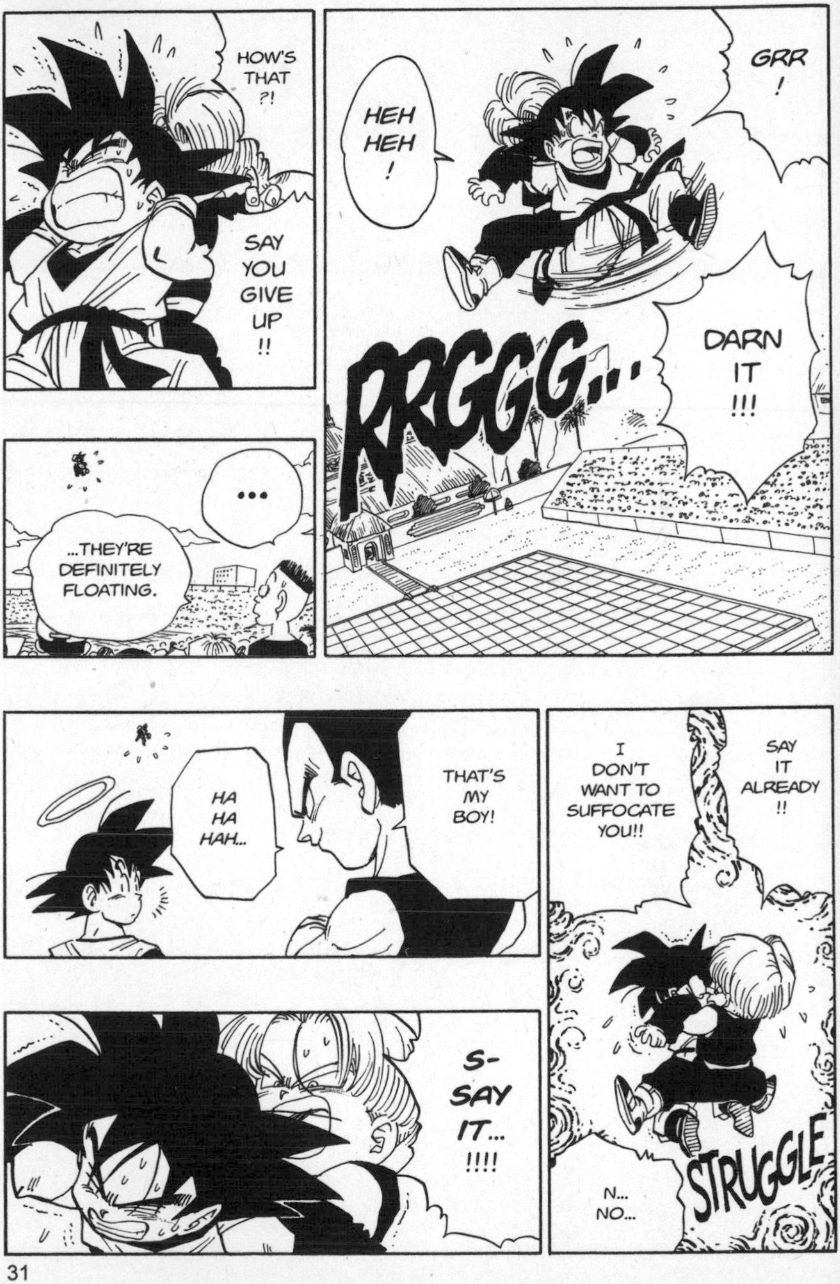

GRR!
HEH HEH!
DARN IT!!!
RRGGG...
HOW'S THAT?!
SAY YOU GIVE UP!!
...
...THEY'RE DEFINITELY FLOATING.
SAY IT ALREADY!!
I DON'T WANT TO SUFFOCATE YOU!!
STRUGGLE
N... NO...
THAT'S MY BOY!
HA HA HAH...
S-SAY IT...!!!!

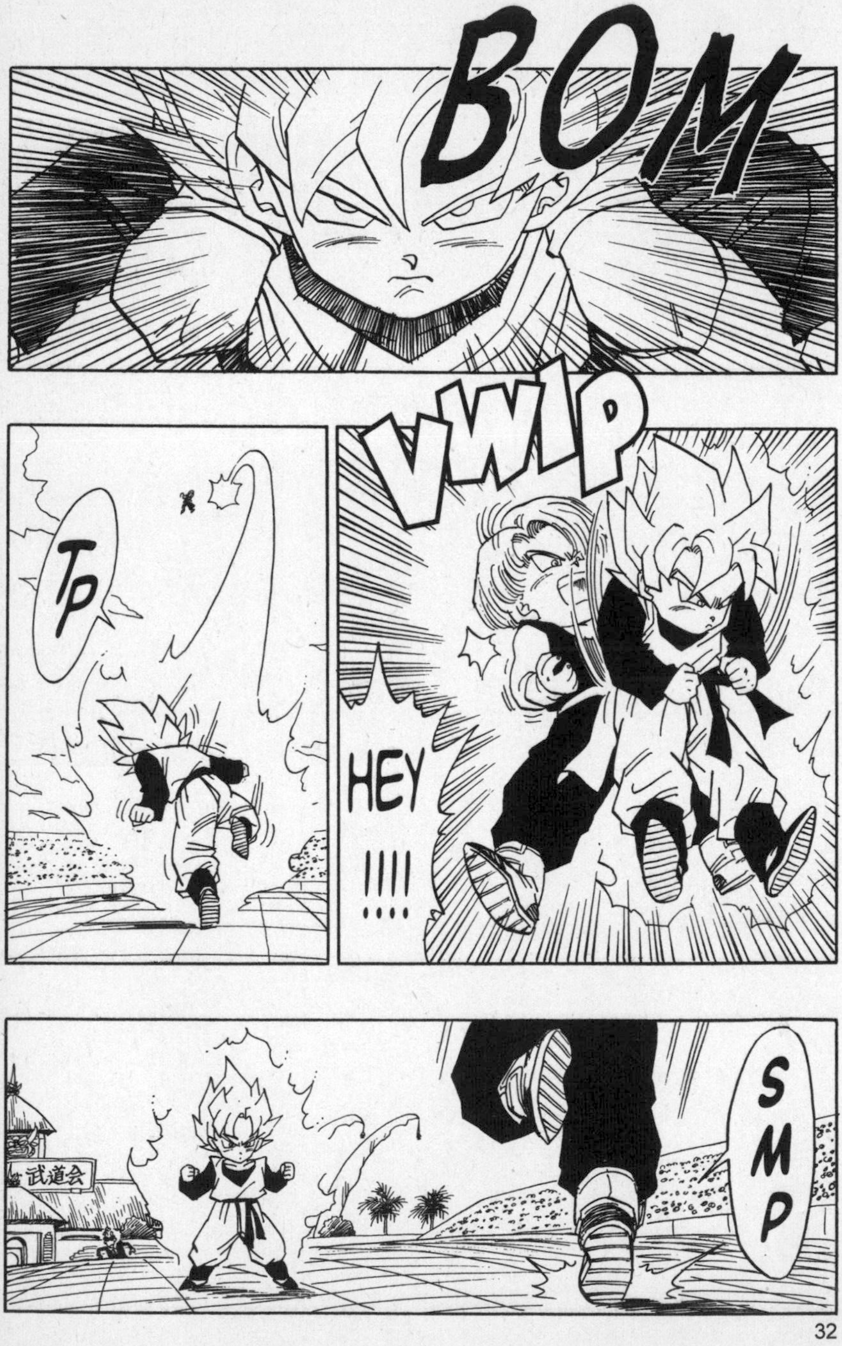
BOM
VWIP
HEY!!!!
TP
SMP
武道会

READ THIS WAY

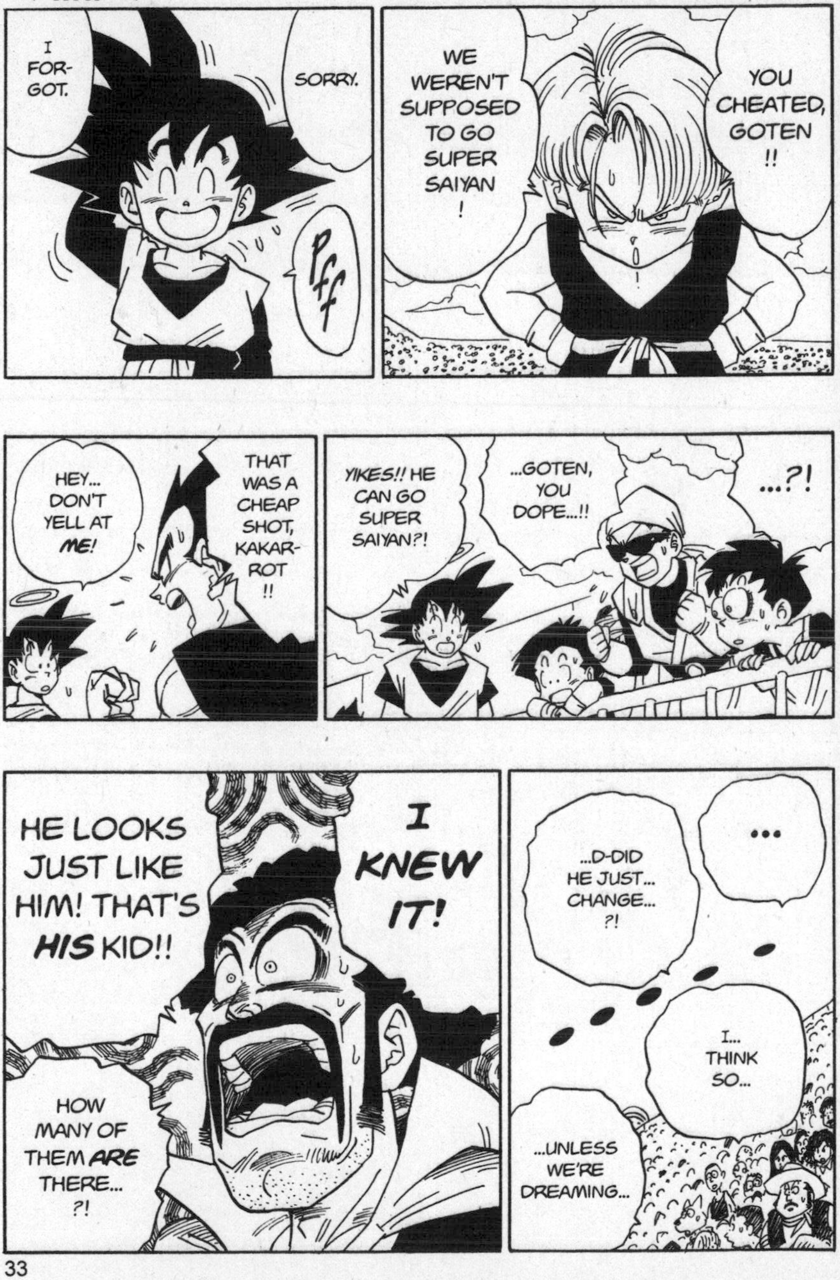

YOU CHEATED, GOTEN!!
WE WEREN'T SUPPOSED TO GO SUPER SAIYAN!
Pff
SORRY.
I FORGOT.
...?!
...GOTEN, YOU DOPE...!!
YIKES!! HE CAN GO SUPER SAIYAN?!
THAT WAS A CHEAP SHOT, KAKARROT!!
HEY... DON'T YELL AT ME!
...
...D-DID HE JUST... CHANGE...?!
I... THINK SO...
...UNLESS WE'RE DREAMING...
I KNEW IT!
HE LOOKS JUST LIKE HIM! THAT'S HIS KID!!
HOW MANY OF THEM ARE THERE...?!

DBZ:241 • The Winner!

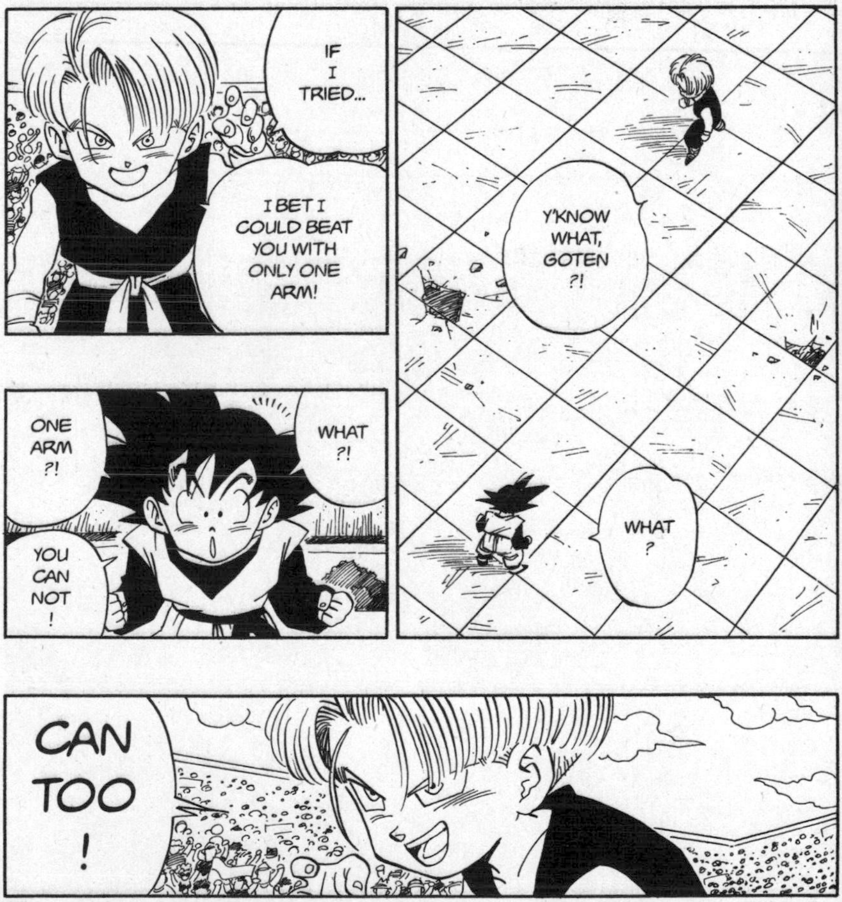

Y'KNOW WHAT, GOTEN ?!
WHAT ?
IF I TRIED...
I BET I COULD BEAT YOU WITH ONLY ONE ARM!
WHAT ?!
ONE ARM ?!
YOU CAN NOT !
CAN TOO !

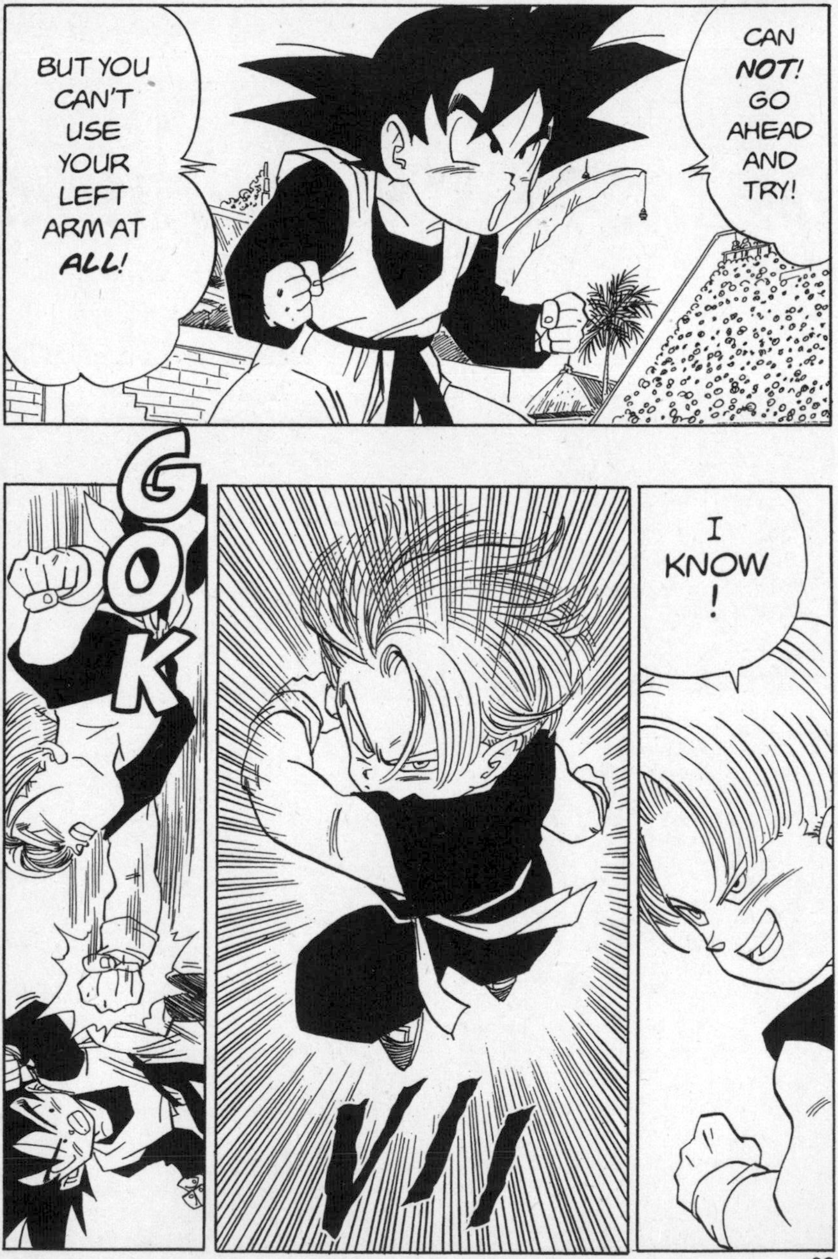
CAN NOT! GO AHEAD AND TRY!
BUT YOU CAN'T USE YOUR LEFT ARM AT ALL!
I KNOW!
GOK

READ THIS WAY

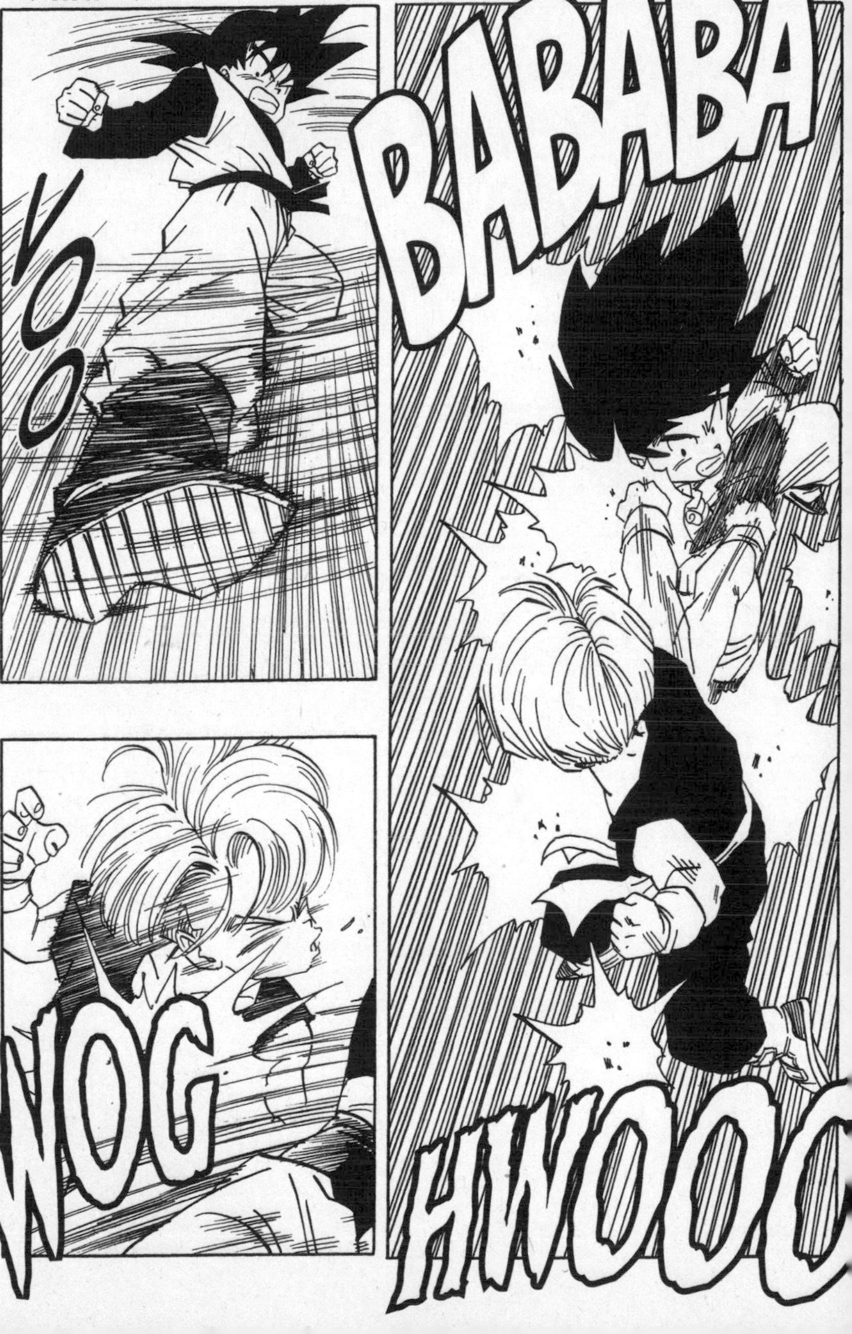
BABABA
HWOOO
VOOO
WOG

READ THIS WAY

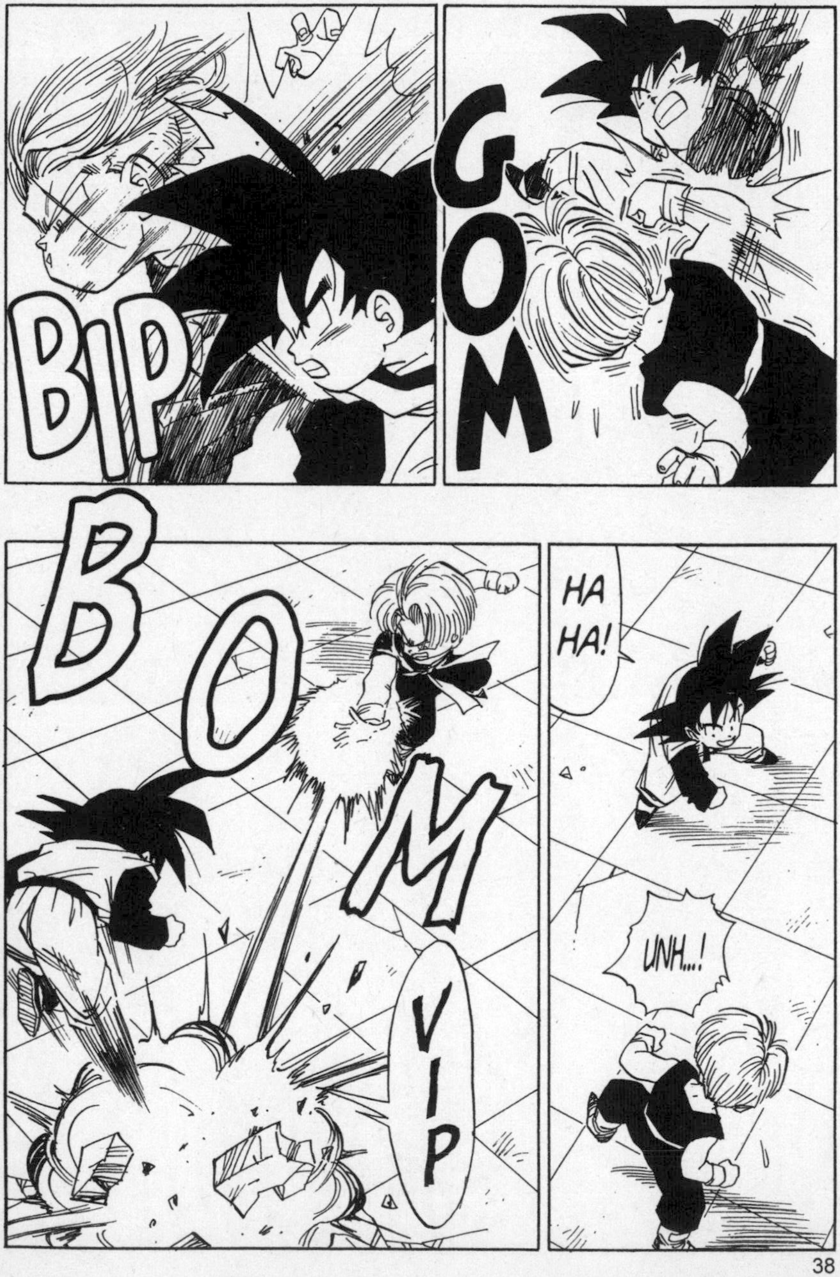
GOM
BIP
HA HA!
UNH...!
BOM
VIP

READ THIS WAY

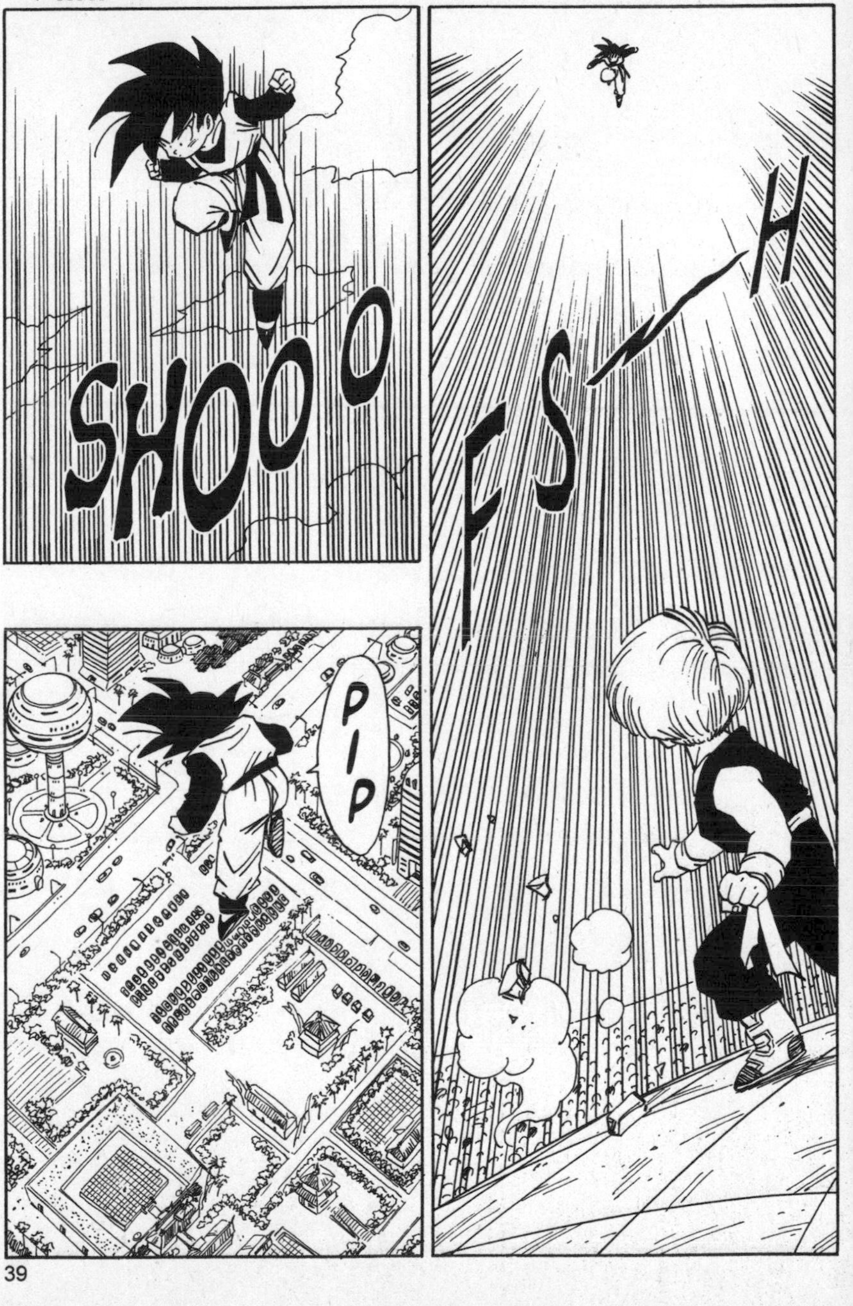
FSH
SHOOOO
PIP

READ THIS WAY

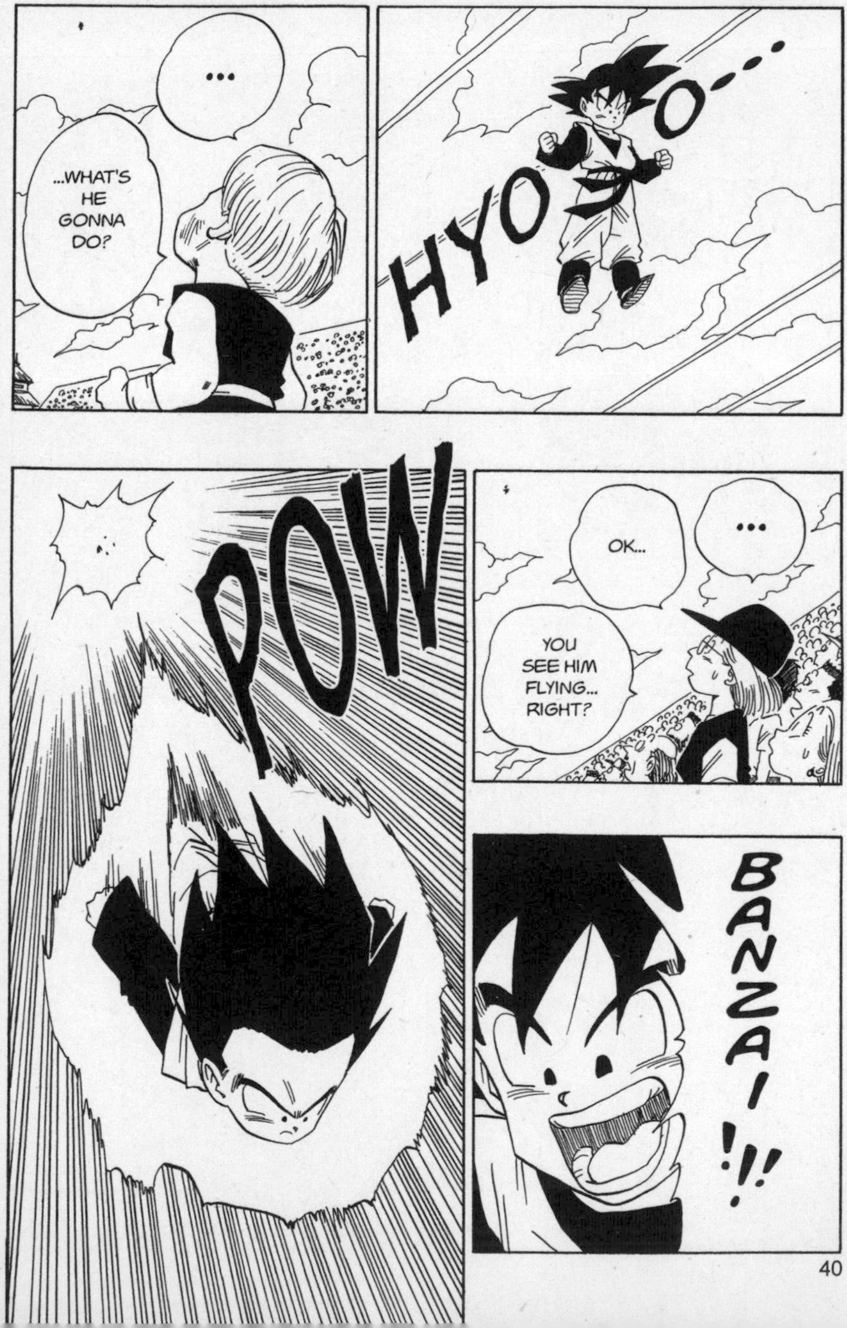
HYO O...
...
...WHAT'S HE GONNA DO?
...
OK...
YOU SEE HIM FLYING... RIGHT?
BANZAI!!!
POW

READ THIS WAY

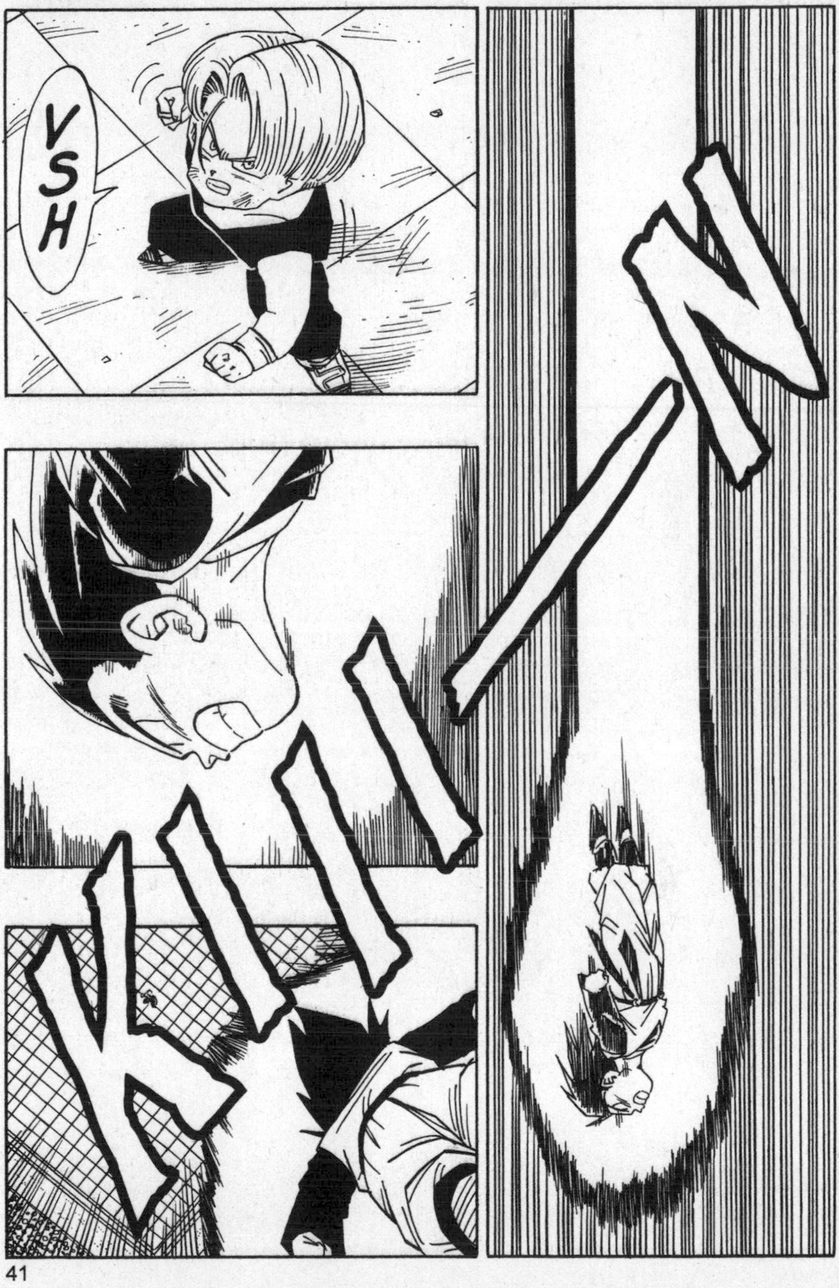

VSH
KIIIIN

READ THIS WAY

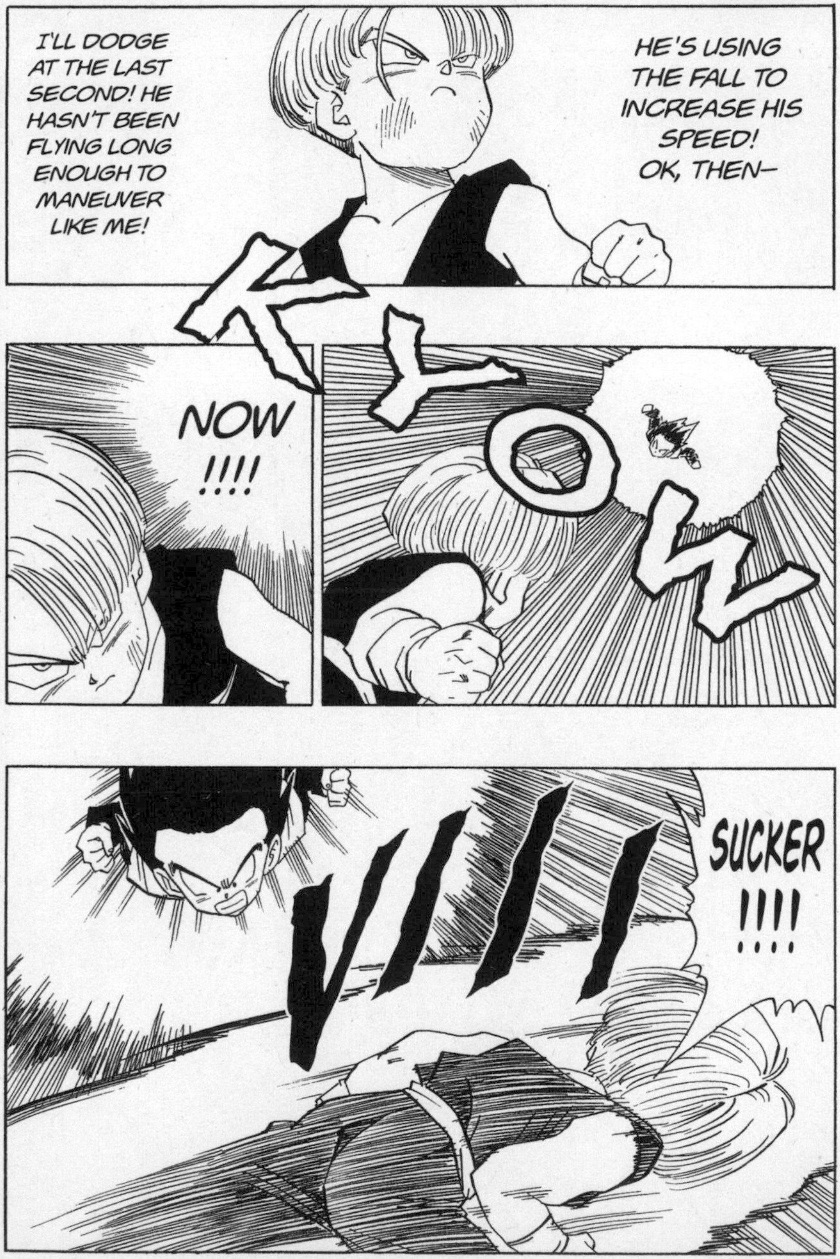
HE'S USING THE FALL TO INCREASE HIS SPEED! OK, THEN–
I'LL DODGE AT THE LAST SECOND! HE HASN'T BEEN FLYING LONG ENOUGH TO MANEUVER LIKE ME!
KYON
NOW !!!!
SUCKER !!!!

READ THIS WAY

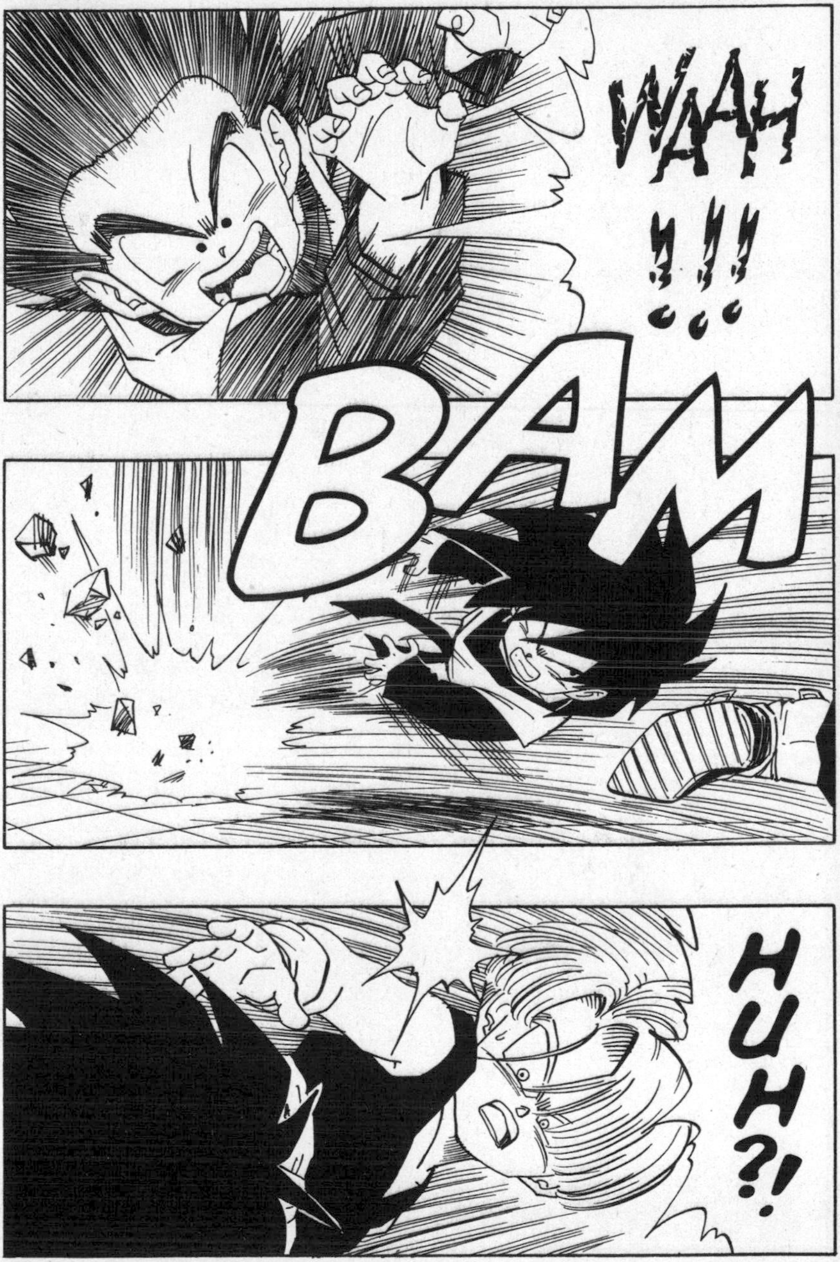
WAAH!!!...
BAM
HUH?!

READ THIS WAY

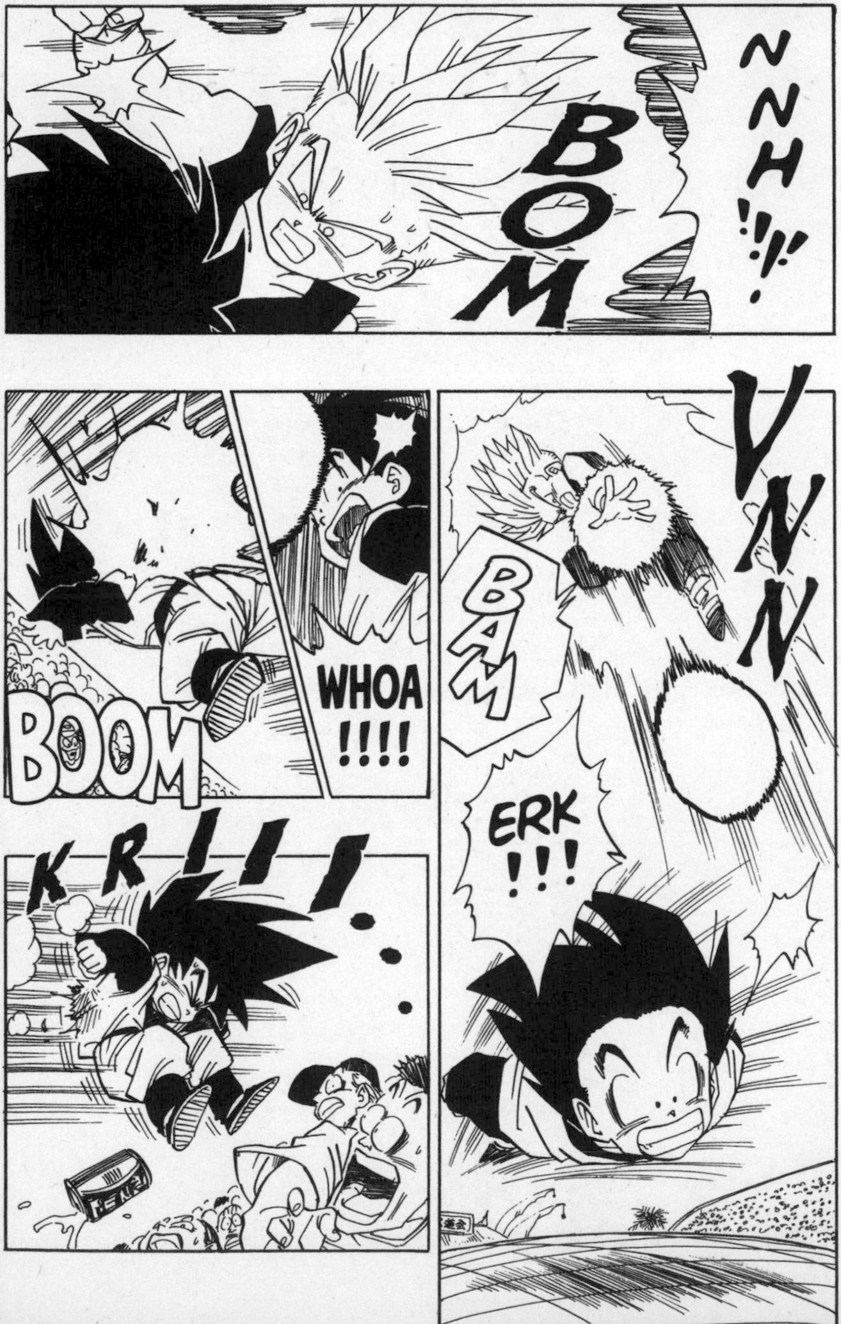
NNH!!!!
BOM
VNN
BAM
ERK!!!
WHOA!!!!
BOOM
KRIII

READ THIS WAY

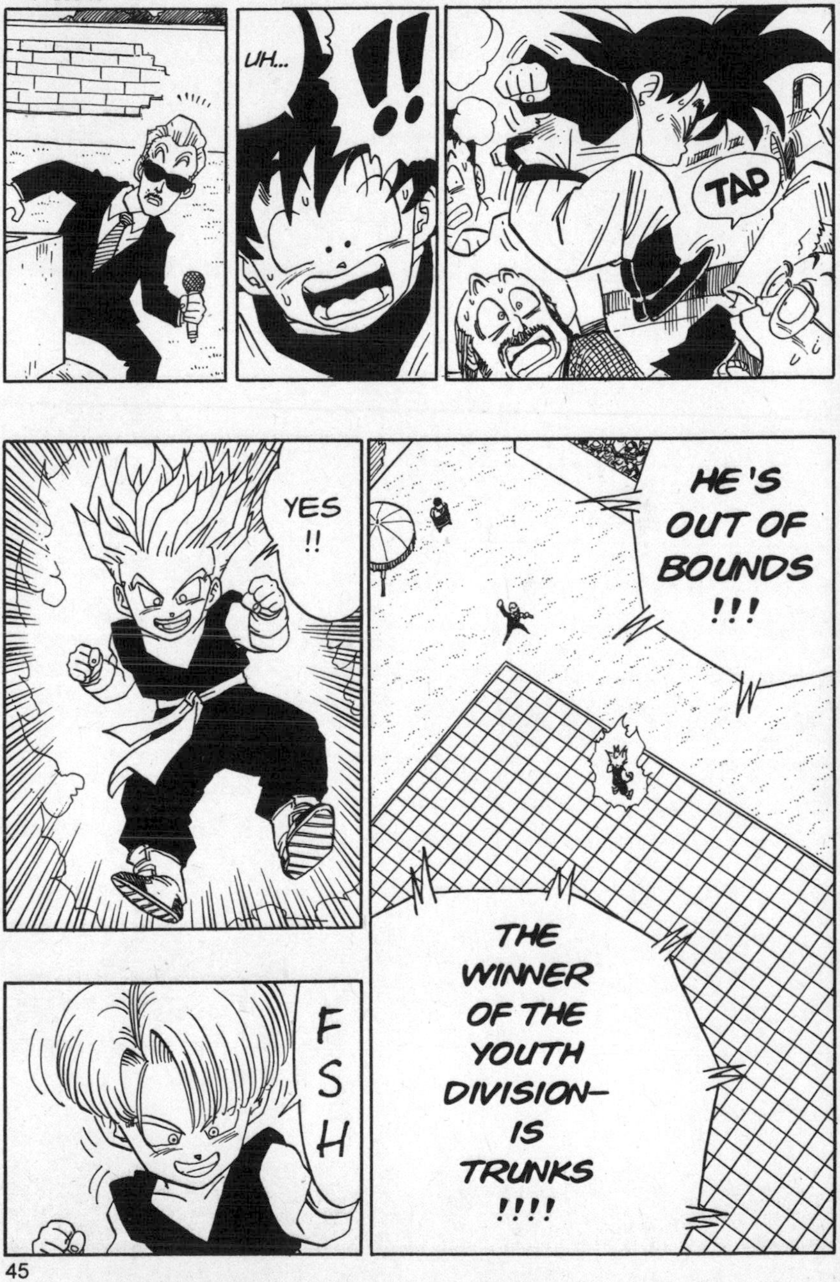

TAP
UH...
!!
HE'S OUT OF BOUNDS !!!
THE WINNER OF THE YOUTH DIVISION-IS TRUNKS !!!!
YES !!
FSH

READ THIS WAY

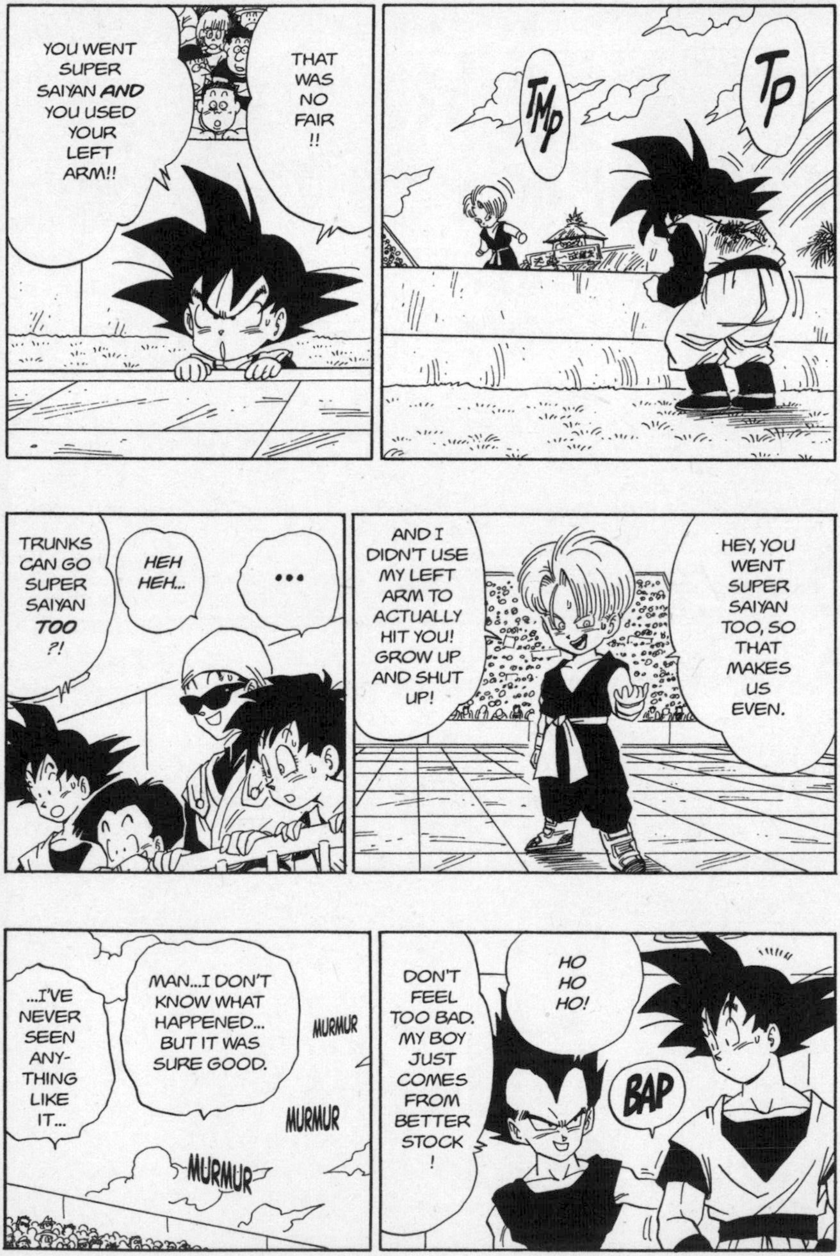
TP
TMP
YOU WENT SUPER SAIYAN AND YOU USED YOUR LEFT ARM!!
THAT WAS NO FAIR!!
HEY, YOU WENT SUPER SAIYAN TOO, SO THAT MAKES US EVEN.
AND I DIDN'T USE MY LEFT ARM TO ACTUALLY HIT YOU! GROW UP AND SHUT UP!
...
HEH HEH...
TRUNKS CAN GO SUPER SAIYAN TOO ?!
HO HO HO!
BAP
DON'T FEEL TOO BAD. MY BOY JUST COMES FROM BETTER STOCK!
MURMUR
MAN...I DON'T KNOW WHAT HAPPENED... BUT IT WAS SURE GOOD.
...I'VE NEVER SEEN ANY-THING LIKE IT...
MURMUR
MURMUR

READ THIS WAY

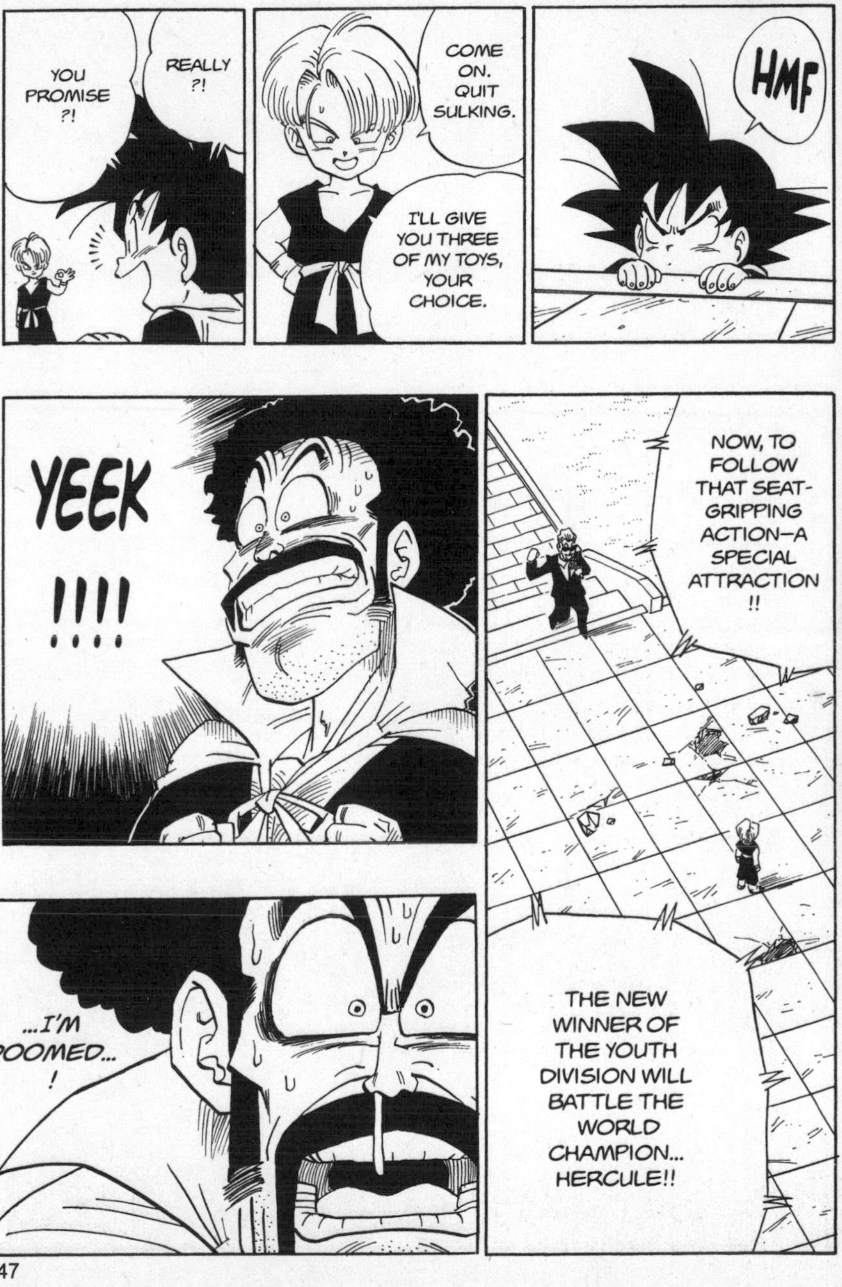
HMF
COME ON. QUIT SULKING.
I'LL GIVE YOU THREE OF MY TOYS, YOUR CHOICE.
REALLY ?!
YOU PROMISE ?!
NOW, TO FOLLOW THAT SEAT-GRIPPING ACTION—A SPECIAL ATTRACTION !!
THE NEW WINNER OF THE YOUTH DIVISION WILL BATTLE THE WORLD CHAMPION... HERCULE!!
YEEK !!!!
...I'M DOOMED... !

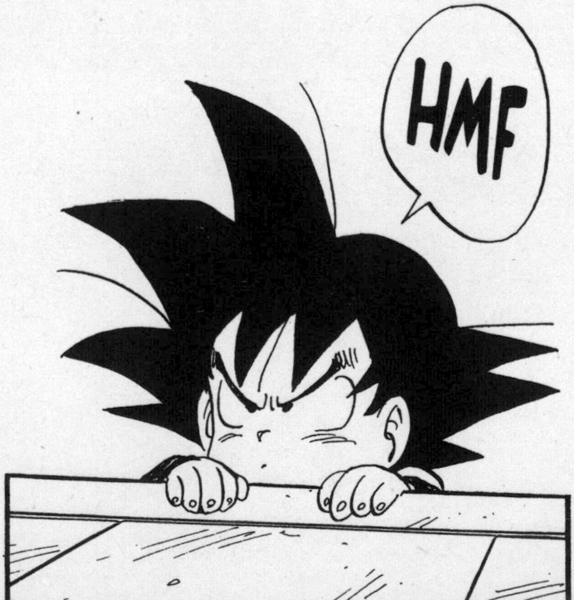
HMF

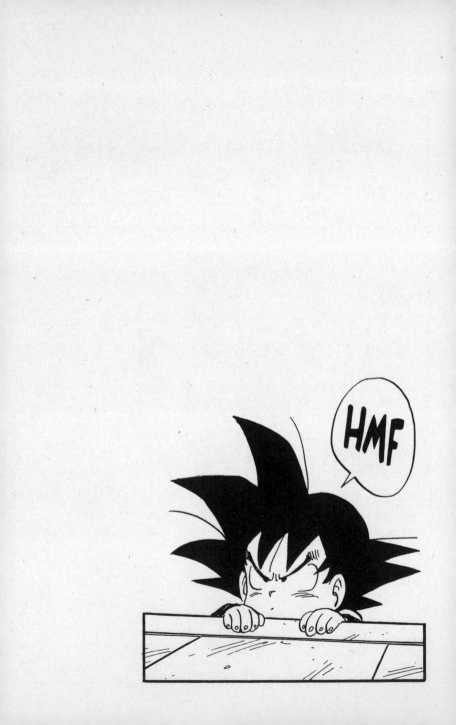

DBZ:242 • Hercule's Courage!

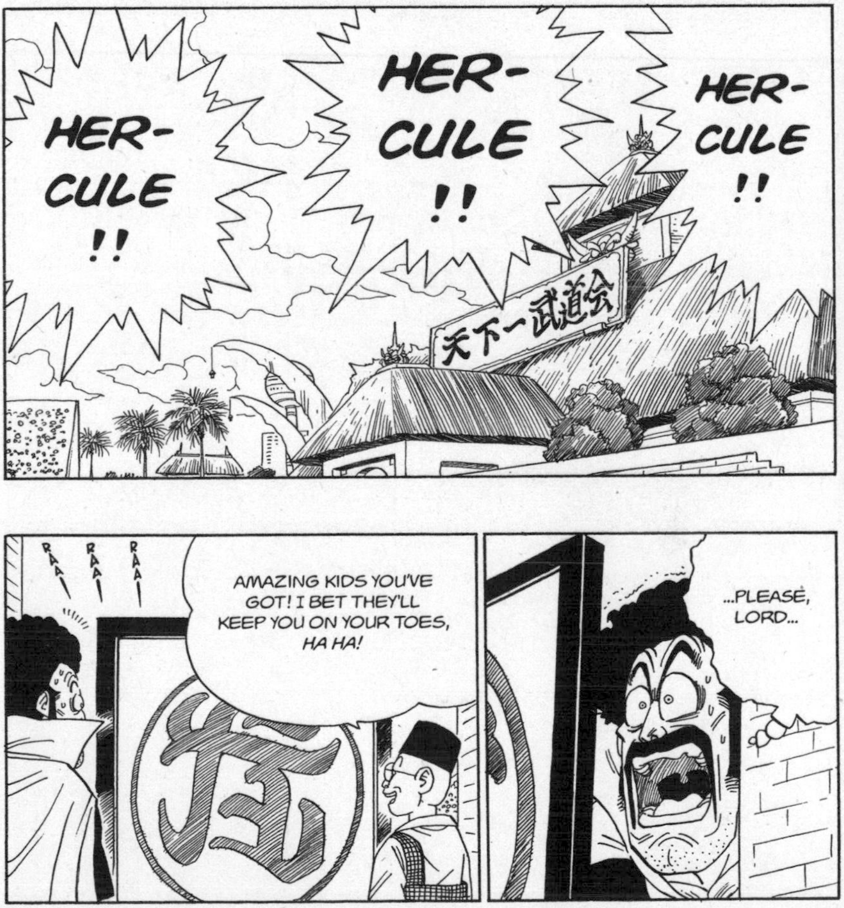

HER-CULE!!
HER-CULE!!
HER-CULE!!
天下一武道会
...PLEASE, LORD...
AMAZING KIDS YOU'VE GOT! I BET THEY'LL KEEP YOU ON YOUR TOES, HA HA!
RAA!
RAA!
RAA!

READ THIS WAY

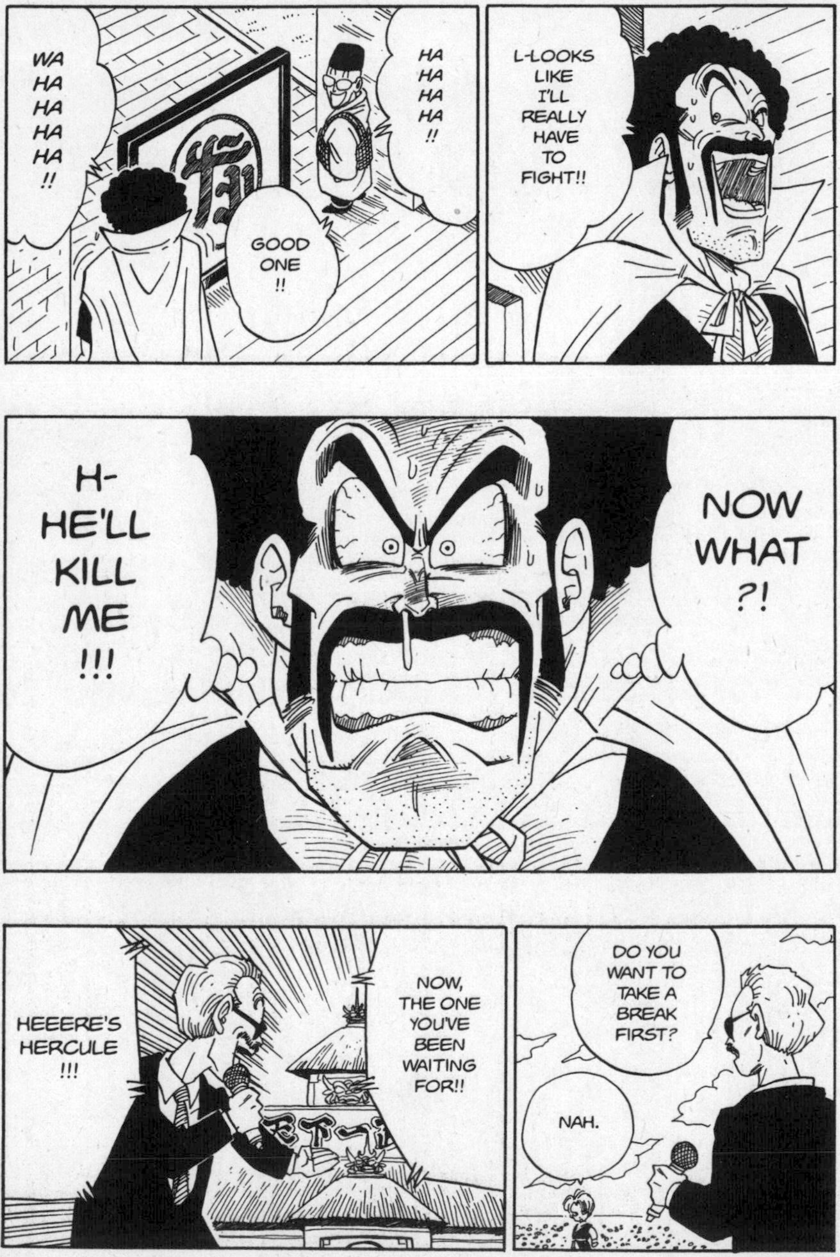
L-LOOKS LIKE I'LL REALLY HAVE TO FIGHT!!
HA HA HA HA !!
WA HA HA HA HA !!
GOOD ONE !!
NOW WHAT ?!
H-HE'LL KILL ME !!!
DO YOU WANT TO TAKE A BREAK FIRST?
NAH.
NOW, THE ONE YOU'VE BEEN WAITING FOR!!
HEEERE'S HERCULE !!!

READ THIS WAY

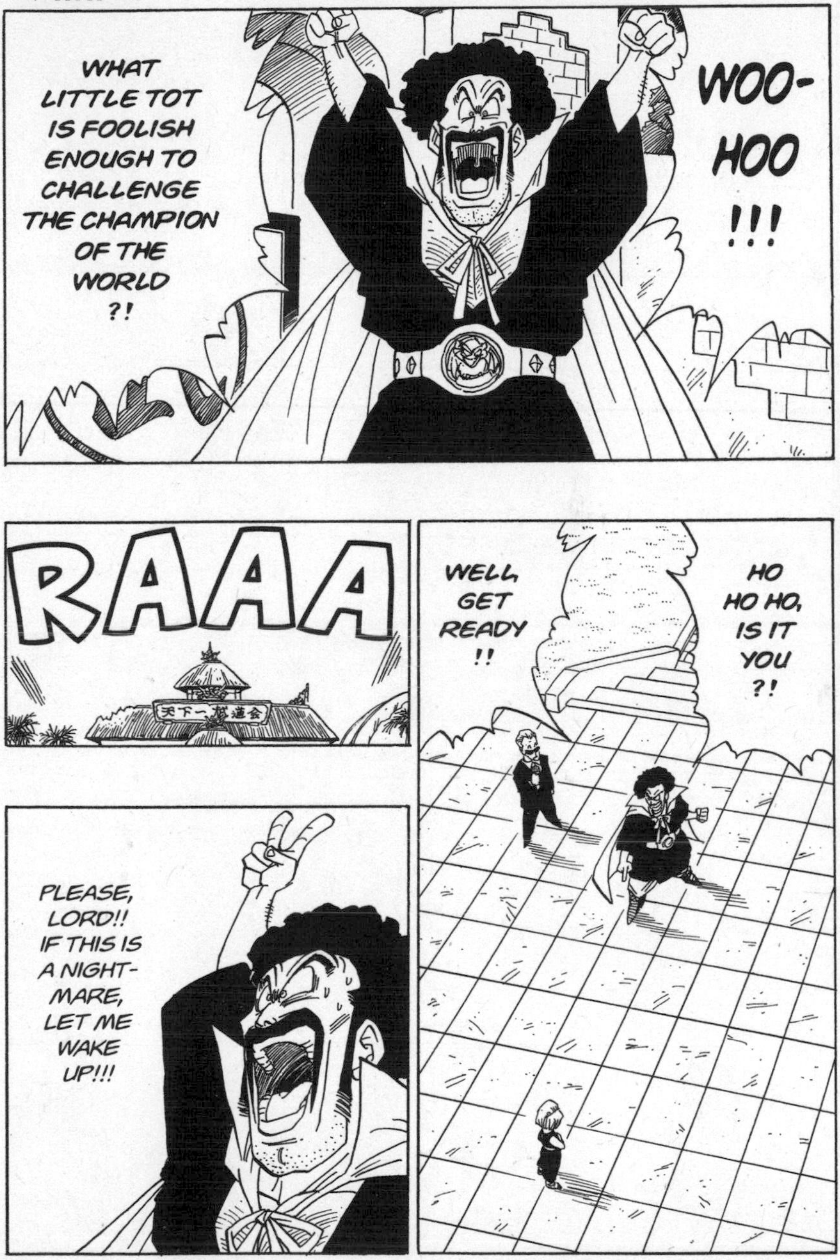
WOO-HOO!!!
WHAT LITTLE TOT IS FOOLISH ENOUGH TO CHALLENGE THE CHAMPION OF THE WORLD?!
HO HO HO, IS IT YOU?!
WELL, GET READY!!
RAAA
天下一武道会
PLEASE, LORD!! IF THIS IS A NIGHTMARE, LET ME WAKE UP!!!

READ THIS WAY

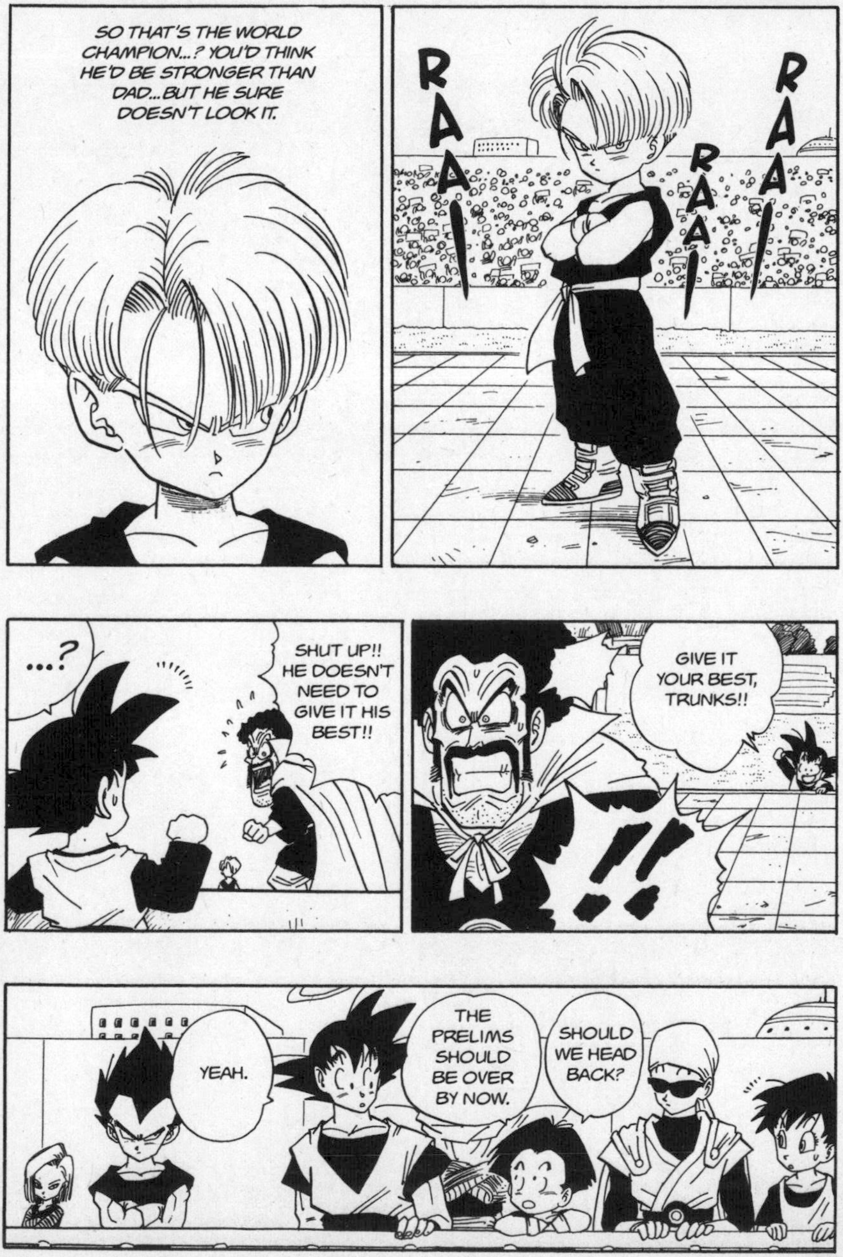
RAA
RAA
RAA
SO THAT'S THE WORLD CHAMPION...? YOU'D THINK HE'D BE STRONGER THAN DAD...BUT HE SURE DOESN'T LOOK IT.
GIVE IT YOUR BEST, TRUNKS!!
!!
SHUT UP!! HE DOESN'T NEED TO GIVE IT HIS BEST!!
...?
SHOULD WE HEAD BACK?
THE PRELIMS SHOULD BE OVER BY NOW.
YEAH.

READ THIS WAY

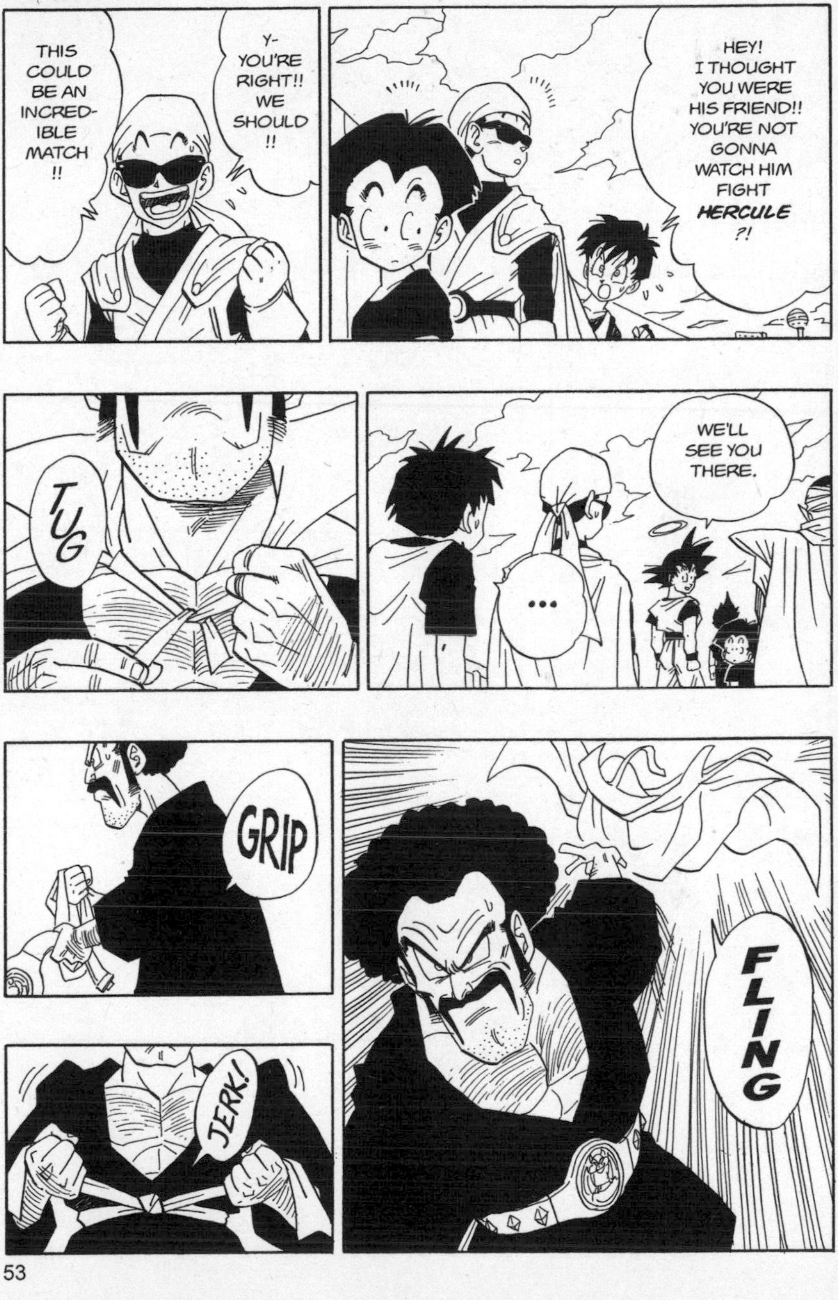
HEY! I THOUGHT YOU WERE HIS FRIEND!! YOU'RE NOT GONNA WATCH HIM FIGHT **HERCULE** ?!
THIS COULD BE AN INCRED-IBLE MATCH !!
Y-YOU'RE RIGHT!! WE SHOULD !!
WE'LL SEE YOU THERE.
...
TUG
FLING
GRIP
JERK!

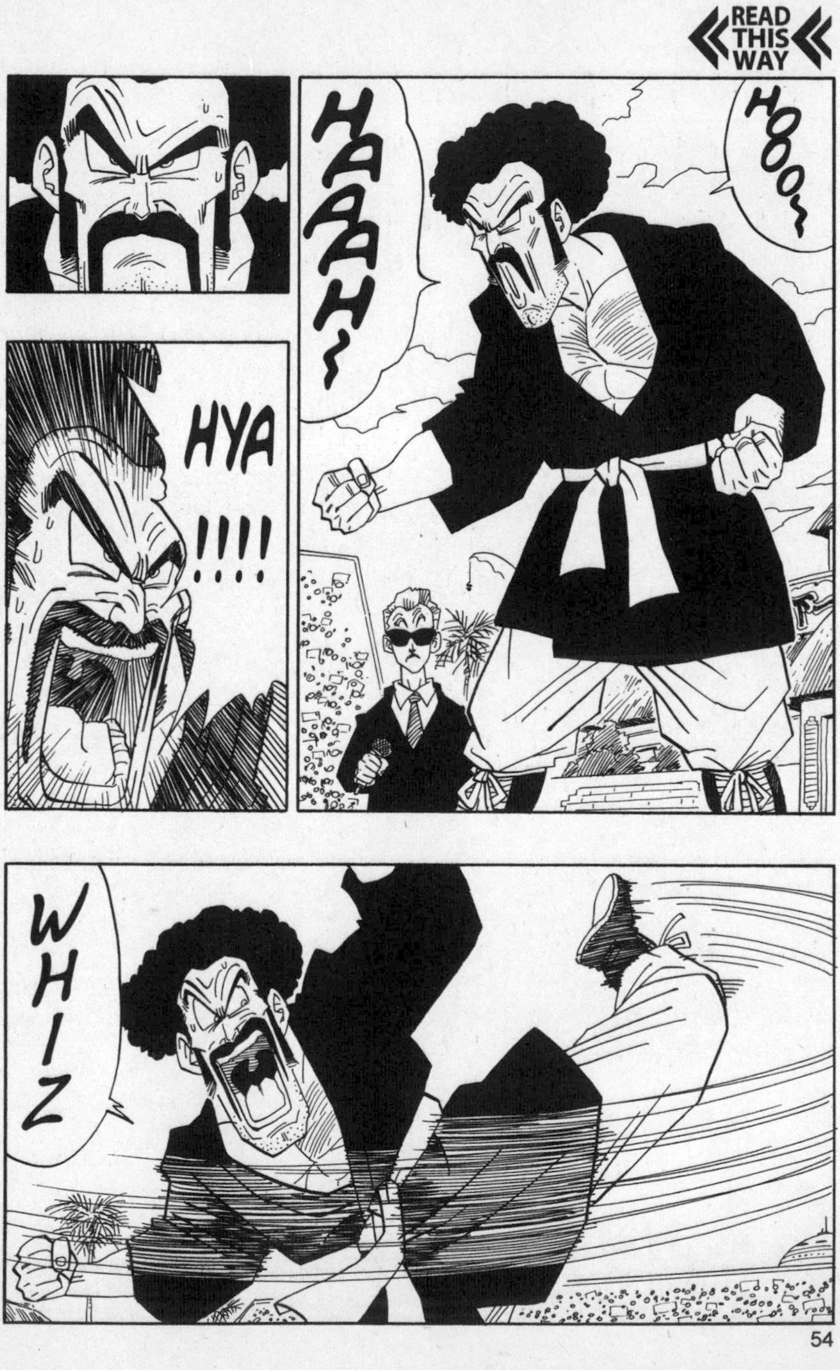
READ THIS WAY
HOOO~
HAAAH~
HYA
!!!!
WHIZ

READ THIS WAY

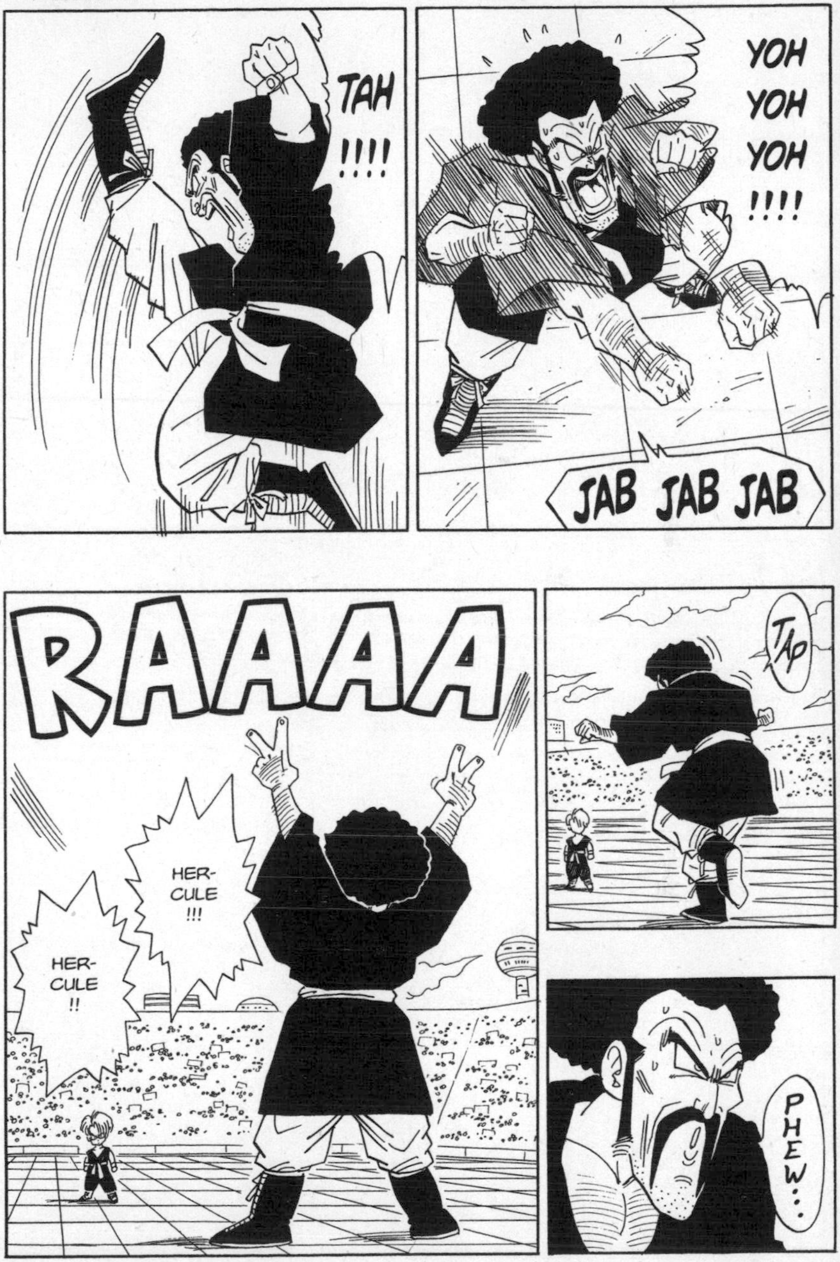
YOH YOH YOH !!!!
JAB JAB JAB
TAH !!!!
TAP
PHEW...
RAAAA
HER-CULE !!!
HER-CULE !!

READ THIS WAY

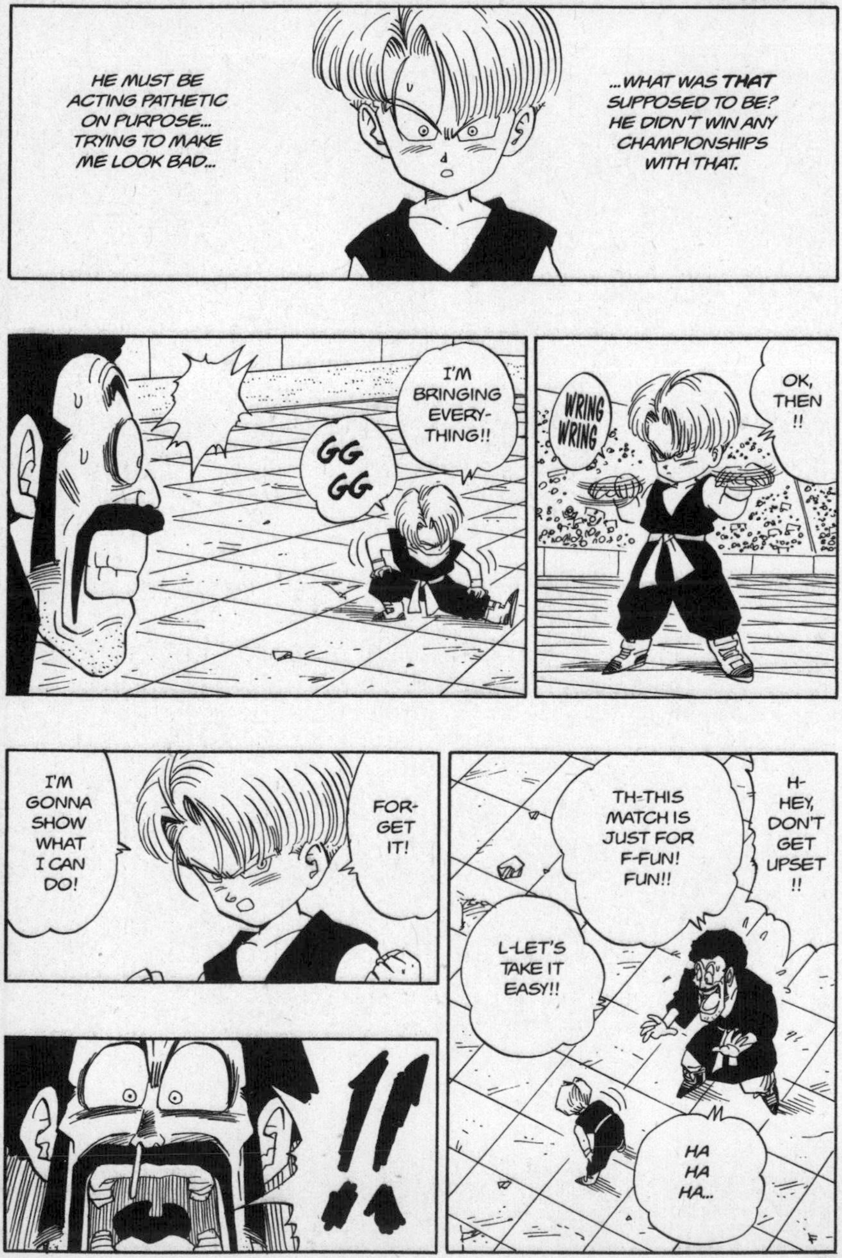
...WHAT WAS THAT SUPPOSED TO BE? HE DIDN'T WIN ANY CHAMPIONSHIPS WITH THAT.
HE MUST BE ACTING PATHETIC ON PURPOSE... TRYING TO MAKE ME LOOK BAD...
OK, THEN !!
WRING WRING
I'M BRINGING EVERY-THING!!
GG GG
H-HEY, DON'T GET UPSET !!
TH-THIS MATCH IS JUST FOR F-FUN! FUN!!
L-LET'S TAKE IT EASY!!
HA HA HA...
FOR-GET IT!
I'M GONNA SHOW WHAT I CAN DO!
!!

READ THIS WAY

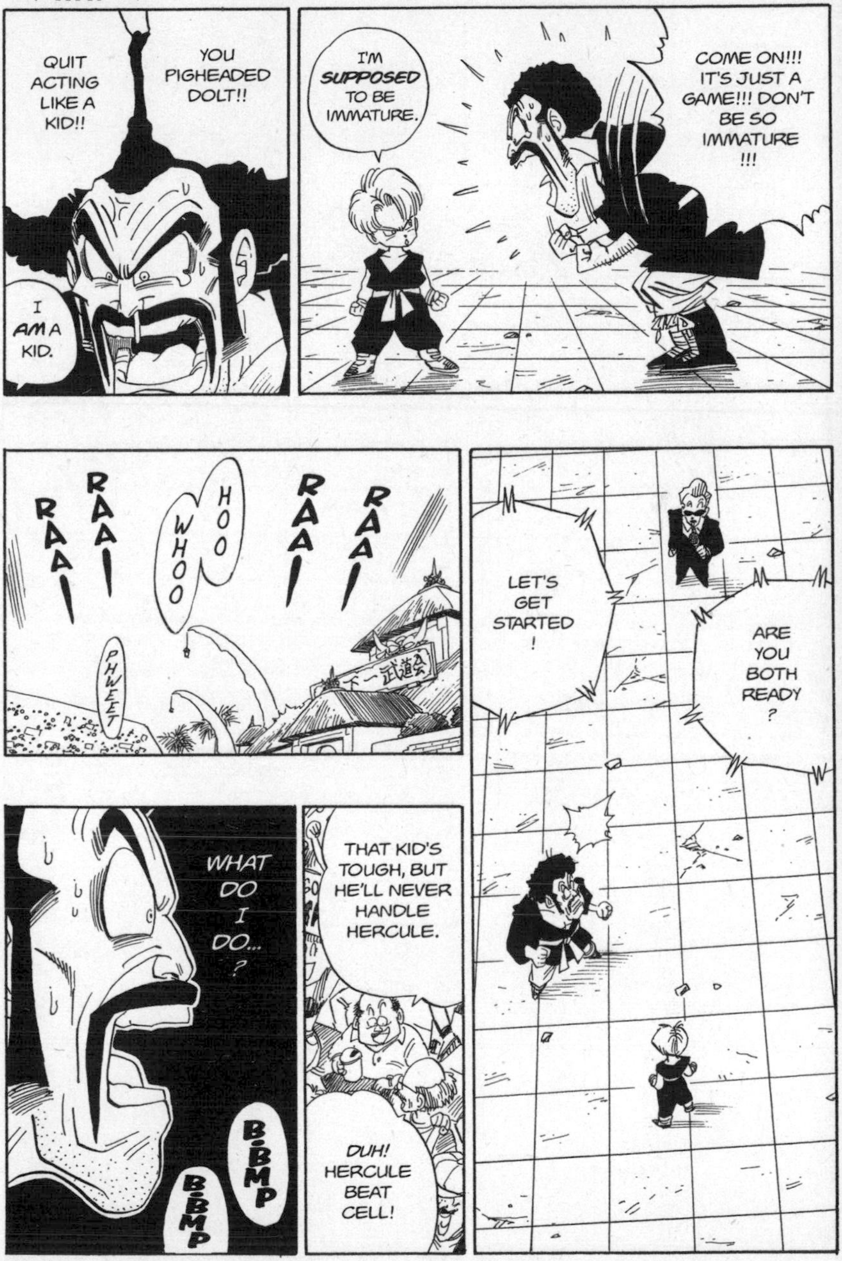

COME ON!!! IT'S JUST A GAME!!! DON'T BE SO IMMATURE!!!
I'M *SUPPOSED* TO BE IMMATURE.
YOU PIGHEADED DOLT!!
QUIT ACTING LIKE A KID!!
I *AM* A KID.
ARE YOU BOTH READY?
LET'S GET STARTED!
RAA!
RAA!
WHOO HOO
RAA!
RAA!
PHWEET
THAT KID'S TOUGH, BUT HE'LL NEVER HANDLE HERCULE.
DUH! HERCULE BEAT CELL!
WHAT DO I DO...?
B-BMP
B-BMP

READ THIS WAY

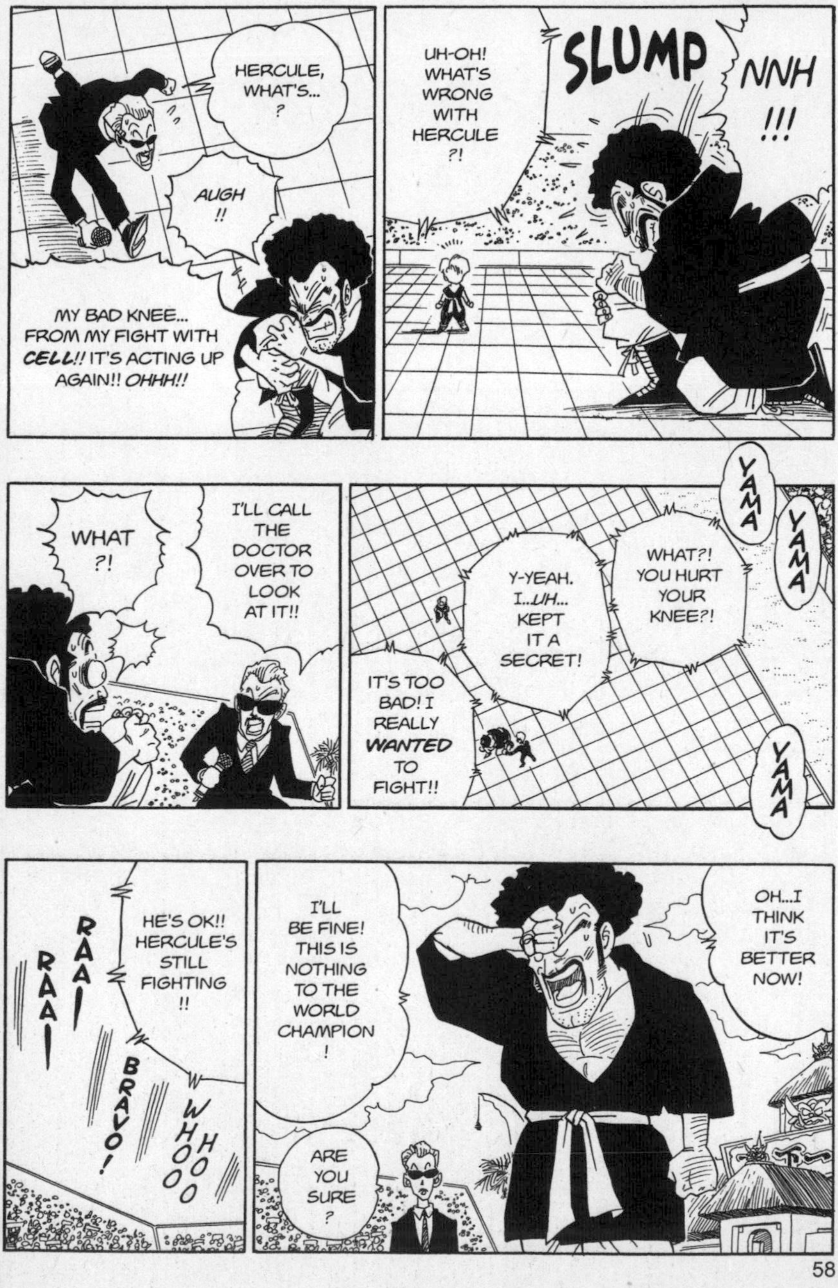

NNH!!!
SLUMP
UH-OH! WHAT'S WRONG WITH HERCULE?!
HERCULE, WHAT'S...?
AUGH!!
MY BAD KNEE... FROM MY FIGHT WITH *CELL!!* IT'S ACTING UP AGAIN!! *OHHH!!*
YAMA
YAMA
WHAT?! YOU HURT YOUR KNEE?!
Y-YEAH. I...*UH*... KEPT IT A SECRET!
IT'S TOO BAD! I REALLY ***WANTED*** TO FIGHT!!
YAMA
I'LL CALL THE DOCTOR OVER TO LOOK AT IT!!
WHAT?!
OH...I THINK IT'S BETTER NOW!
I'LL BE FINE! THIS IS NOTHING TO THE WORLD CHAMPION!
ARE YOU SURE?
HE'S OK!! HERCULE'S STILL FIGHTING!!
RAA!
RAA!
BRAVO!
WHOOO
HOOO

READ THIS WAY

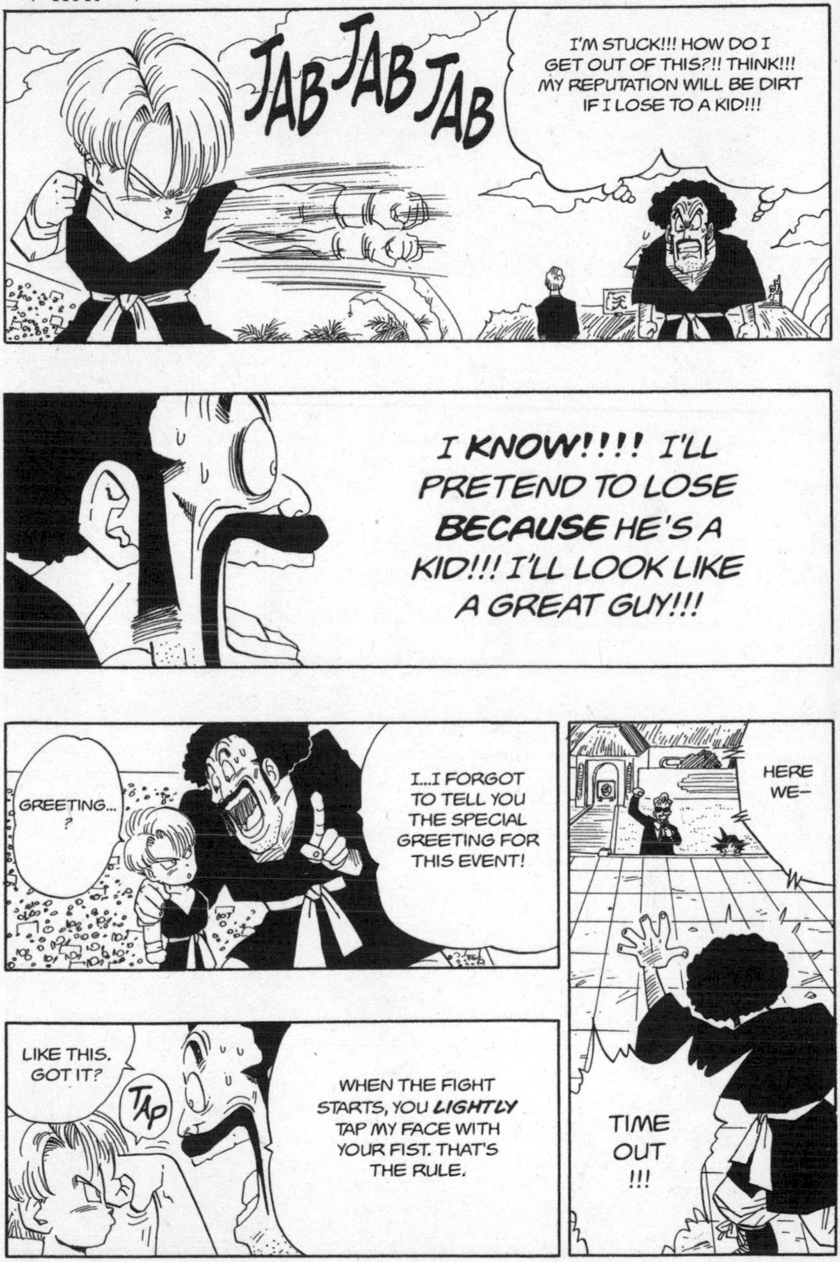

I'M STUCK!!! HOW DO I GET OUT OF THIS?!! THINK!!! MY REPUTATION WILL BE DIRT IF I LOSE TO A KID!!!
JAB JAB JAB
I KNOW!!!! I'LL PRETEND TO LOSE BECAUSE HE'S A KID!!! I'LL LOOK LIKE A GREAT GUY!!!
HERE WE—
TIME OUT !!!
I...I FORGOT TO TELL YOU THE SPECIAL GREETING FOR THIS EVENT!
GREETING... ?
WHEN THE FIGHT STARTS, YOU LIGHTLY TAP MY FACE WITH YOUR FIST. THAT'S THE RULE.
LIKE THIS. GOT IT?
TAP

READ THIS WAY

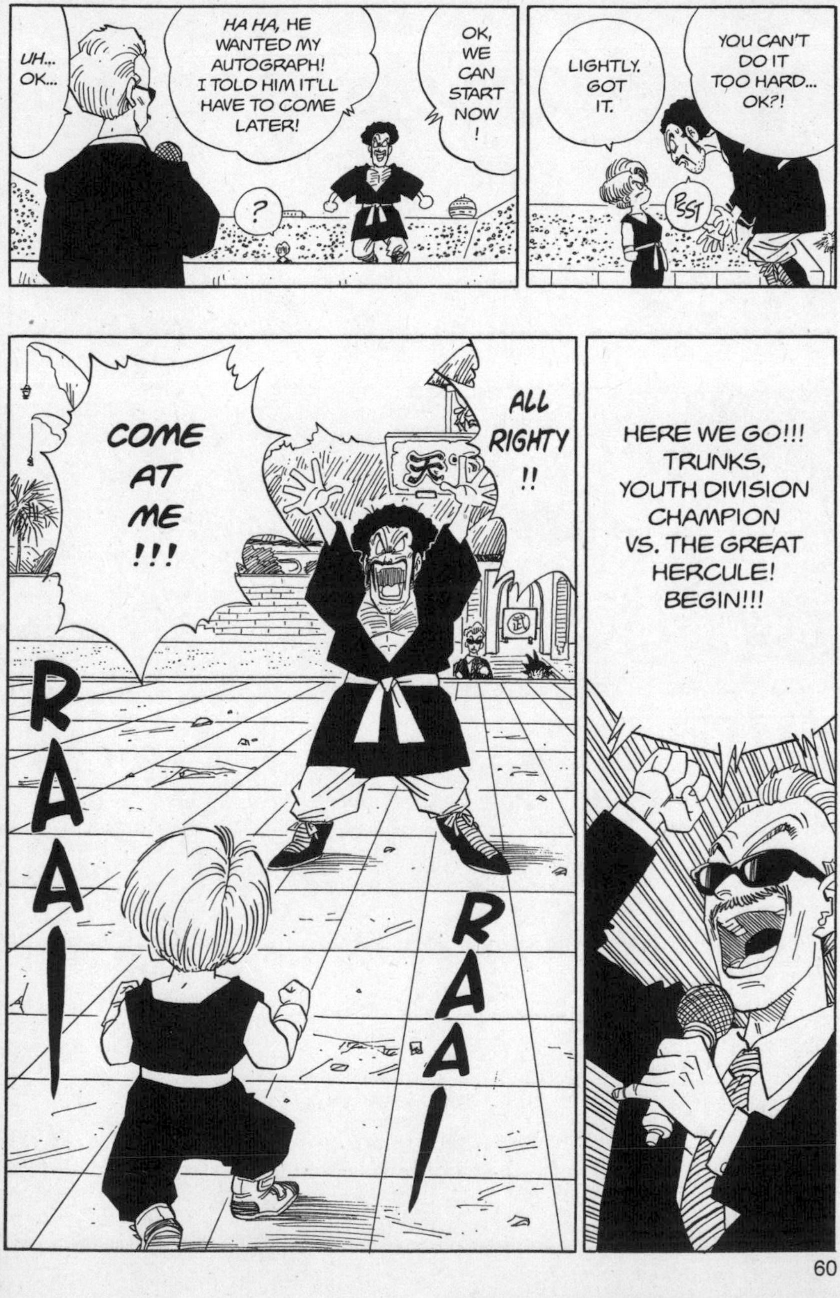

YOU CAN'T DO IT TOO HARD... OK?!
LIGHTLY. GOT IT.
PSST
OK, WE CAN START NOW!
HA HA, HE WANTED MY AUTOGRAPH! I TOLD HIM IT'LL HAVE TO COME LATER!
?
UH... OK...
HERE WE GO!!! TRUNKS, YOUTH DIVISION CHAMPION VS. THE GREAT HERCULE! BEGIN!!!
ALL RIGHTY!!
COME AT ME!!!
RAAA!
RAAA!

READ THIS WAY

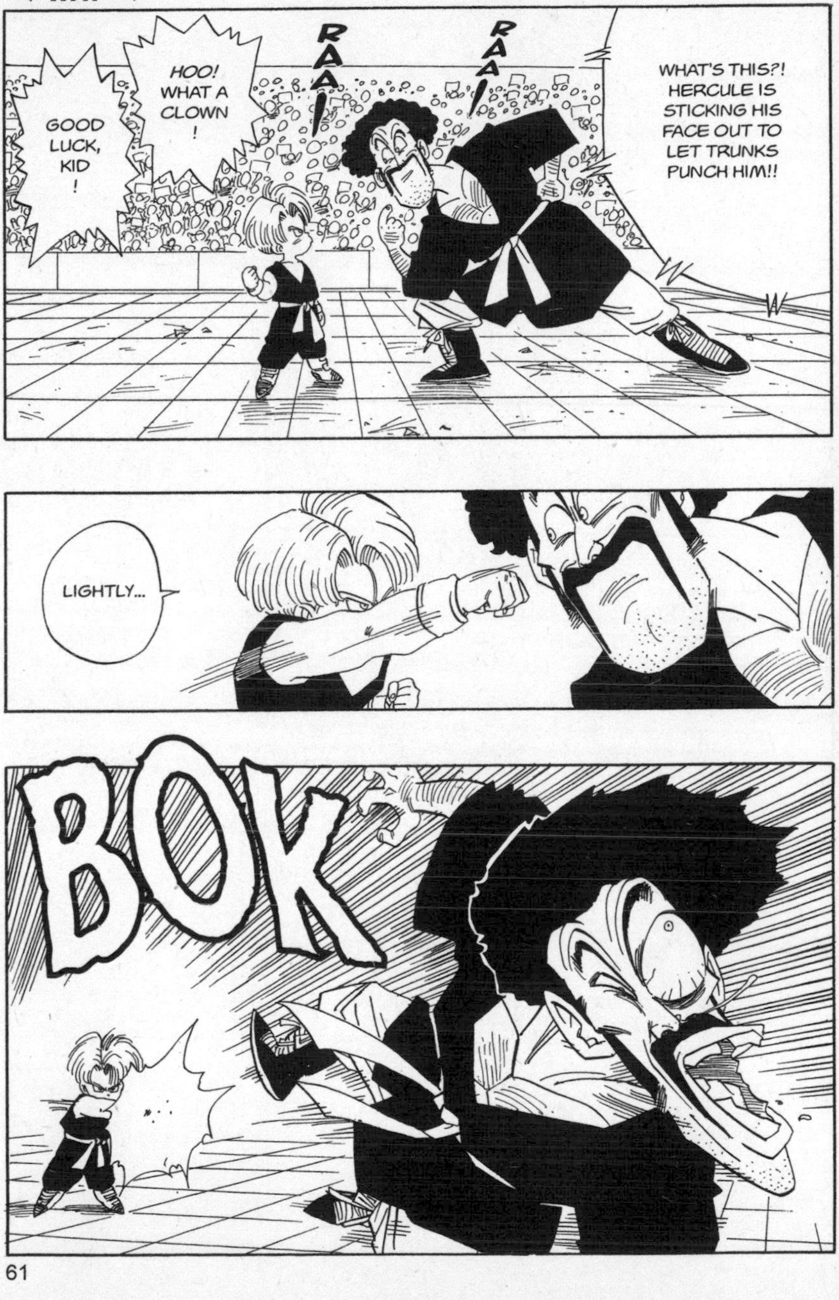
WHAT'S THIS?! HERCULE IS STICKING HIS FACE OUT TO LET TRUNKS PUNCH HIM!!
RAA!
RAA!
HOO! WHAT A CLOWN!
GOOD LUCK, KID!
LIGHTLY...
BOK

READ THIS WAY

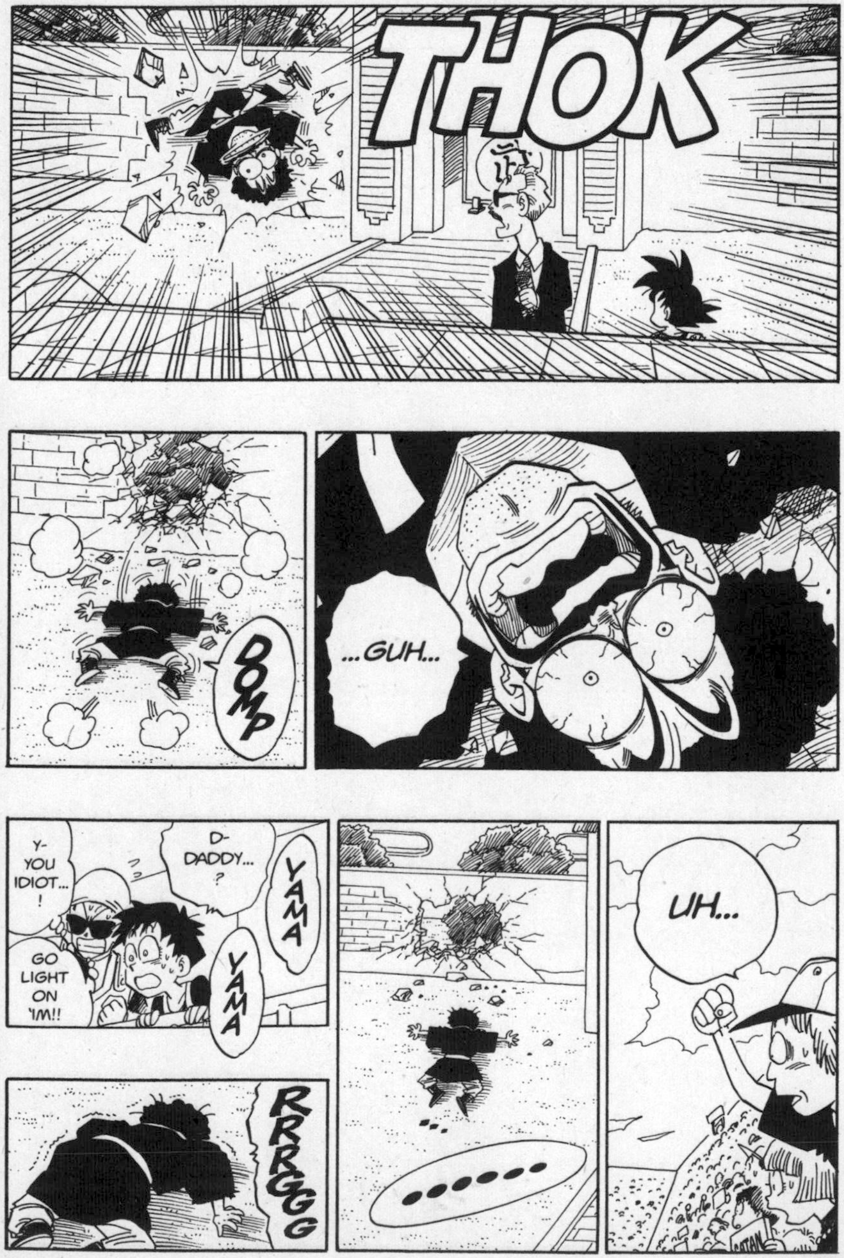
THOK
...GUH...
DOMP
UH...
......
YAMA YAMA
D-DADDY...?
Y-YOU IDIOT...!
GO LIGHT ON 'IM!!
RRRGGG

READ THIS WAY

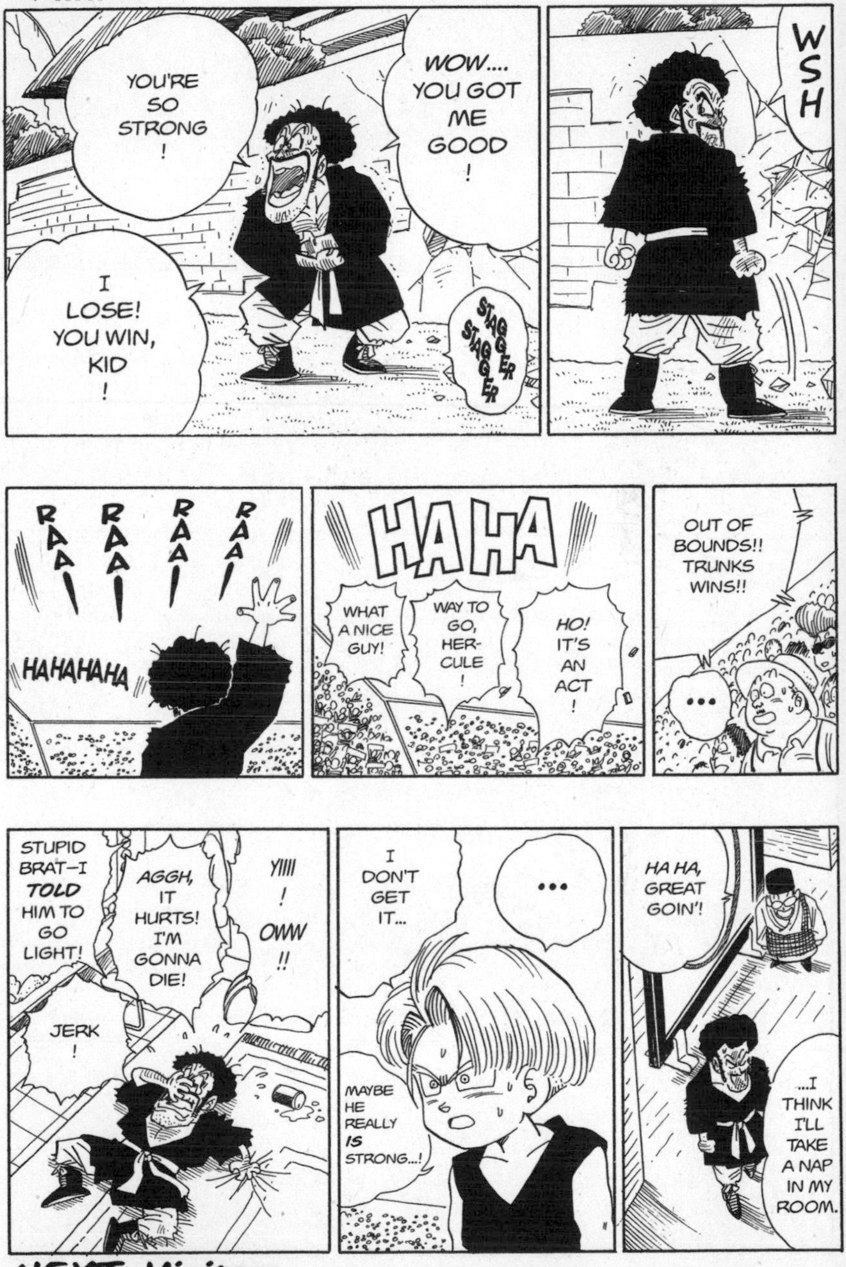
WSH
WOW.... YOU GOT ME GOOD!
YOU'RE SO STRONG!
STAGGER STAGGER
I LOSE! YOU WIN, KID!
OUT OF BOUNDS!! TRUNKS WINS!!
...
HAHA
HO! IT'S AN ACT!
WAY TO GO, HERCULE!
WHAT A NICE GUY!
RAAA RAAA RAAA RAA
HAHAHAHA
HA HA, GREAT GOIN'!
...I THINK I'LL TAKE A NAP IN MY ROOM.
...
I DON'T GET IT...
MAYBE HE REALLY *IS* STRONG...!
YIIII! OWW!!
AGGH, IT HURTS! I'M GONNA DIE!
STUPID BRAT—I *TOLD* HIM TO GO LIGHT!
JERK!

NEXT: Visitors

DBZ:243 • The Mysterious Duo

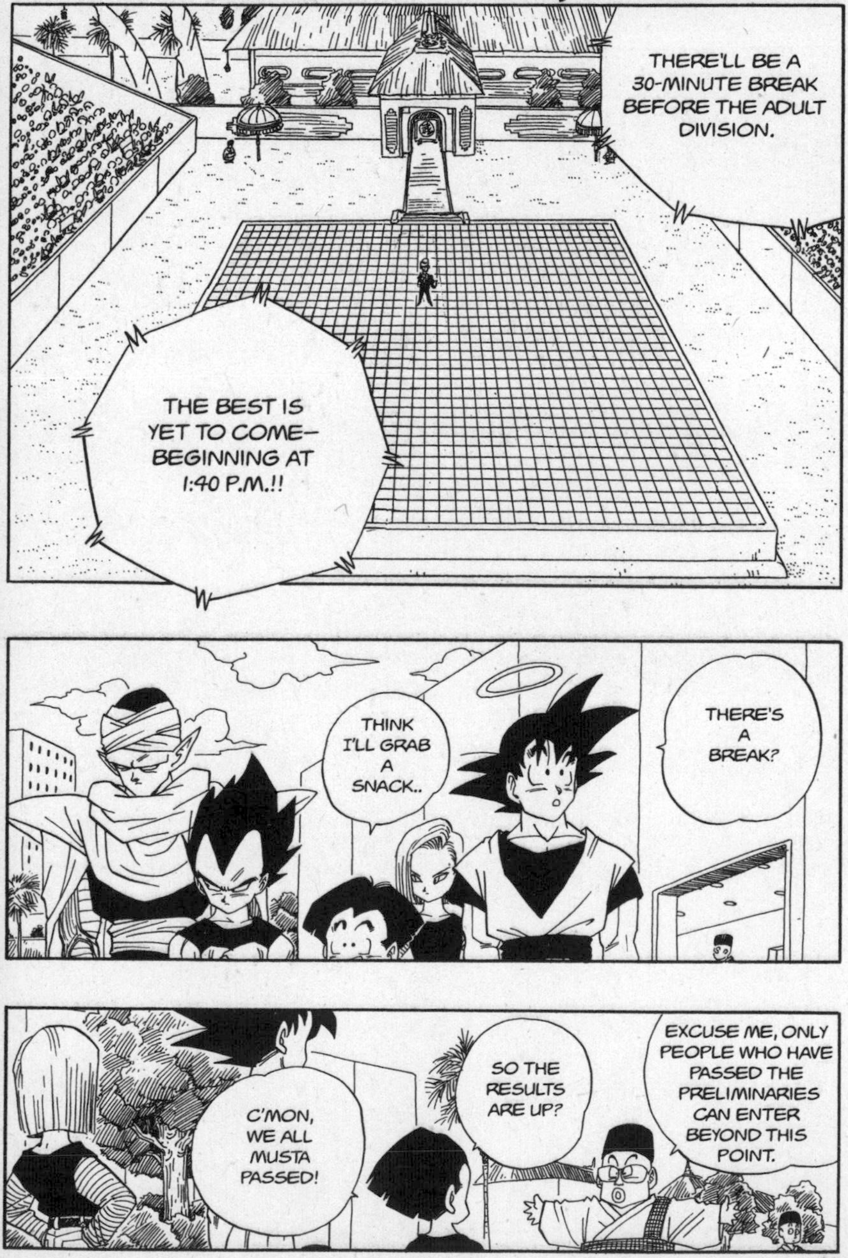
THERE'LL BE A 30-MINUTE BREAK BEFORE THE ADULT DIVISION.
THE BEST IS YET TO COME— BEGINNING AT 1:40 P.M.!!
THERE'S A BREAK?
THINK I'LL GRAB A SNACK..
EXCUSE ME, ONLY PEOPLE WHO HAVE PASSED THE PRELIMINARIES CAN ENTER BEYOND THIS POINT.
SO THE RESULTS ARE UP?
C'MON, WE ALL MUSTA PASSED!

READ THIS WAY

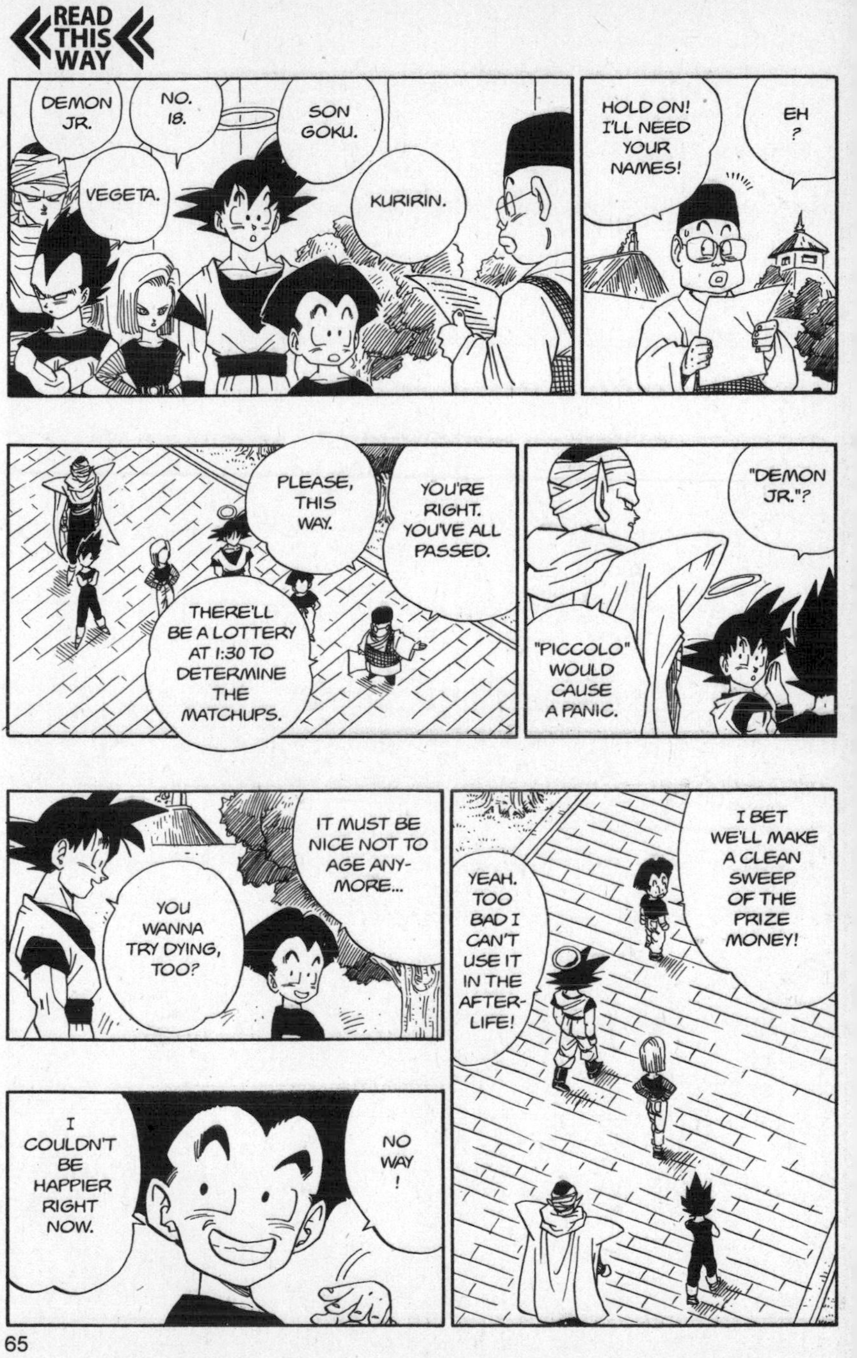
EH ?
HOLD ON! I'LL NEED YOUR NAMES!
SON GOKU.
NO. 18.
DEMON JR.
KURIRIN.
VEGETA.
"DEMON JR."?
"PICCOLO" WOULD CAUSE A PANIC.
YOU'RE RIGHT. YOU'VE ALL PASSED.
PLEASE, THIS WAY.
THERE'LL BE A LOTTERY AT 1:30 TO DETERMINE THE MATCHUPS.
I BET WE'LL MAKE A CLEAN SWEEP OF THE PRIZE MONEY!
YEAH. TOO BAD I CAN'T USE IT IN THE AFTER-LIFE!
IT MUST BE NICE NOT TO AGE ANY-MORE...
YOU WANNA TRY DYING, TOO?
NO WAY !
I COULDN'T BE HAPPIER RIGHT NOW.

READ THIS WAY

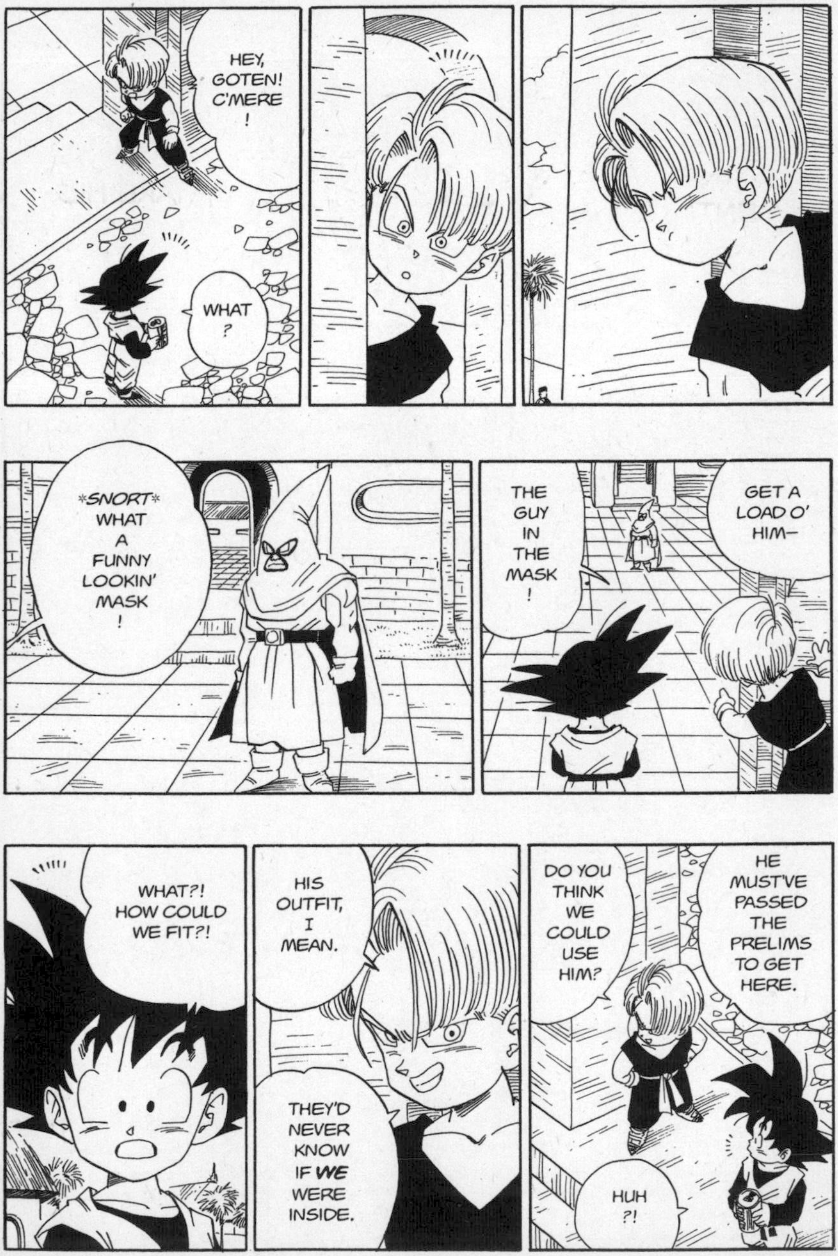
HEY, GOTEN! C'MERE!
WHAT?
GET A LOAD O' HIM—
THE GUY IN THE MASK!
SNORT WHAT A FUNNY LOOKIN' MASK!
HE MUST'VE PASSED THE PRELIMS TO GET HERE.
DO YOU THINK WE COULD USE HIM?
HUH?!
HIS OUTFIT, I MEAN.
THEY'D NEVER KNOW IF ***WE*** WERE INSIDE.
WHAT?! HOW COULD WE FIT?!

READ THIS WAY

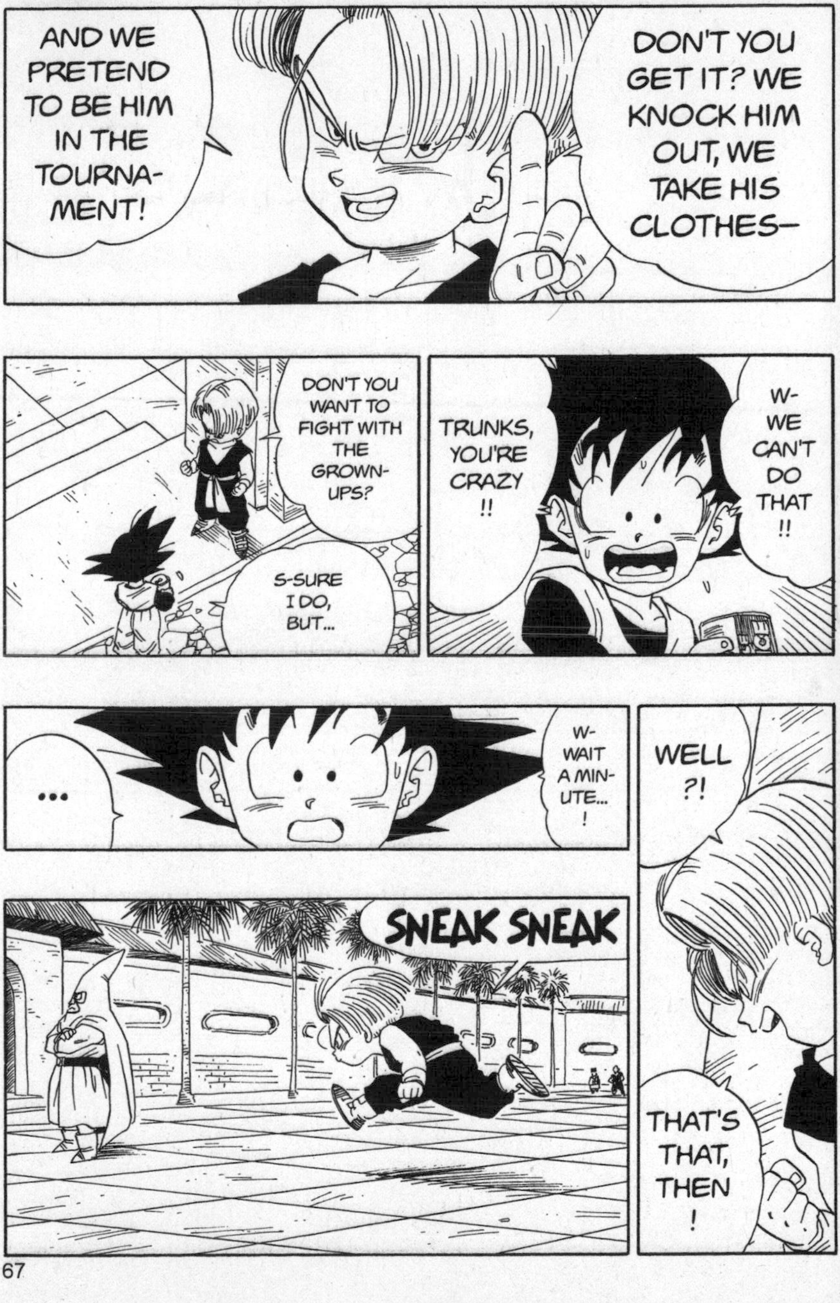
DON'T YOU GET IT? WE KNOCK HIM OUT, WE TAKE HIS CLOTHES—
AND WE PRETEND TO BE HIM IN THE TOURNA-MENT!
W-WE CAN'T DO THAT!!
TRUNKS, YOU'RE CRAZY!!
DON'T YOU WANT TO FIGHT WITH THE GROWN-UPS?
S-SURE I DO, BUT...
WELL?!
THAT'S THAT, THEN!
W-WAIT A MIN-UTE...!
...
SNEAK SNEAK

READ THIS WAY

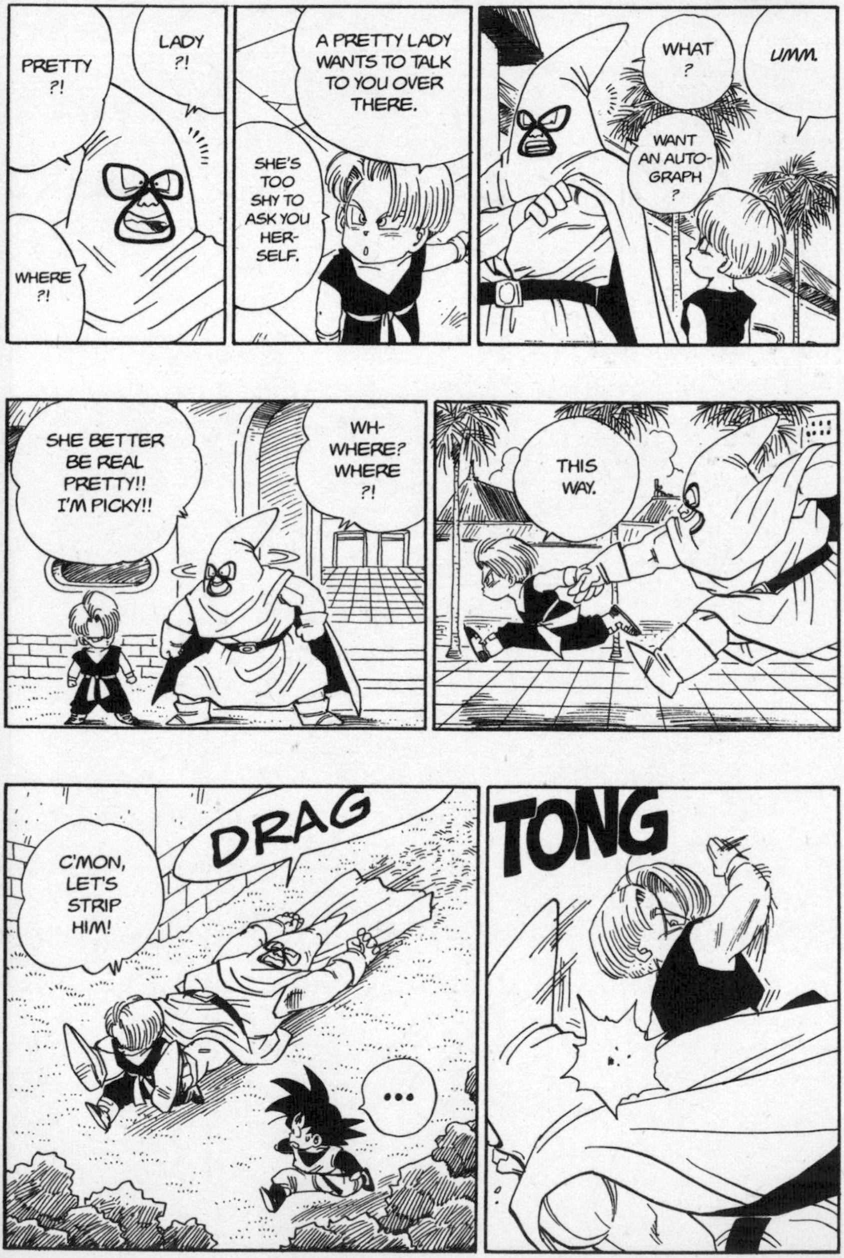
UMM.
WHAT ?
WANT AN AUTO-GRAPH ?
A PRETTY LADY WANTS TO TALK TO YOU OVER THERE.
SHE'S TOO SHY TO ASK YOU HER-SELF.
LADY ?!
PRETTY ?!
WHERE ?!
THIS WAY.
WH- WHERE? WHERE ?!
SHE BETTER BE REAL PRETTY!! I'M PICKY!!
TONG
DRAG
C'MON, LET'S STRIP HIM!
...

READ THIS WAY

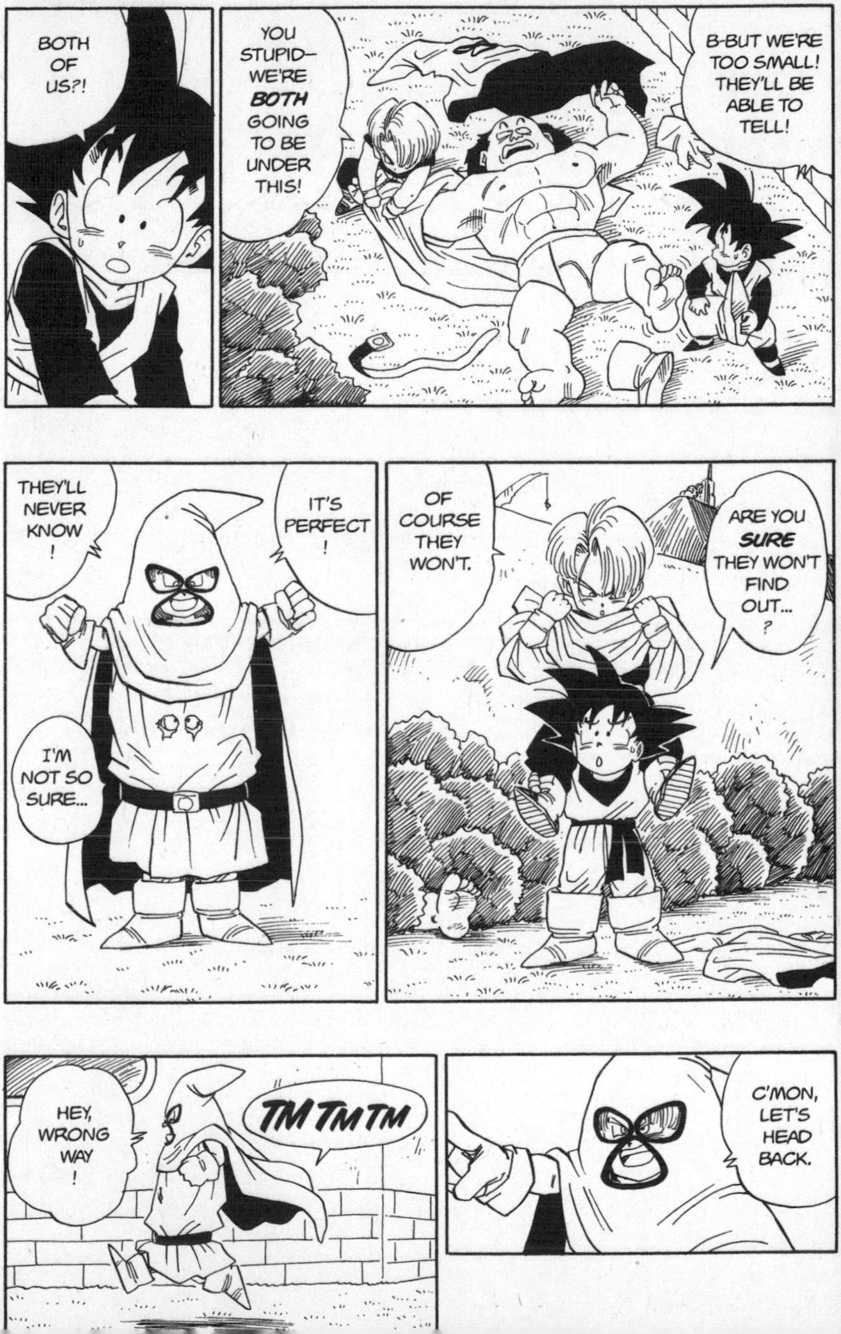
B-BUT WE'RE TOO SMALL! THEY'LL BE ABLE TO TELL!
YOU STUPID— WE'RE *BOTH* GOING TO BE UNDER THIS!
BOTH OF US?!
ARE YOU *SURE* THEY WON'T FIND OUT...?
OF COURSE THEY WON'T.
IT'S PERFECT!
THEY'LL NEVER KNOW!
I'M NOT SO SURE...
C'MON, LET'S HEAD BACK.
TM TM TM
HEY, WRONG WAY!

READ THIS WAY

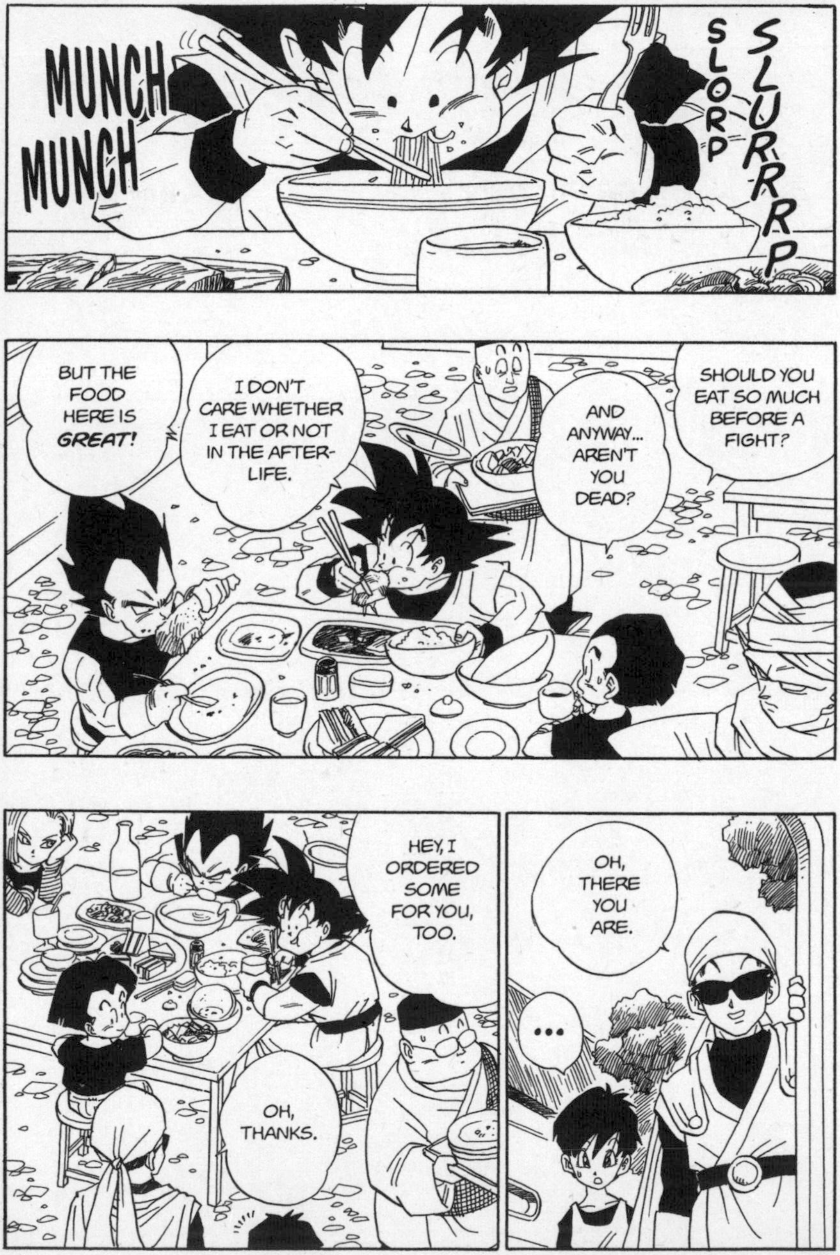
SLURRRP
SLORP
MUNCH MUNCH
SHOULD YOU EAT SO MUCH BEFORE A FIGHT?
AND ANYWAY... AREN'T YOU DEAD?
I DON'T CARE WHETHER I EAT OR NOT IN THE AFTER-LIFE.
BUT THE FOOD HERE IS *GREAT!*
OH, THERE YOU ARE.
...
HEY, I ORDERED SOME FOR YOU, TOO.
OH, THANKS.

READ THIS WAY

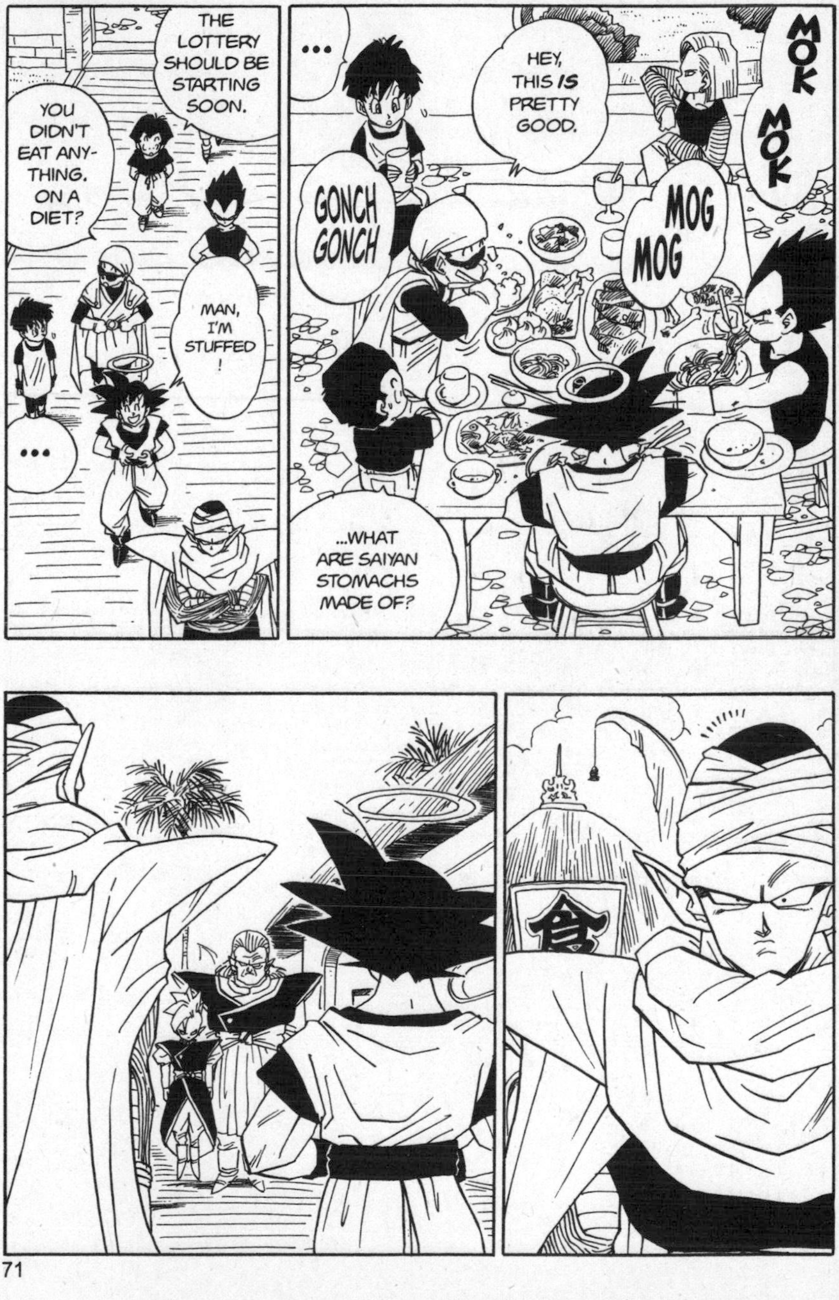
MOK MOK
HEY, THIS IS PRETTY GOOD.
...
MOG MOG
GONCH GONCH
...WHAT ARE SAIYAN STOMACHS MADE OF?
THE LOTTERY SHOULD BE STARTING SOON.
YOU DIDN'T EAT ANY-THING. ON A DIET?
MAN, I'M STUFFED!
...

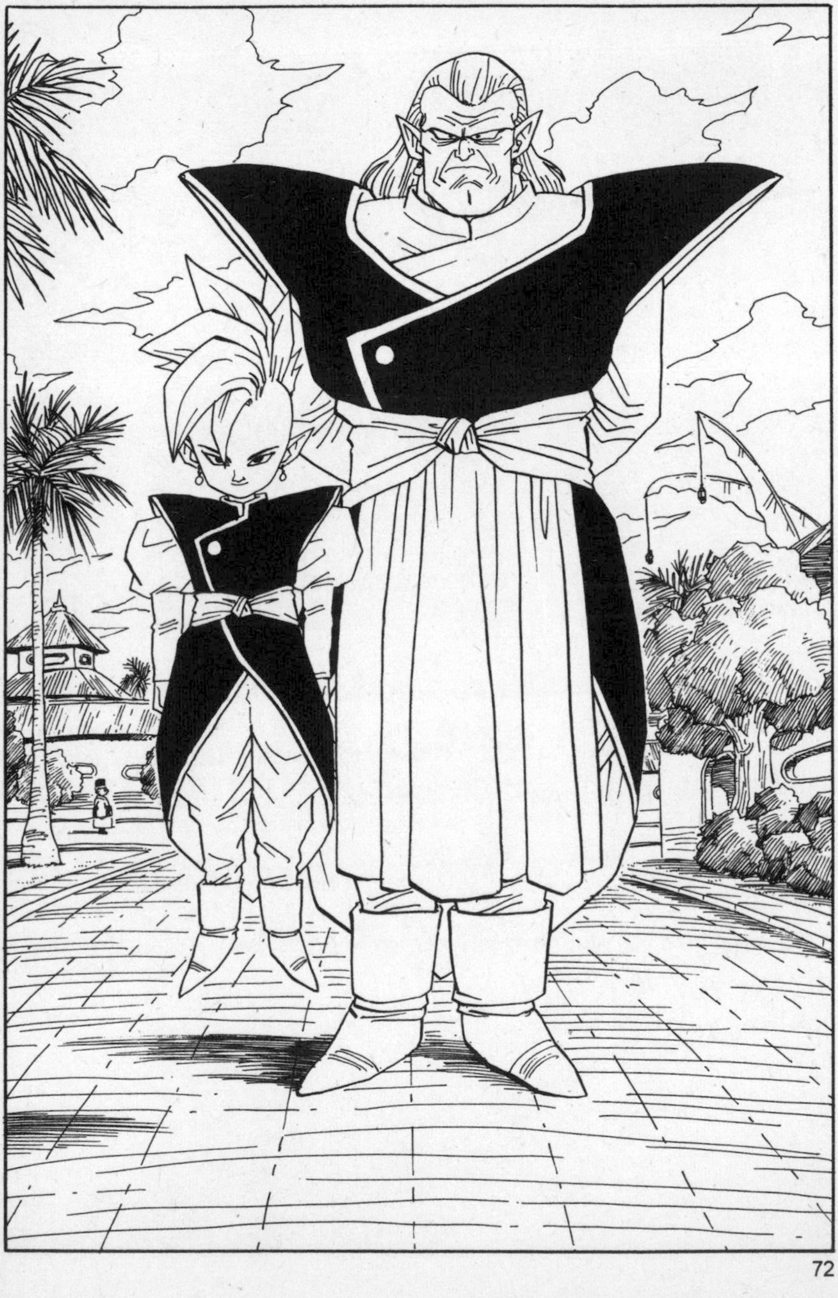

READ THIS WAY

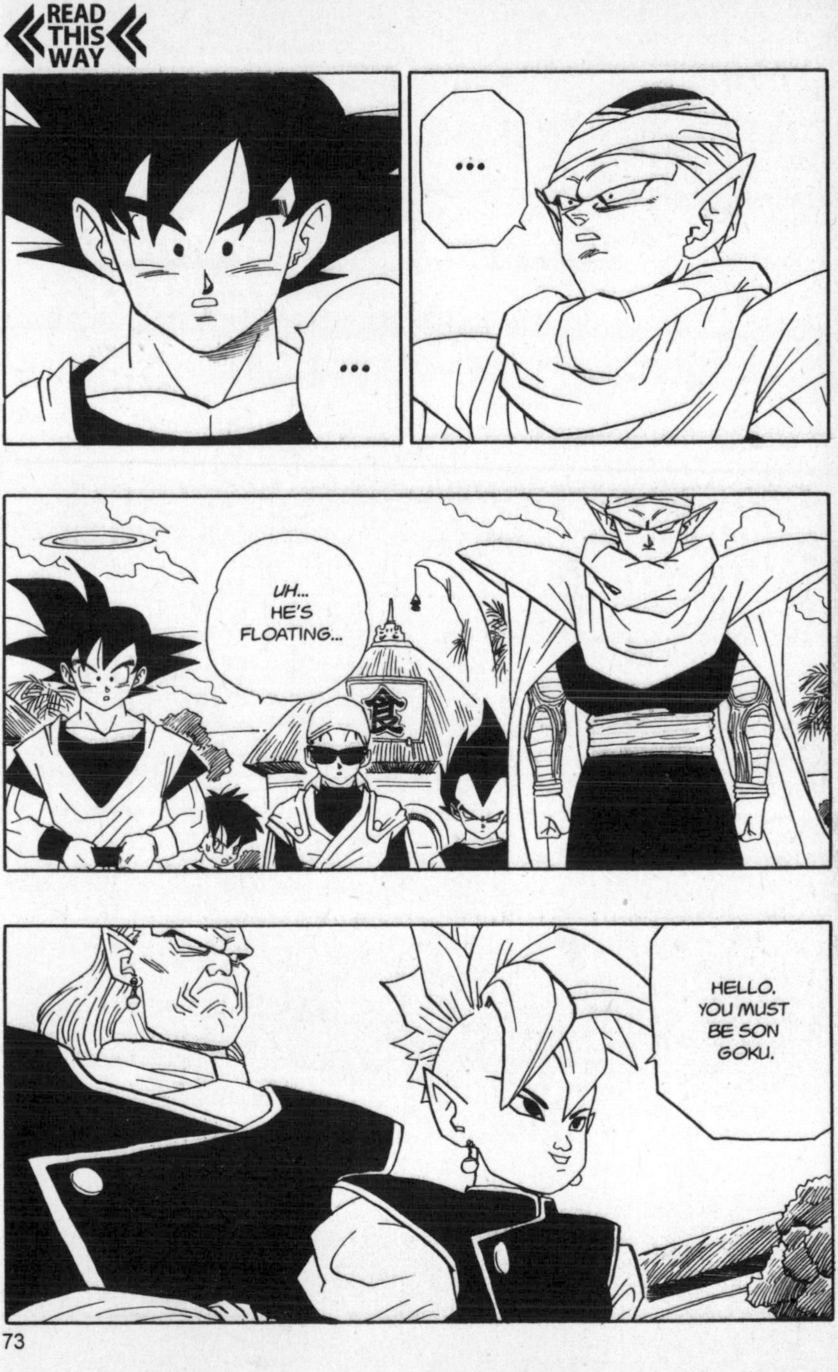
READ THIS WAY
...
...
UH... HE'S FLOATING...
HELLO. YOU MUST BE SON GOKU.

READ THIS WAY

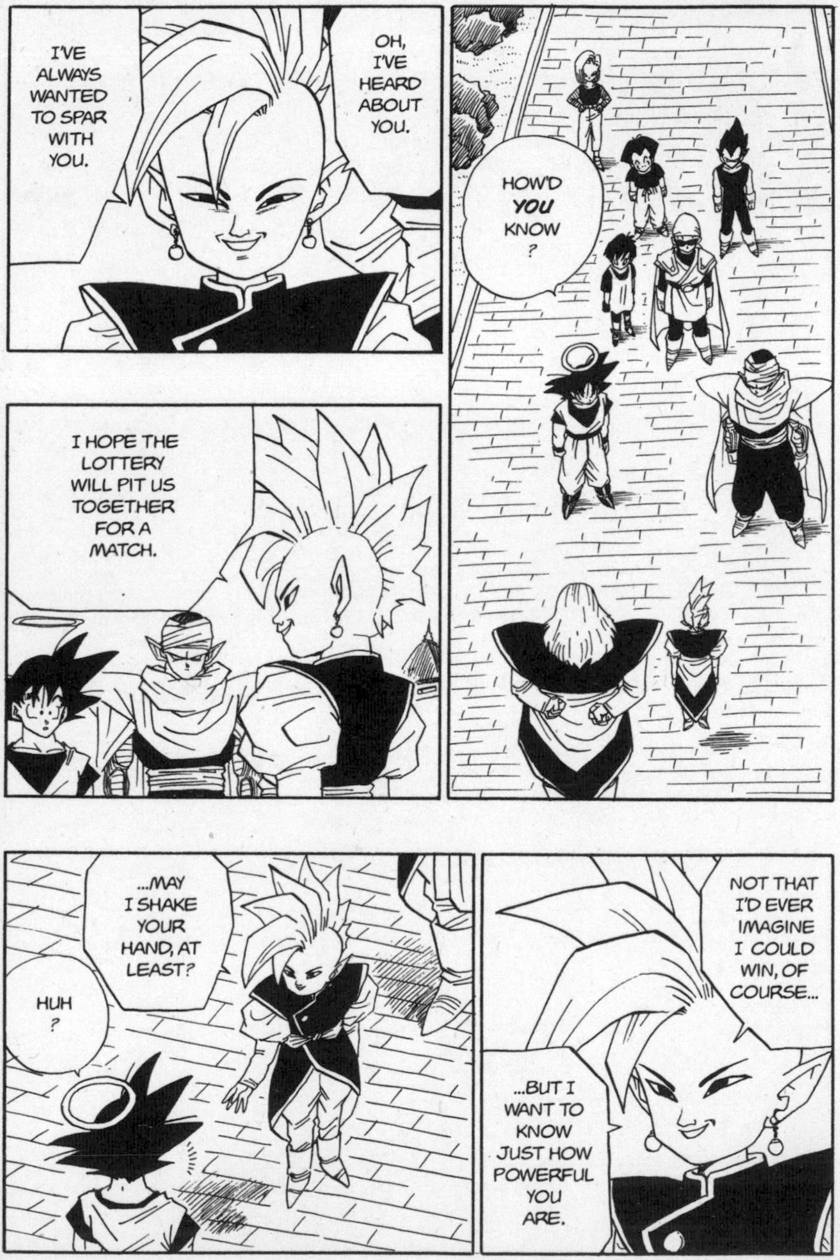

HOW'D ***YOU*** KNOW?
OH, I'VE HEARD ABOUT YOU.
I'VE ALWAYS WANTED TO SPAR WITH YOU.
I HOPE THE LOTTERY WILL PIT US TOGETHER FOR A MATCH.
NOT THAT I'D EVER IMAGINE I COULD WIN, OF COURSE...
...BUT I WANT TO KNOW JUST HOW POWERFUL YOU ARE.
...MAY I SHAKE YOUR HAND, AT LEAST?
HUH?

READ THIS WAY

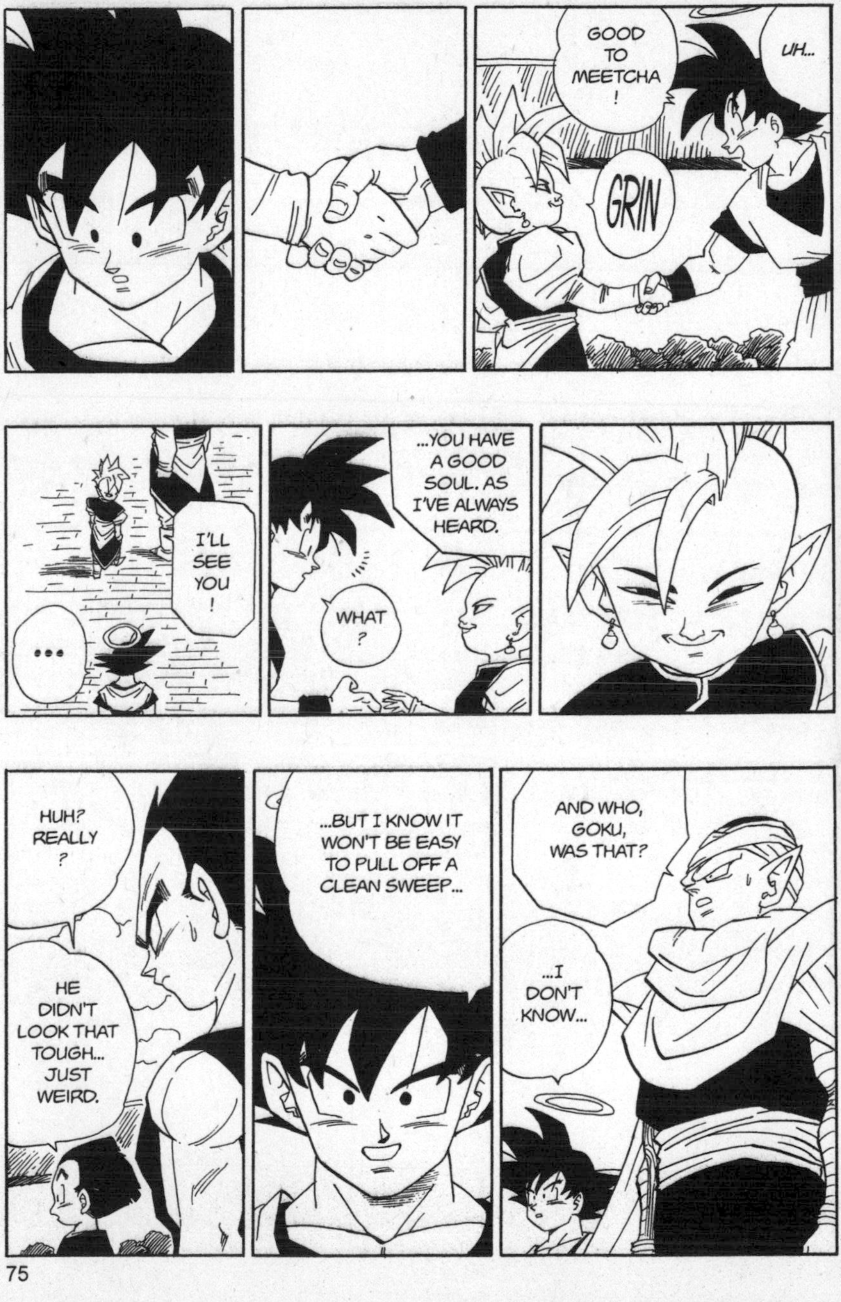

UH...
GOOD TO MEETCHA!
GRIN
...YOU HAVE A GOOD SOUL. AS I'VE ALWAYS HEARD.
WHAT?
I'LL SEE YOU!
...
AND WHO, GOKU, WAS THAT?
...I DON'T KNOW...
...BUT I KNOW IT WON'T BE EASY TO PULL OFF A CLEAN SWEEP...
HUH? REALLY?
HE DIDN'T LOOK THAT TOUGH... JUST WEIRD.

DBZ:244 • The Finalists are Chosen!

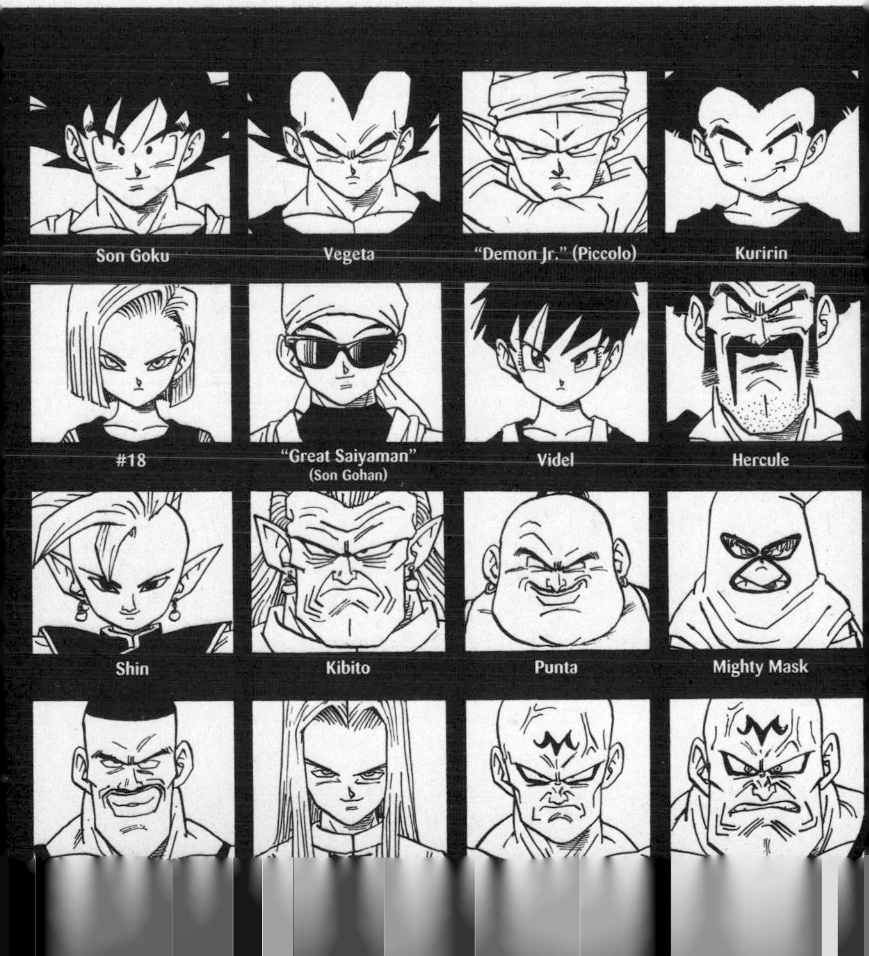

Kuririn
"Demon Jr." (Piccolo)
Vegeta
Son Goku
Hercule
Videl
"Great Saiyaman" (Son Gohan)
#18
Mighty Mask
Punta
Kibito
Shin

READ THIS WAY

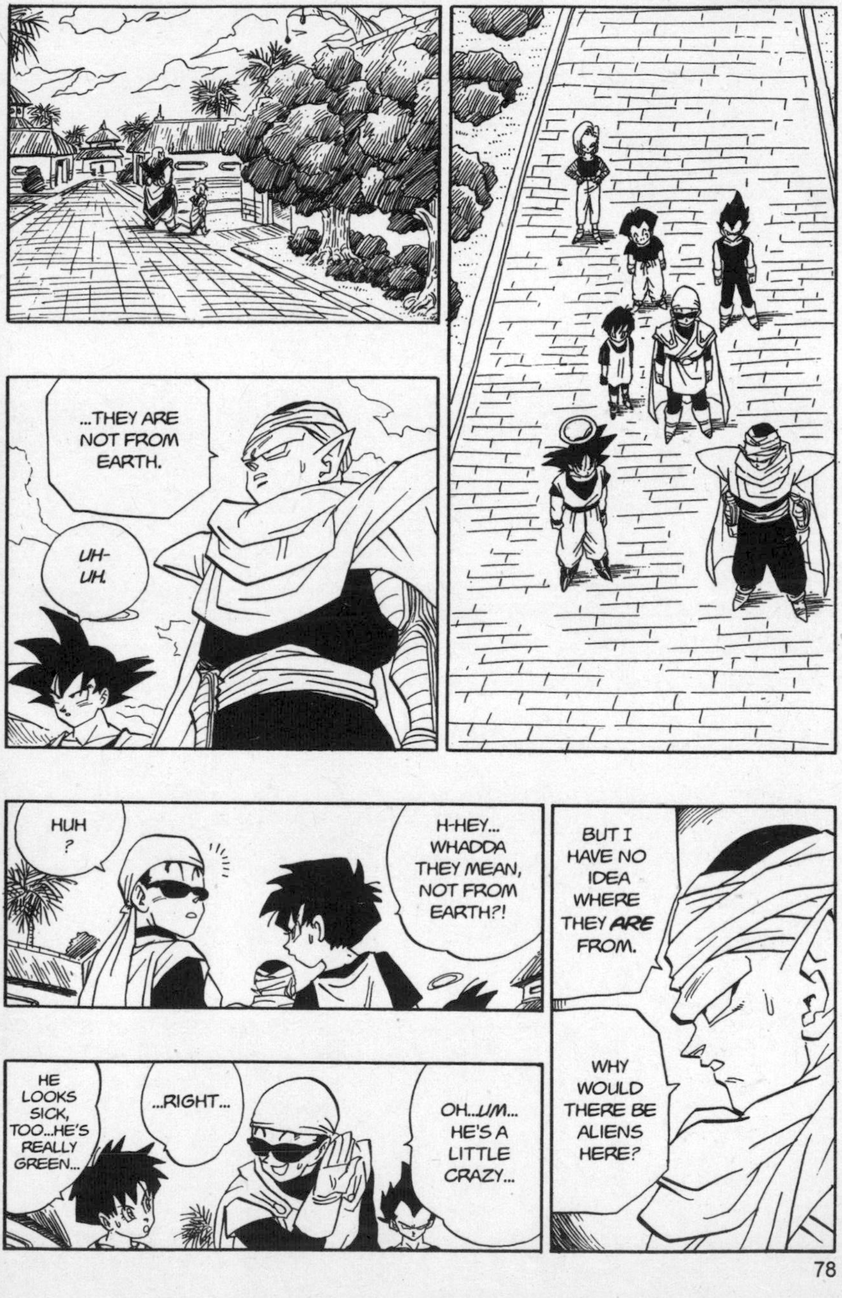

...THEY ARE NOT FROM EARTH.
UH-UH.
BUT I HAVE NO IDEA WHERE THEY *ARE* FROM.
WHY WOULD THERE BE ALIENS HERE?
H-HEY... WHADDA THEY MEAN, NOT FROM EARTH?!
HUH ?
OH...*UM*... HE'S A LITTLE CRAZY...
...RIGHT...
HE LOOKS SICK, TOO...HE'S REALLY GREEN...

READ THIS WAY

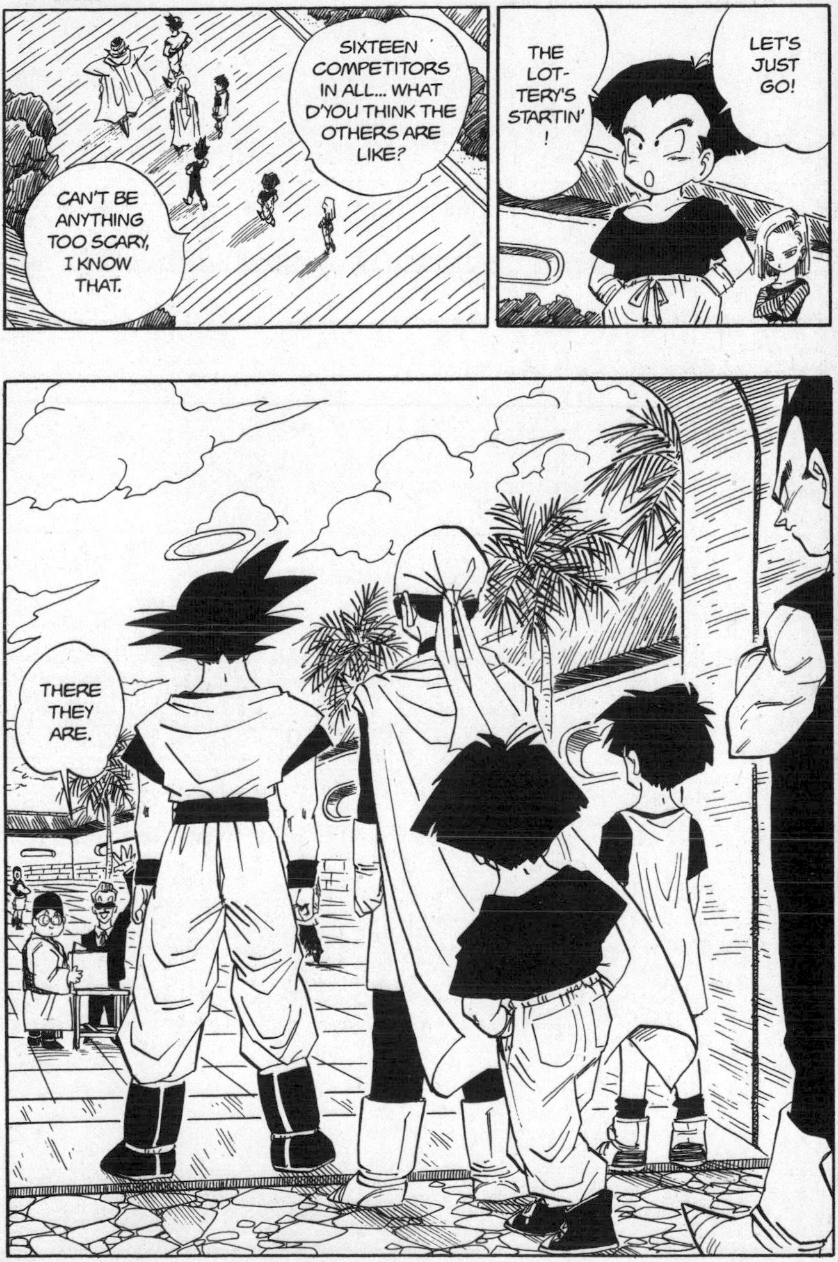
LET'S JUST GO!
THE LOT-TERY'S STARTIN'!
SIXTEEN COMPETITORS IN ALL... WHAT D'YOU THINK THE OTHERS ARE LIKE?
CAN'T BE ANYTHING TOO SCARY, I KNOW THAT.
THERE THEY ARE.

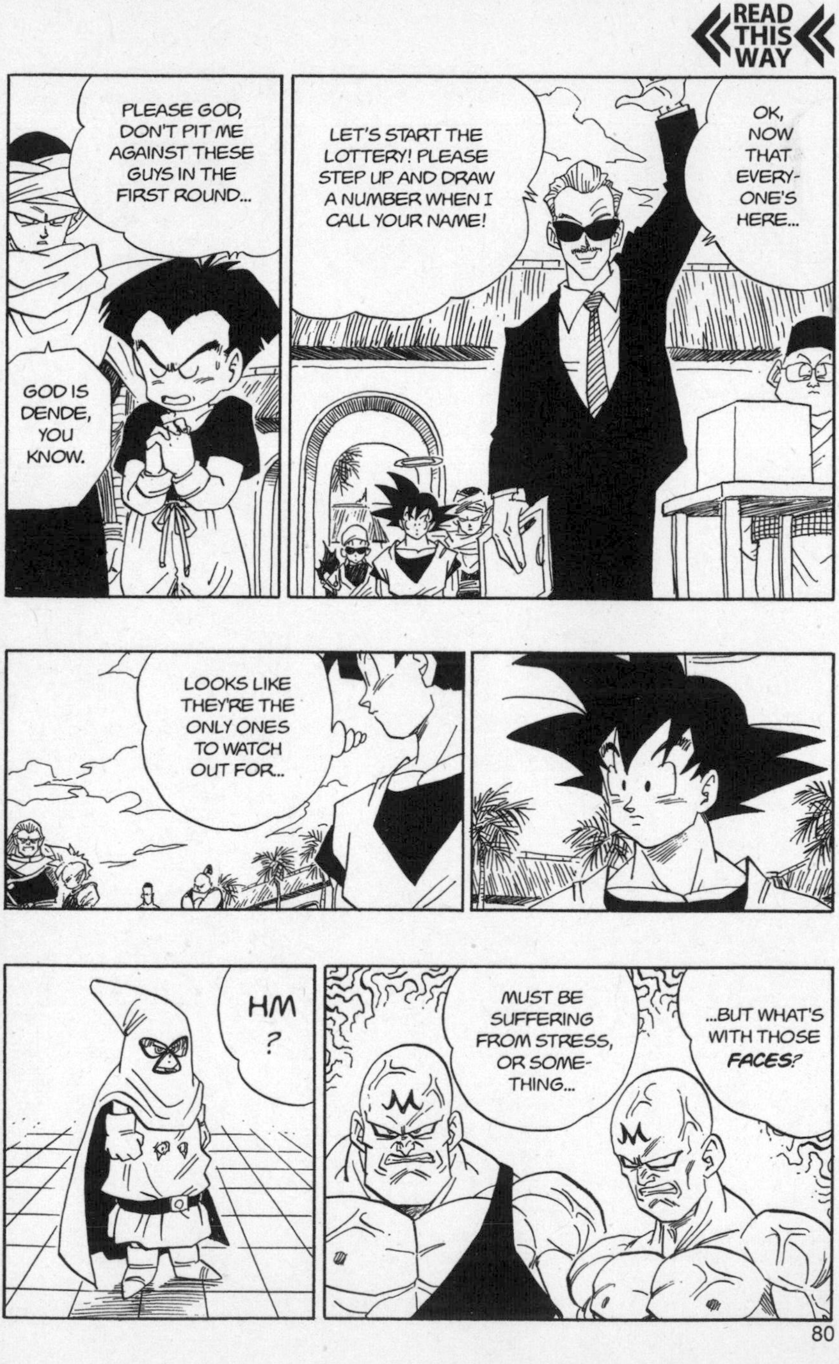
READ THIS WAY
OK, NOW THAT EVERYONE'S HERE...
LET'S START THE LOTTERY! PLEASE STEP UP AND DRAW A NUMBER WHEN I CALL YOUR NAME!
PLEASE GOD, DON'T PIT ME AGAINST THESE GUYS IN THE FIRST ROUND...
GOD IS DENDE, YOU KNOW.
LOOKS LIKE THEY'RE THE ONLY ONES TO WATCH OUT FOR...
...BUT WHAT'S WITH THOSE *FACES?*
MUST BE SUFFERING FROM STRESS, OR SOMETHING...
HM ?

READ THIS WAY

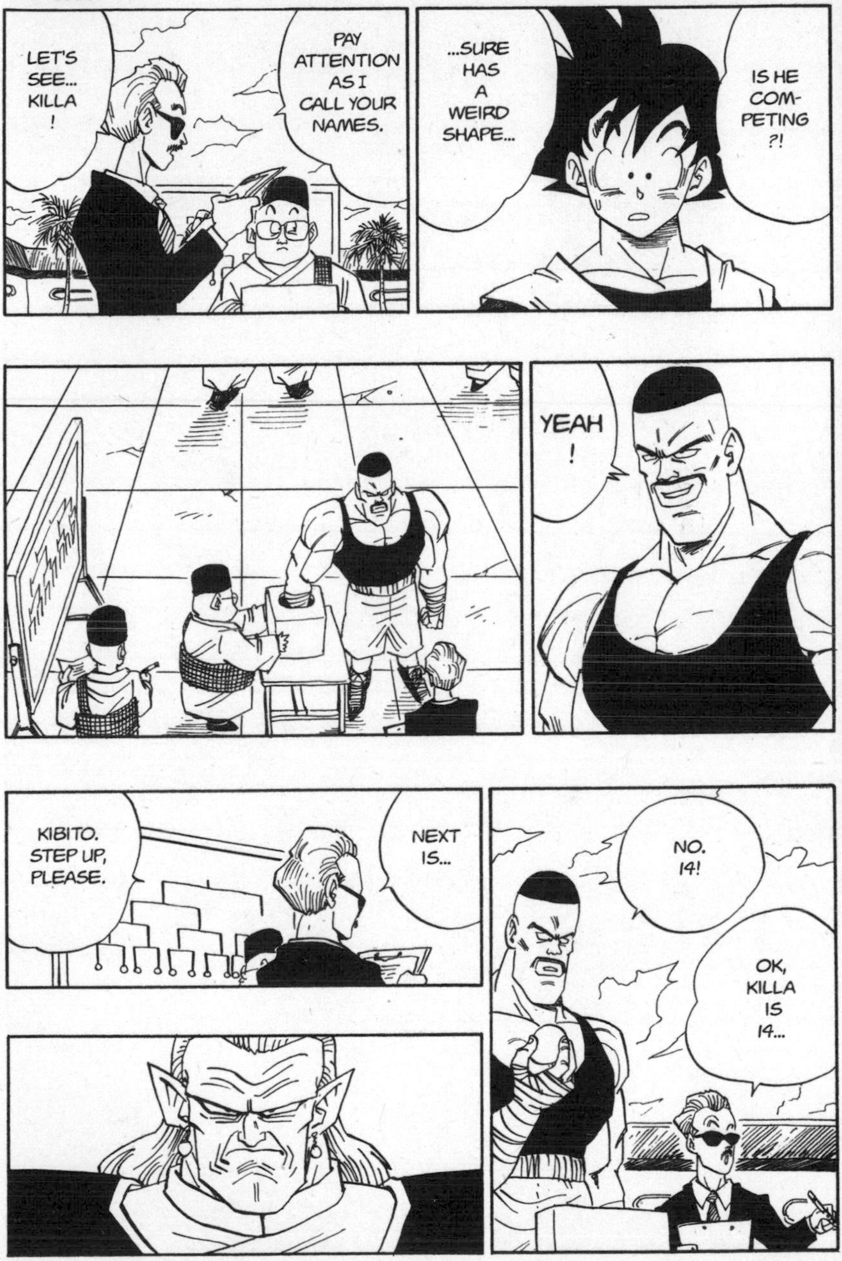
IS HE COMPETING ?!
...SURE HAS A WEIRD SHAPE...
PAY ATTENTION AS I CALL YOUR NAMES.
LET'S SEE... KILLA!
YEAH!
NO. 14!
OK, KILLA IS 14...
NEXT IS...
KIBITO. STEP UP, PLEASE.

READ THIS WAY

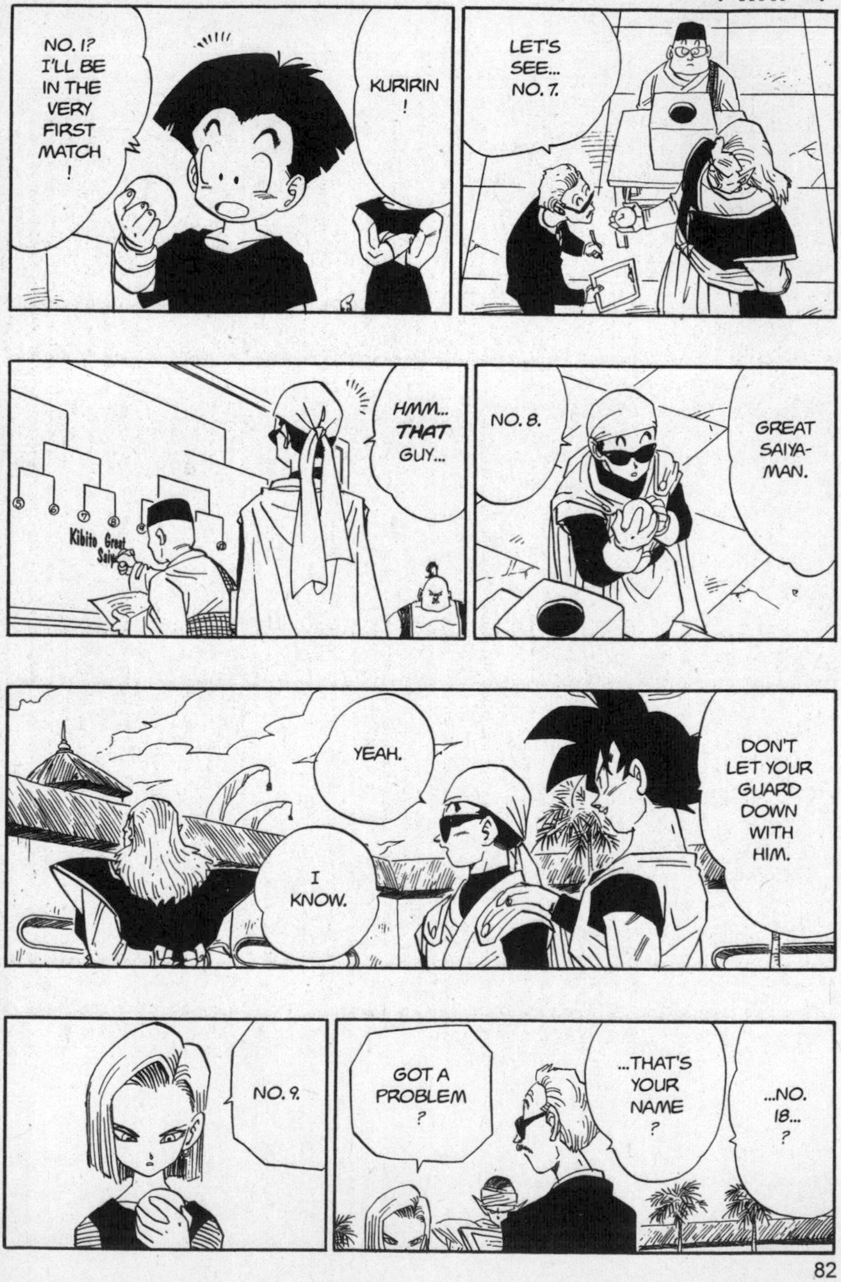
LET'S SEE... NO. 7.
KURIRIN!
NO. 1? I'LL BE IN THE VERY FIRST MATCH!
GREAT SAIYA-MAN.
NO. 8.
HMM... THAT GUY...
Kibito
DON'T LET YOUR GUARD DOWN WITH HIM.
YEAH.
I KNOW.
...NO. 18...?
...THAT'S YOUR NAME?
GOT A PROBLEM?
NO. 9.

READ THIS WAY

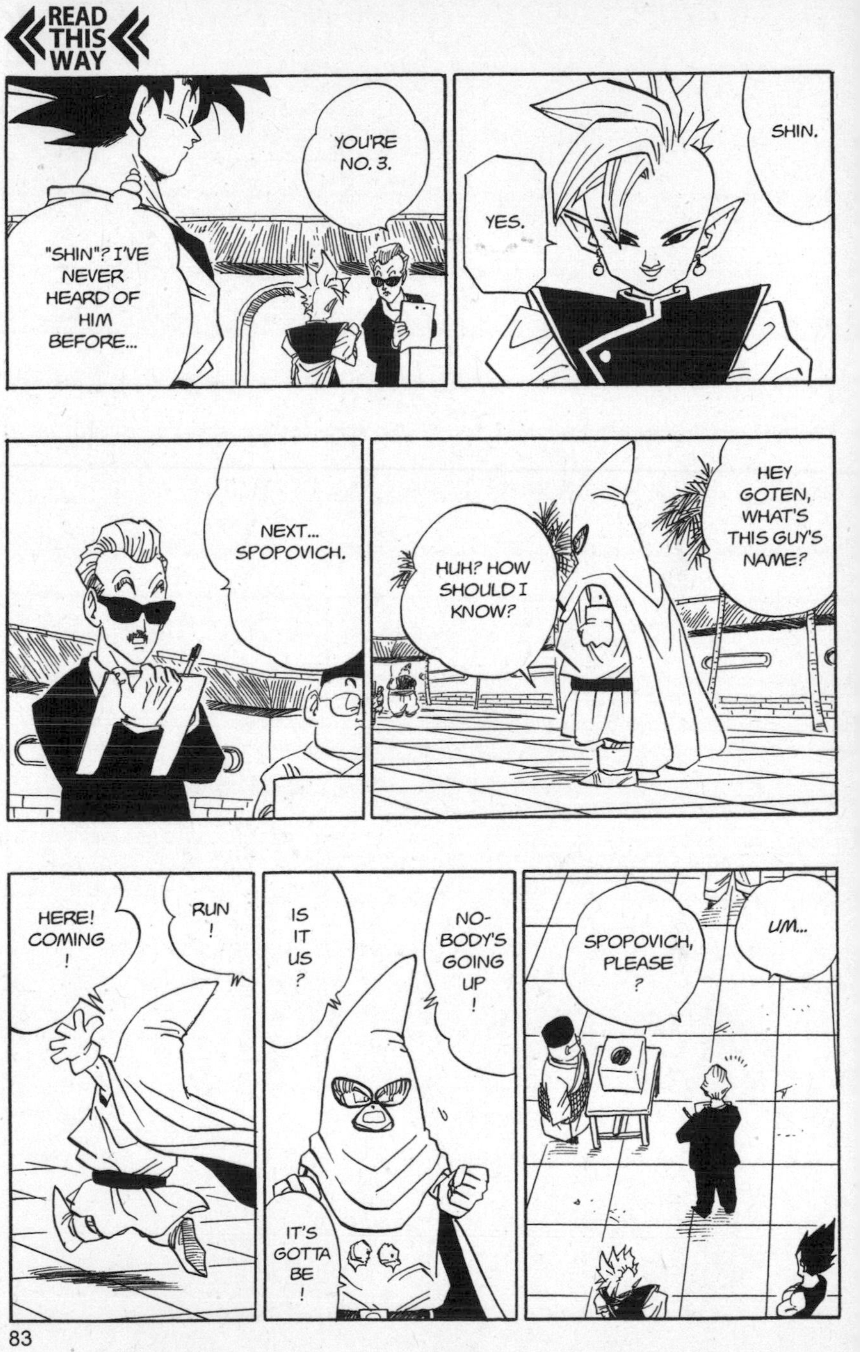
SHIN.
YES.
YOU'RE NO. 3.
"SHIN"? I'VE NEVER HEARD OF HIM BEFORE...
HEY GOTEN, WHAT'S THIS GUY'S NAME?
HUH? HOW SHOULD I KNOW?
NEXT... SPOPOVICH.
UM...
SPOPOVICH, PLEASE?
NO-BODY'S GOING UP!
IS IT US?
IT'S GOTTA BE!
RUN!
HERE! COMING!

READ THIS WAY

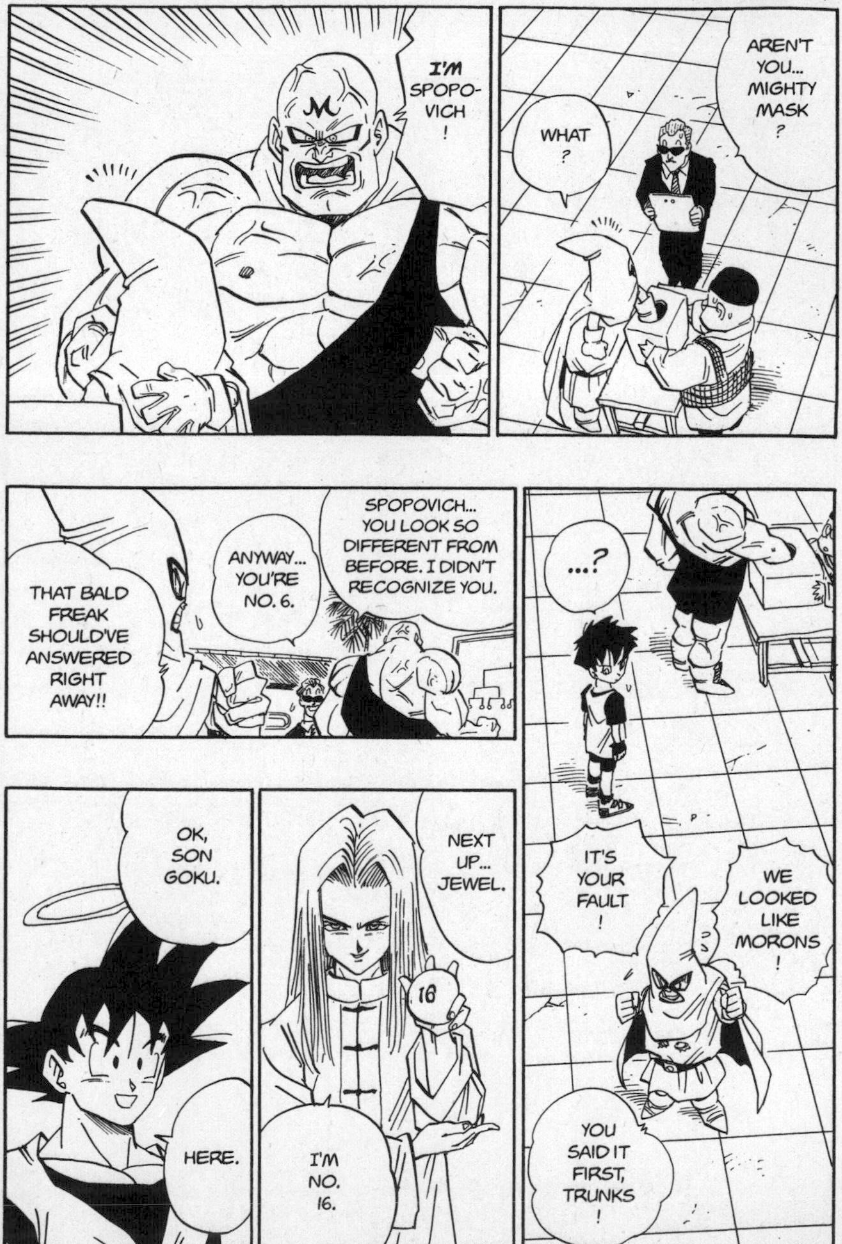
AREN'T YOU... MIGHTY MASK?
WHAT?
I'M SPOPO-VICH!
...?
WE LOOKED LIKE MORONS!
IT'S YOUR FAULT!
YOU SAID IT FIRST, TRUNKS!
SPOPOVICH... YOU LOOK SO DIFFERENT FROM BEFORE. I DIDN'T RECOGNIZE YOU.
ANYWAY... YOU'RE NO. 6.
THAT BALD FREAK SHOULD'VE ANSWERED RIGHT AWAY!!
NEXT UP... JEWEL.
16
I'M NO. 16.
OK, SON GOKU.
HERE.

READ THIS WAY

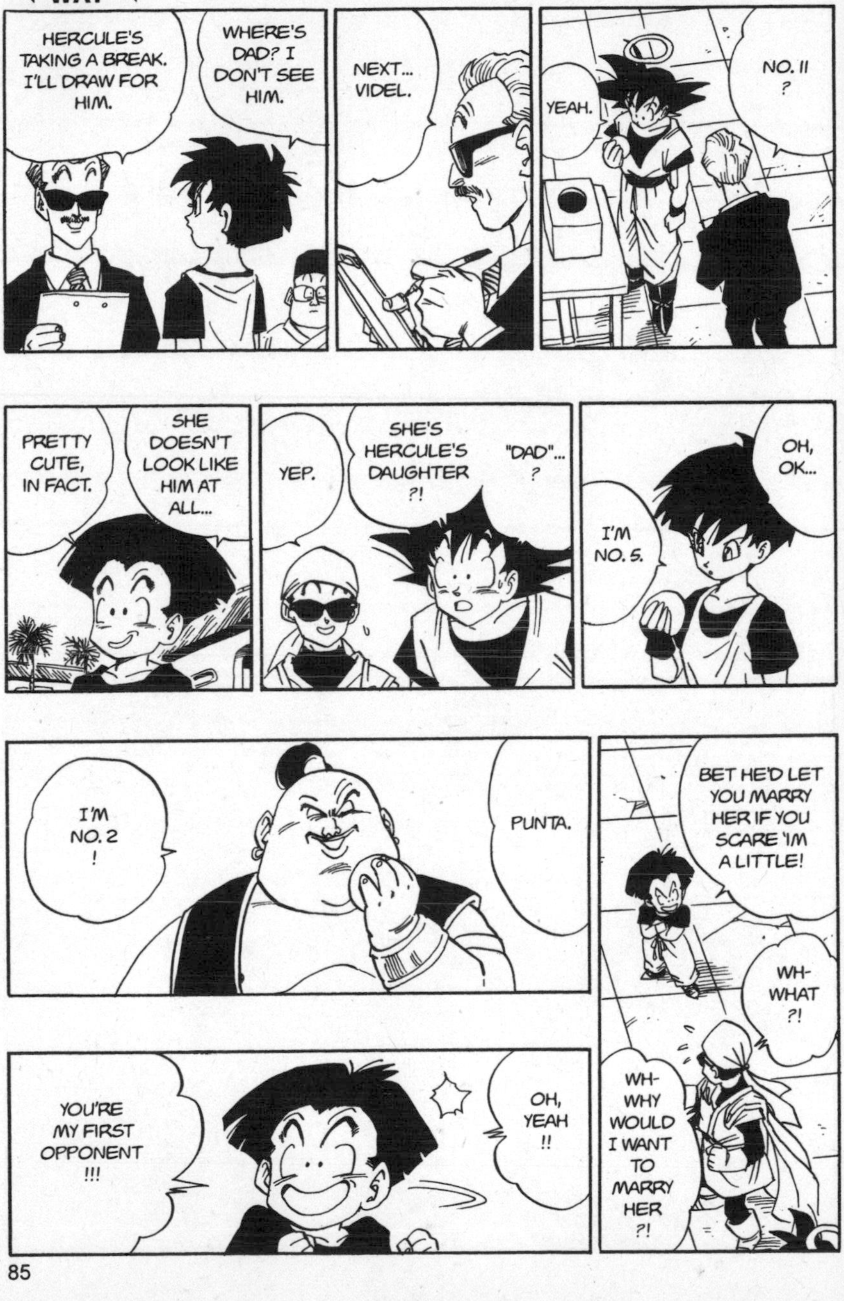
NO. 11 ?
YEAH.
NEXT... VIDEL.
WHERE'S DAD? I DON'T SEE HIM.
HERCULE'S TAKING A BREAK. I'LL DRAW FOR HIM.
OH, OK...
I'M NO. 5.
"DAD"... ?
SHE'S HERCULE'S DAUGHTER ?!
YEP.
SHE DOESN'T LOOK LIKE HIM AT ALL...
PRETTY CUTE, IN FACT.
BET HE'D LET YOU MARRY HER IF YOU SCARE 'IM A LITTLE!
WH-WHAT ?!
WH-WHY WOULD I WANT TO MARRY HER ?!
PUNTA.
I'M NO. 2 !
OH, YEAH !!
YOU'RE MY FIRST OPPONENT !!!

READ THIS WAY

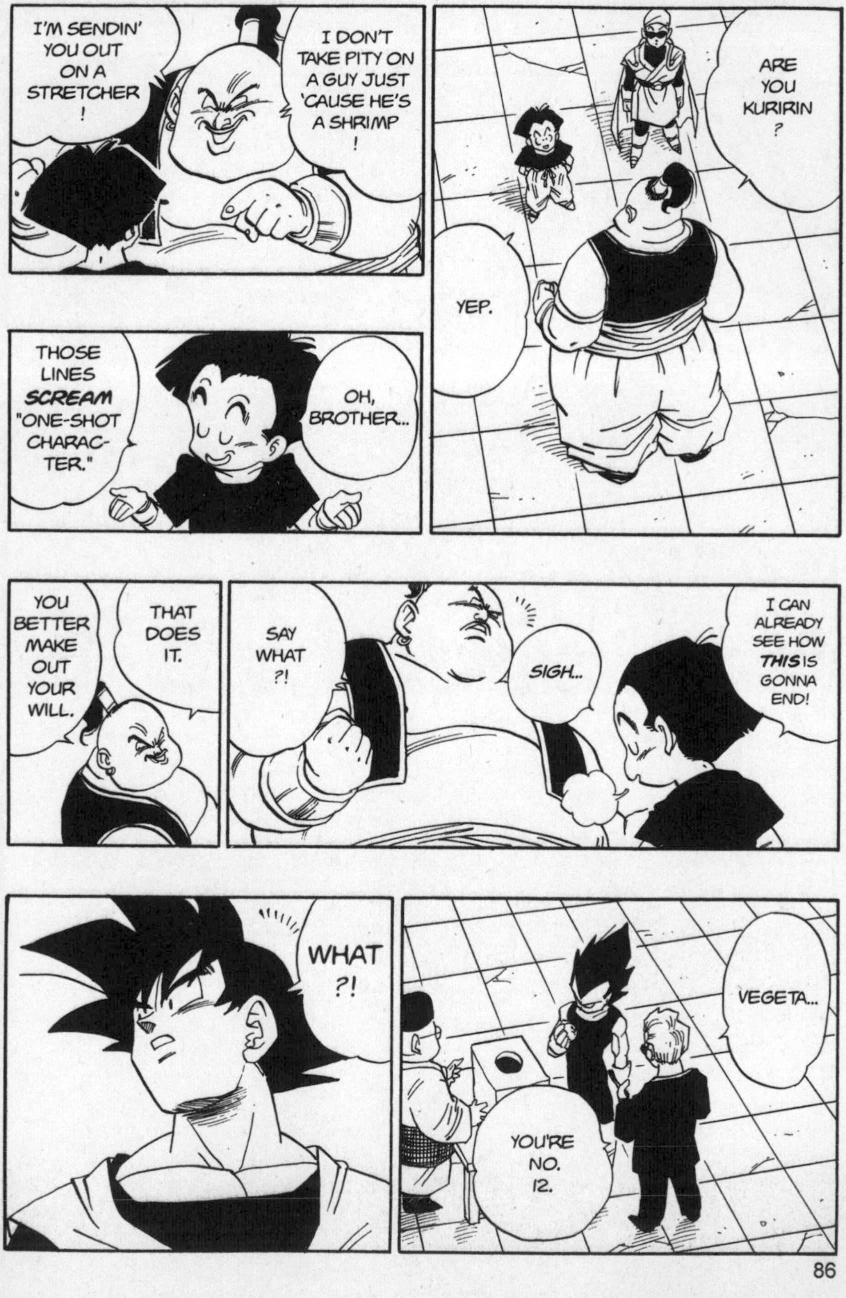
ARE YOU KURIRIN?
YEP.
I DON'T TAKE PITY ON A GUY JUST 'CAUSE HE'S A SHRIMP!
I'M SENDIN' YOU OUT ON A STRETCHER!
OH, BROTHER...
THOSE LINES **SCREAM** "ONE-SHOT CHARACTER."
I CAN ALREADY SEE HOW **THIS** IS GONNA END!
SIGH...
SAY WHAT?!
THAT DOES IT.
YOU BETTER MAKE OUT YOUR WILL.
VEGETA...
YOU'RE NO. 12.
WHAT?!

READ THIS WAY

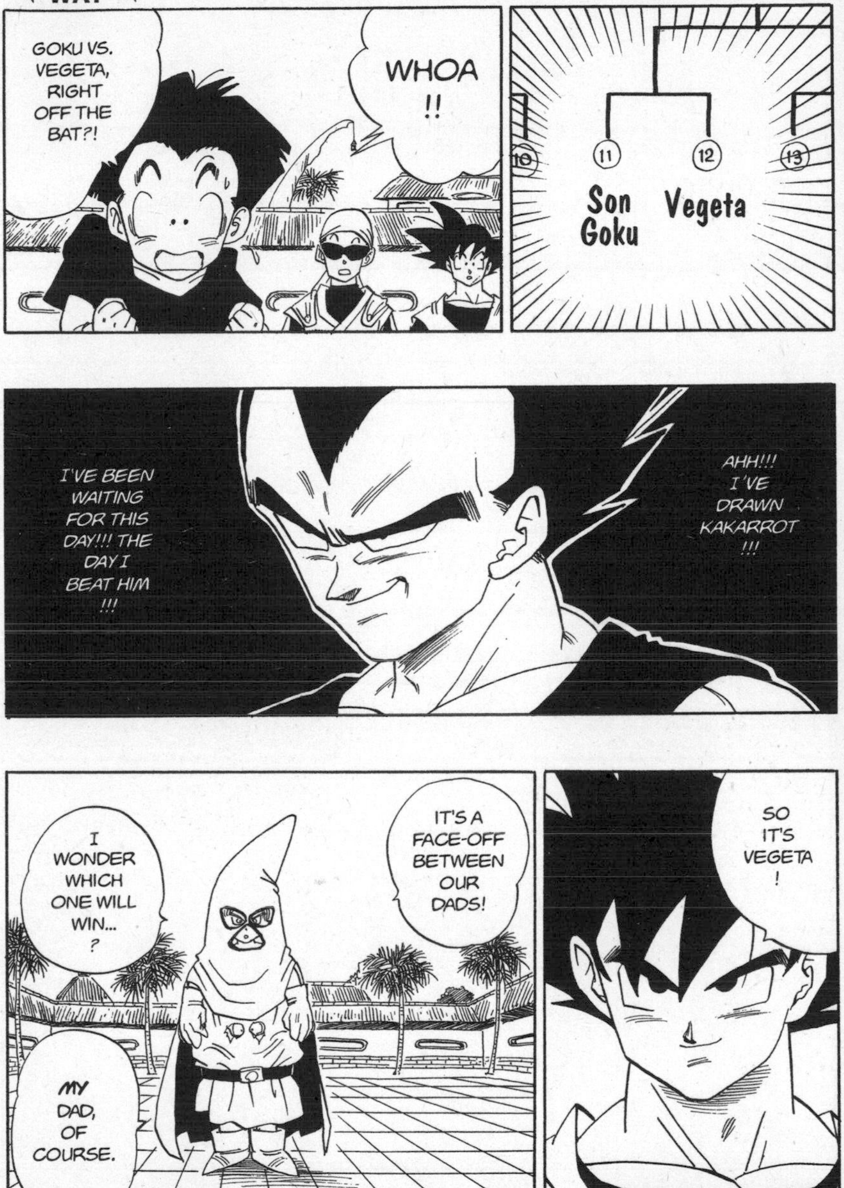

10
11
12
13
Son Goku
Vegeta
WHOA!!
GOKU VS. VEGETA, RIGHT OFF THE BAT?!
AHH!!! I'VE DRAWN KAKARROT!!!
I'VE BEEN WAITING FOR THIS DAY!!! THE DAY I BEAT HIM!!!
SO IT'S VEGETA!
IT'S A FACE-OFF BETWEEN OUR DADS!
I WONDER WHICH ONE WILL WIN...?
MY DAD, OF COURSE.

READ THIS WAY

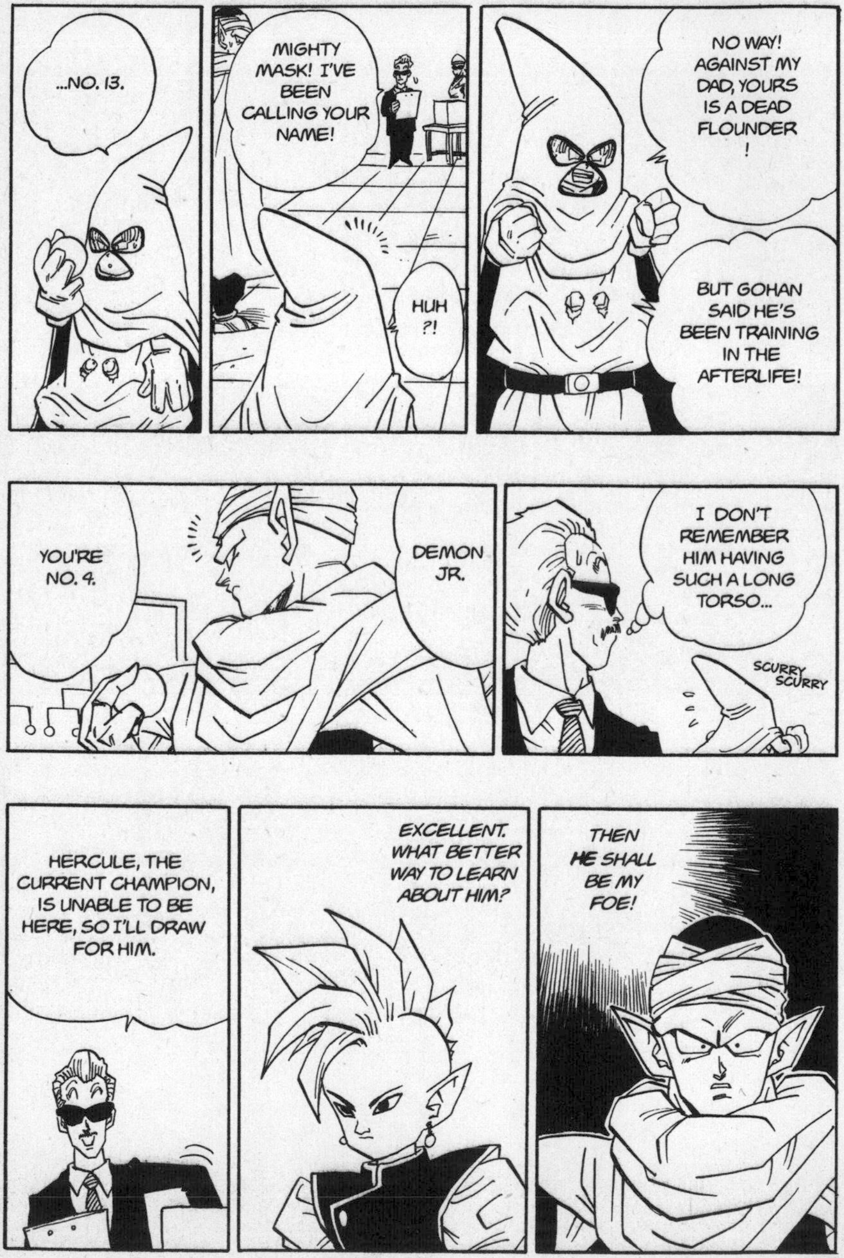

NO WAY! AGAINST MY DAD, YOURS IS A DEAD FLOUNDER!
BUT GOHAN SAID HE'S BEEN TRAINING IN THE AFTERLIFE!
MIGHTY MASK! I'VE BEEN CALLING YOUR NAME!
HUH ?!
...NO. 13.
I DON'T REMEMBER HIM HAVING SUCH A LONG TORSO...
SCURRY SCURRY
DEMON JR.
YOU'RE NO. 4.
THEN HE SHALL BE MY FOE!
EXCELLENT. WHAT BETTER WAY TO LEARN ABOUT HIM?
HERCULE, THE CURRENT CHAMPION, IS UNABLE TO BE HERE, SO I'LL DRAW FOR HIM.

READ THIS WAY

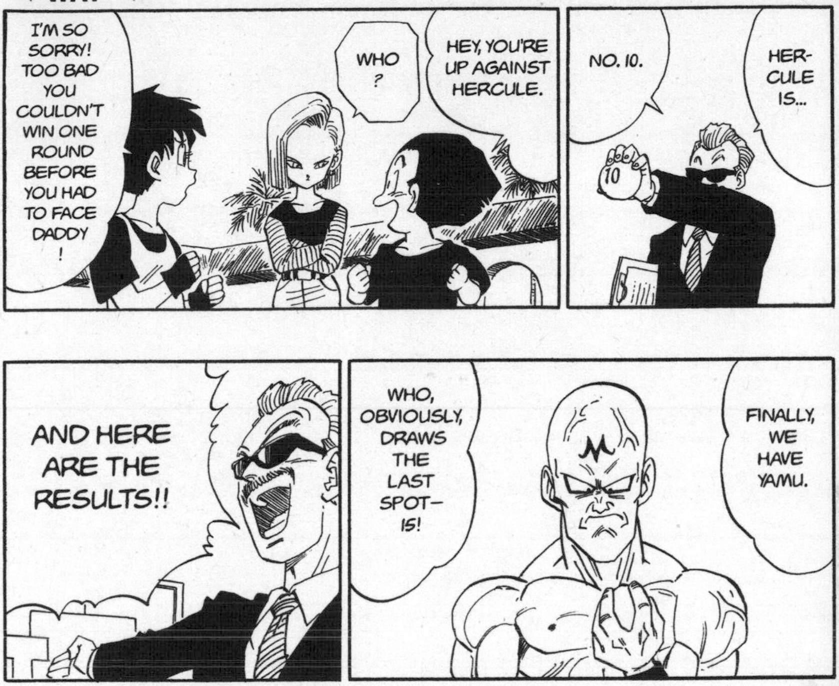
HERCULE IS...
NO. 10.
HEY, YOU'RE UP AGAINST HERCULE.
WHO?
I'M SO SORRY! TOO BAD YOU COULDN'T WIN ONE ROUND BEFORE YOU HAD TO FACE DADDY!
FINALLY, WE HAVE YAMU.
WHO, OBVIOUSLY, DRAWS THE LAST SPOT—IS!
AND HERE ARE THE RESULTS!!

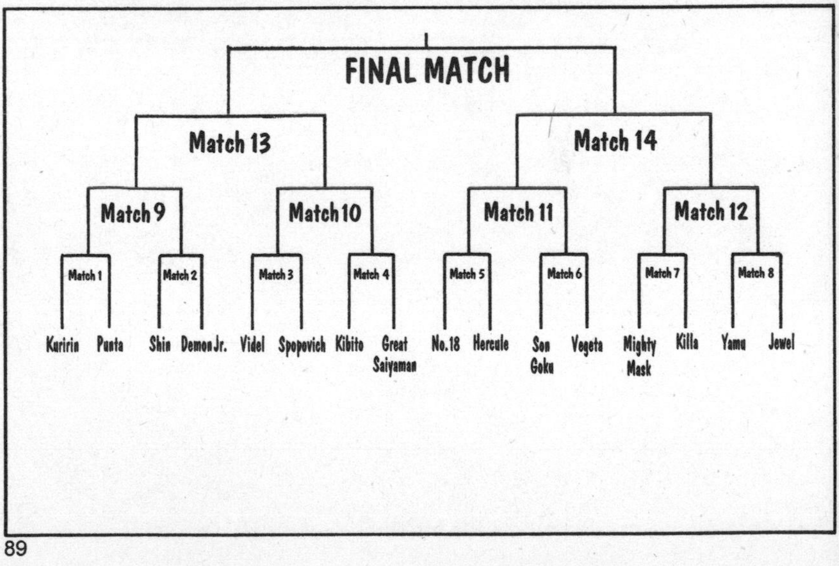
FINAL MATCH
Match 13
Match 14
Match 9
Match 10
Match 11
Match 12
Match 1
Match 2
Match 3
Match 4
Match 5
Match 6
Match 7
Match 8
Kuririn
Punta
Shin
Demon Jr.
Videl
Spopovich
Kibito
Great Saiyaman
No.18
Hercule
Son Goku
Vegeta
Mighty Mask
Killa
Yamu
Jewel

READ THIS WAY

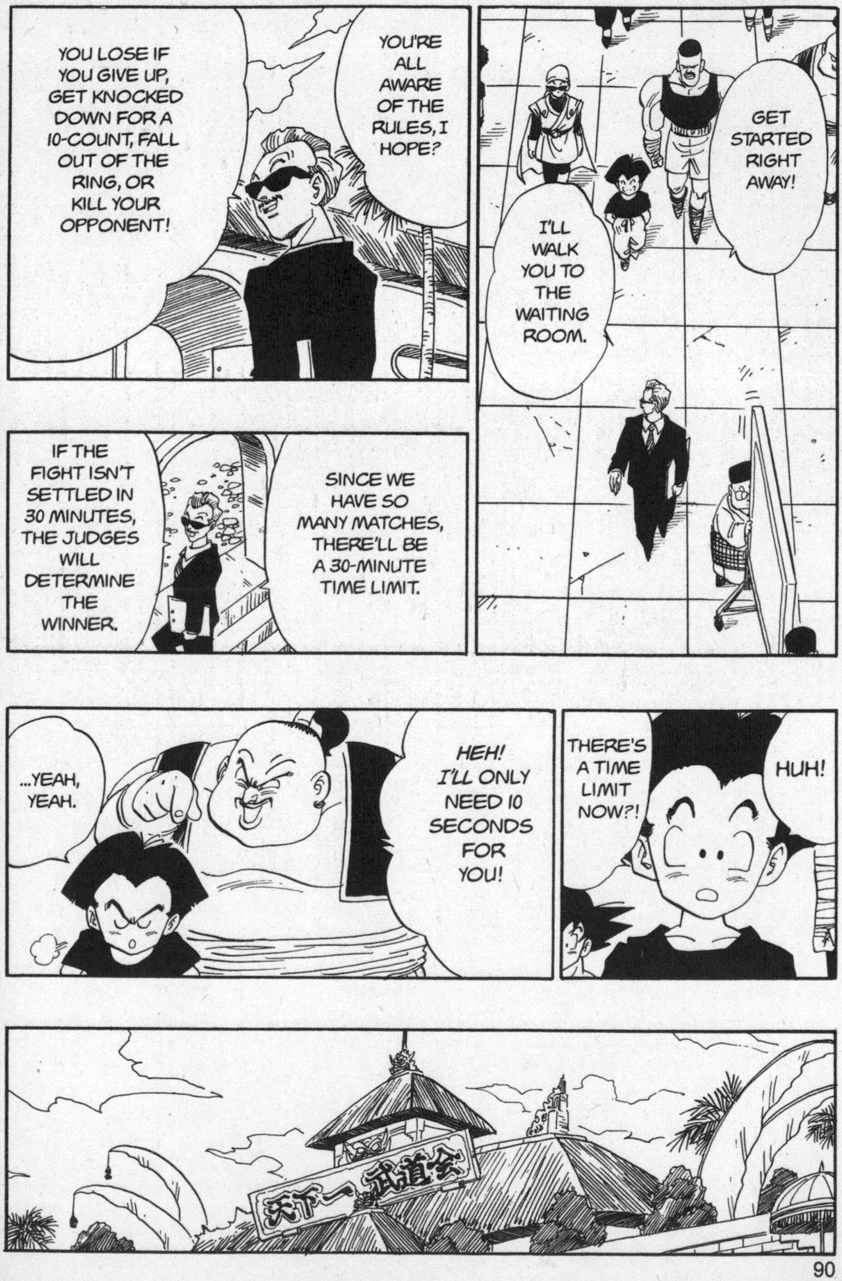
GET STARTED RIGHT AWAY!
I'LL WALK YOU TO THE WAITING ROOM.
YOU'RE ALL AWARE OF THE RULES, I HOPE?
YOU LOSE IF YOU GIVE UP, GET KNOCKED DOWN FOR A 10-COUNT, FALL OUT OF THE RING, OR KILL YOUR OPPONENT!
SINCE WE HAVE SO MANY MATCHES, THERE'LL BE A 30-MINUTE TIME LIMIT.
IF THE FIGHT ISN'T SETTLED IN 30 MINUTES, THE JUDGES WILL DETERMINE THE WINNER.
HUH!
THERE'S A TIME LIMIT NOW?!
HEH! I'LL ONLY NEED 10 SECONDS FOR YOU!
...YEAH, YEAH.
天下一武道会

READ THIS WAY

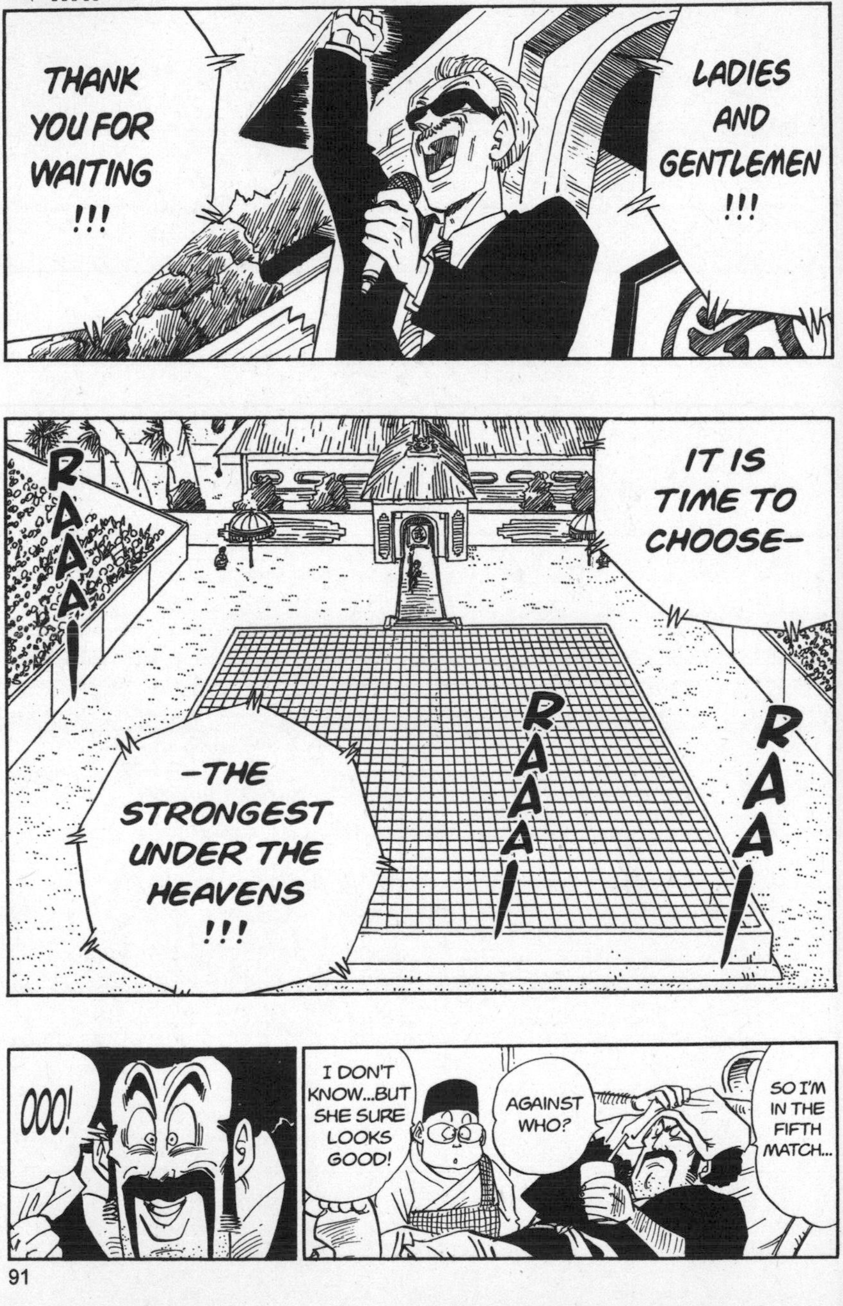
LADIES AND GENTLEMEN !!!
THANK YOU FOR WAITING !!!
IT IS TIME TO CHOOSE—
RAAAA!
RAAAA!
RAAAA!
—THE STRONGEST UNDER THE HEAVENS !!!
SO I'M IN THE FIFTH MATCH...
AGAINST WHO?
I DON'T KNOW...BUT SHE SURE LOOKS GOOD!
OOO!

DBZ:245 • The First Two Fights

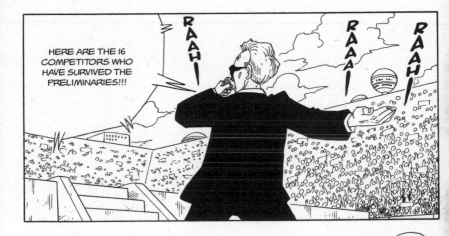

HERE ARE THE 16 COMPETITORS WHO HAVE SURVIVED THE PRELIMINARIES!!!
RAAAH!
RAAAA!
RAAH!

RATTLE RATTLE

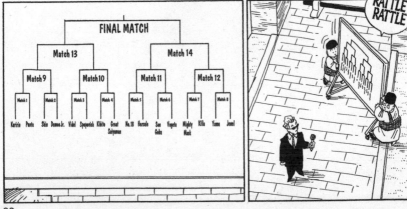

FINAL MATCH
Match 13
Match 14
Match 9
Match 10
Match 11
Match 12
Match 1
Match 2
Match 3
Match 4
Match 5
Match 6
Match 7
Match 8
Kuririn
Punta
Shin
Demon Jr.
Videl
Spopovich
Kibito
Great Saiyaman
No.18
Hercule
Son Goku
Vegeta
Mighty Mask
Killa
Yamu
Jewel

READ THIS WAY

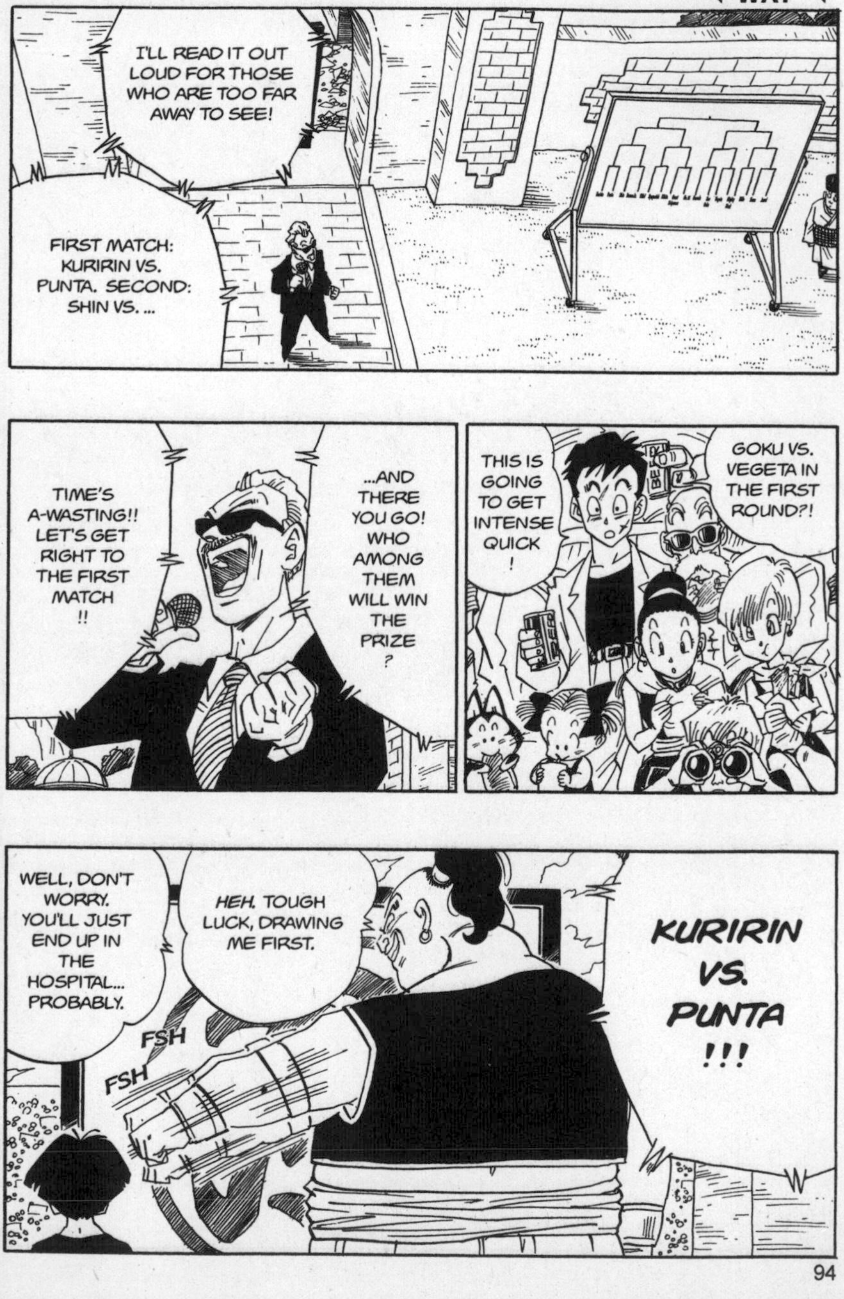

I'LL READ IT OUT LOUD FOR THOSE WHO ARE TOO FAR AWAY TO SEE!
FIRST MATCH: KURIRIN VS. PUNTA. SECOND: SHIN VS. ...
GOKU VS. VEGETA IN THE FIRST ROUND?!
THIS IS GOING TO GET INTENSE QUICK!
...AND THERE YOU GO! WHO AMONG THEM WILL WIN THE PRIZE?
TIME'S A-WASTING!! LET'S GET RIGHT TO THE FIRST MATCH!!
KURIRIN VS. PUNTA!!!
HEH. TOUGH LUCK, DRAWING ME FIRST.
WELL, DON'T WORRY. YOU'LL JUST END UP IN THE HOSPITAL... PROBABLY.
FSH
FSH

READ THIS WAY

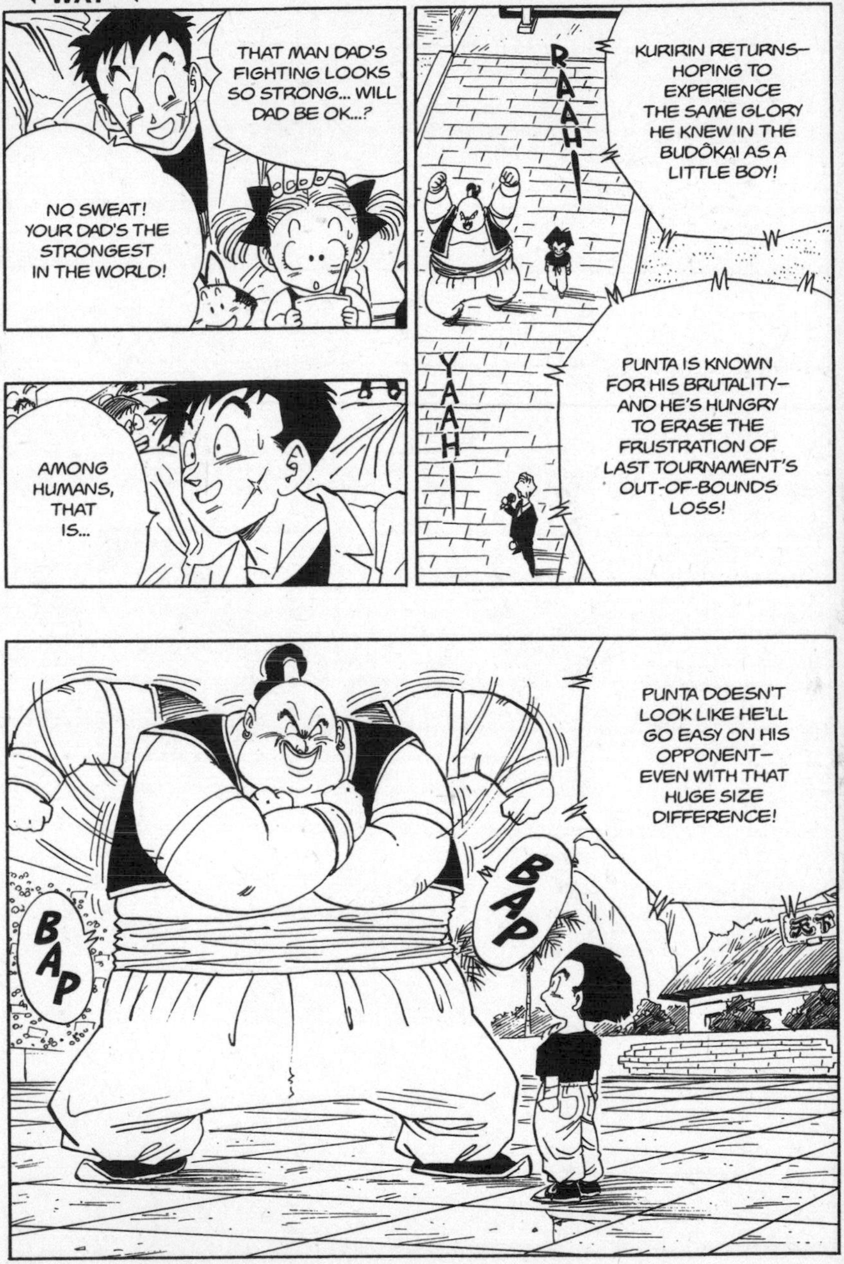
RAAH!
KURIRIN RETURNS—HOPING TO EXPERIENCE THE SAME GLORY HE KNEW IN THE BUDÔKAI AS A LITTLE BOY!
YAAH!
PUNTA IS KNOWN FOR HIS BRUTALITY—AND HE'S HUNGRY TO ERASE THE FRUSTRATION OF LAST TOURNAMENT'S OUT-OF-BOUNDS LOSS!
THAT MAN DAD'S FIGHTING LOOKS SO STRONG... WILL DAD BE OK...?
NO SWEAT! YOUR DAD'S THE STRONGEST IN THE WORLD!
AMONG HUMANS, THAT IS...
PUNTA DOESN'T LOOK LIKE HE'LL GO EASY ON HIS OPPONENT—EVEN WITH THAT HUGE SIZE DIFFERENCE!
BAP
BAP

READ THIS WAY

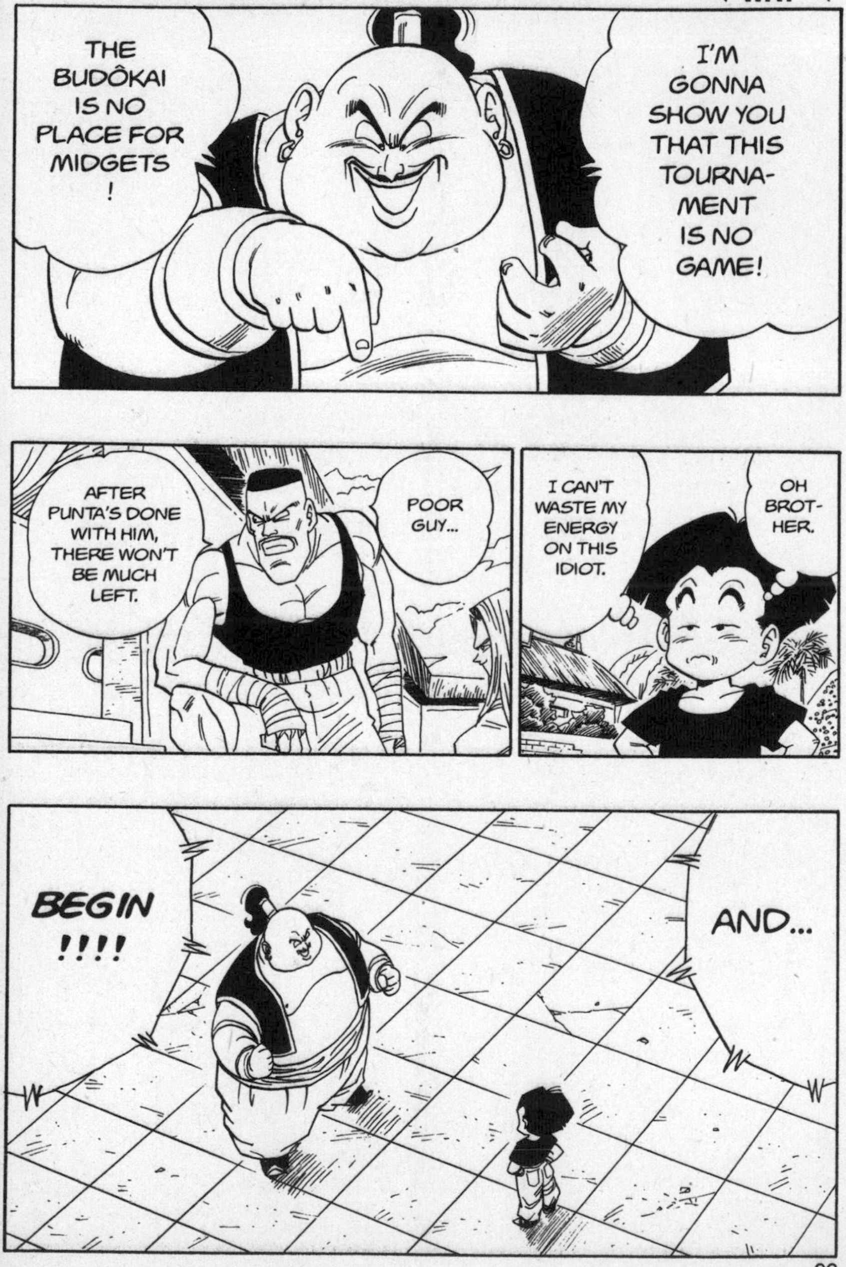
I'M GONNA SHOW YOU THAT THIS TOURNAMENT IS NO GAME!
THE BUDÔKAI IS NO PLACE FOR MIDGETS!
OH BROTHER.
I CAN'T WASTE MY ENERGY ON THIS IDIOT.
POOR GUY...
AFTER PUNTA'S DONE WITH HIM, THERE WON'T BE MUCH LEFT.
AND...
BEGIN!!!!

READ THIS WAY

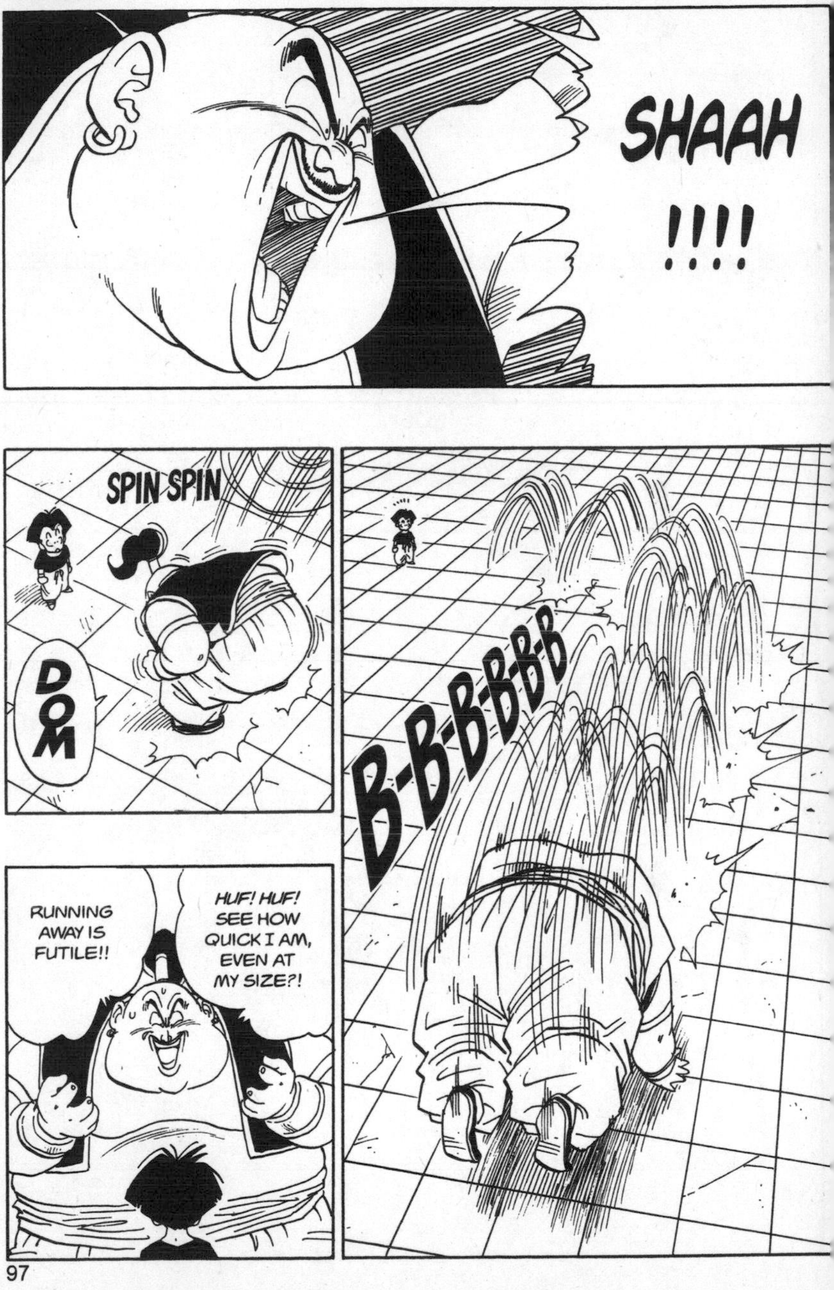
SHAAH
!!!!
B-B-B-B-B-B
SPIN SPIN
DOM
HUF! HUF! SEE HOW QUICK I AM, EVEN AT MY SIZE?!
RUNNING AWAY IS FUTILE!!

READ THIS WAY

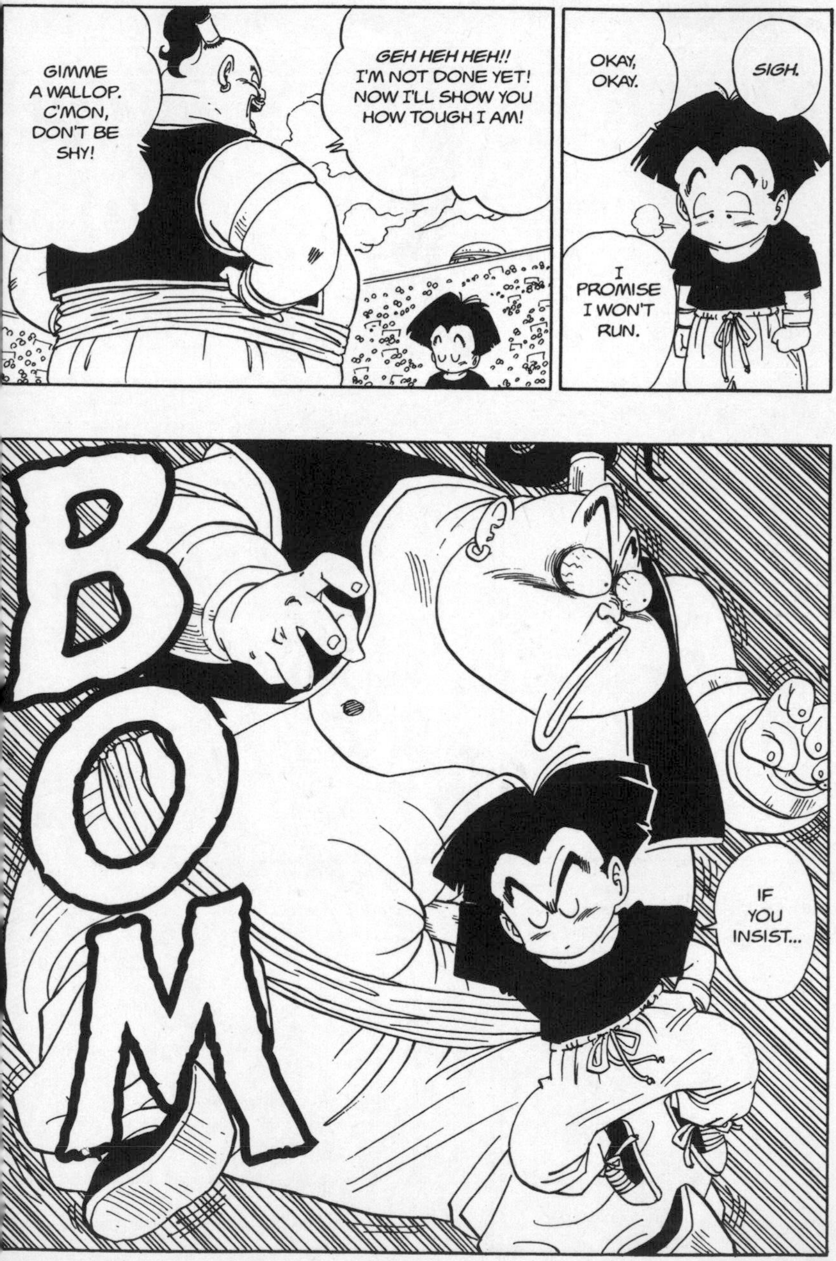
SIGH.
OKAY, OKAY.
I PROMISE I WON'T RUN.
GEH HEH HEH!! I'M NOT DONE YET! NOW I'LL SHOW YOU HOW TOUGH I AM!
GIMME A WALLOP. C'MON, DON'T BE SHY!
IF YOU INSIST...
BOM

READ THIS WAY

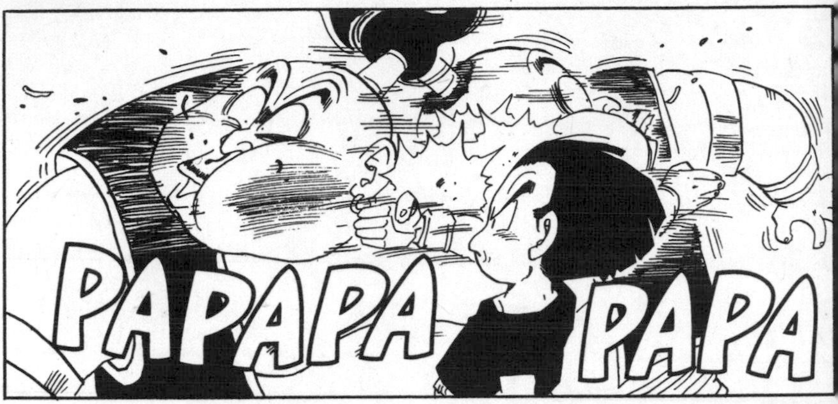
PAPAPA PAPA

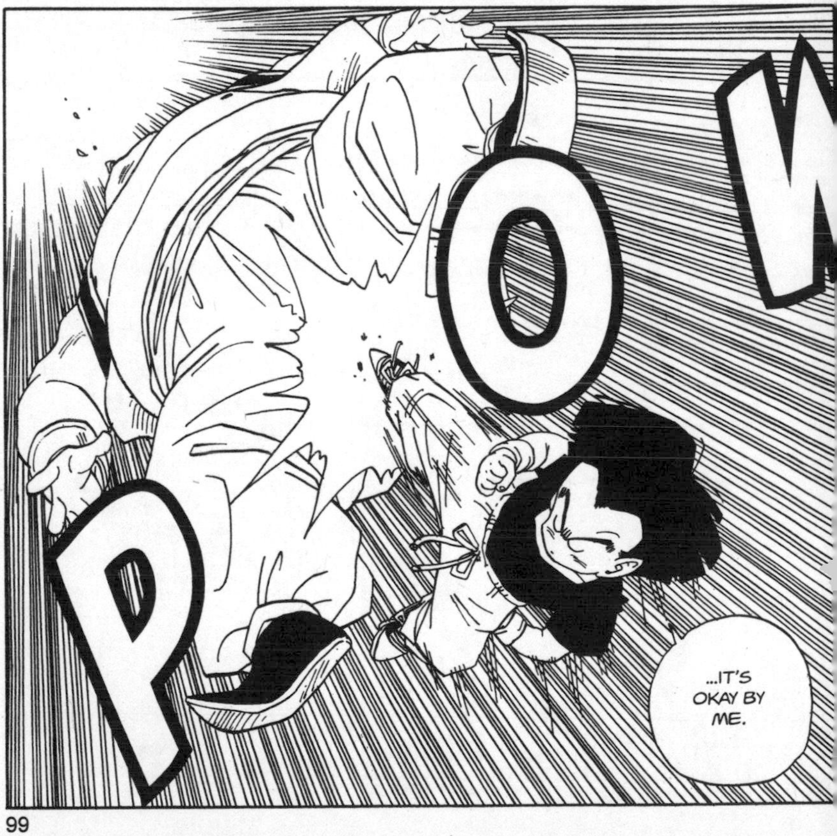
POW
...IT'S OKAY BY ME.

READ THIS WAY

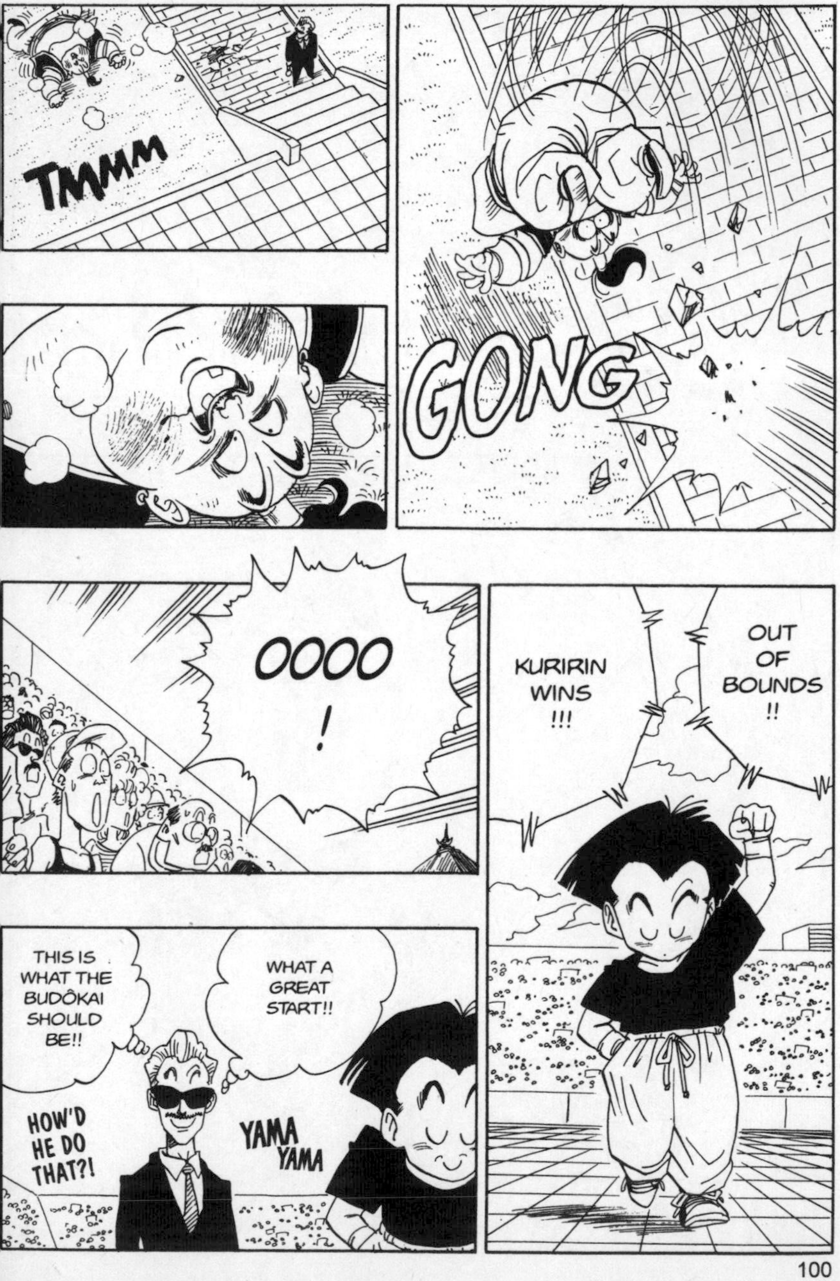
GONG
TMMM
OUT OF BOUNDS!!
KURIRIN WINS!!!
OOOO!
WHAT A GREAT START!!
THIS IS WHAT THE BUDÔKAI SHOULD BE!!
YAMA YAMA
HOW'D HE DO THAT?!

READ THIS WAY

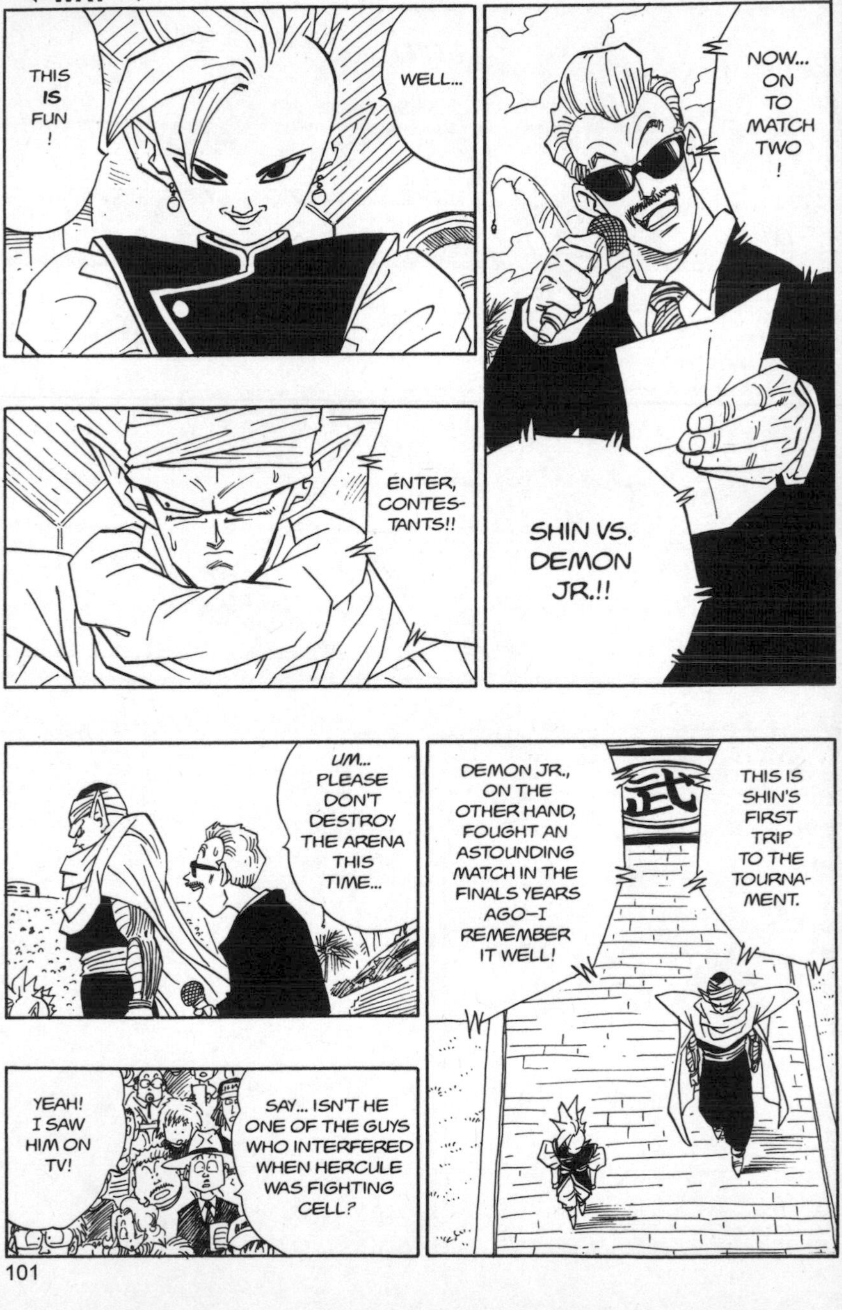

NOW... ON TO MATCH TWO!
SHIN VS. DEMON JR.!!
WELL...
THIS IS FUN!
ENTER, CONTESTANTS!!
THIS IS SHIN'S FIRST TRIP TO THE TOURNAMENT.
DEMON JR., ON THE OTHER HAND, FOUGHT AN ASTOUNDING MATCH IN THE FINALS YEARS AGO—I REMEMBER IT WELL!
UM... PLEASE DON'T DESTROY THE ARENA THIS TIME...
SAY... ISN'T HE ONE OF THE GUYS WHO INTERFERED WHEN HERCULE WAS FIGHTING CELL?
YEAH! I SAW HIM ON TV!

READ THIS WAY

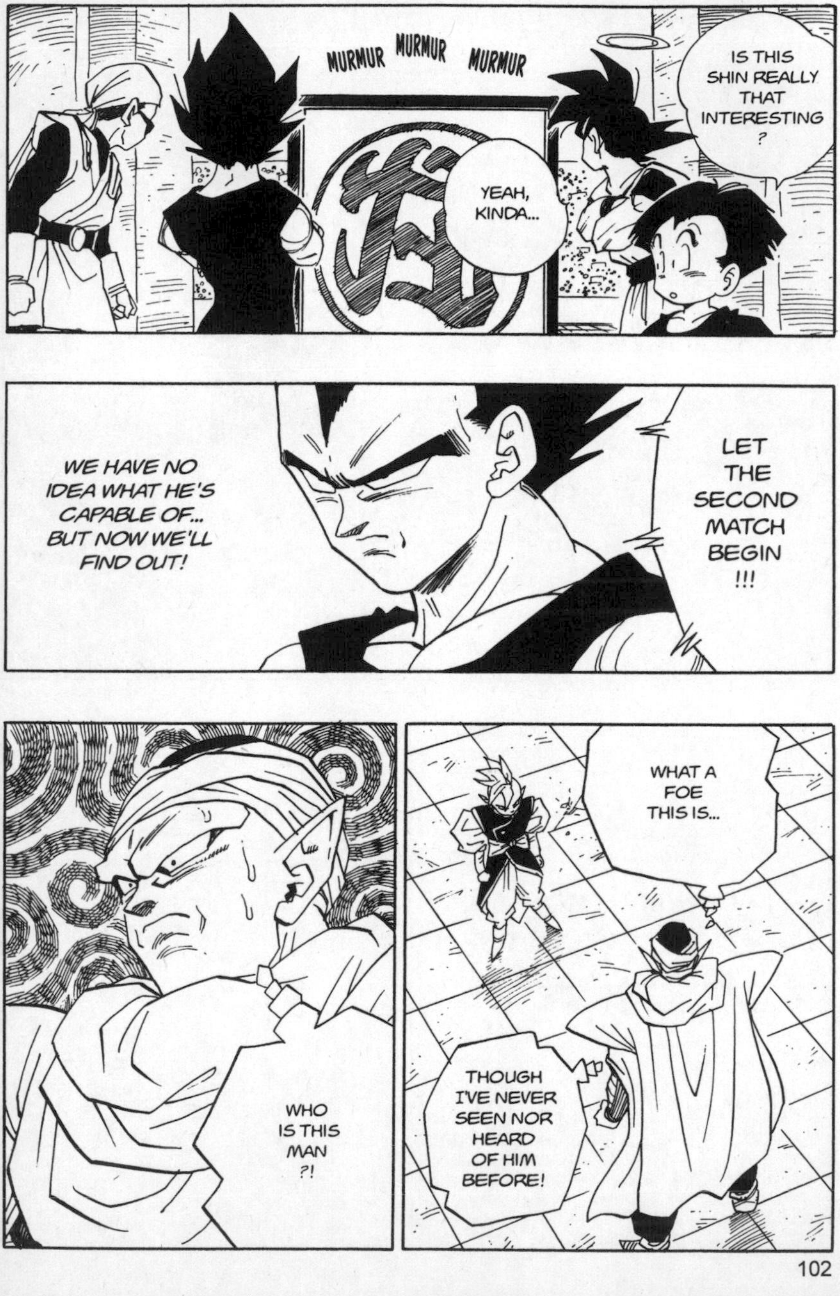
IS THIS SHIN REALLY THAT INTERESTING?
MURMUR MURMUR MURMUR
YEAH, KINDA...
LET THE SECOND MATCH BEGIN!!!
WE HAVE NO IDEA WHAT HE'S CAPABLE OF... BUT NOW WE'LL FIND OUT!
WHAT A FOE THIS IS...
THOUGH I'VE NEVER SEEN NOR HEARD OF HIM BEFORE!
WHO IS THIS MAN?!

READ THIS WAY

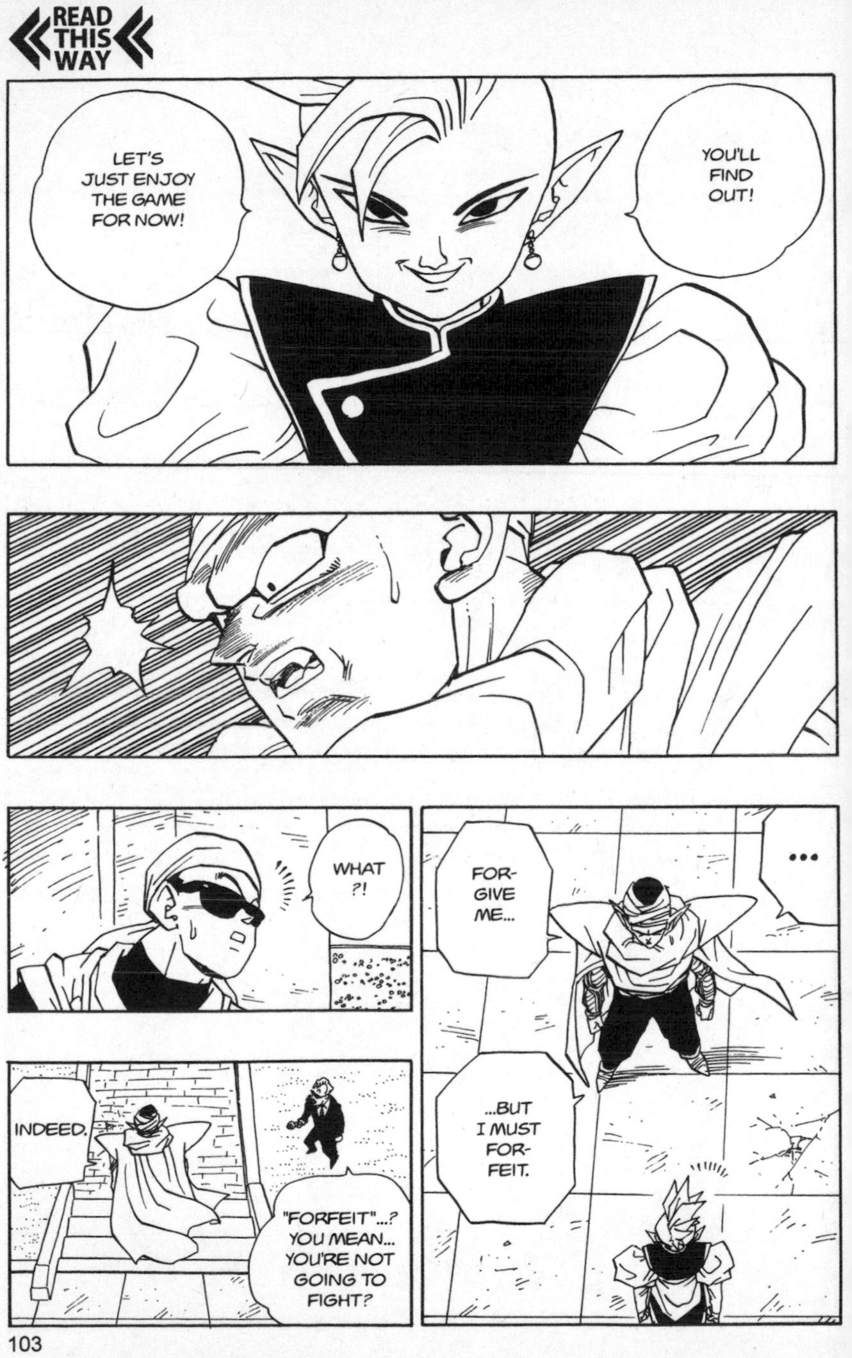
YOU'LL FIND OUT!
LET'S JUST ENJOY THE GAME FOR NOW!
...
FOR-GIVE ME...
...BUT I MUST FOR-FEIT.
WHAT?!
"FORFEIT"...? YOU MEAN... YOU'RE NOT GOING TO FIGHT?
INDEED.

READ THIS WAY

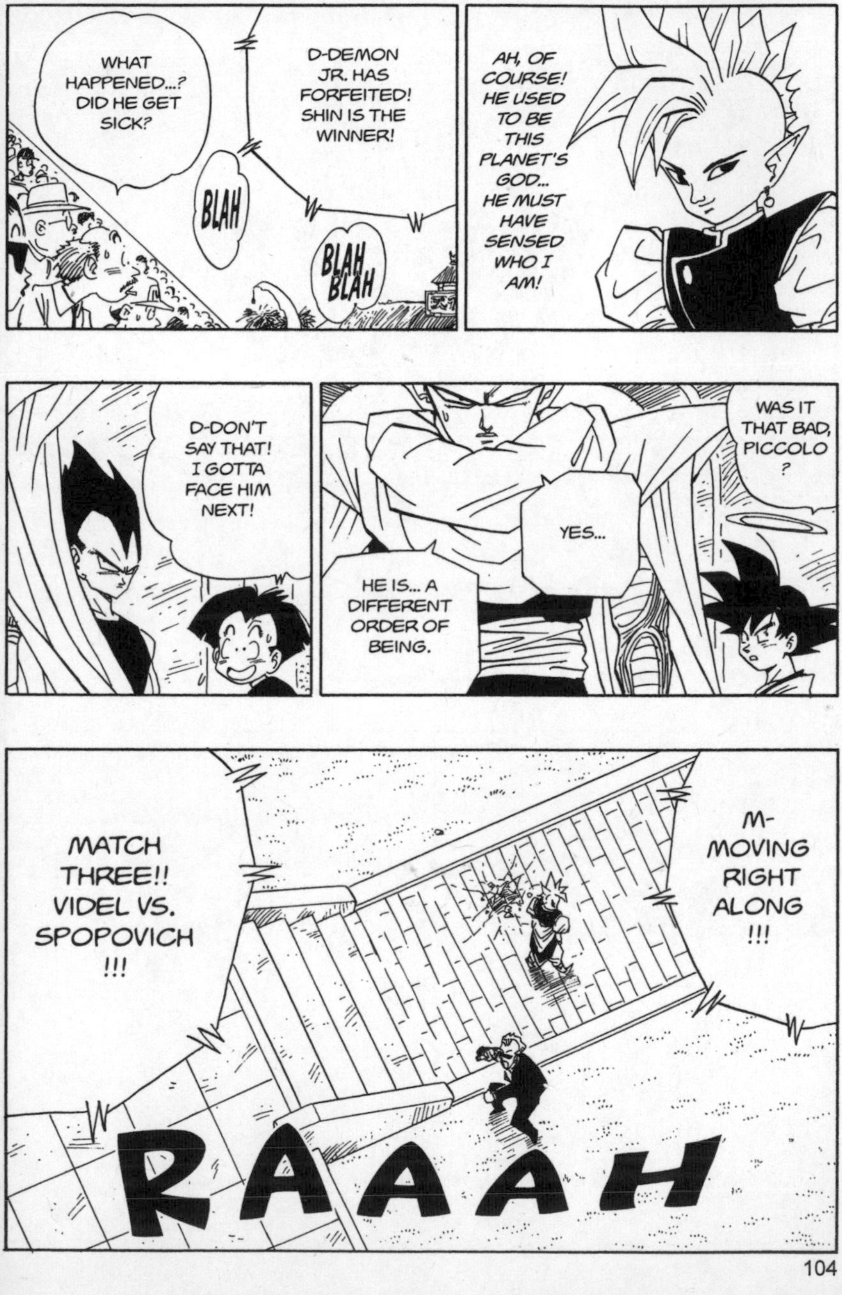
AH, OF COURSE! HE USED TO BE THIS PLANET'S GOD... HE MUST HAVE SENSED WHO I AM!
D-DEMON JR. HAS FORFEITED! SHIN IS THE WINNER!
WHAT HAPPENED...? DID HE GET SICK?
BLAH
BLAH BLAH
WAS IT THAT BAD, PICCOLO?
YES...
HE IS... A DIFFERENT ORDER OF BEING.
D-DON'T SAY THAT! I GOTTA FACE HIM NEXT!
M-MOVING RIGHT ALONG!!!
MATCH THREE!! VIDEL VS. SPOPOVICH!!!
RAAAH

READ THIS WAY

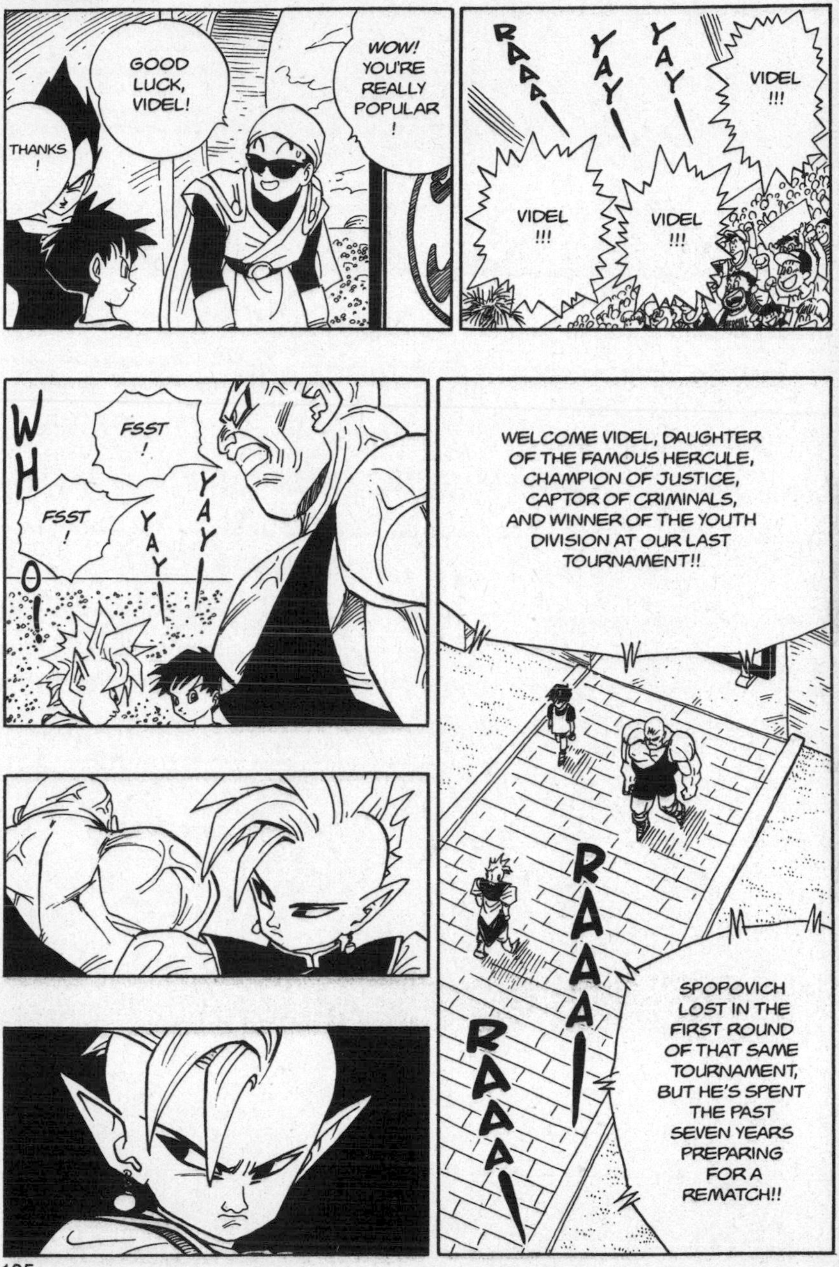

VIDEL!!!
YAY!
YAY!
RAAA!
VIDEL!!!
VIDEL!!!
WOW! YOU'RE REALLY POPULAR!
GOOD LUCK, VIDEL!
THANKS!
WELCOME VIDEL, DAUGHTER OF THE FAMOUS HERCULE, CHAMPION OF JUSTICE, CAPTOR OF CRIMINALS, AND WINNER OF THE YOUTH DIVISION AT OUR LAST TOURNAMENT!!
SPOPOVICH LOST IN THE FIRST ROUND OF THAT SAME TOURNAMENT, BUT HE'S SPENT THE PAST SEVEN YEARS PREPARING FOR A REMATCH!!
RAAA!
RAAA!
FSST!
YAY!
YAY!
FSST!
WHOO!

DBZ:246 • Shin's Surprise

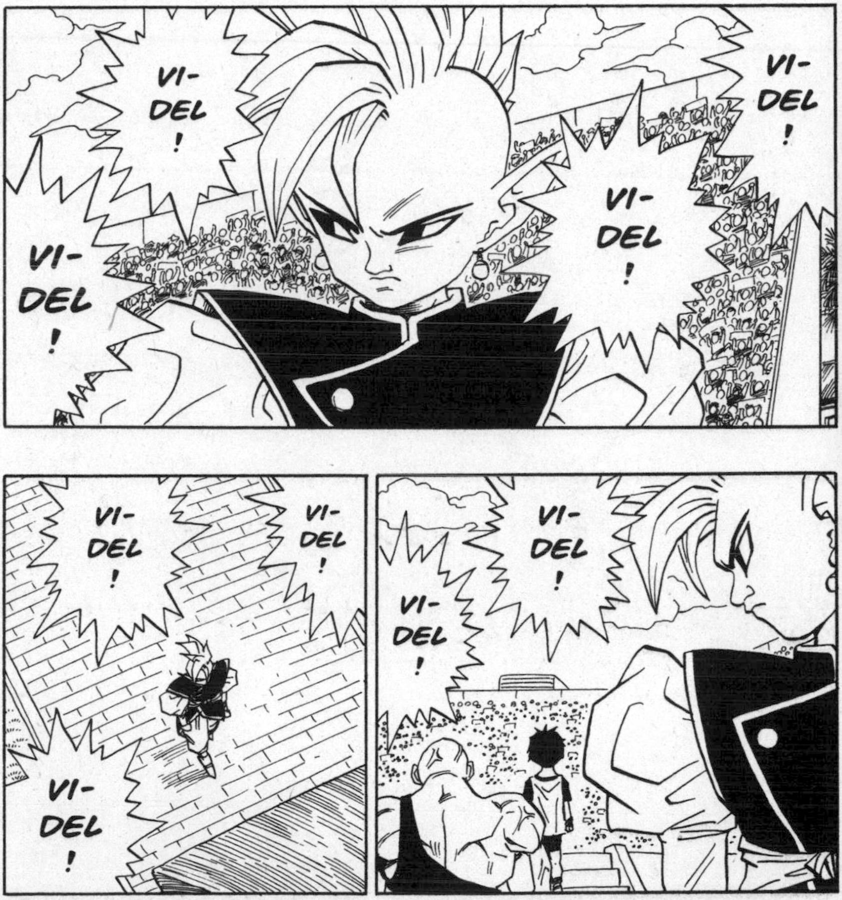
VI-DEL!
VI-DEL!
VI-DEL!
VI-DEL!
VI-DEL!
VI-DEL!
VI-DEL!
VI-DEL!
VI-DEL!

READ THIS WAY

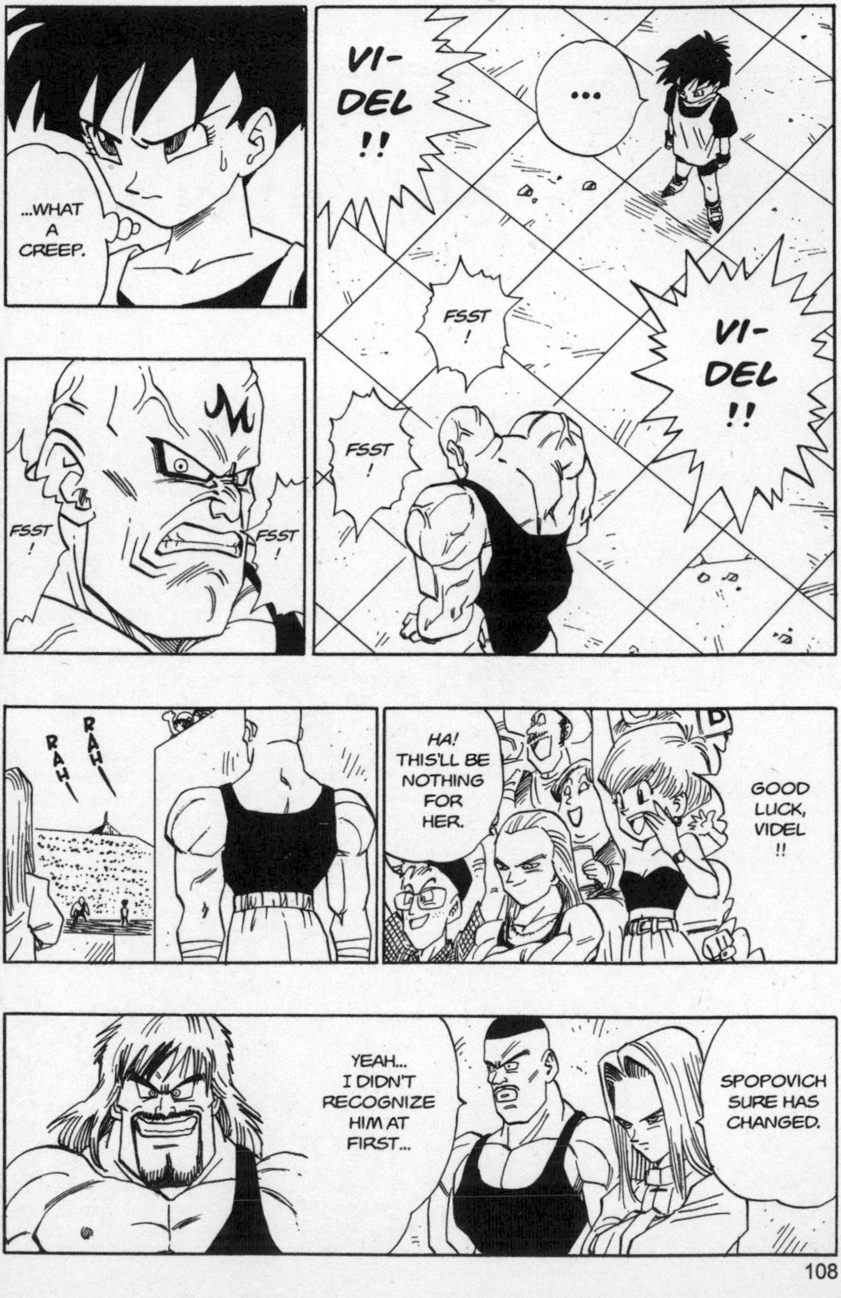
...
VI-DEL !!
VI-DEL !!
FSST !
FSST !
...WHAT A CREEP.
FSST !
FSST !
GOOD LUCK, VIDEL !!
HA! THIS'LL BE NOTHING FOR HER.
RAH RAH
SPOPOVICH SURE HAS CHANGED.
YEAH... I DIDN'T RECOGNIZE HIM AT FIRST...

READ THIS WAY

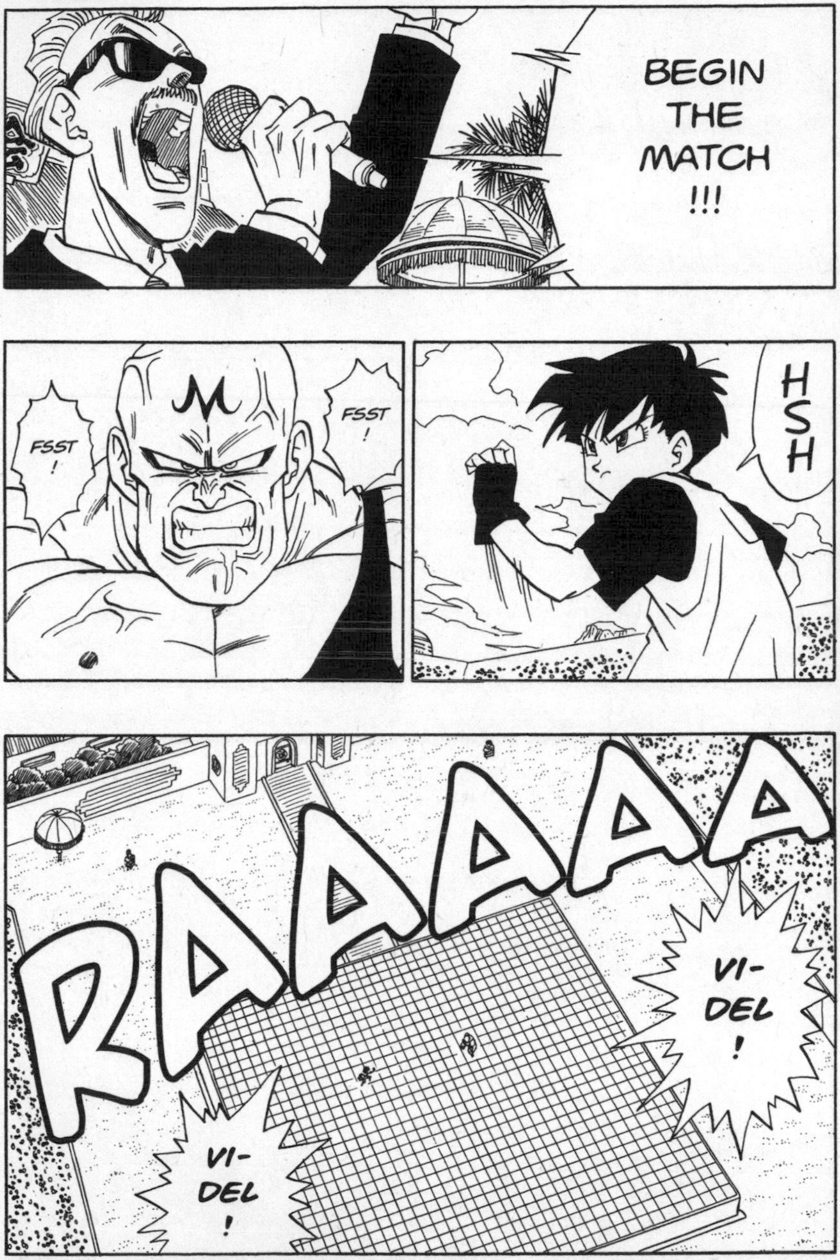
BEGIN THE MATCH !!!
HSH
FSST !
FSST !
VI-DEL !
RAAAAA
VI-DEL !

READ THIS WAY

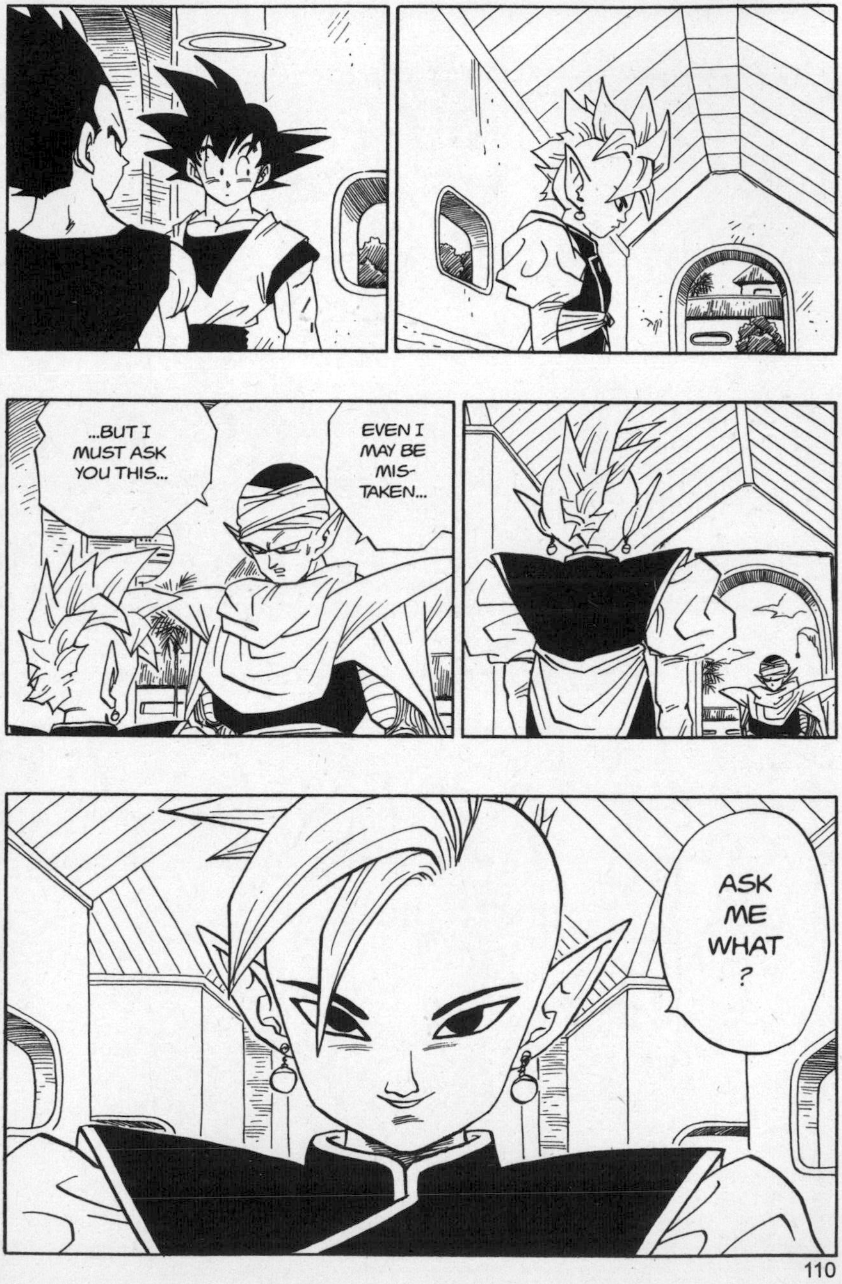
EVEN I MAY BE MIS-TAKEN...
...BUT I MUST ASK YOU THIS...
ASK ME WHAT?

READ THIS WAY

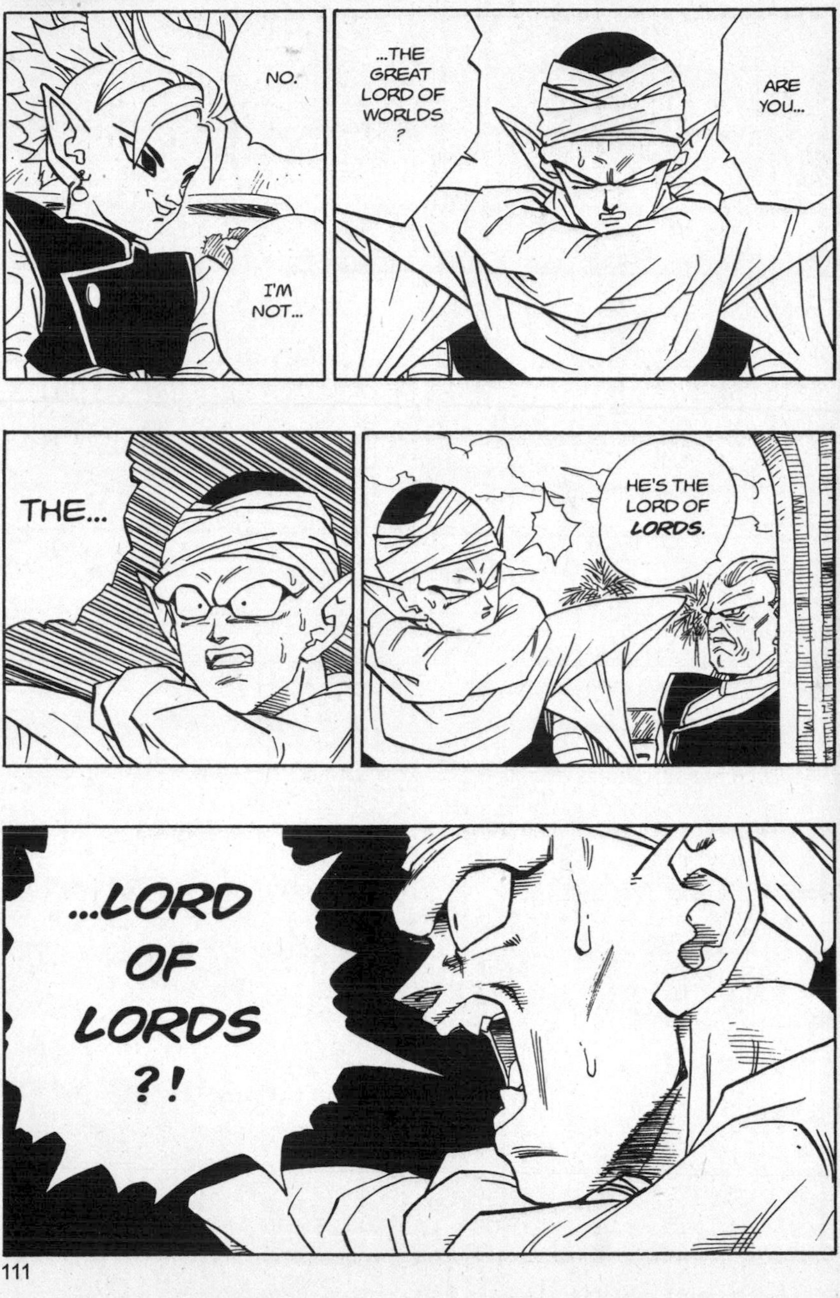
ARE YOU...
...THE GREAT LORD OF WORLDS ?
NO.
I'M NOT...
HE'S THE LORD OF LORDS.
THE...
...LORD OF LORDS ?!

READ THIS WAY

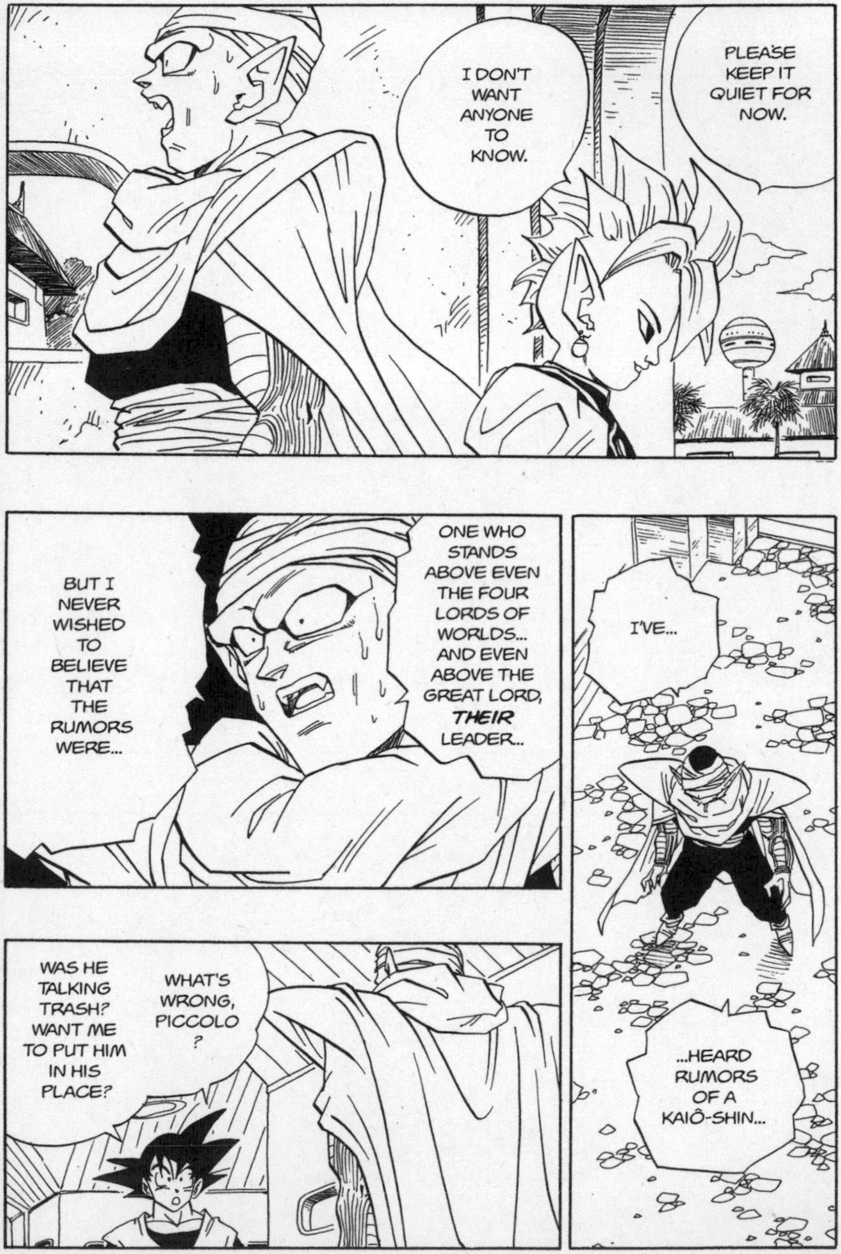
PLEASE KEEP IT QUIET FOR NOW.
I DON'T WANT ANYONE TO KNOW.
I'VE...
...HEARD RUMORS OF A KAIÔ-SHIN...
ONE WHO STANDS ABOVE EVEN THE FOUR LORDS OF WORLDS... AND EVEN ABOVE THE GREAT LORD, ***THEIR*** LEADER...
BUT I NEVER WISHED TO BELIEVE THAT THE RUMORS WERE...
WHAT'S WRONG, PICCOLO?
WAS HE TALKING TRASH? WANT ME TO PUT HIM IN HIS PLACE?

READ THIS WAY

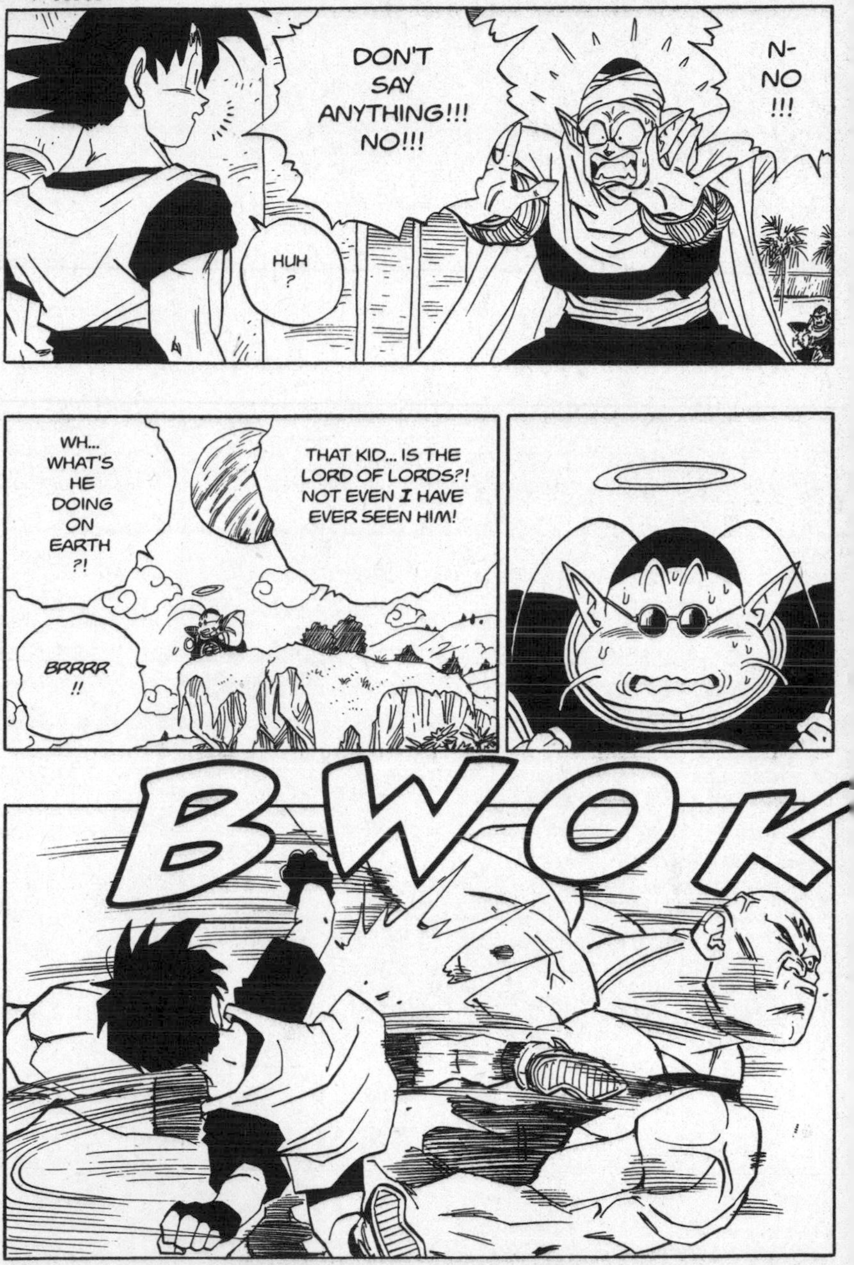
N-NO!!!
DON'T SAY ANYTHING!!! NO!!!
HUH?
THAT KID... IS THE LORD OF LORDS?! NOT EVEN I HAVE EVER SEEN HIM!
WH... WHAT'S HE DOING ON EARTH?!
BRRRR!!
BWOK

READ THIS WAY

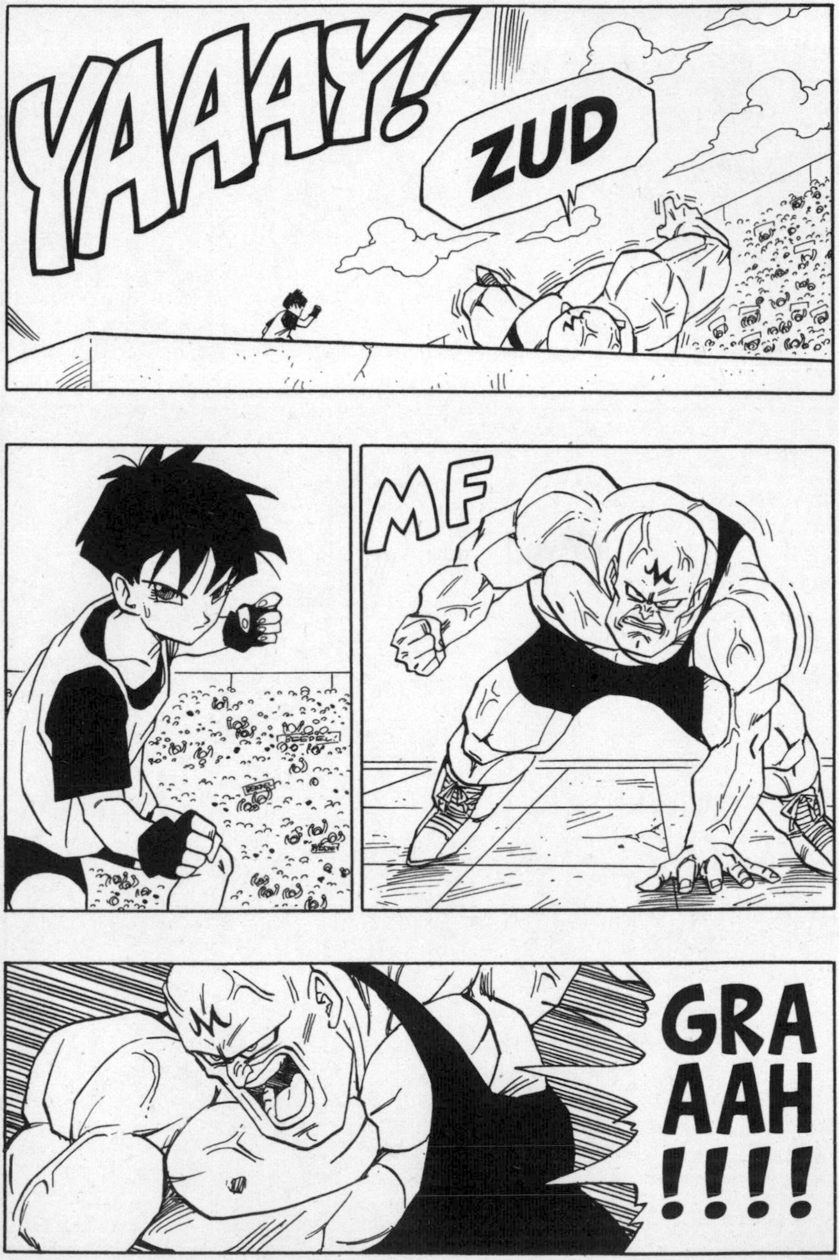
YAAAY!
ZUD
MF
GRA
AAH
!!!!

READ THIS WAY

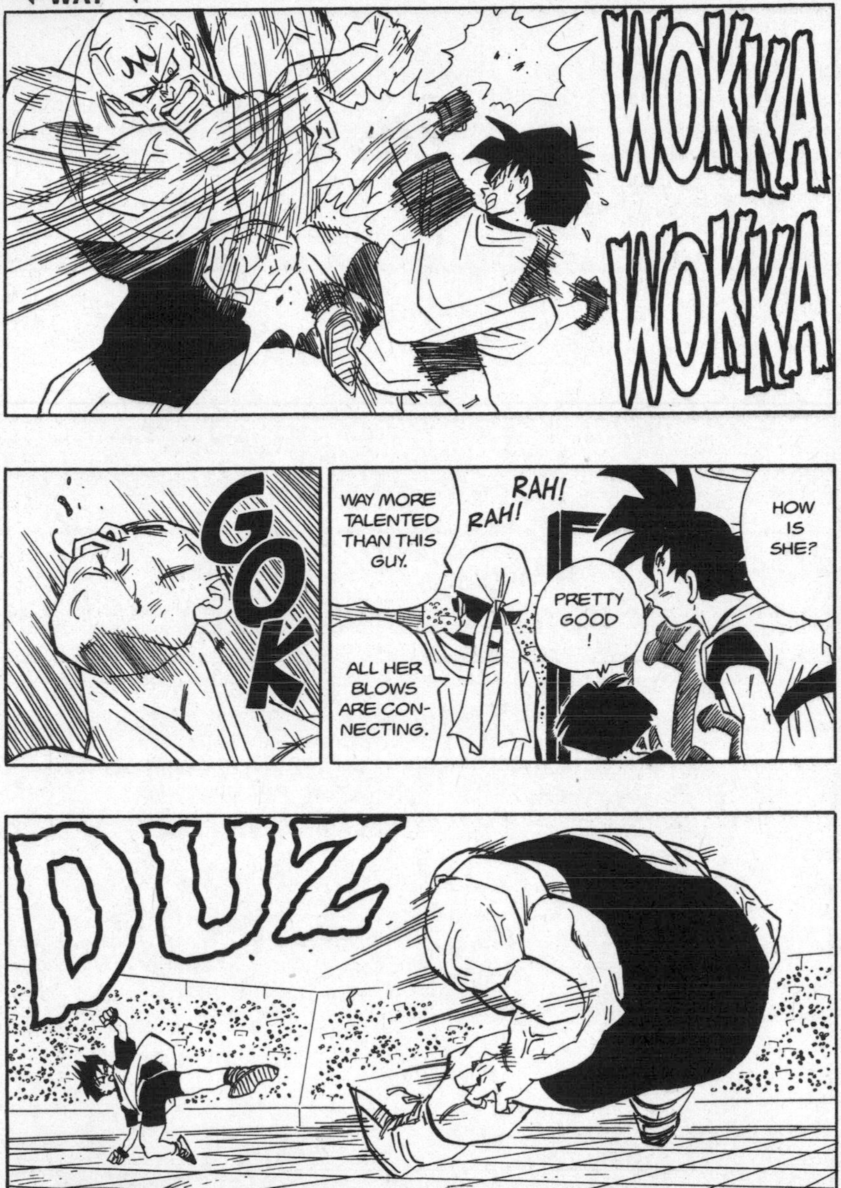

WOKKA WOKKA
HOW IS SHE?
RAH! RAH!
PRETTY GOOD!
ALL HER BLOWS ARE CON-NECTING.
WAY MORE TALENTED THAN THIS GUY.
GOK
DUZ

READ THIS WAY

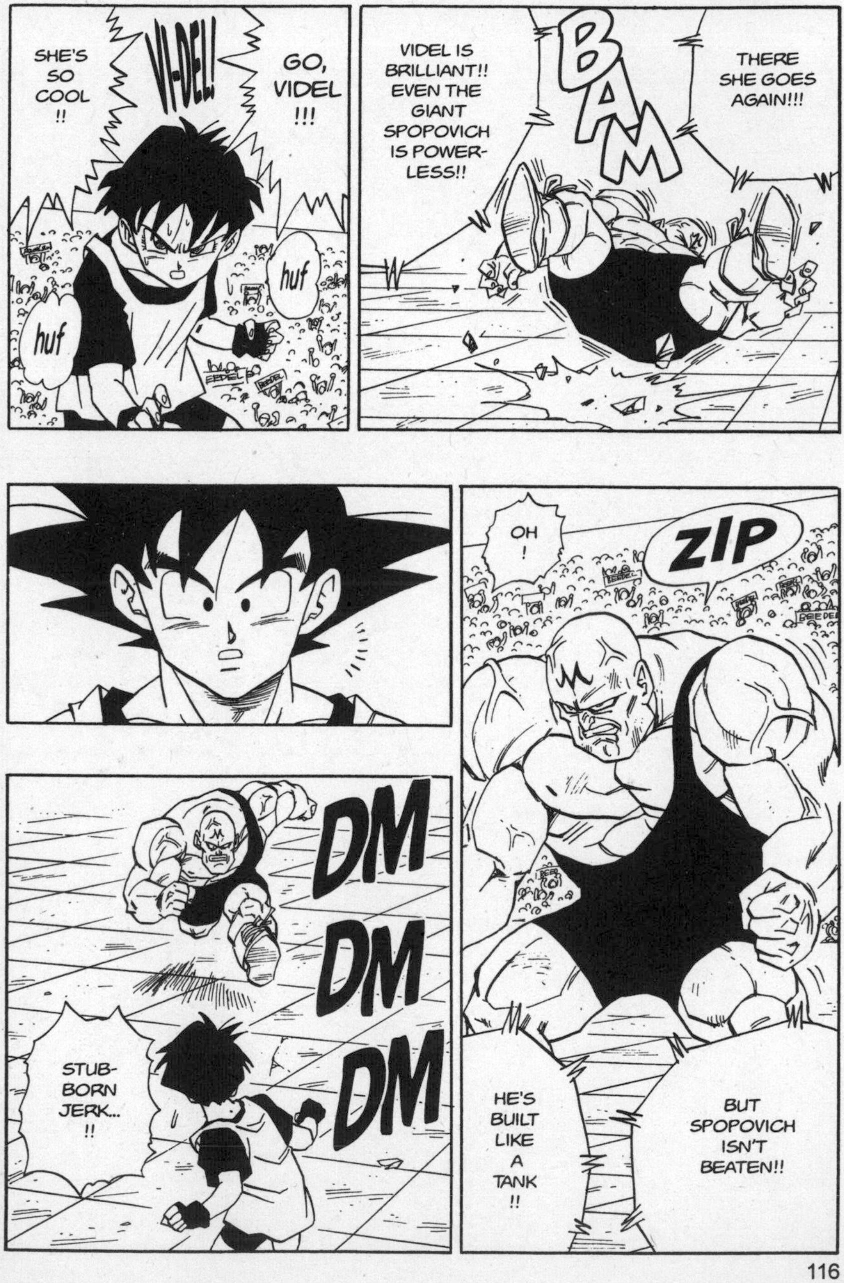
THERE SHE GOES AGAIN!!!
BAM
VIDEL IS BRILLIANT!! EVEN THE GIANT SPOPOVICH IS POWER-LESS!!
GO, VIDEL !!!
VI-DEL!
SHE'S SO COOL !!
huf
huf
ZIP
OH !
BUT SPOPOVICH ISN'T BEATEN!!
HE'S BUILT LIKE A TANK !!
DM DM DM
STUB-BORN JERK... !!

READ THIS WAY

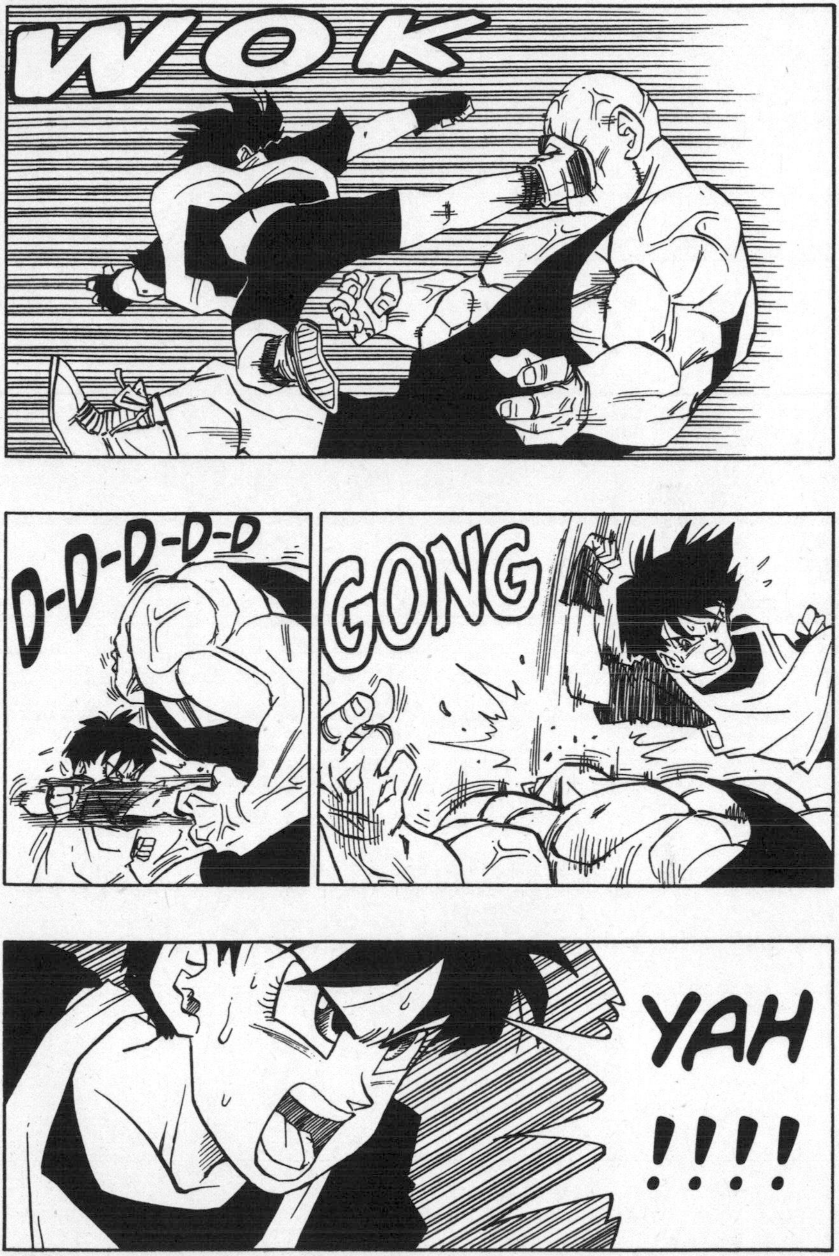
WOK
GONG
D-D-D-D-D
YAH
!!!!

READ THIS WAY

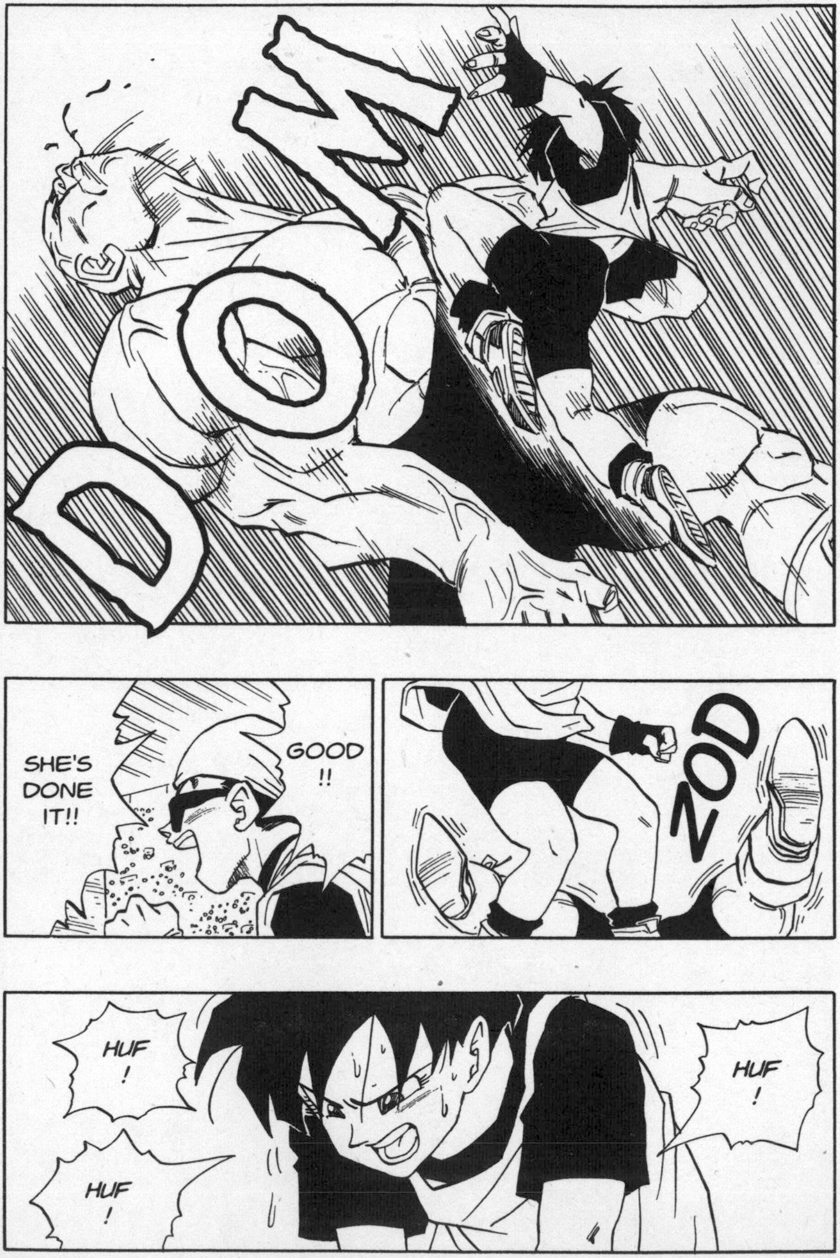

DOM
ZOD
GOOD !!
SHE'S DONE IT!!
HUF !
HUF !
HUF !

READ THIS WAY

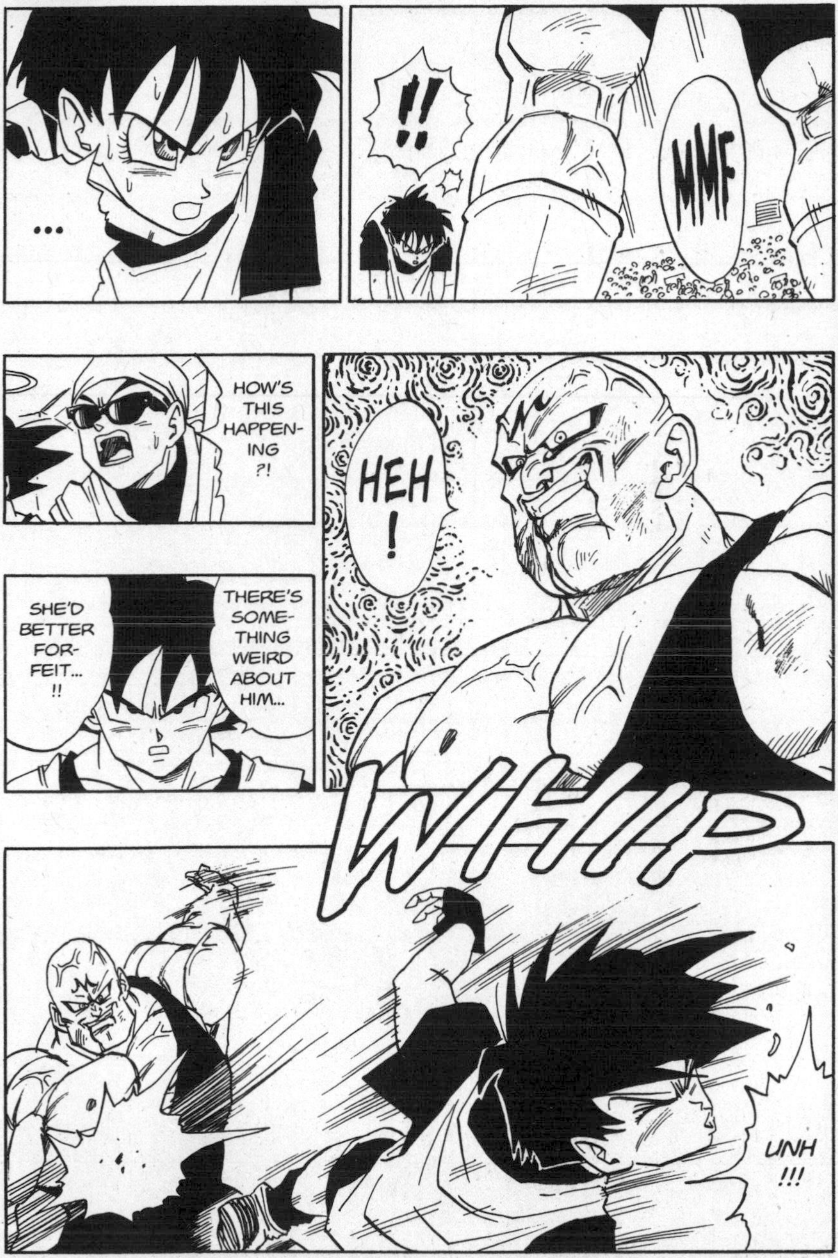

!!
MMF
...
HEH !
HOW'S THIS HAPPEN-ING ?!
THERE'S SOME-THING WEIRD ABOUT HIM...
SHE'D BETTER FOR-FEIT... !!
WHIP
UNH !!!

DBZ:247 • Videl...Battered

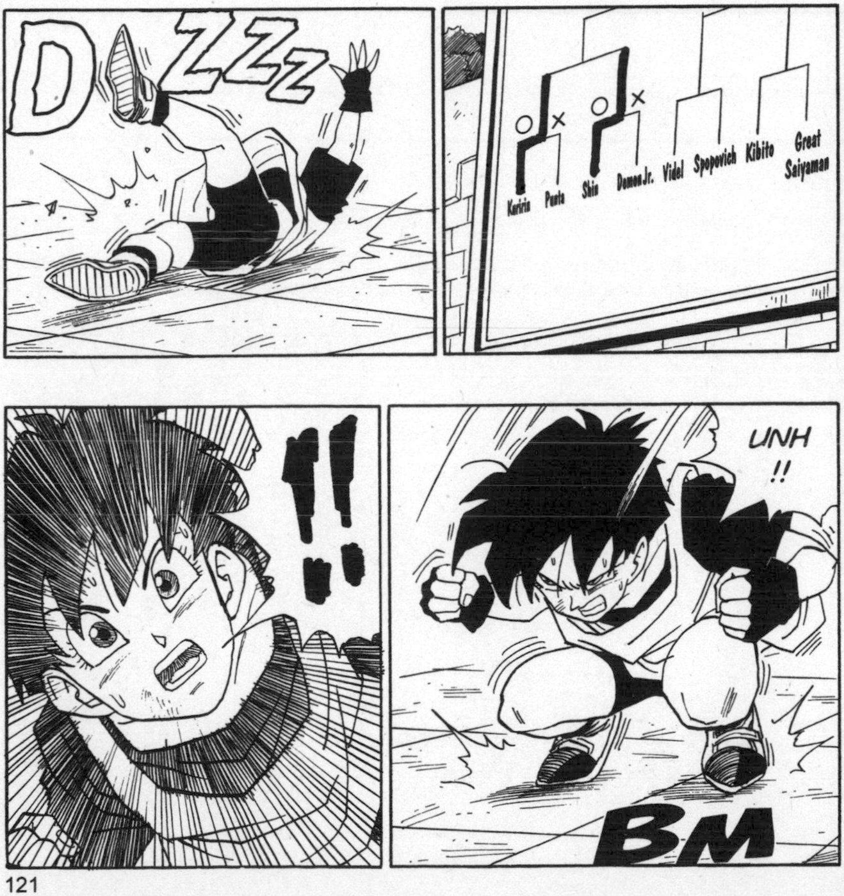
Kuririn
Punta
Shin
Demon Jr.
Videl
Spopovich
Kibito
Great Saiyaman
DZZZ
UNH !!
BM
!!

READ THIS WAY

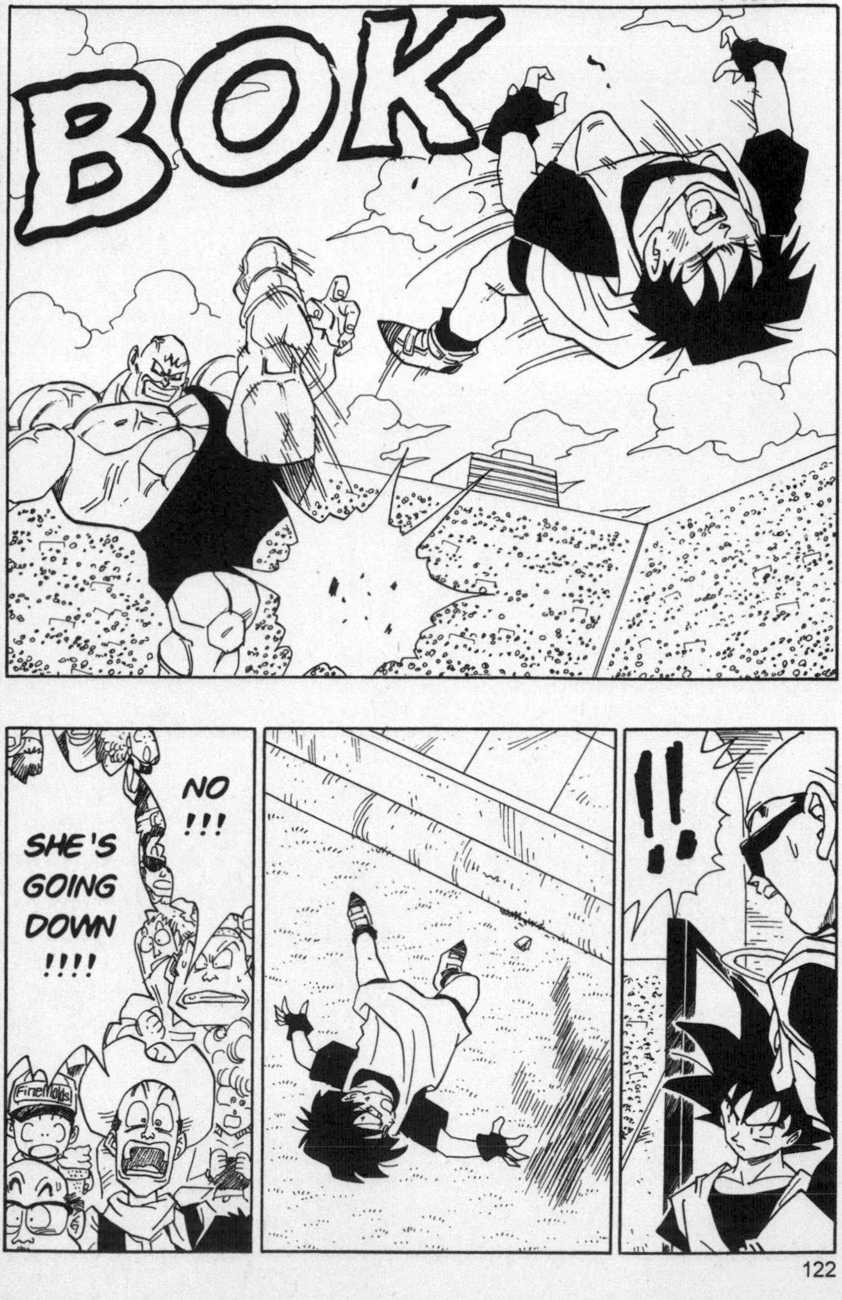
BOK
!!
NO !!!
SHE'S GOING DOWN !!!!
FineMolds

READ THIS WAY

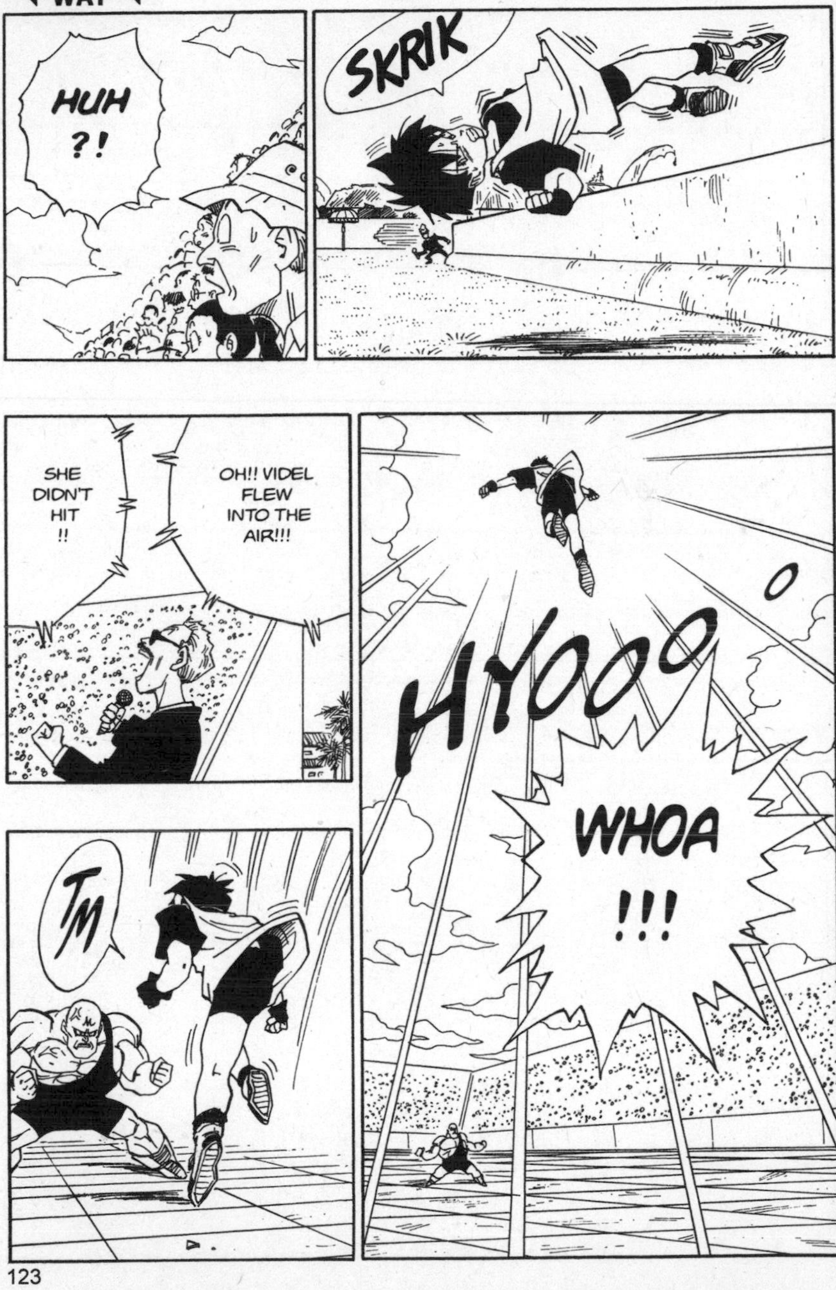
SKRIK
HUH ?!
HYOOO
WHOA !!!
OH!! VIDEL FLEW INTO THE AIR!!!
SHE DIDN'T HIT !!
TM

READ THIS WAY

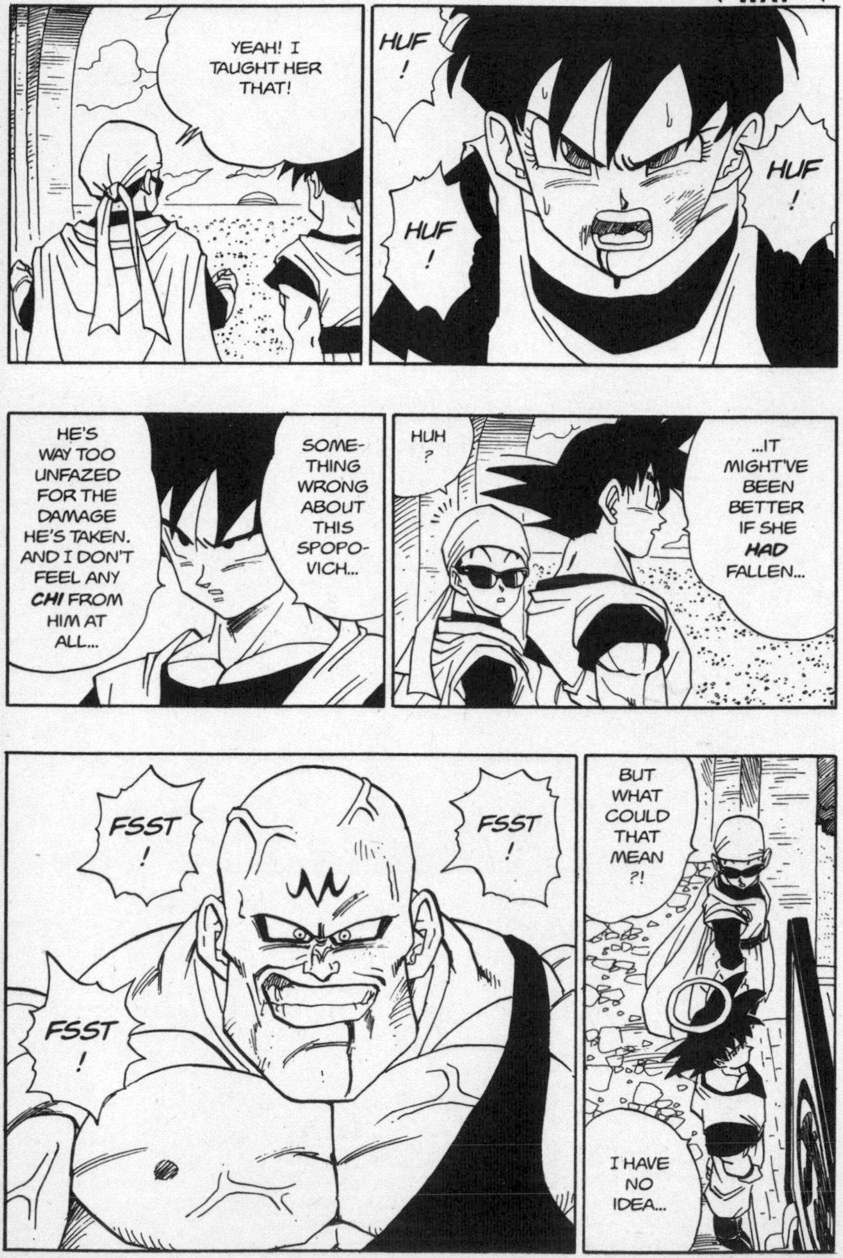
HUF!
HUF!
HUF!
YEAH! I TAUGHT HER THAT!
...IT MIGHT'VE BEEN BETTER IF SHE **HAD** FALLEN...
HUH?
SOME-THING WRONG ABOUT THIS SPOPO-VICH...
HE'S WAY TOO UNFAZED FOR THE DAMAGE HE'S TAKEN. AND I DON'T FEEL ANY **CHI** FROM HIM AT ALL...
BUT WHAT COULD THAT MEAN?!
I HAVE NO IDEA...
FSST!
FSST!
FSST!

READ THIS WAY

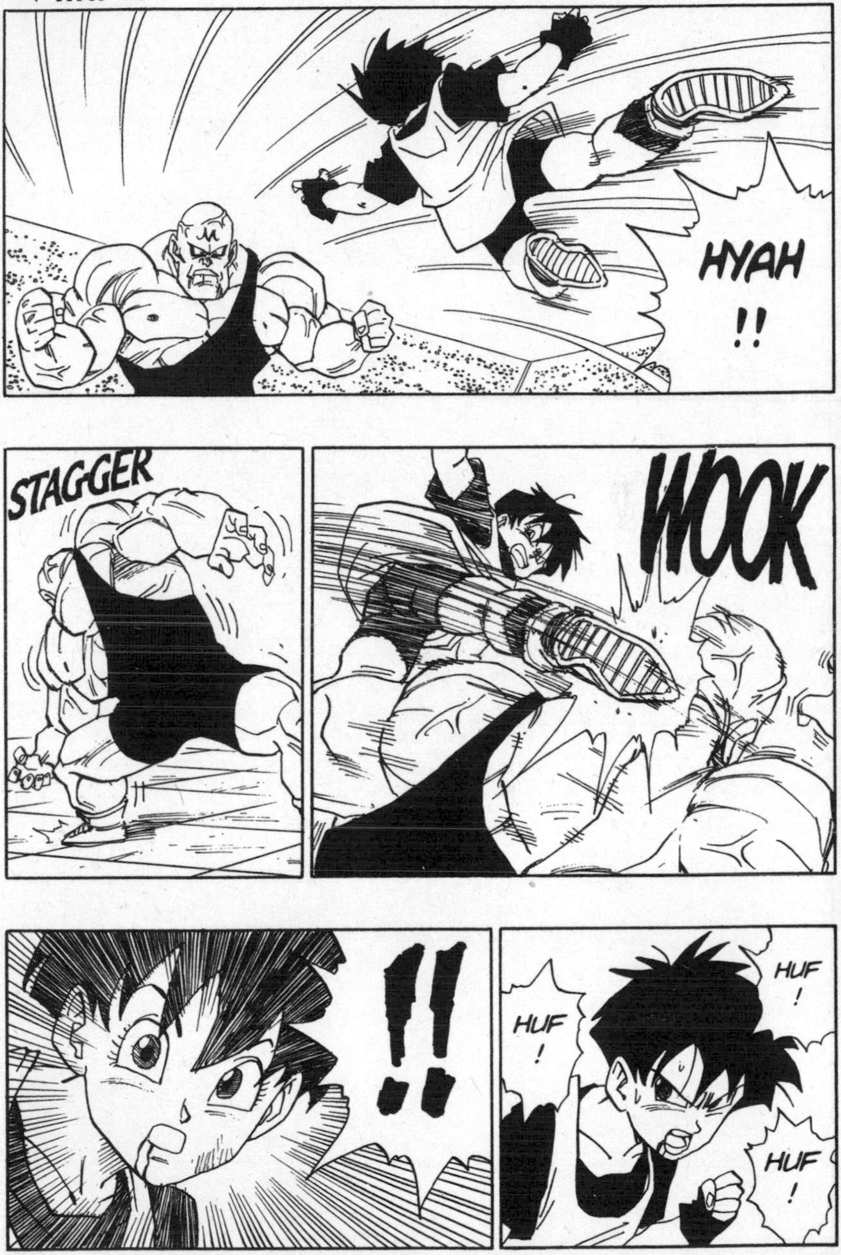
HYAH !!
WOOK
STAGGER
HUF !
HUF !
HUF !
!!

READ THIS WAY

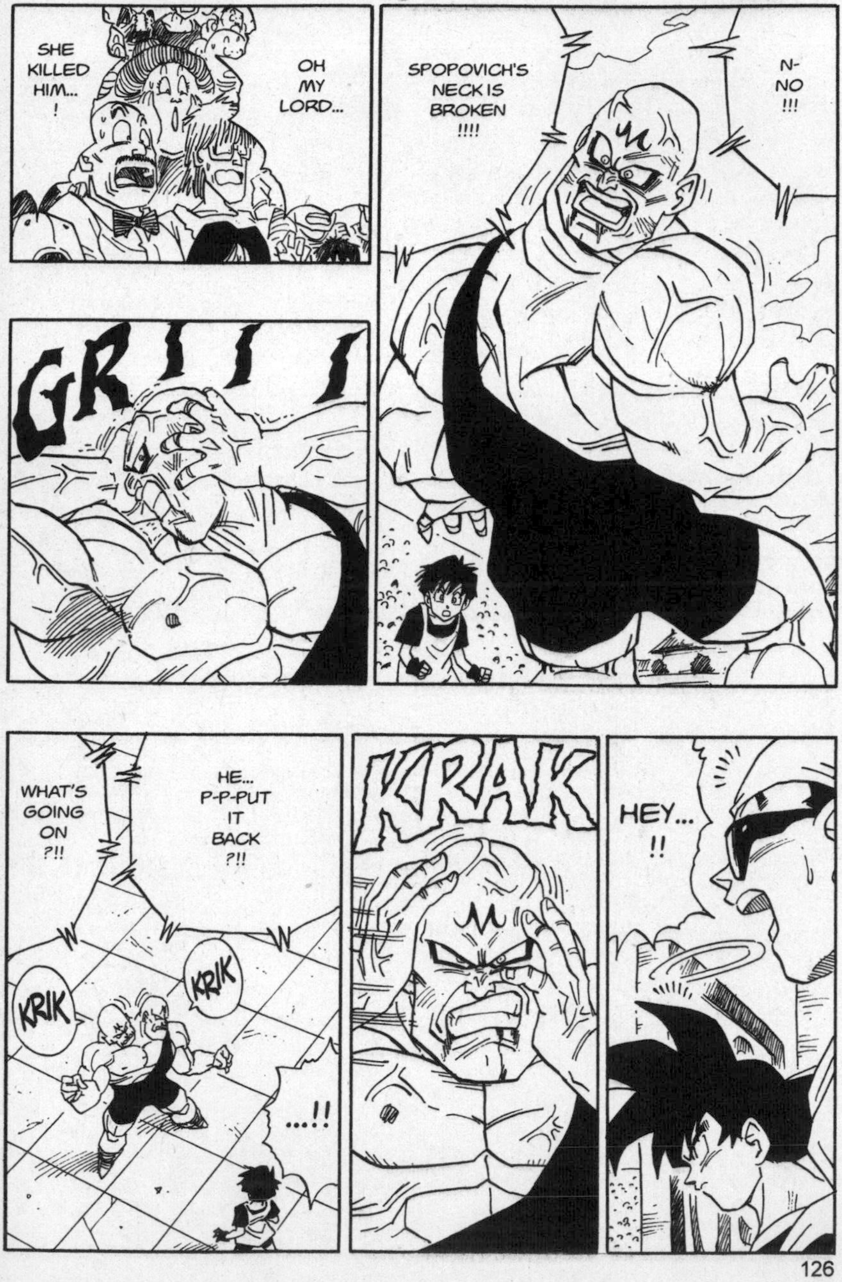
N-NO!!!
SPOPOVICH'S NECK IS BROKEN!!!!
OH MY LORD...
SHE KILLED HIM...!
GRIII
HEY...!!
KRAK
HE... P-P-PUT IT BACK?!!
WHAT'S GOING ON?!!
KRIK
KRIK
...!!

READ THIS WAY

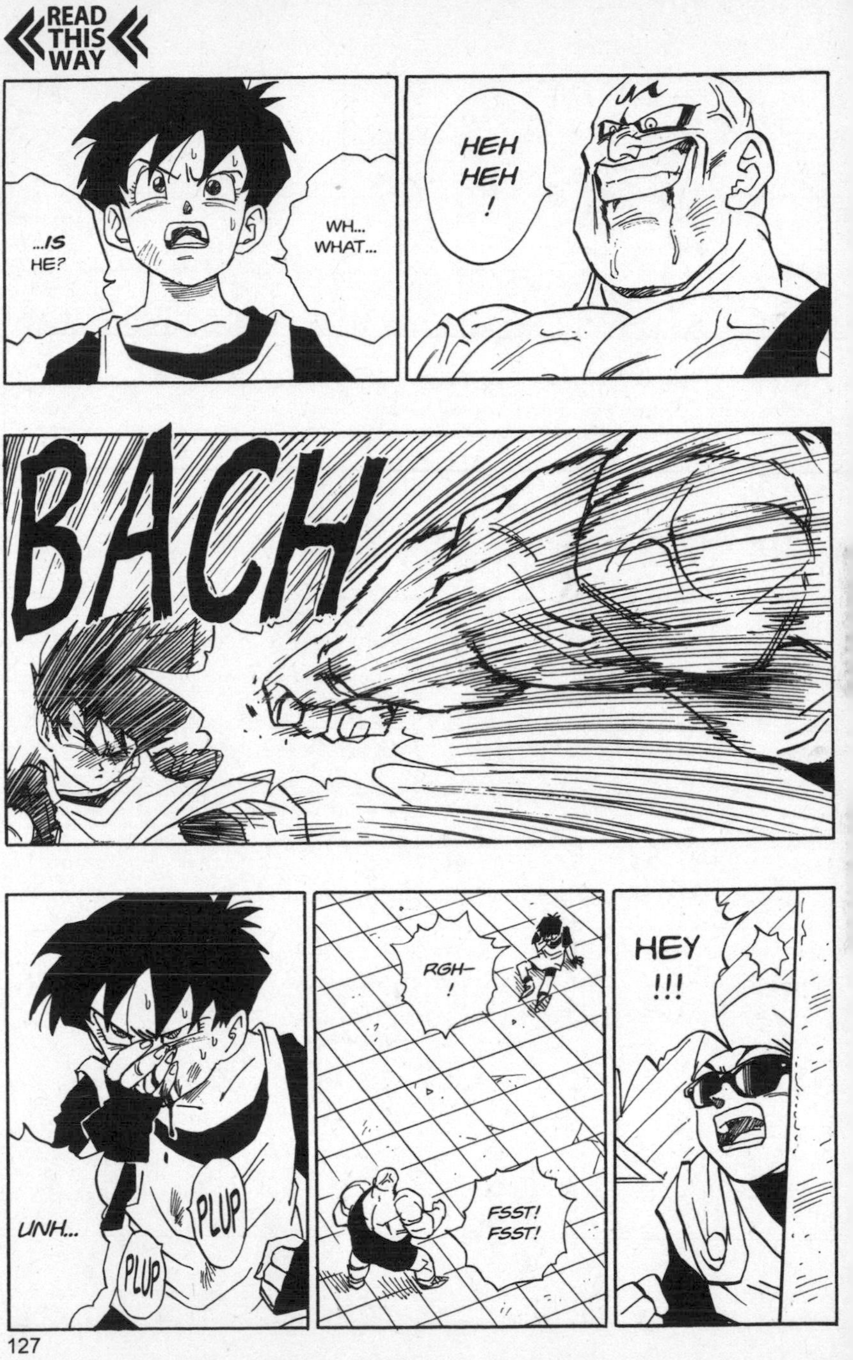

HEH HEH !
WH... WHAT...
...IS HE?
BACH
HEY !!!
RGH- !
FSST! FSST!
PLUP
PLUP
UNH...

READ THIS WAY

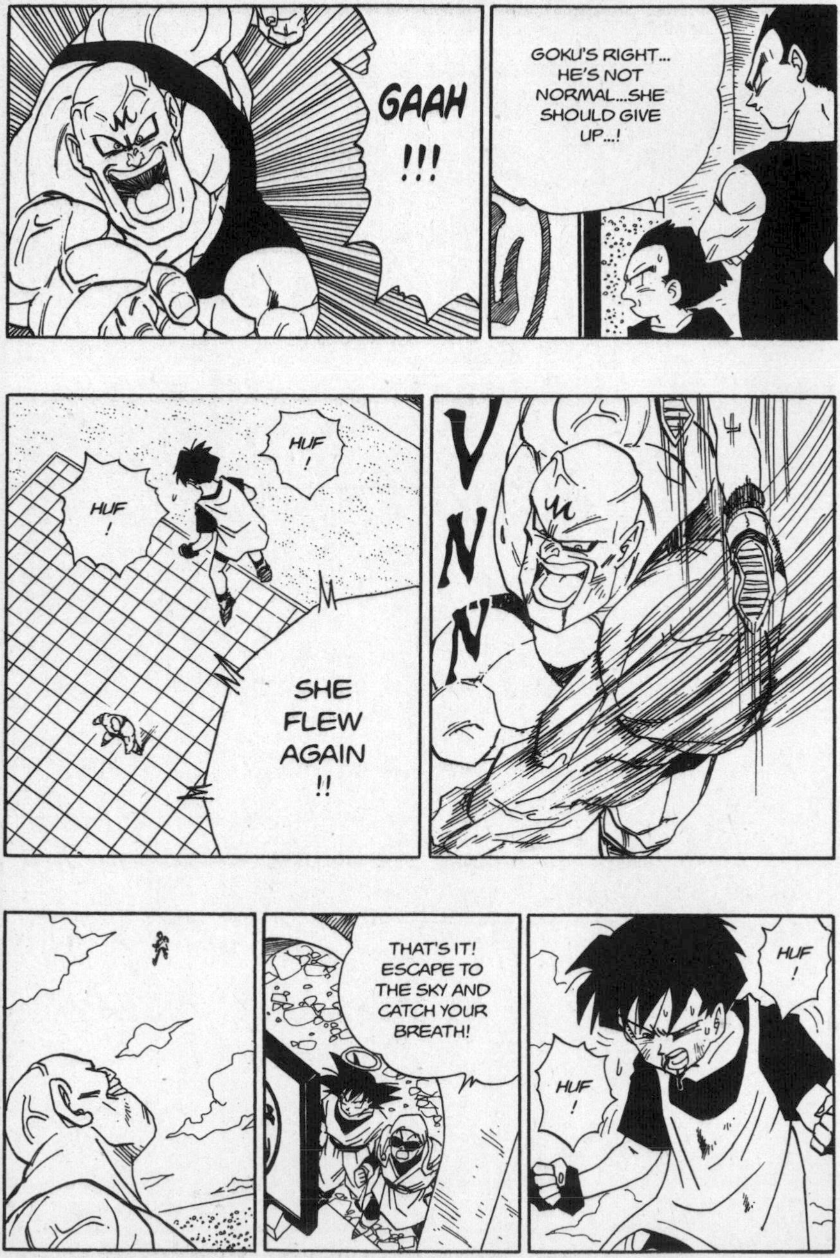
GOKU'S RIGHT... HE'S NOT NORMAL...SHE SHOULD GIVE UP...!
GAAH !!!
VNN
HUF !
HUF !
SHE FLEW AGAIN !!
HUF !
HUF !
THAT'S IT! ESCAPE TO THE SKY AND CATCH YOUR BREATH!

READ THIS WAY

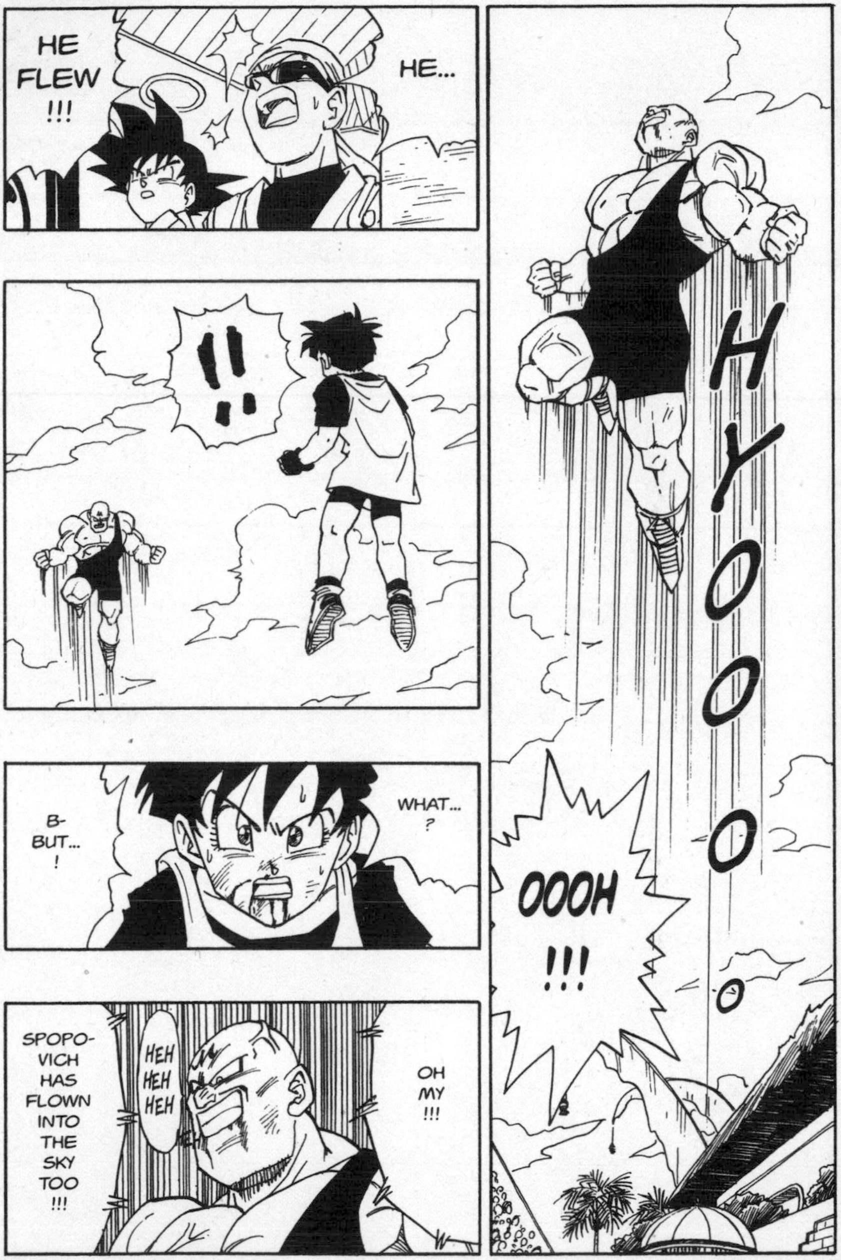
HYOOOO
OOOH !!!
HE...
HE FLEW !!!
!!
WHAT... ?
B-BUT... !
OH MY !!!
HEH HEH HEH
SPOPOVICH HAS FLOWN INTO THE SKY TOO !!!

READ THIS WAY

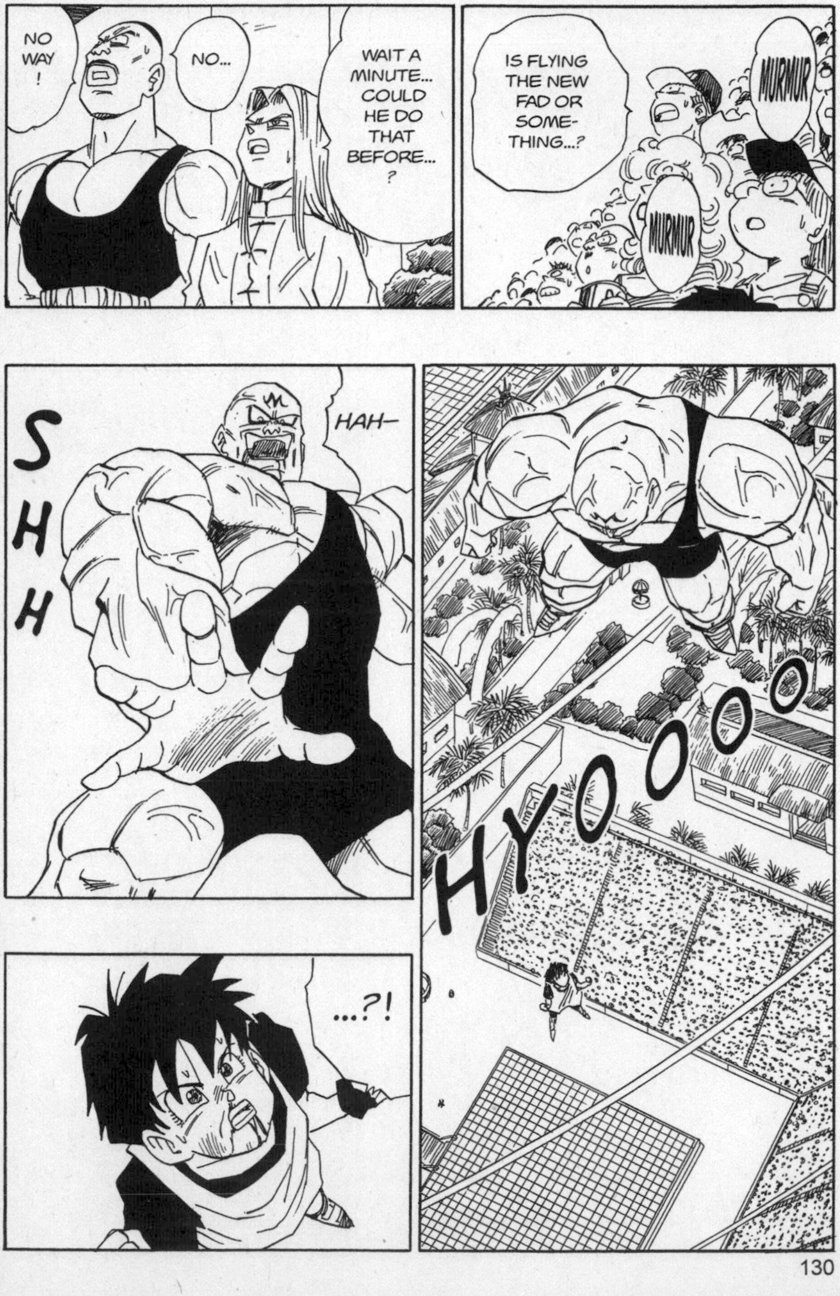
IS FLYING THE NEW FAD OR SOME-THING...?
MURMUR
MURMUR
WAIT A MINUTE... COULD HE DO THAT BEFORE... ?
NO...
NO WAY !
HYOOOOOO
HAH-
SHHH
...?!

READ THIS WAY

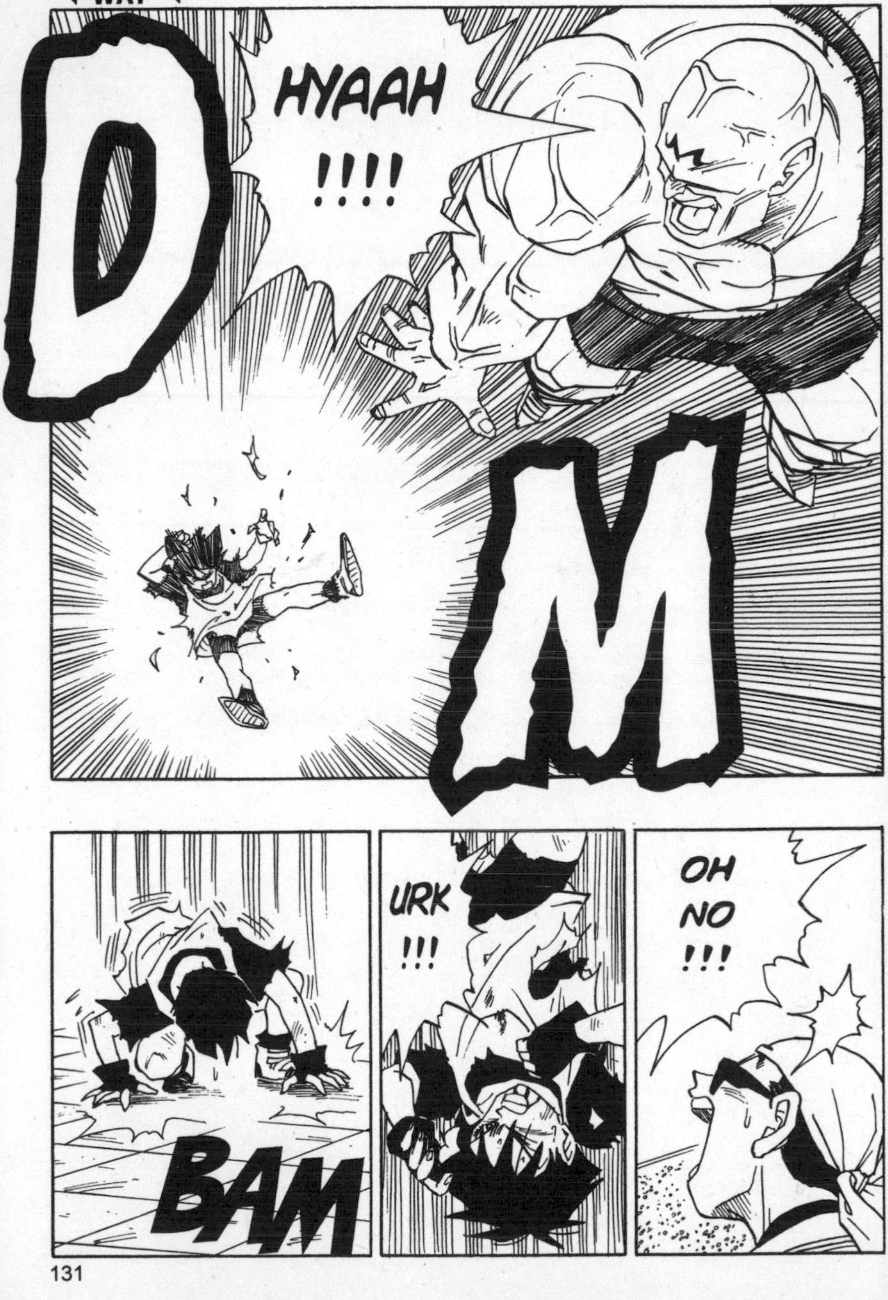
HYAAH !!!!
D
M
OH NO !!!
URK !!!
BAM

READ THIS WAY

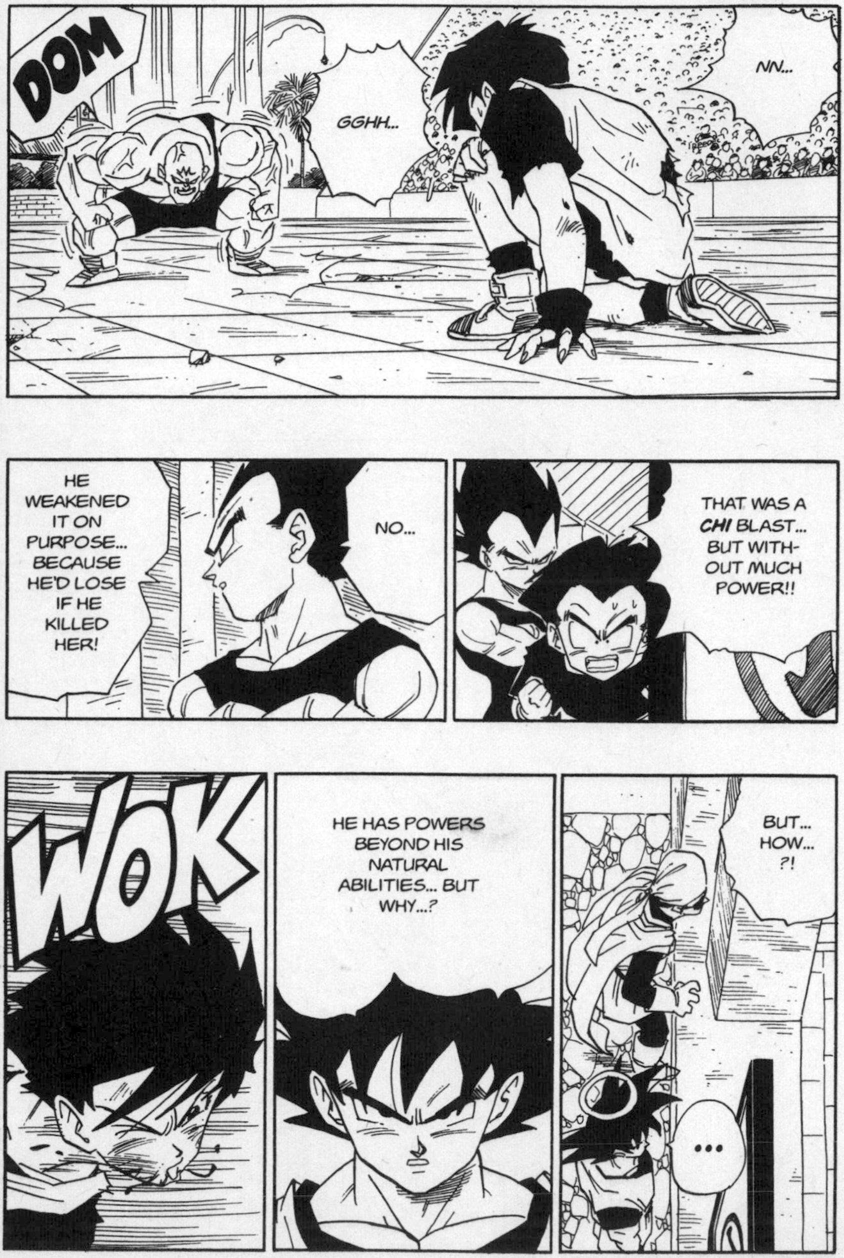

NN...
DOM
GGHH...
THAT WAS A CHI BLAST... BUT WITH-OUT MUCH POWER!!
NO...
HE WEAKENED IT ON PURPOSE... BECAUSE HE'D LOSE IF HE KILLED HER!
BUT... HOW... ?!
...
HE HAS POWERS BEYOND HIS NATURAL ABILITIES... BUT WHY...?
WOK

READ THIS WAY

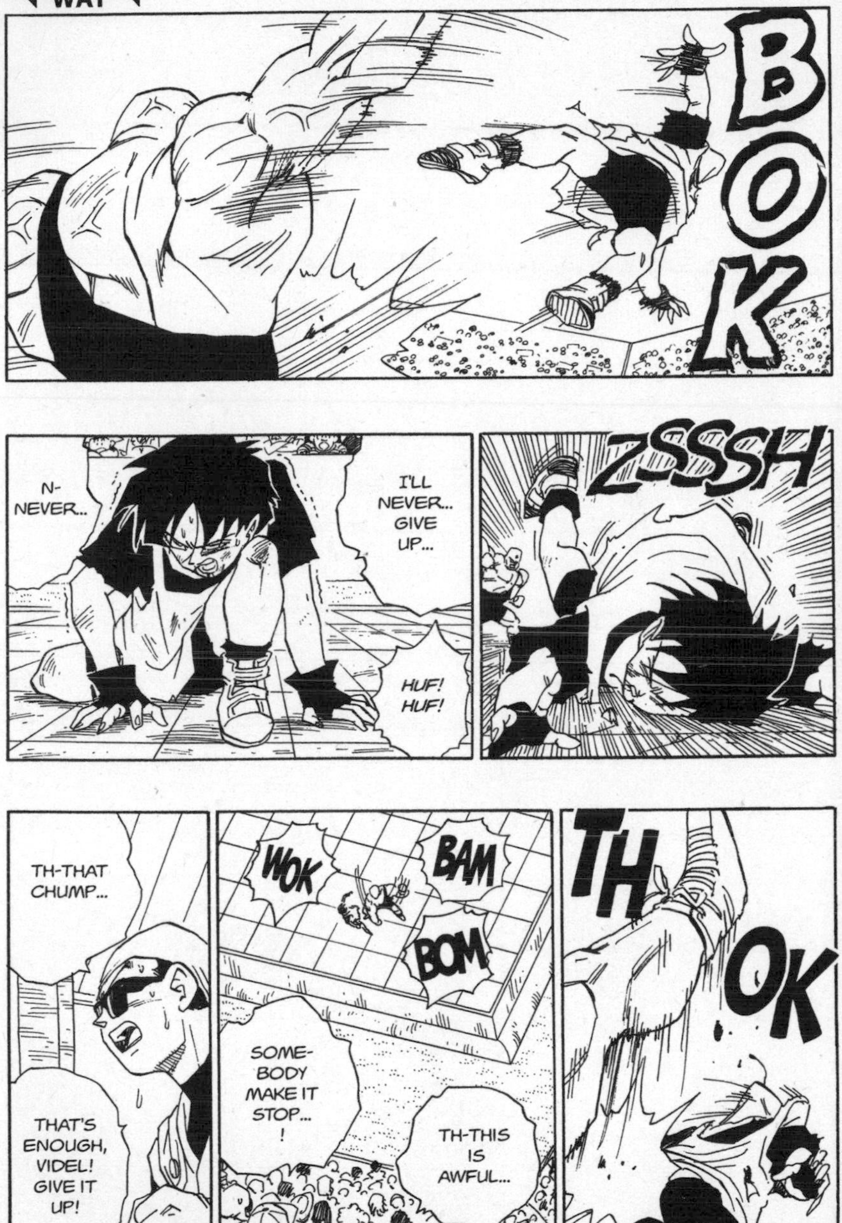

BOK
ZSSSH
I'LL NEVER... GIVE UP...
N-NEVER..
HUF! HUF!
THOK
BAM
WOK
BOM
SOME-BODY MAKE IT STOP... !
TH-THIS IS AWFUL...
TH-THAT CHUMP...
THAT'S ENOUGH, VIDEL! GIVE IT UP!

DBZ:248 · Gohan Gets Mad!!

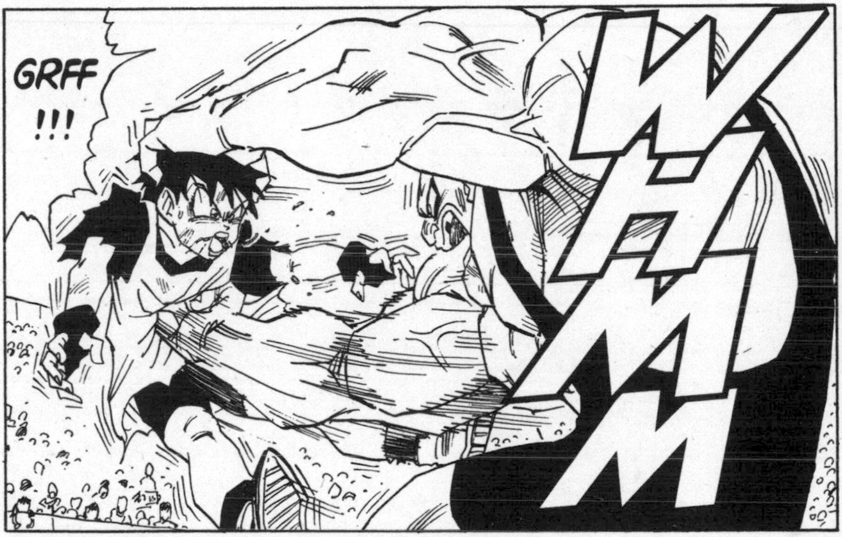
WHAMM
GRFF !!!

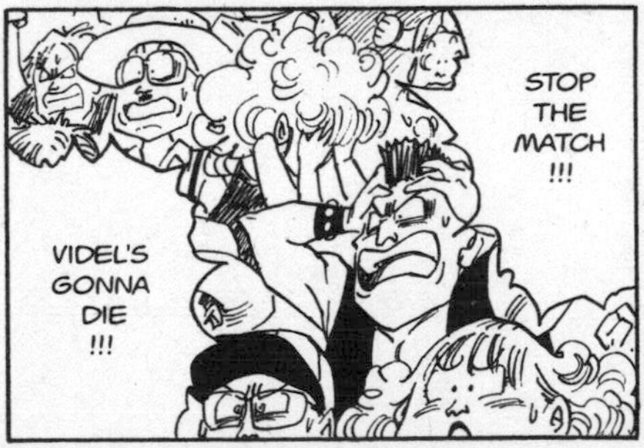
STOP THE MATCH !!!
VIDEL'S GONNA DIE !!!

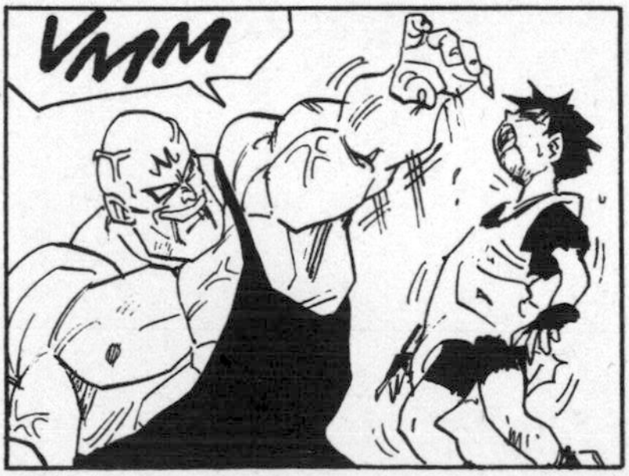
VMM

READ THIS WAY

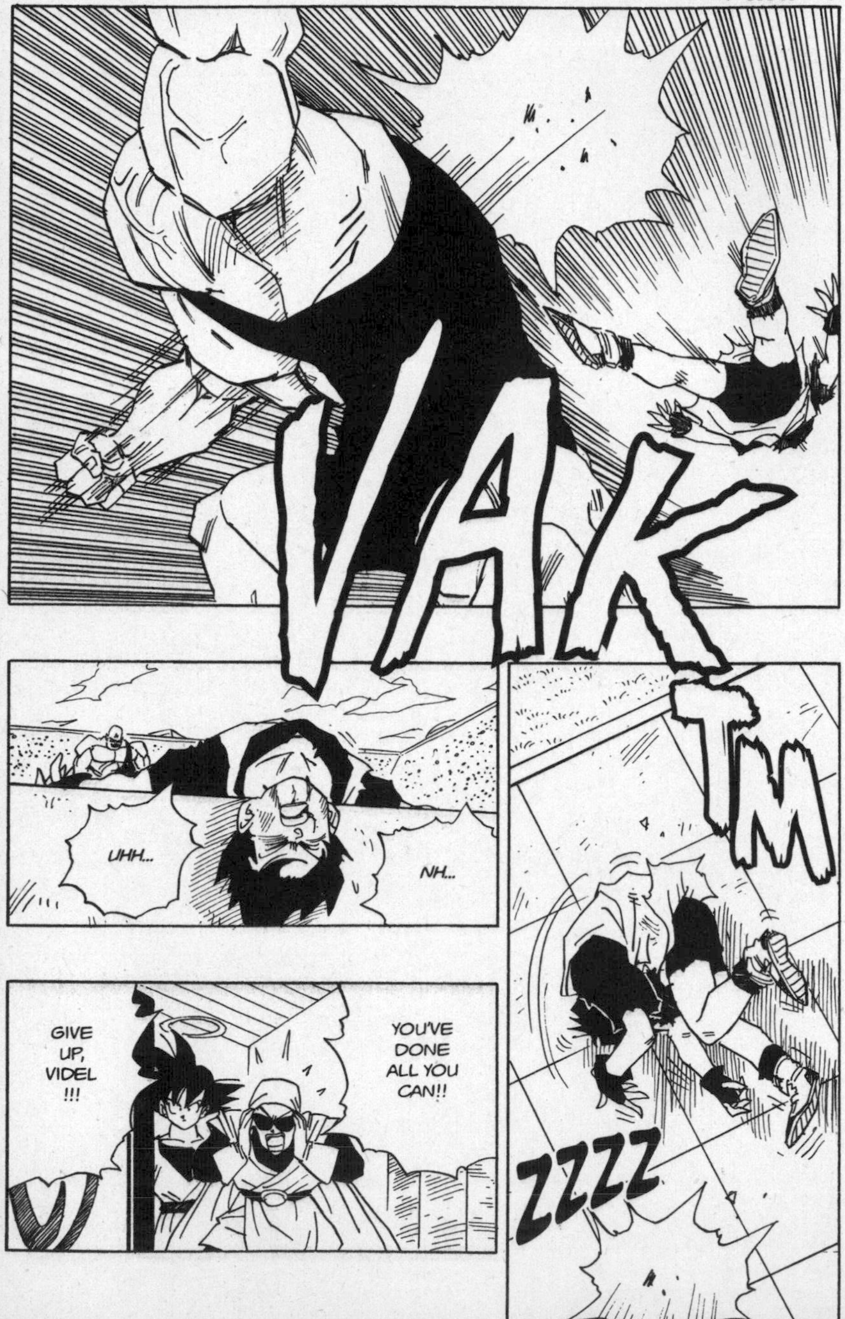
VAK
TM
ZZZZ
NH...
UHH...
YOU'VE DONE ALL YOU CAN!!
GIVE UP, VIDEL !!!

READ THIS WAY

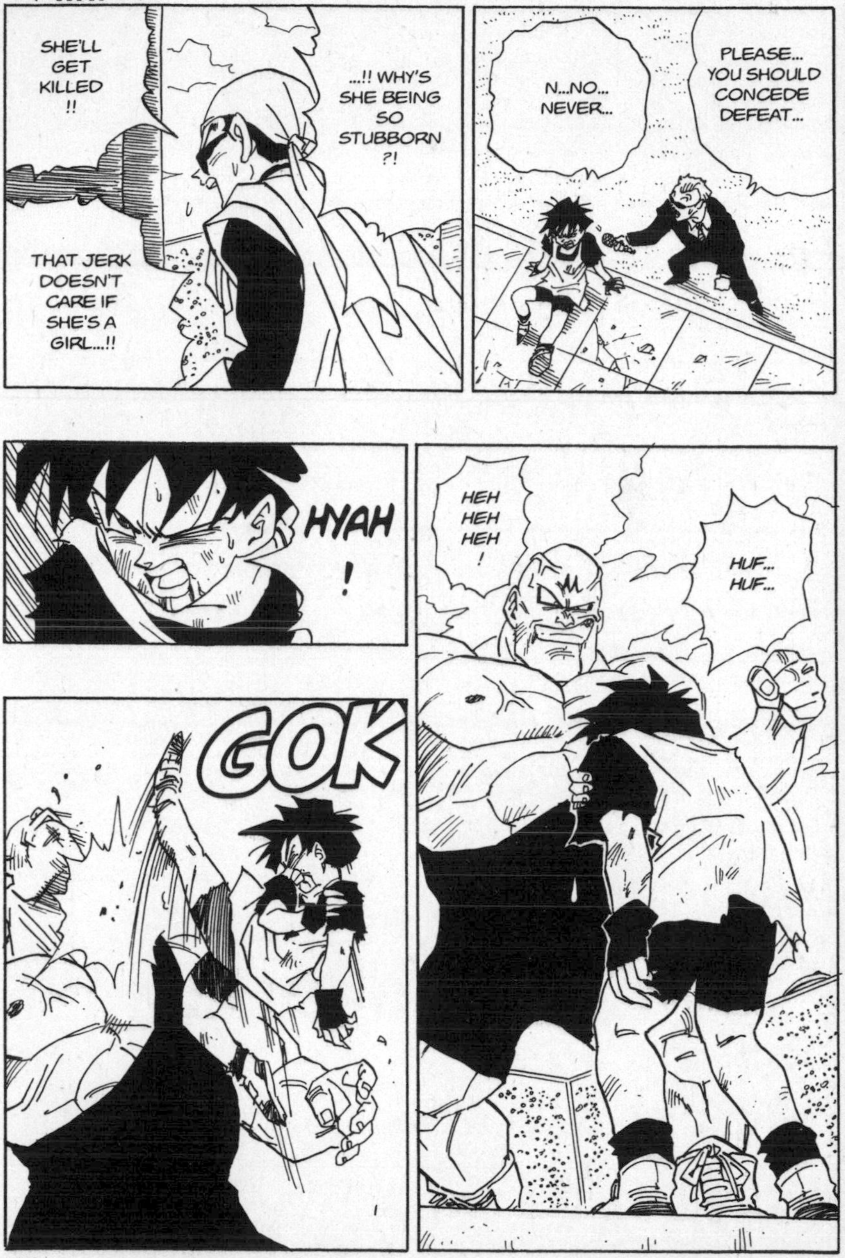

PLEASE... YOU SHOULD CONCEDE DEFEAT...
N...NO... NEVER...
...!! WHY'S SHE BEING SO STUBBORN ?!
SHE'LL GET KILLED !!
THAT JERK DOESN'T CARE IF SHE'S A GIRL...!!
HUF... HUF...
HEH HEH HEH !
HYAH !
GOK

READ THIS WAY

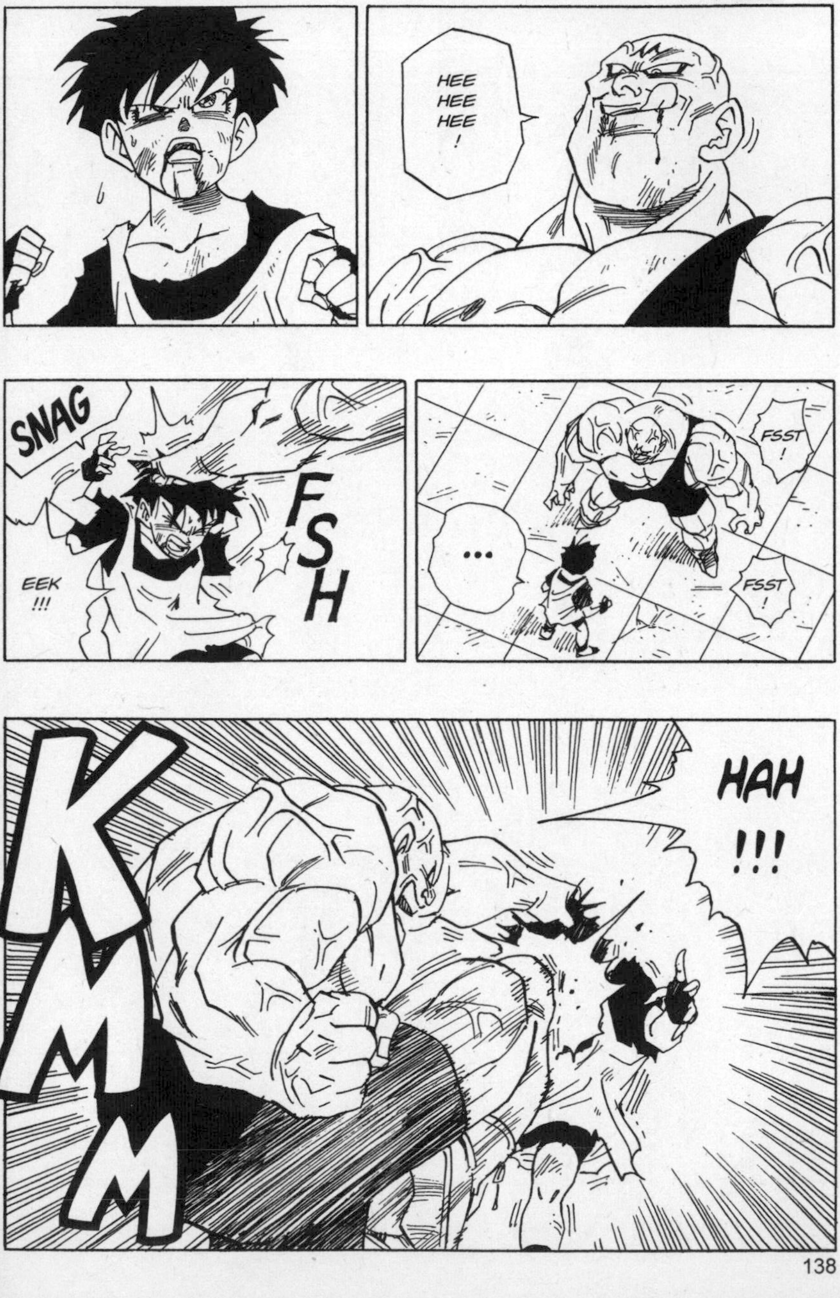
HEE HEE HEE !
FSST !
...
FSST !
SNAG
FSH
EEK !!!
HAH !!!
KMM

READ THIS WAY

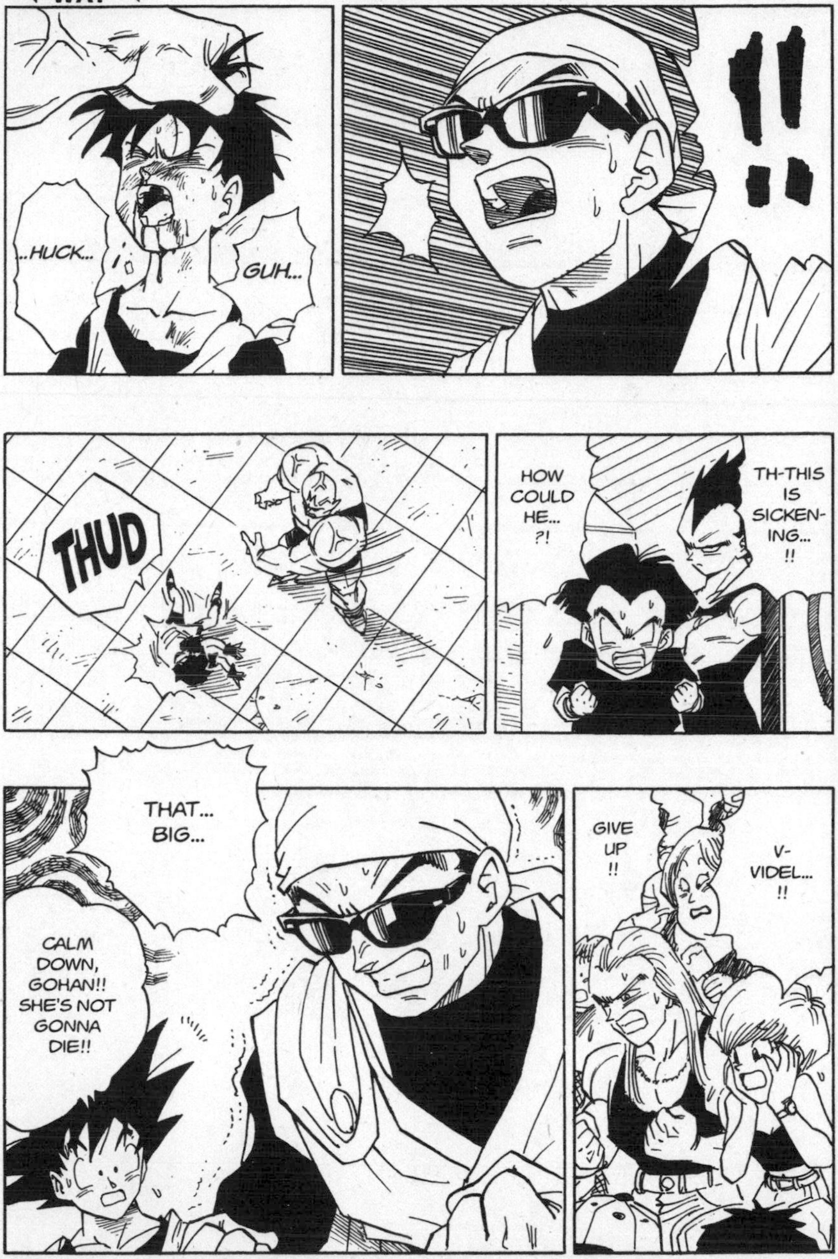
!!
GUH...
...HUCK...
TH-THIS IS SICKENING...!!
HOW COULD HE...?!
THUD
V-VIDEL...!!
GIVE UP!!
THAT... BIG...
CALM DOWN, GOHAN!! SHE'S NOT GONNA DIE!!

READ THIS WAY

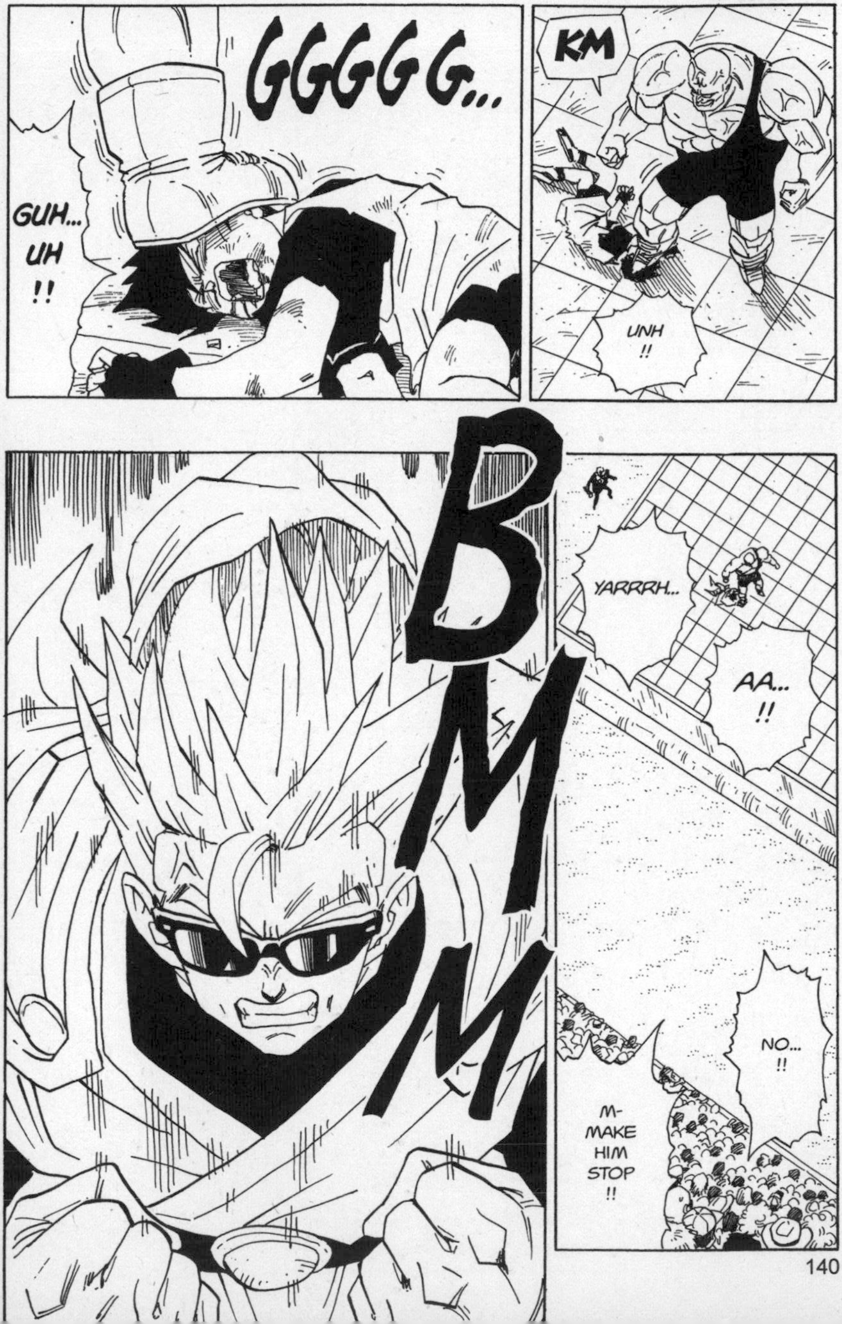
KM
UNH !!
GGGGG...
GUH... UH !!
YARRRH...
AA... !!
NO... !!
M-MAKE HIM STOP !!
BMM

READ THIS WAY

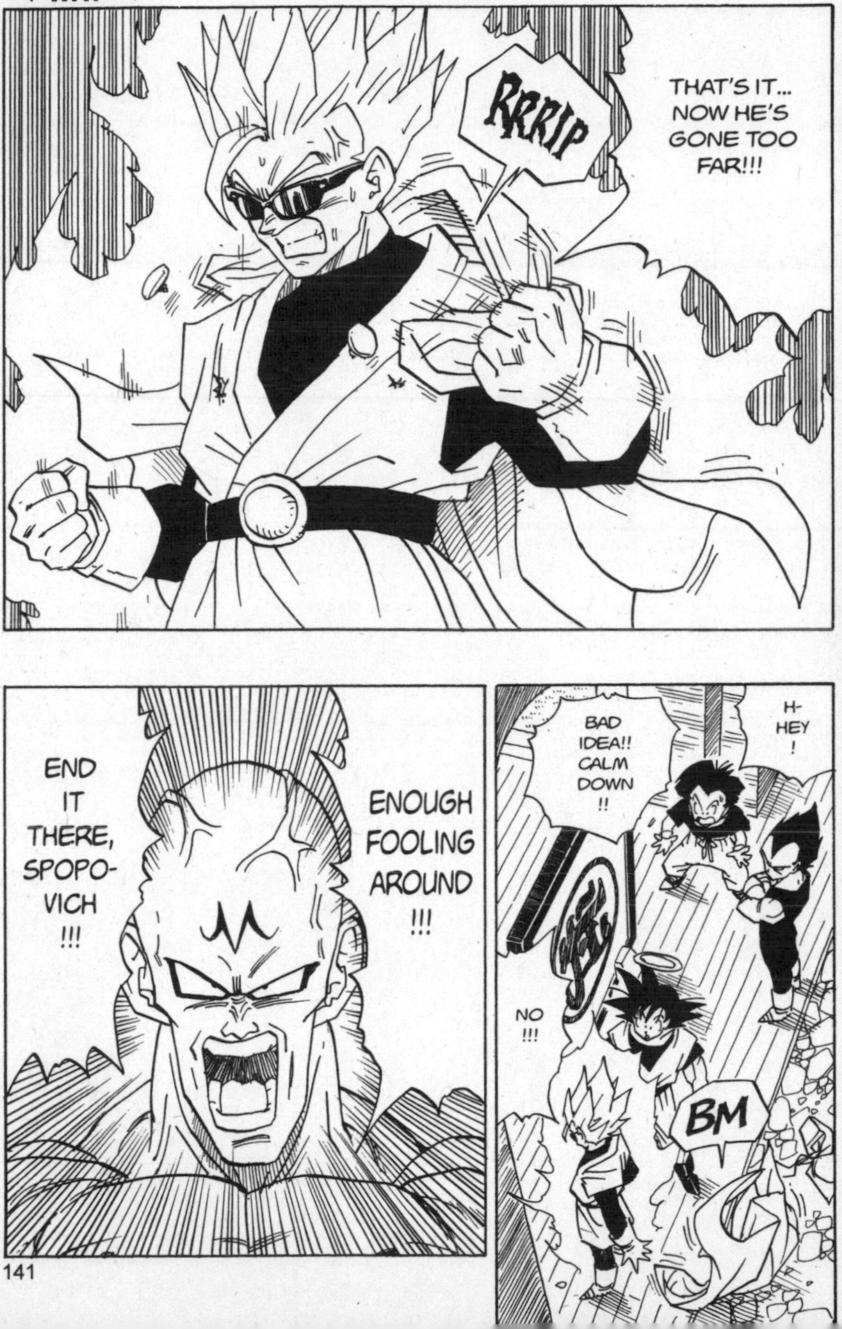

THAT'S IT... NOW HE'S GONE TOO FAR!!!
RRRIP
H-HEY!
BAD IDEA!! CALM DOWN!!
NO!!!
BM
ENOUGH FOOLING AROUND!!!
END IT THERE, SPOPOVICH!!!

READ THIS WAY

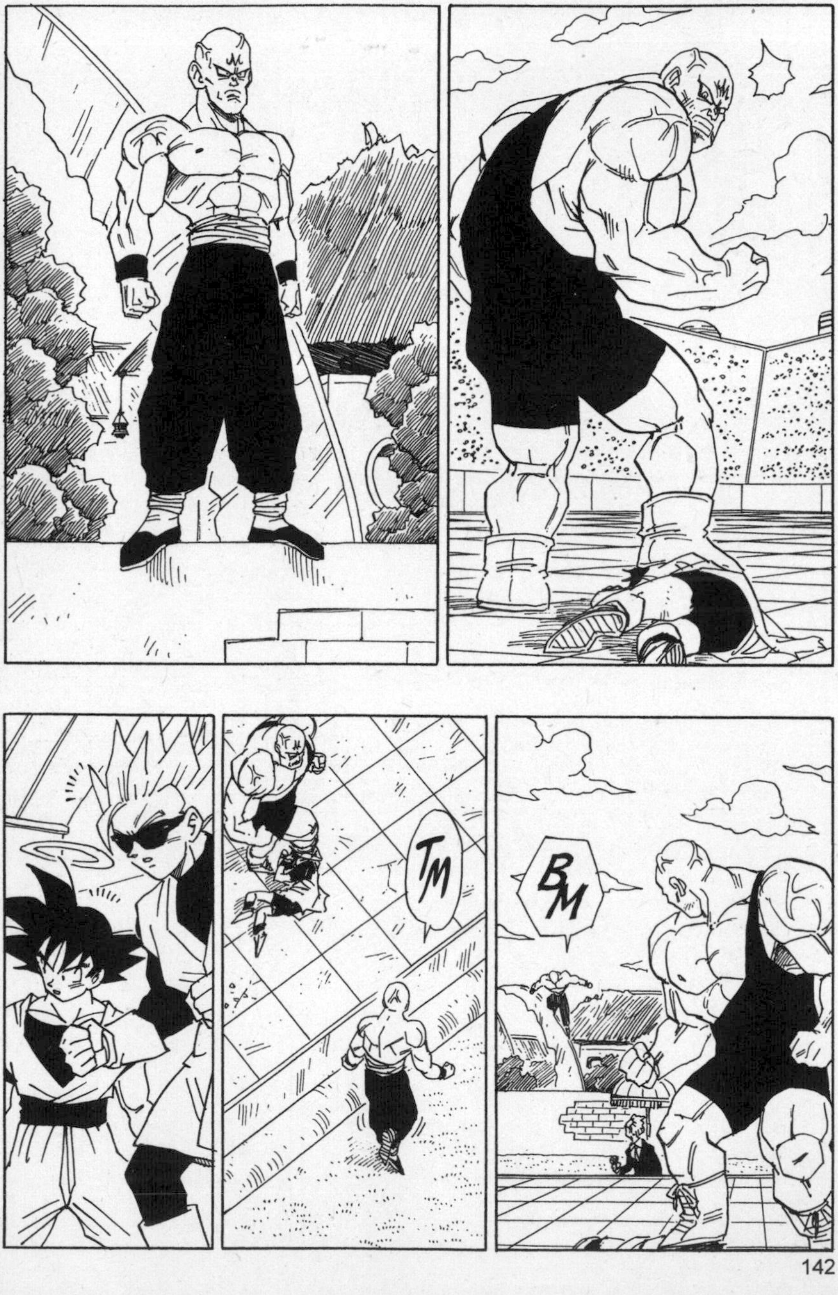
BM
TM

READ THIS WAY

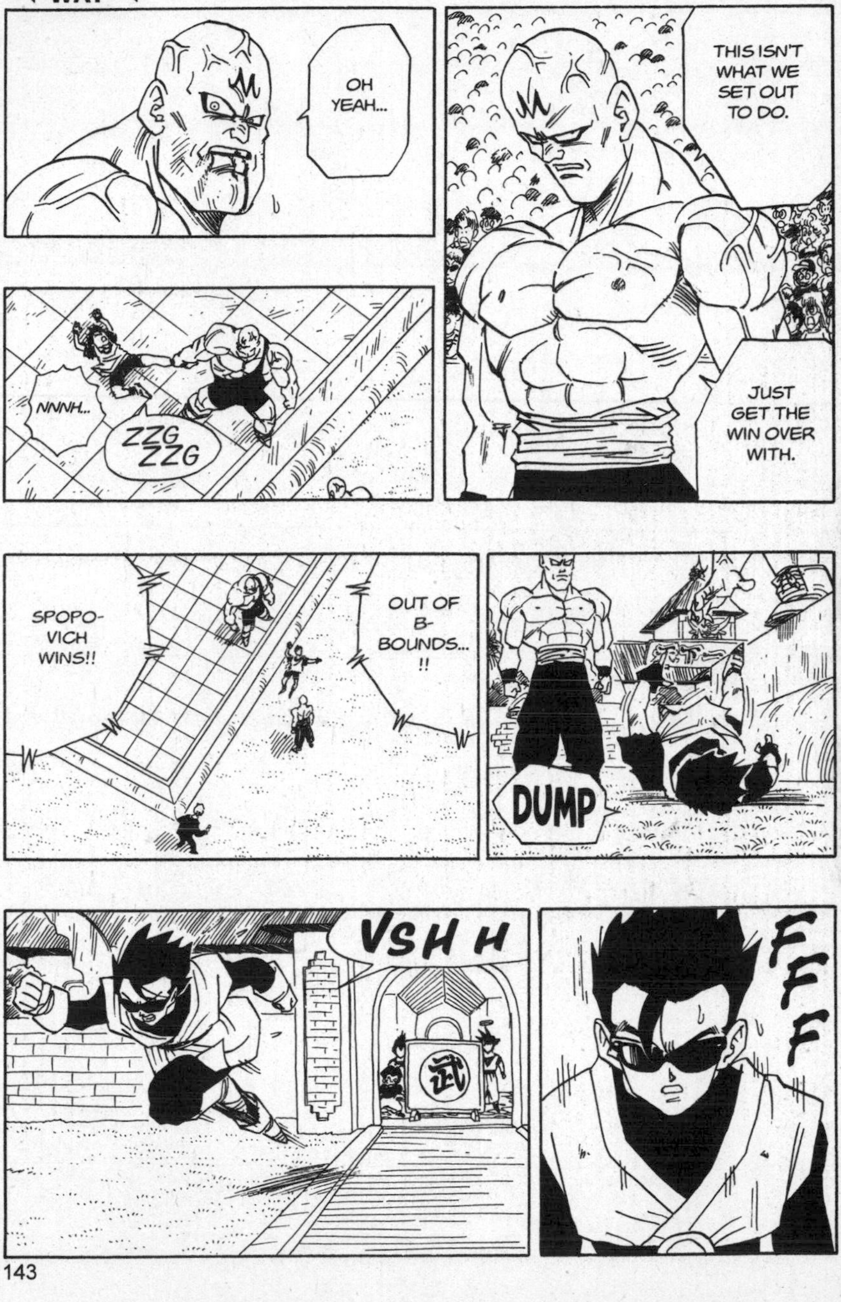
THIS ISN'T WHAT WE SET OUT TO DO.
JUST GET THE WIN OVER WITH.
OH YEAH...
NNNH...
ZZG ZZG
DUMP
OUT OF B-BOUNDS... !!
SPOPO-VICH WINS!!
FFF
VSH H

READ THIS WAY

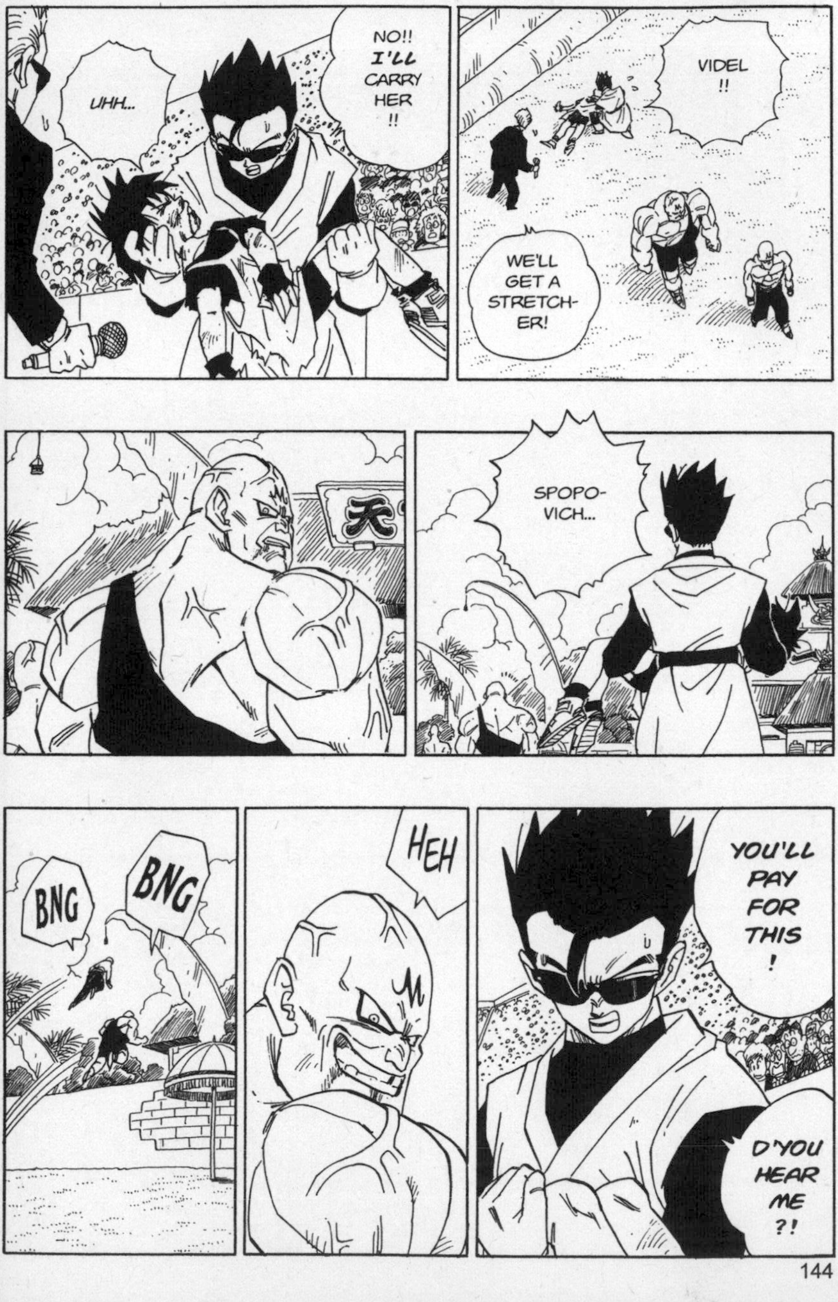

VIDEL !!
WE'LL GET A STRETCHER!
NO!! I'LL CARRY HER !!
UHH...
SPOPOVICH...
YOU'LL PAY FOR THIS !
D'YOU HEAR ME ?!
HEH
BNG
BNG

READ THIS WAY

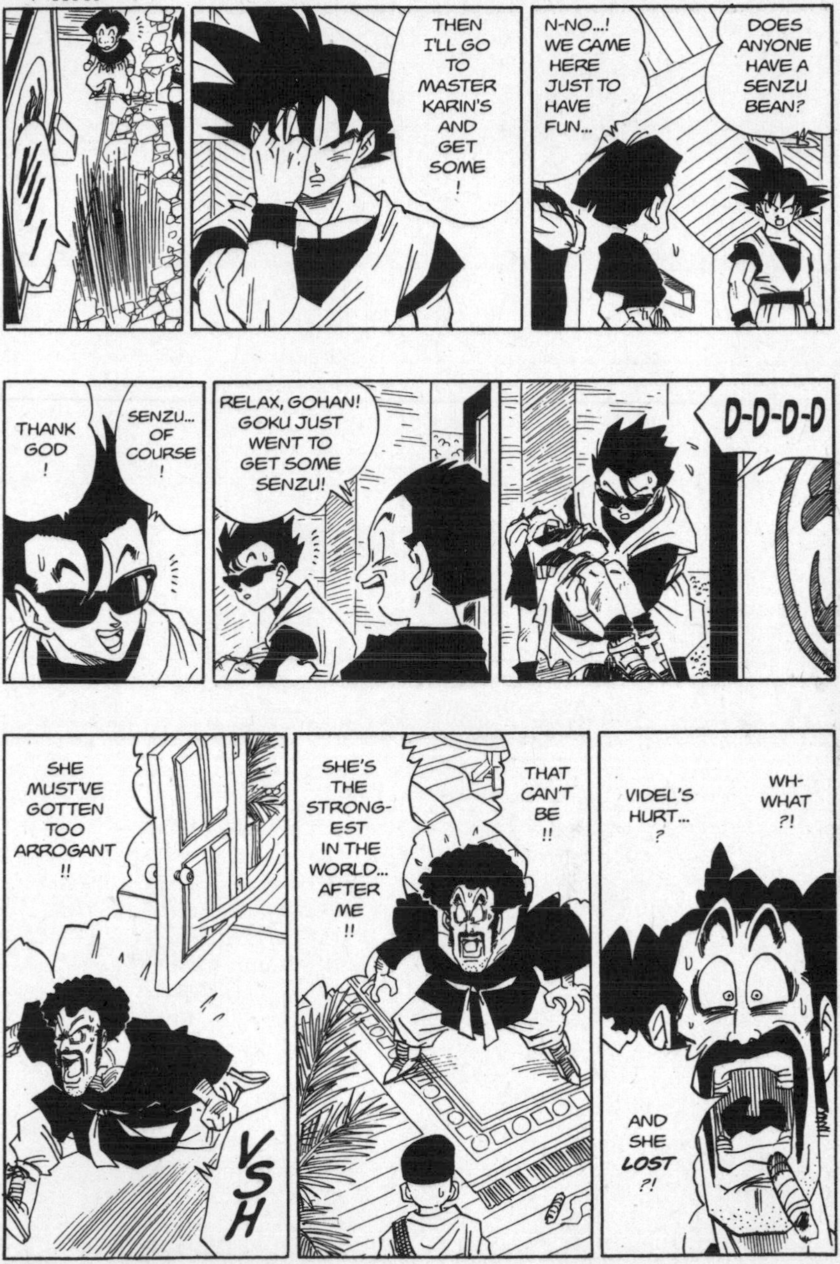
DOES ANYONE HAVE A SENZU BEAN?
N-NO...! WE CAME HERE JUST TO HAVE FUN...
THEN I'LL GO TO MASTER KARIN'S AND GET SOME!
D-D-D-D
RELAX, GOHAN! GOKU JUST WENT TO GET SOME SENZU!
SENZU... OF COURSE!
THANK GOD!
WH-WHAT?!
VIDEL'S HURT...?
AND SHE *LOST*?!
THAT CAN'T BE!!
SHE'S THE STRONGEST IN THE WORLD... AFTER ME!!
SHE MUST'VE GOTTEN TOO ARROGANT!!
VSH

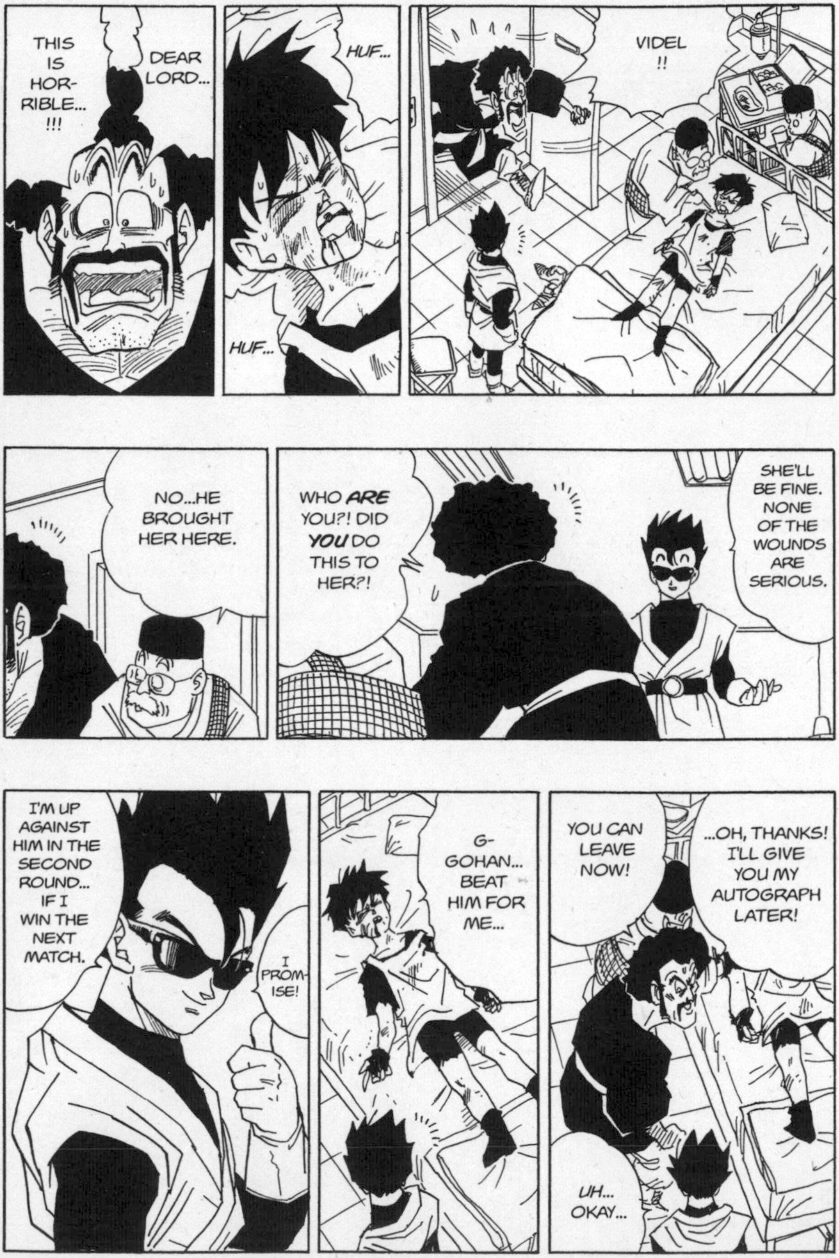
VIDEL !!
HUF...
HUF...
DEAR LORD...
THIS IS HOR-RIBLE... !!!
SHE'LL BE FINE. NONE OF THE WOUNDS ARE SERIOUS.
WHO **ARE** YOU?! DID **YOU** DO THIS TO HER?!
NO...HE BROUGHT HER HERE.
...OH, THANKS! I'LL GIVE YOU MY AUTOGRAPH LATER!
YOU CAN LEAVE NOW!
UH... OKAY...
G-GOHAN... BEAT HIM FOR ME...
I PROM-ISE!
I'M UP AGAINST HIM IN THE SECOND ROUND... IF I WIN THE NEXT MATCH.

READ THIS WAY

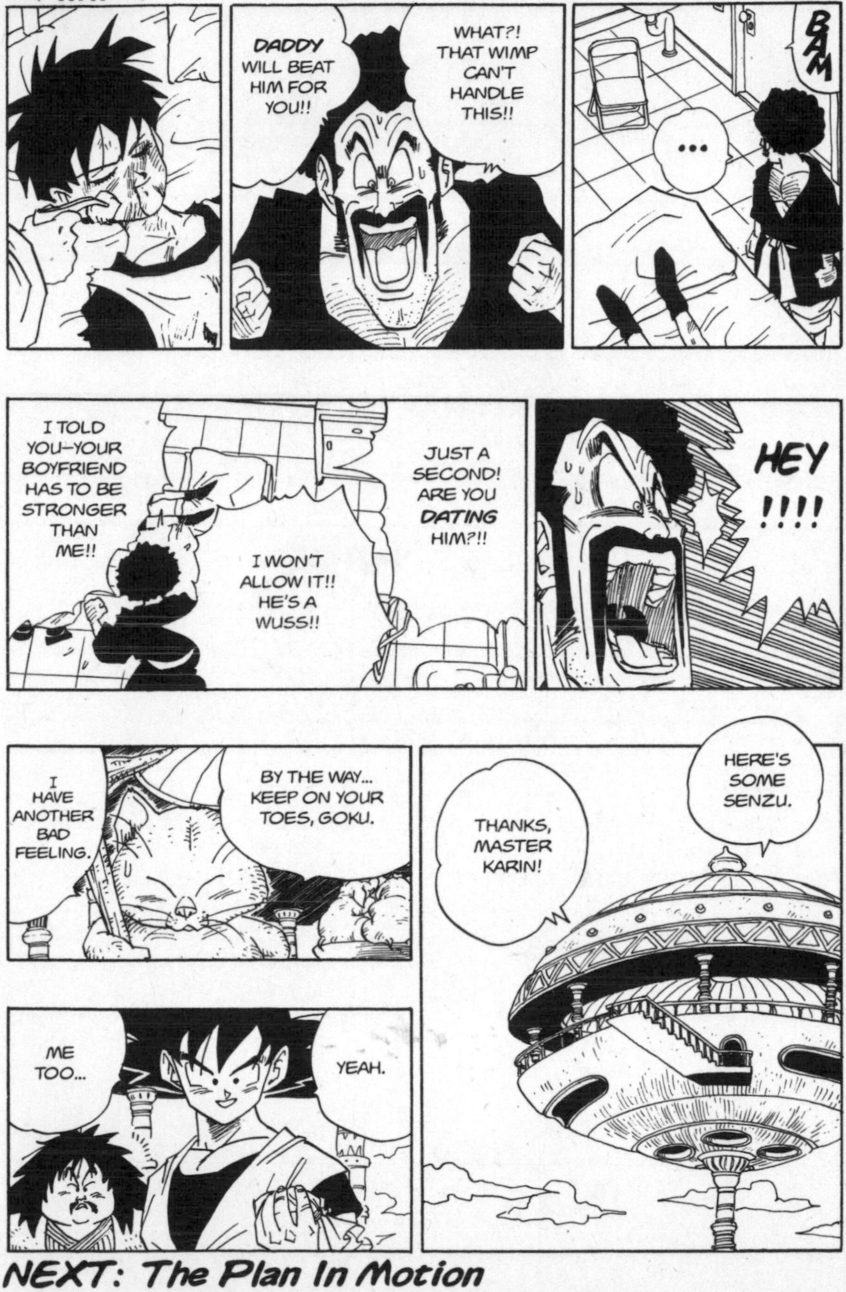
BAM
...
WHAT?! THAT WIMP CAN'T HANDLE THIS!!
DADDY WILL BEAT HIM FOR YOU!!
HEY !!!!
JUST A SECOND! ARE YOU DATING HIM?!!
I WON'T ALLOW IT!! HE'S A WUSS!!
I TOLD YOU—YOUR BOYFRIEND HAS TO BE STRONGER THAN ME!!
HERE'S SOME SENZU.
THANKS, MASTER KARIN!
BY THE WAY... KEEP ON YOUR TOES, GOKU.
I HAVE ANOTHER BAD FEELING.
YEAH.
ME TOO...

NEXT: The Plan In Motion

DBZ:249 • The Plot of the Lords

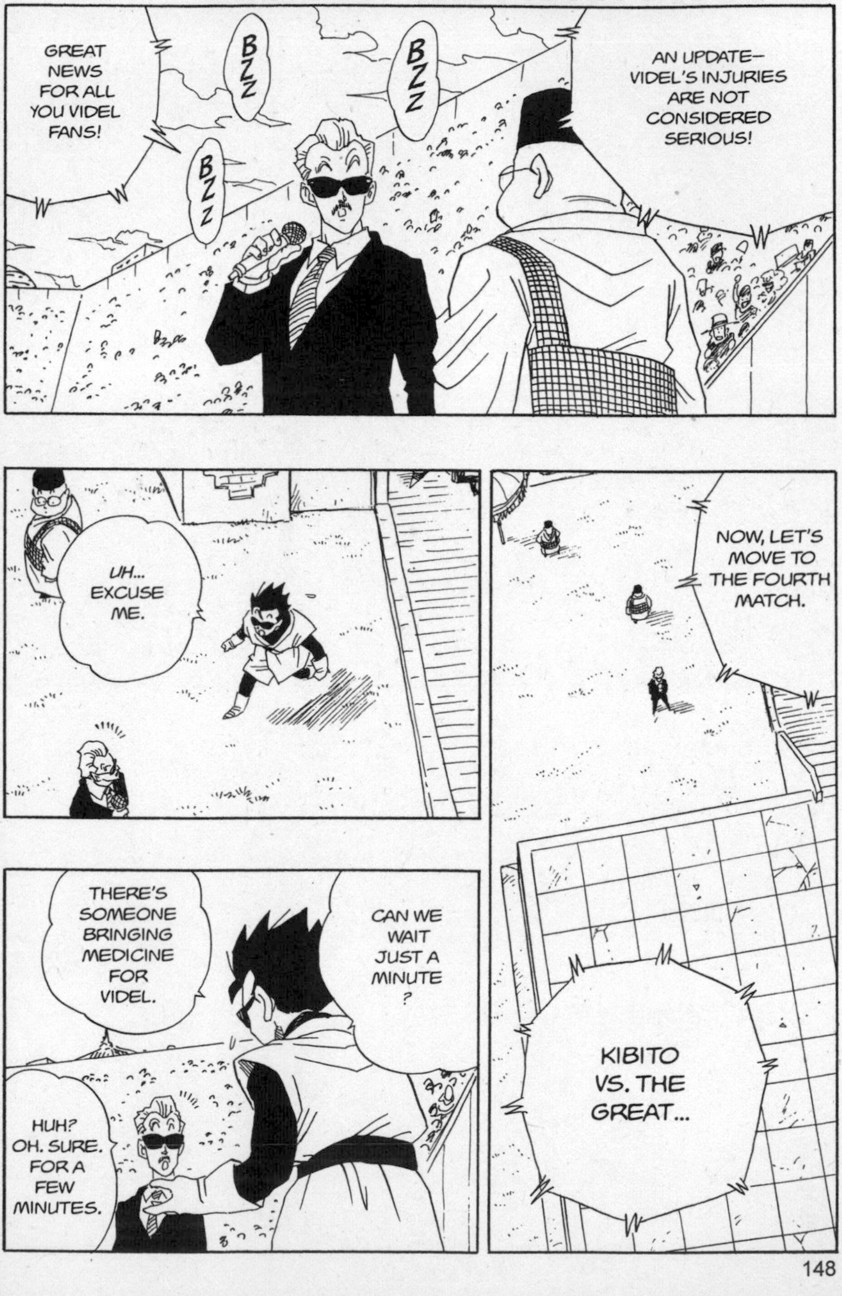
AN UPDATE—VIDEL'S INJURIES ARE NOT CONSIDERED SERIOUS!
BZZ
BZZ
GREAT NEWS FOR ALL YOU VIDEL FANS!
BZZ
NOW, LET'S MOVE TO THE FOURTH MATCH.
KIBITO VS. THE GREAT...
UH... EXCUSE ME.
CAN WE WAIT JUST A MINUTE?
THERE'S SOMEONE BRINGING MEDICINE FOR VIDEL.
HUH? OH. SURE. FOR A FEW MINUTES.

READ THIS WAY

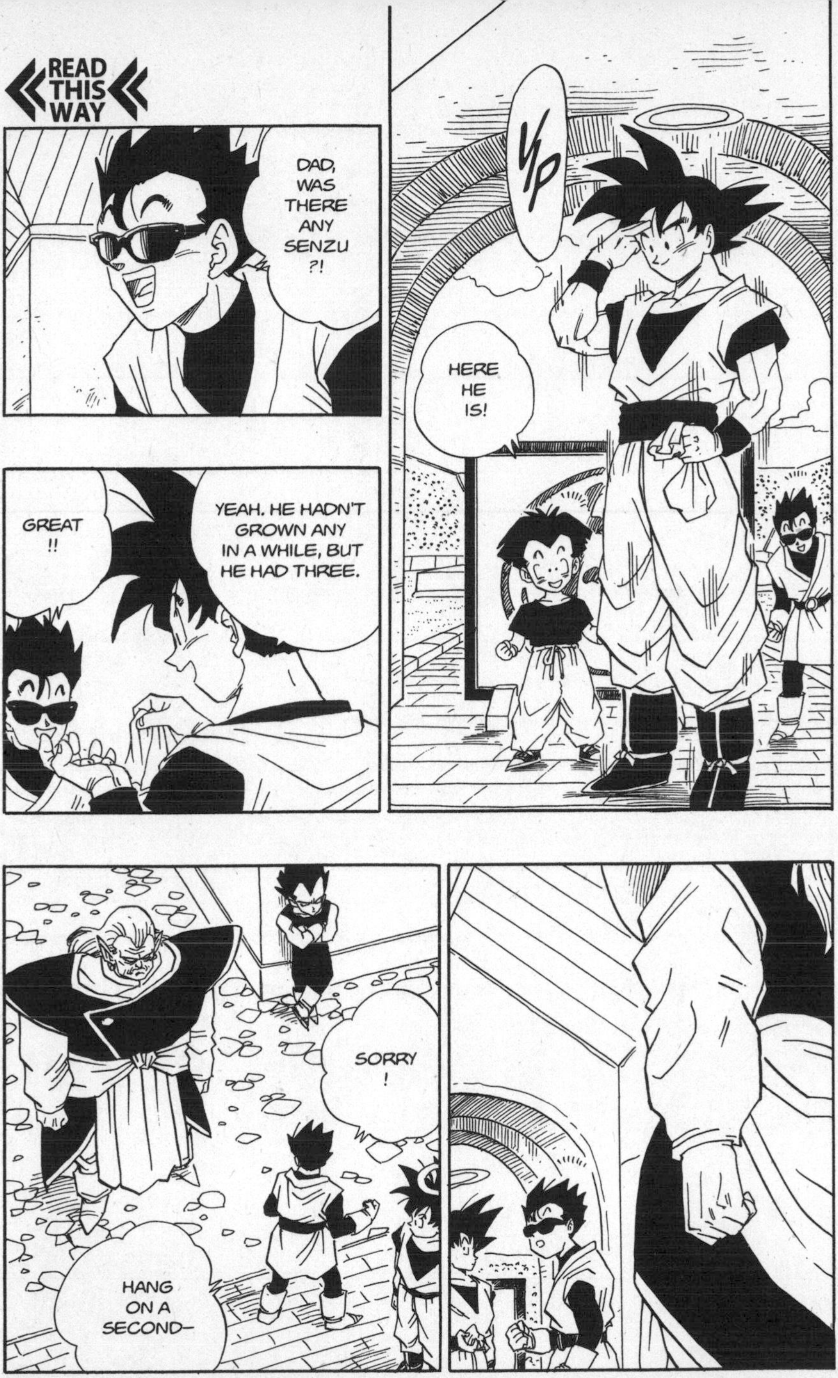

UP
HERE HE IS!
DAD, WAS THERE ANY SENZU ?!
YEAH. HE HADN'T GROWN ANY IN A WHILE, BUT HE HAD THREE.
GREAT !!
SORRY !
HANG ON A SECOND—

READ THIS WAY

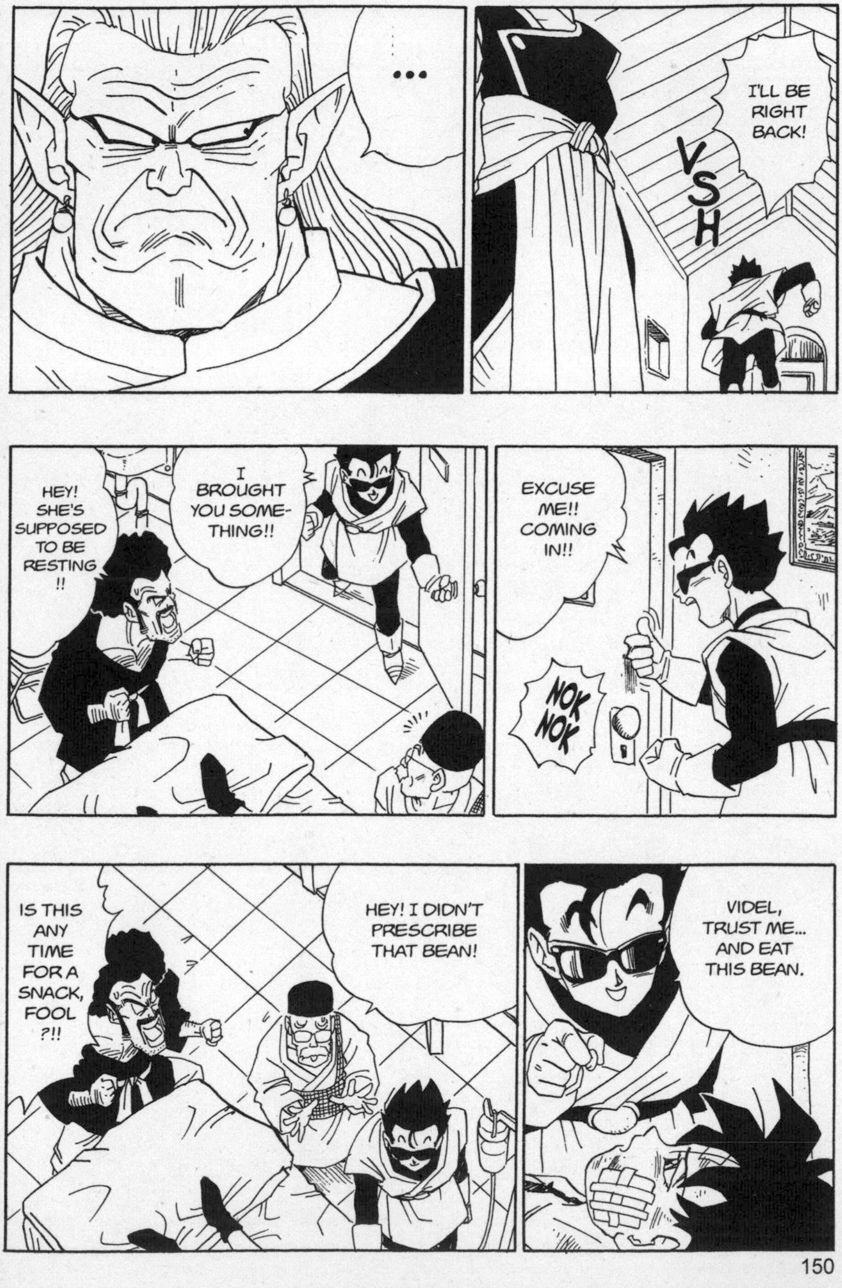
I'LL BE RIGHT BACK!
VSH
...
EXCUSE ME!! COMING IN!!
NOK NOK
I BROUGHT YOU SOME-THING!!
HEY! SHE'S SUPPOSED TO BE RESTING !!
VIDEL, TRUST ME... AND EAT THIS BEAN.
HEY! I DIDN'T PRESCRIBE THAT BEAN!
IS THIS ANY TIME FOR A SNACK, FOOL ?!!

READ THIS WAY

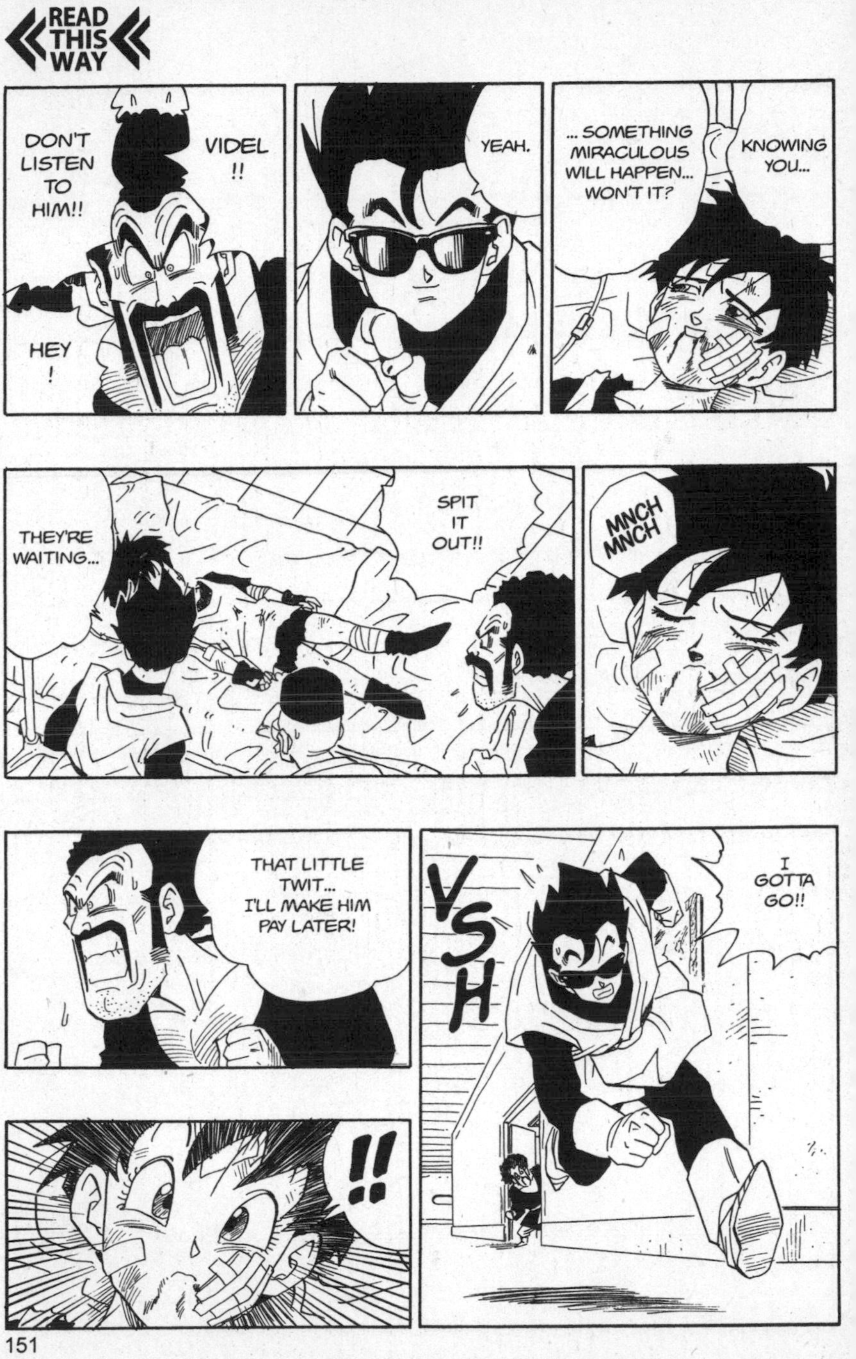
KNOWING YOU...
... SOMETHING MIRACULOUS WILL HAPPEN... WON'T IT?
YEAH.
VIDEL !!
DON'T LISTEN TO HIM!!
HEY !
MNCH MNCH
SPIT IT OUT!!
THEY'RE WAITING...
I GOTTA GO!!
VSH
THAT LITTLE TWIT... I'LL MAKE HIM PAY LATER!
!!

READ THIS WAY

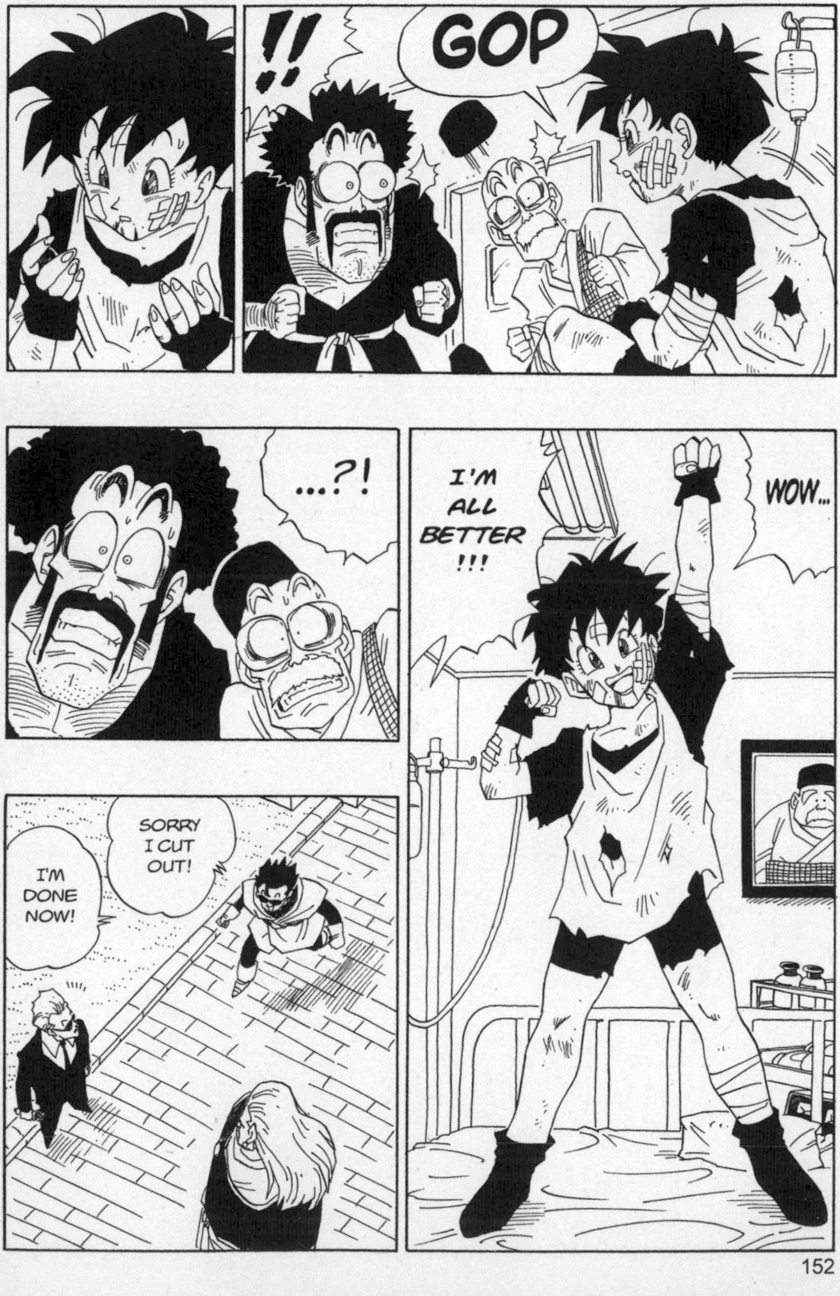
GOP
!!
WOW...
I'M ALL BETTER !!!
...?!
SORRY I CUT OUT!
I'M DONE NOW!

READ THIS WAY

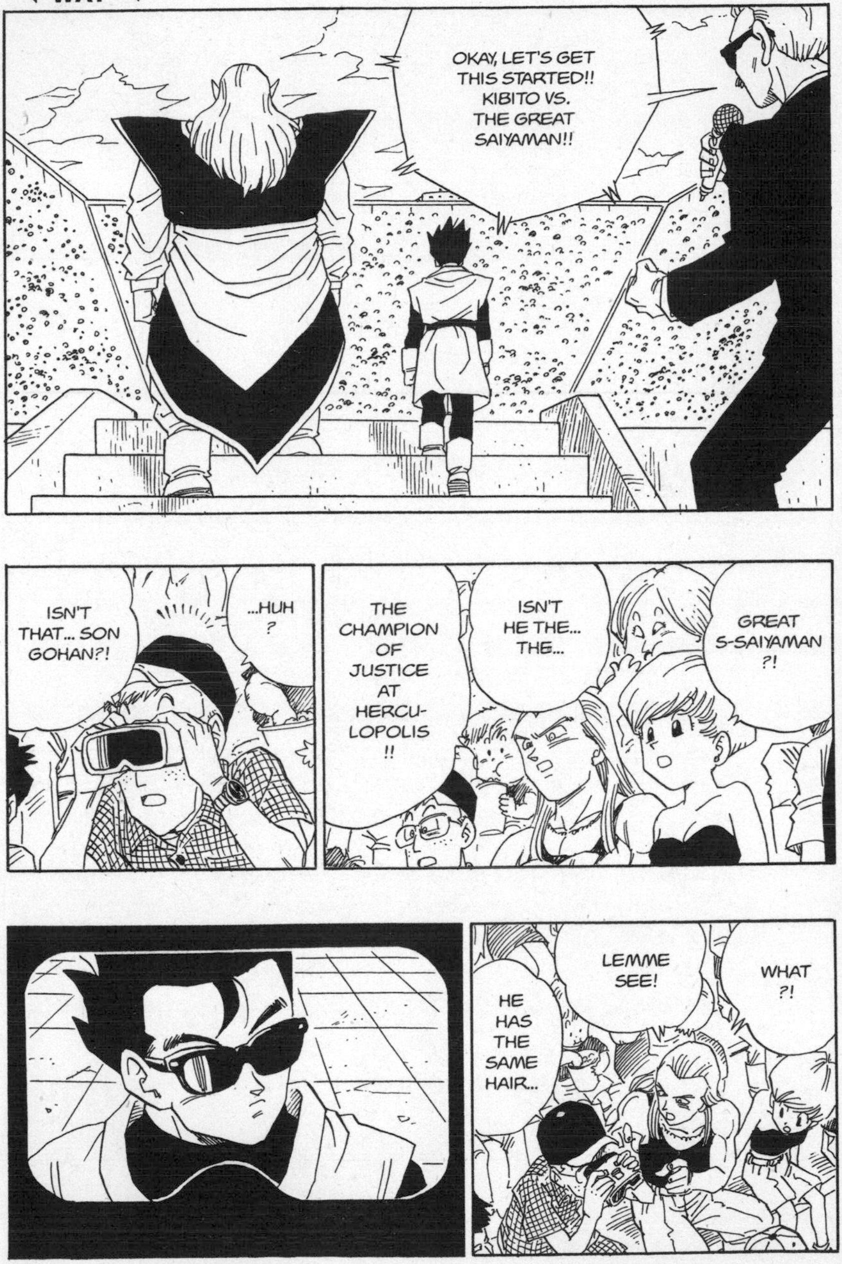
OKAY, LET'S GET THIS STARTED!! KIBITO VS. THE GREAT SAIYAMAN!!
GREAT S-SAIYAMAN ?!
ISN'T HE THE... THE...
THE CHAMPION OF JUSTICE AT HERCU-LOPOLIS !!
...HUH ?
ISN'T THAT... SON GOHAN?!
WHAT ?!
LEMME SEE!
HE HAS THE SAME HAIR...

READ THIS WAY

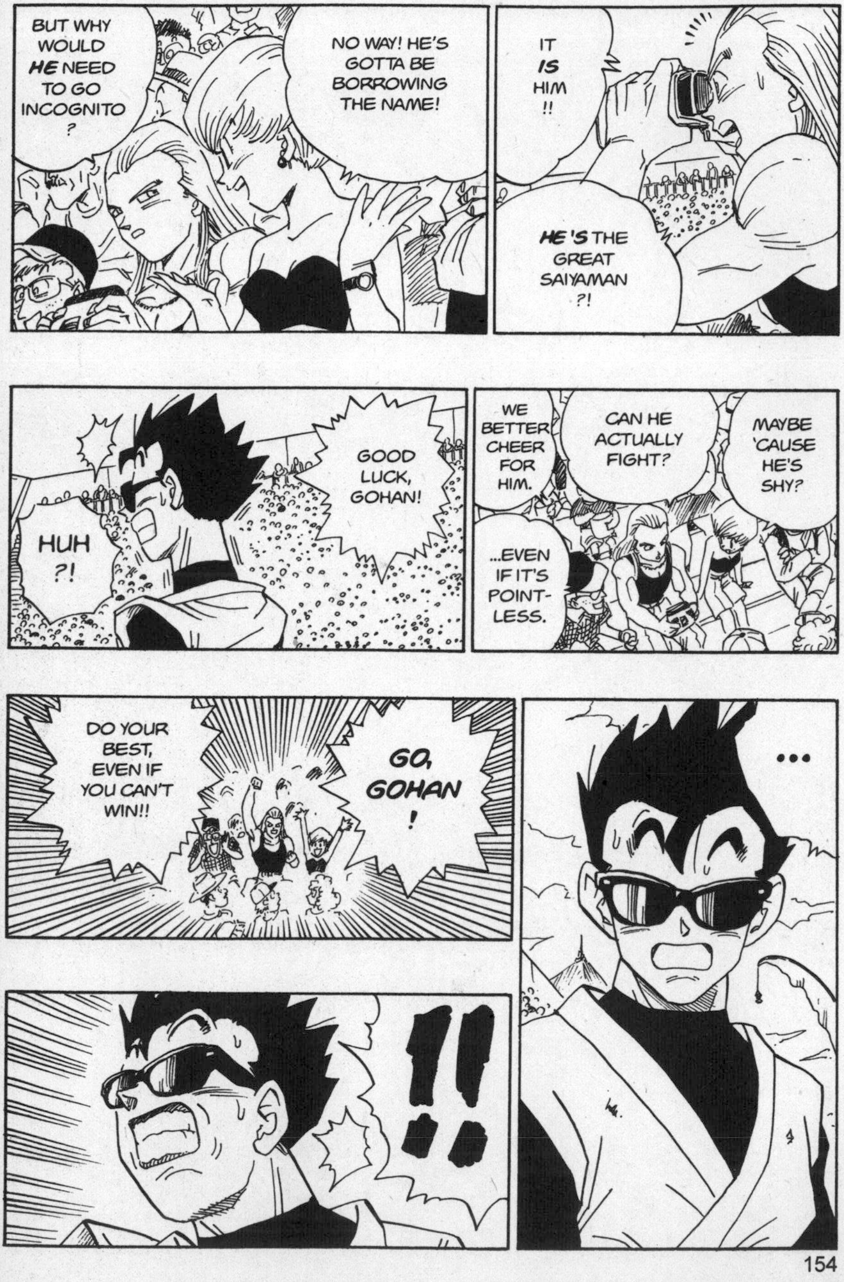
IT IS HIM!!
HE'S THE GREAT SAIYAMAN?!
NO WAY! HE'S GOTTA BE BORROWING THE NAME!
BUT WHY WOULD HE NEED TO GO INCOGNITO?
MAYBE 'CAUSE HE'S SHY?
CAN HE ACTUALLY FIGHT?
WE BETTER CHEER FOR HIM.
...EVEN IF IT'S POINTLESS.
GOOD LUCK, GOHAN!
HUH?!
...
GO, GOHAN!
DO YOUR BEST, EVEN IF YOU CAN'T WIN!!
!!

READ THIS WAY

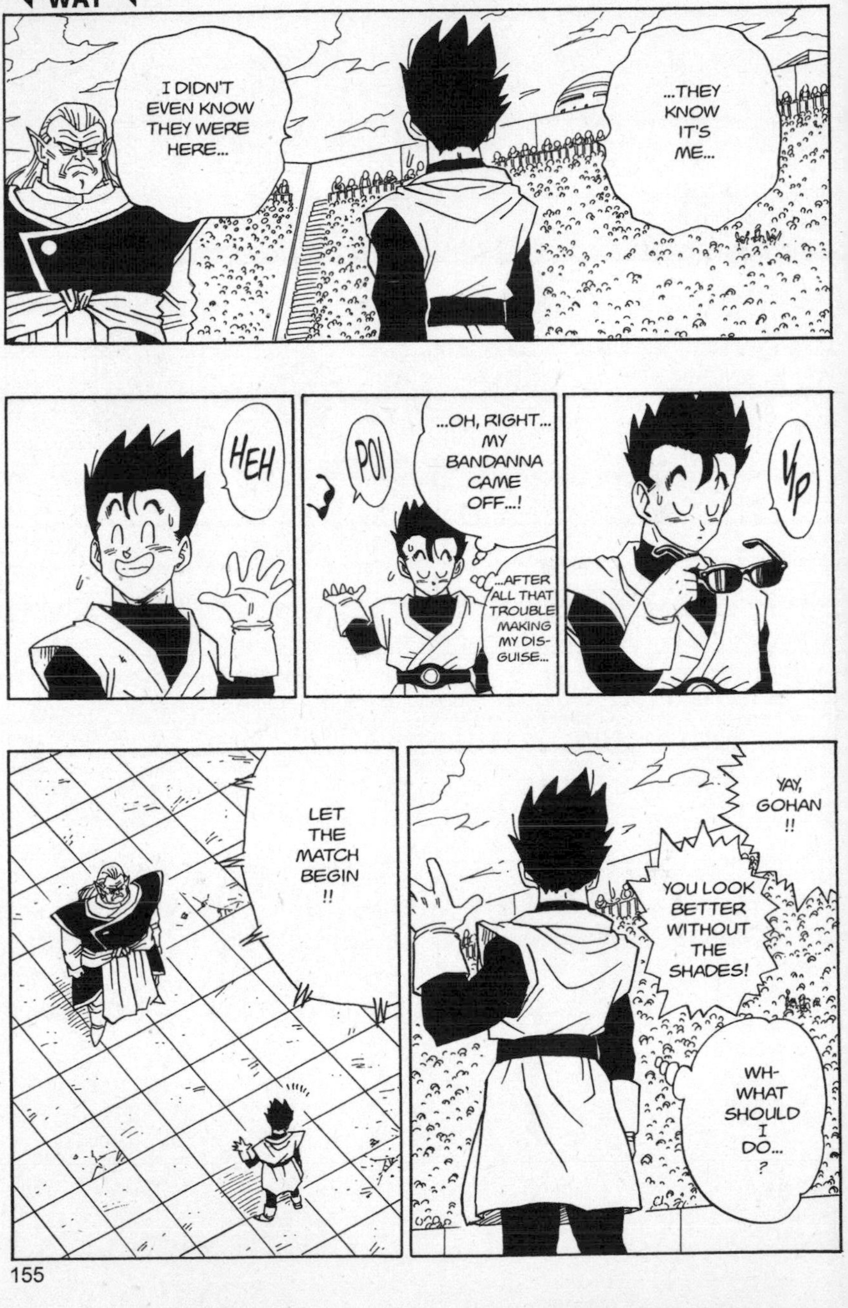

...THEY KNOW IT'S ME...
I DIDN'T EVEN KNOW THEY WERE HERE...
YIP
POI
...OH, RIGHT... MY BANDANNA CAME OFF...!
...AFTER ALL THAT TROUBLE MAKING MY DIS-GUISE...
HEH
YAY, GOHAN !!
YOU LOOK BETTER WITHOUT THE SHADES!
WH-WHAT SHOULD I DO...?
LET THE MATCH BEGIN !!

READ THIS WAY

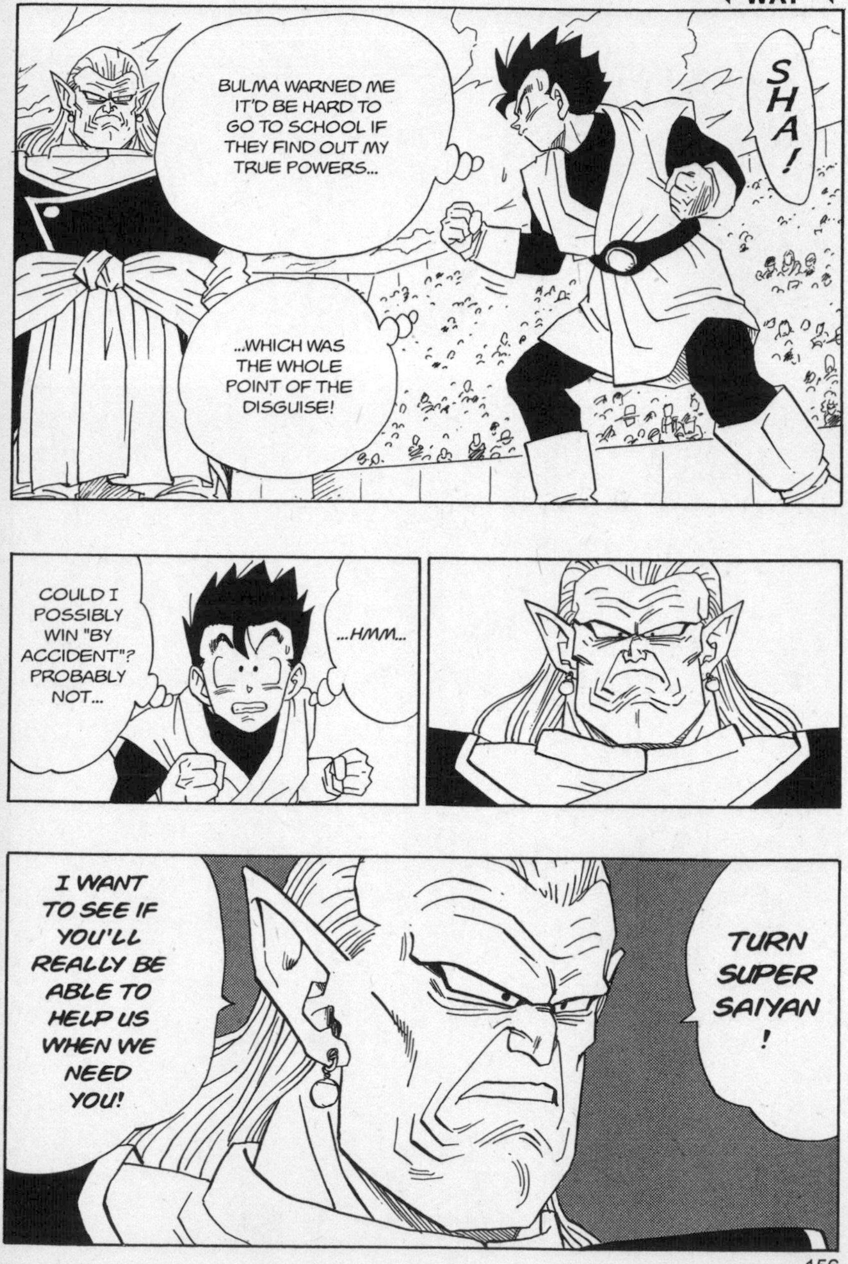
SHA!
BULMA WARNED ME IT'D BE HARD TO GO TO SCHOOL IF THEY FIND OUT MY TRUE POWERS...
...WHICH WAS THE WHOLE POINT OF THE DISGUISE!
...HMM...
COULD I POSSIBLY WIN "BY ACCIDENT"? PROBABLY NOT...
TURN SUPER SAIYAN!
I WANT TO SEE IF YOU'LL REALLY BE ABLE TO HELP US WHEN WE NEED YOU!

READ THIS WAY

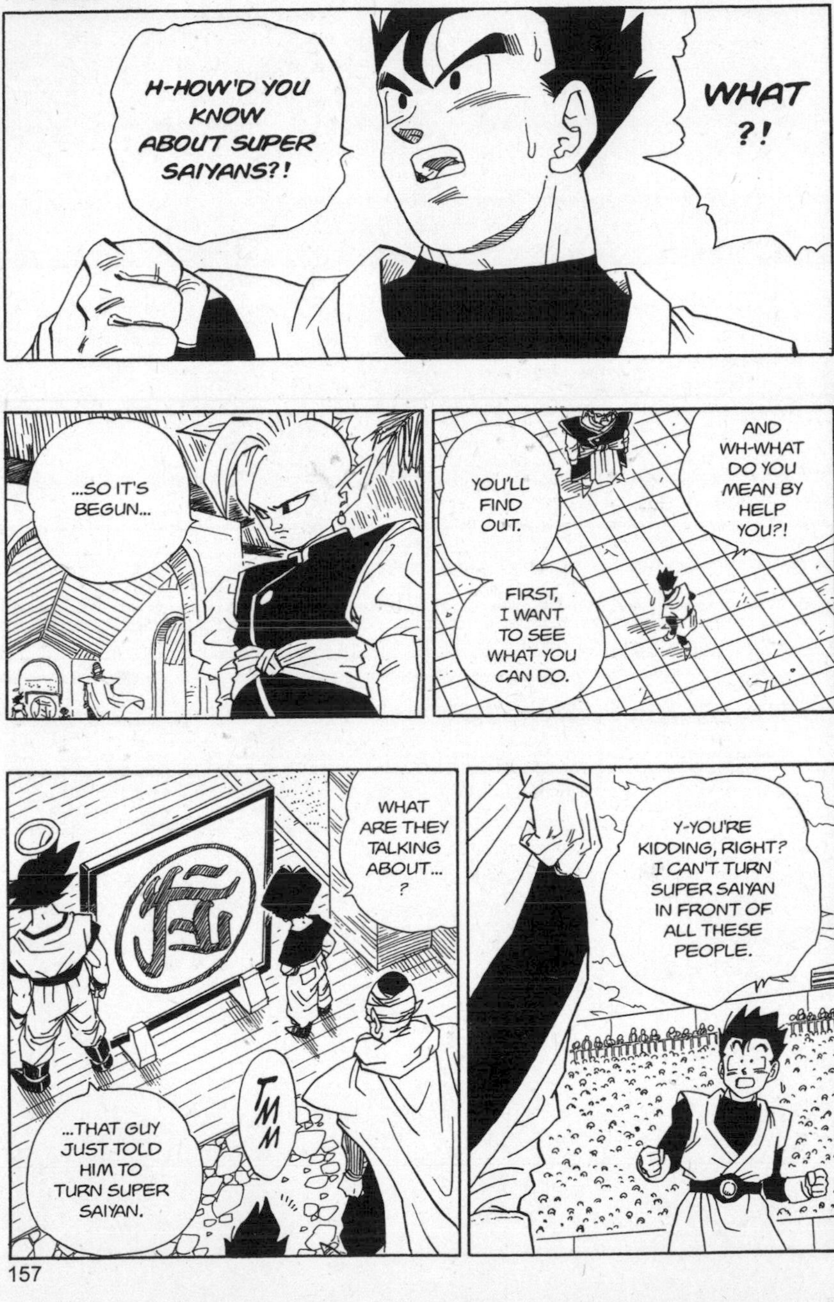
WHAT?!
H-HOW'D YOU KNOW ABOUT SUPER SAIYANS?!
AND WH-WHAT DO YOU MEAN BY HELP YOU?!
YOU'LL FIND OUT.
FIRST, I WANT TO SEE WHAT YOU CAN DO.
...SO IT'S BEGUN...
Y-YOU'RE KIDDING, RIGHT? I CAN'T TURN SUPER SAIYAN IN FRONT OF ALL THESE PEOPLE.
WHAT ARE THEY TALKING ABOUT...?
TMM
...THAT GUY JUST TOLD HIM TO TURN SUPER SAIYAN.

READ THIS WAY

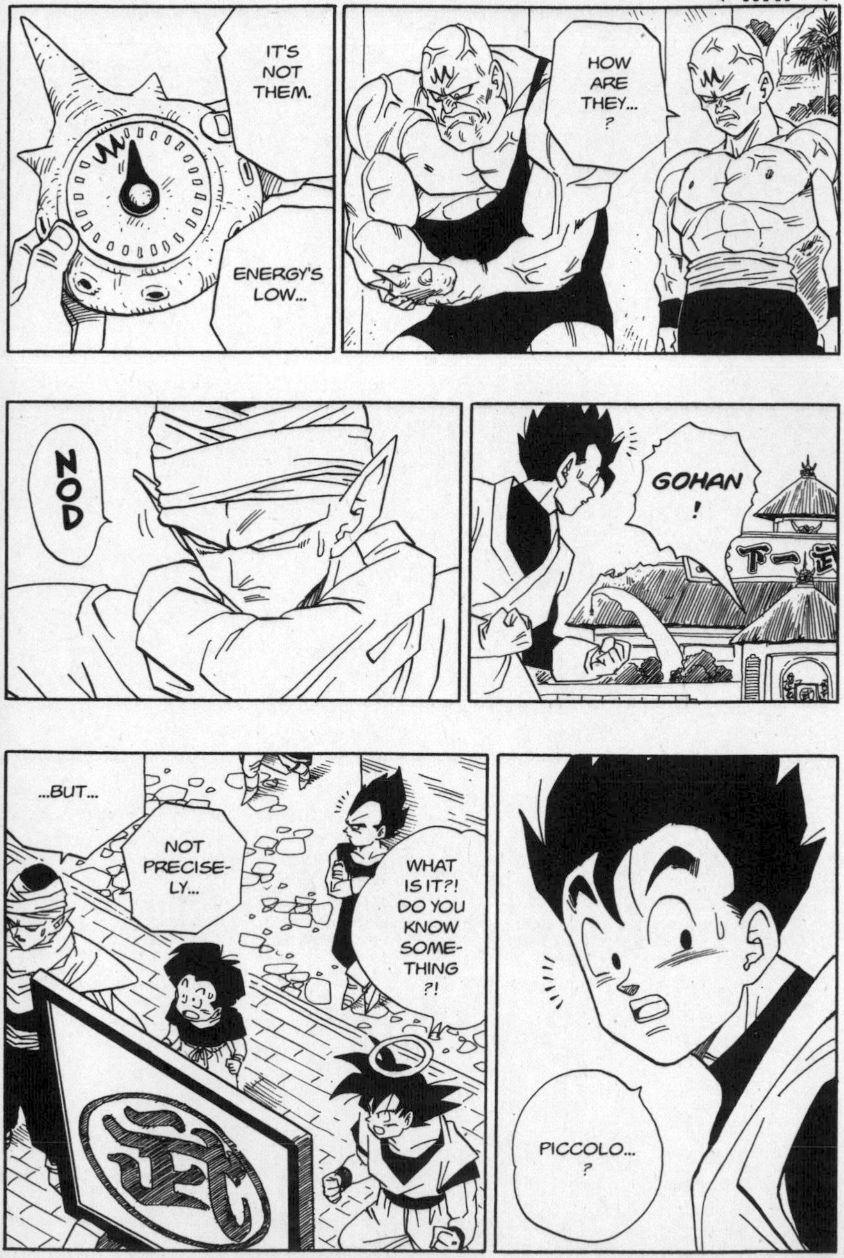
HOW ARE THEY... ?
IT'S NOT THEM.
ENERGY'S LOW...
GOHAN !
NOD
PICCOLO... ?
WHAT IS IT?! DO YOU KNOW SOMETHING ?!
NOT PRECISE-LY...
...BUT...

READ THIS WAY

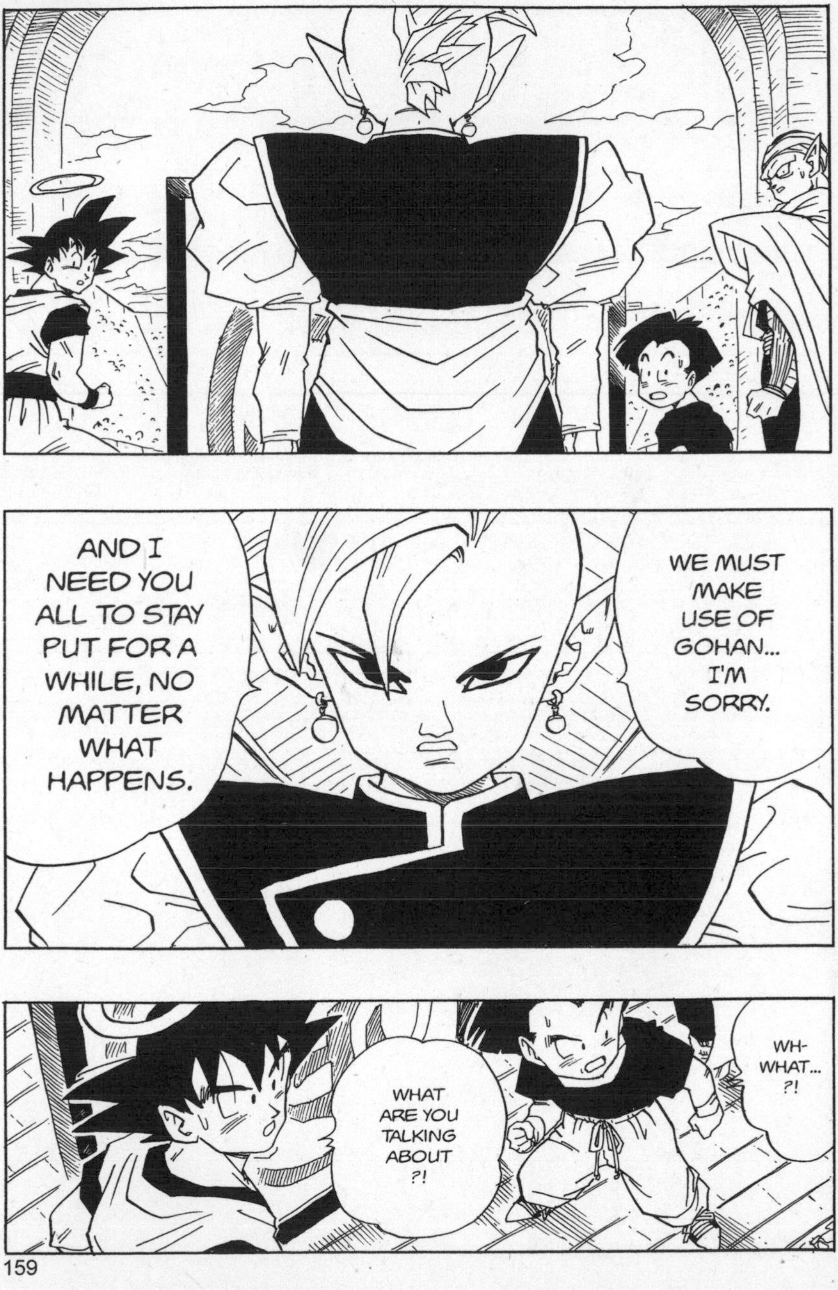

WE MUST MAKE USE OF GOHAN... I'M SORRY.
AND I NEED YOU ALL TO STAY PUT FOR A WHILE, NO MATTER WHAT HAPPENS.
WH- WHAT... ?!
WHAT ARE YOU TALKING ABOUT ?!

READ THIS WAY

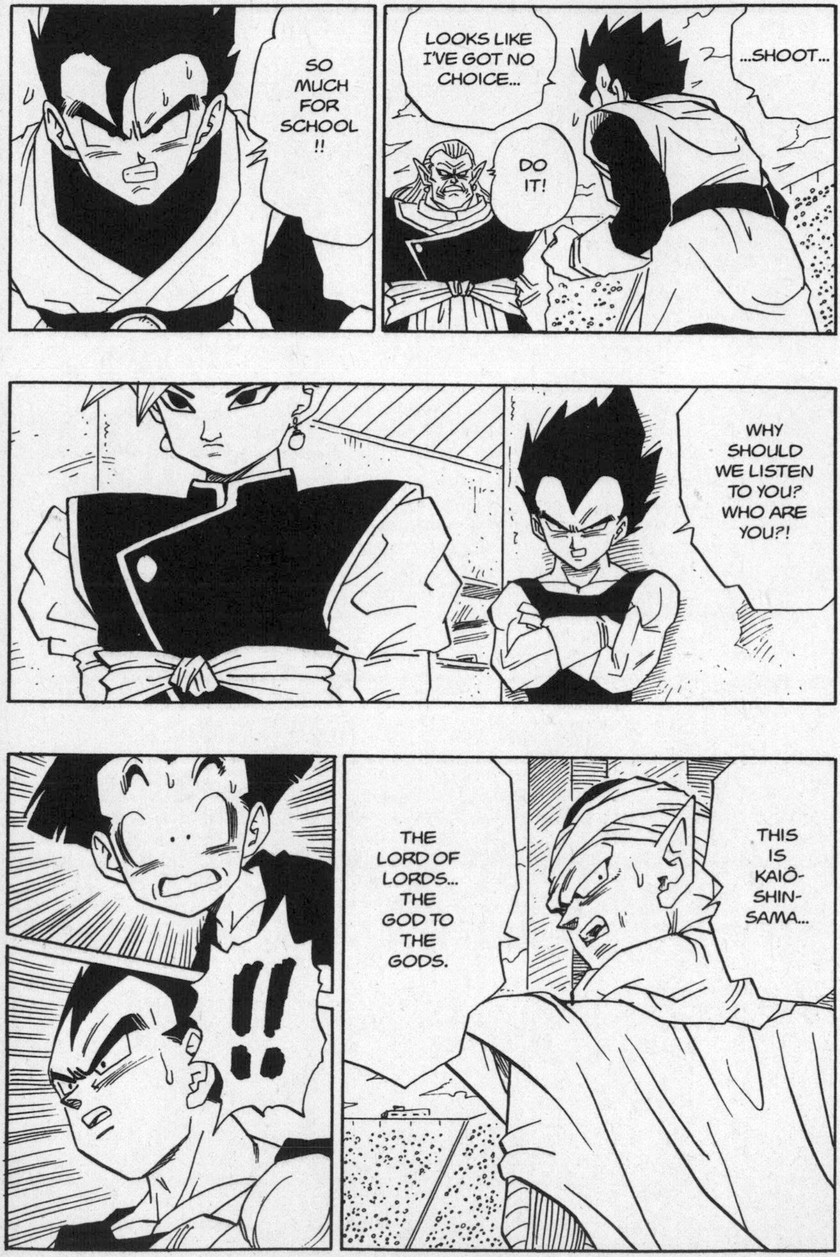
...SHOOT...
LOOKS LIKE I'VE GOT NO CHOICE...
DO IT!
SO MUCH FOR SCHOOL !!
WHY SHOULD WE LISTEN TO YOU? WHO ARE YOU?!
THIS IS KAIÔ-SHIN-SAMA...
THE LORD OF LORDS... THE GOD TO THE GODS.
!!

READ THIS WAY

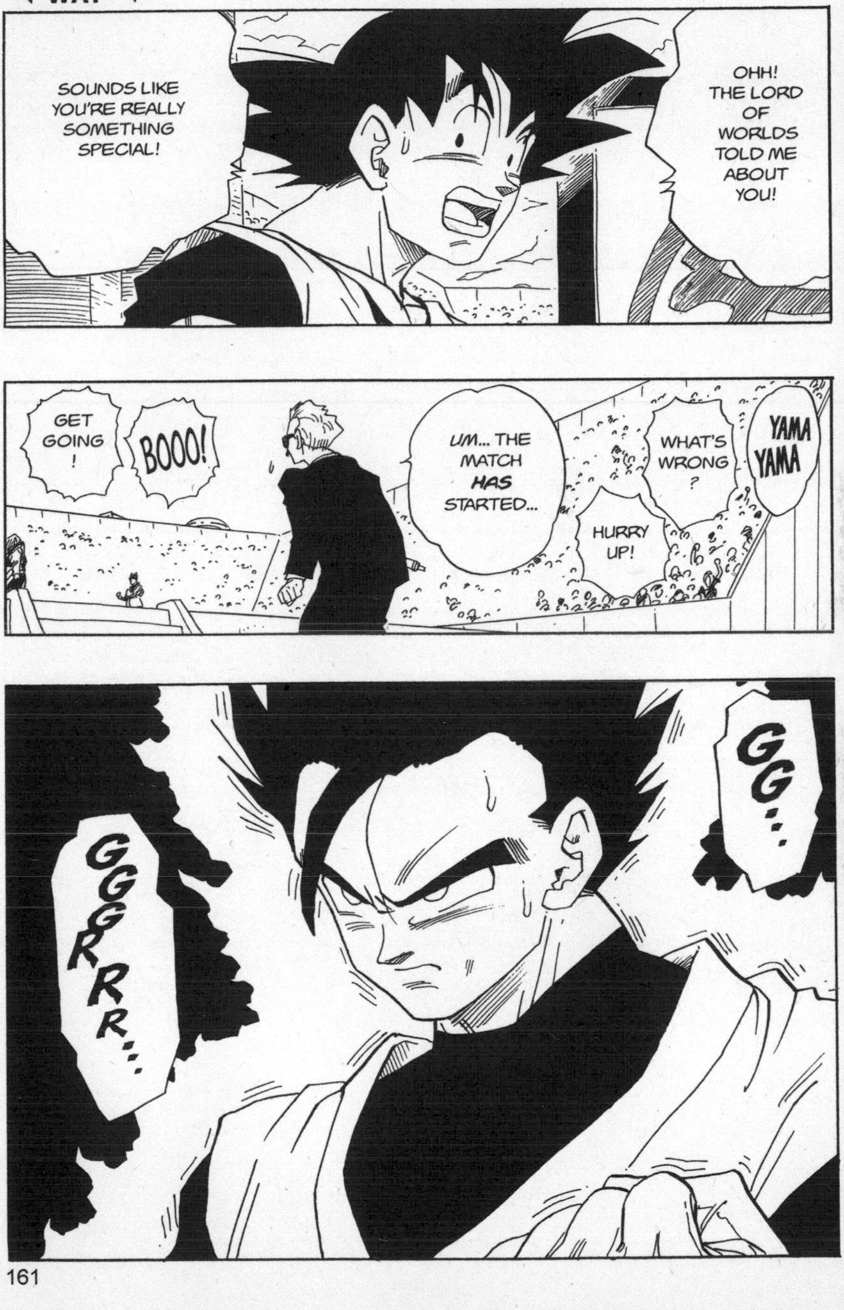
OHH! THE LORD OF WORLDS TOLD ME ABOUT YOU!
SOUNDS LIKE YOU'RE REALLY SOMETHING SPECIAL!
YAMA YAMA
WHAT'S WRONG?
HURRY UP!
UM... THE MATCH HAS STARTED...
BOOO!
GET GOING!
GG...
GGGRRR...

DBZ:250 • The Stolen Energy

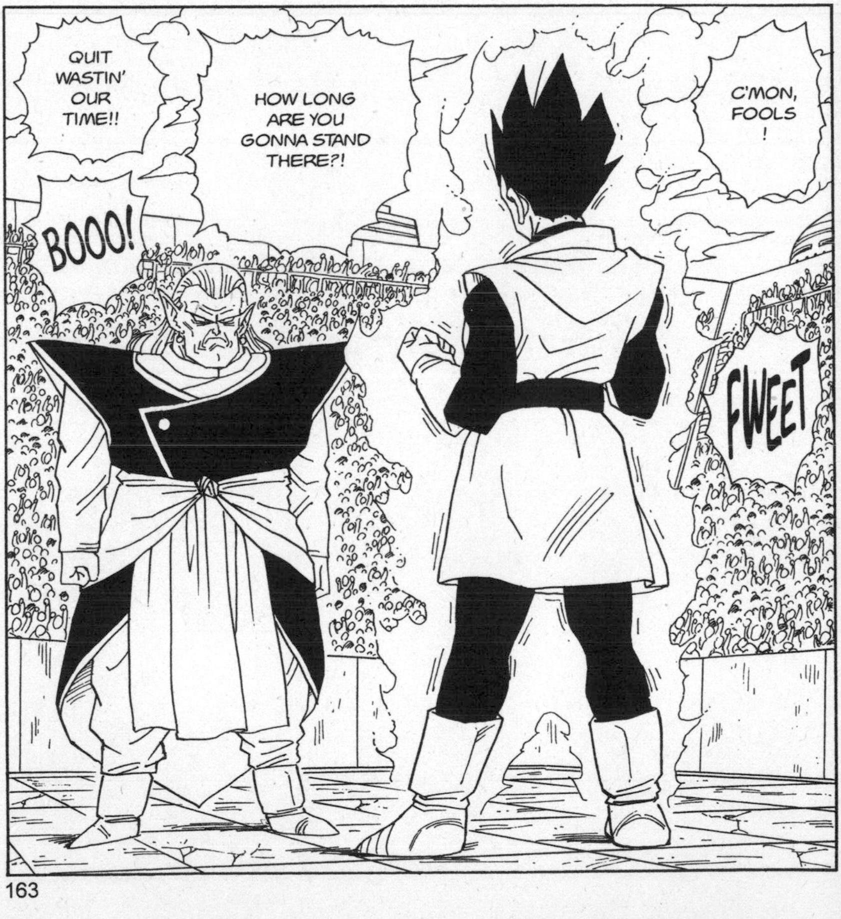
C'MON, FOOLS!
HOW LONG ARE YOU GONNA STAND THERE?!
QUIT WASTIN' OUR TIME!!
BOOO!
FWEET

READ THIS WAY

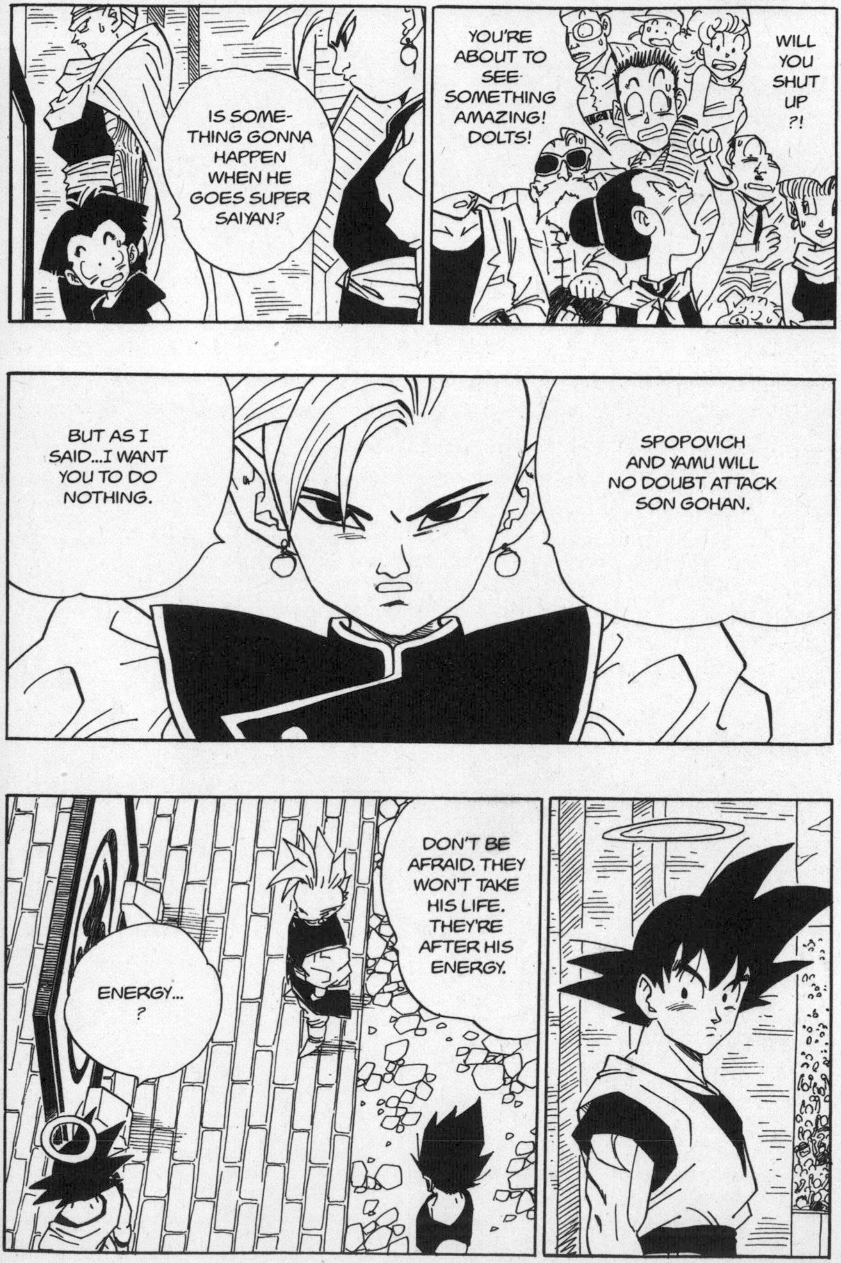
WILL YOU SHUT UP ?!
YOU'RE ABOUT TO SEE SOMETHING AMAZING! DOLTS!
IS SOME-THING GONNA HAPPEN WHEN HE GOES SUPER SAIYAN?
SPOPOVICH AND YAMU WILL NO DOUBT ATTACK SON GOHAN.
BUT AS I SAID...I WANT YOU TO DO NOTHING.
DON'T BE AFRAID. THEY WON'T TAKE HIS LIFE. THEY'RE AFTER HIS ENERGY.
ENERGY... ?

READ THIS WAY

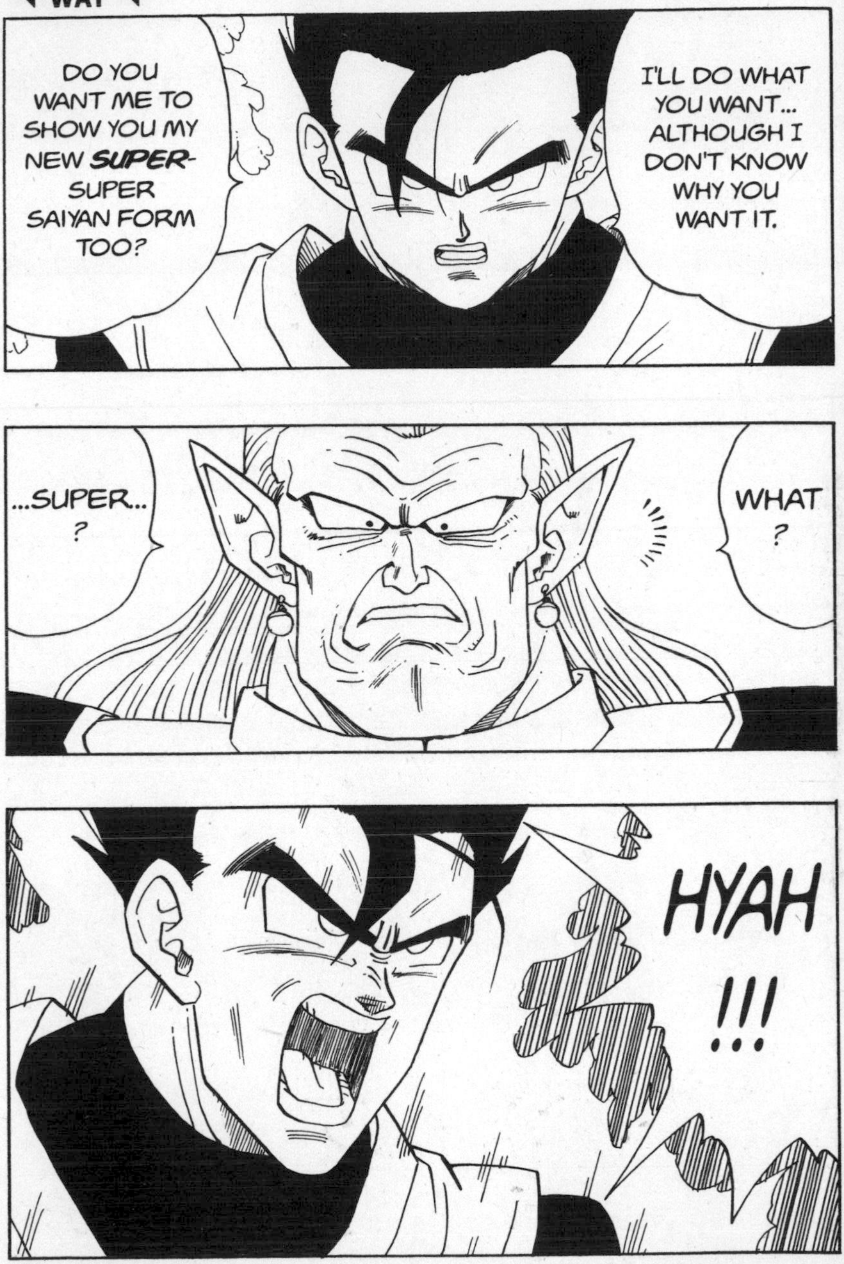
I'LL DO WHAT YOU WANT... ALTHOUGH I DON'T KNOW WHY YOU WANT IT.
DO YOU WANT ME TO SHOW YOU MY NEW **SUPER**-SUPER SAIYAN FORM TOO?
WHAT ?
...SUPER... ?
HYAH !!!

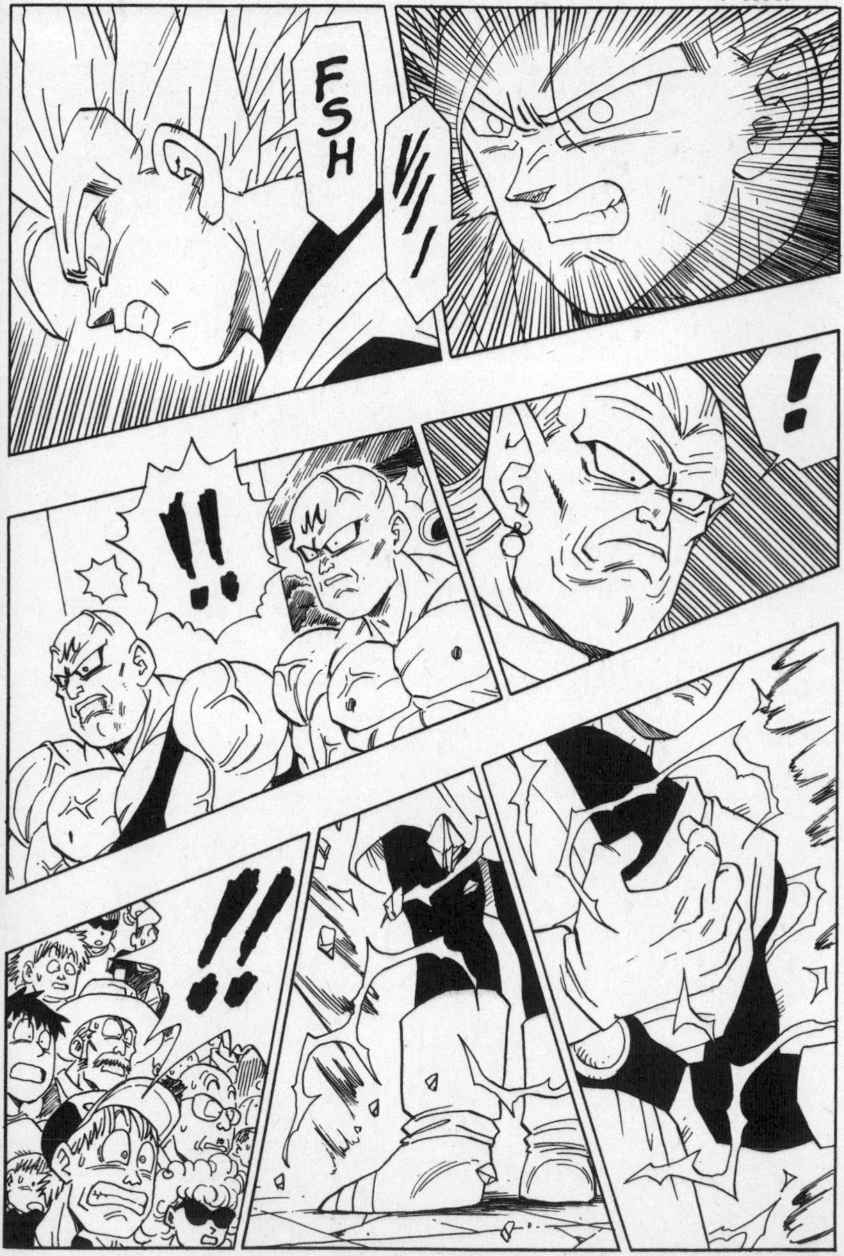
FSH
!
!!
!!

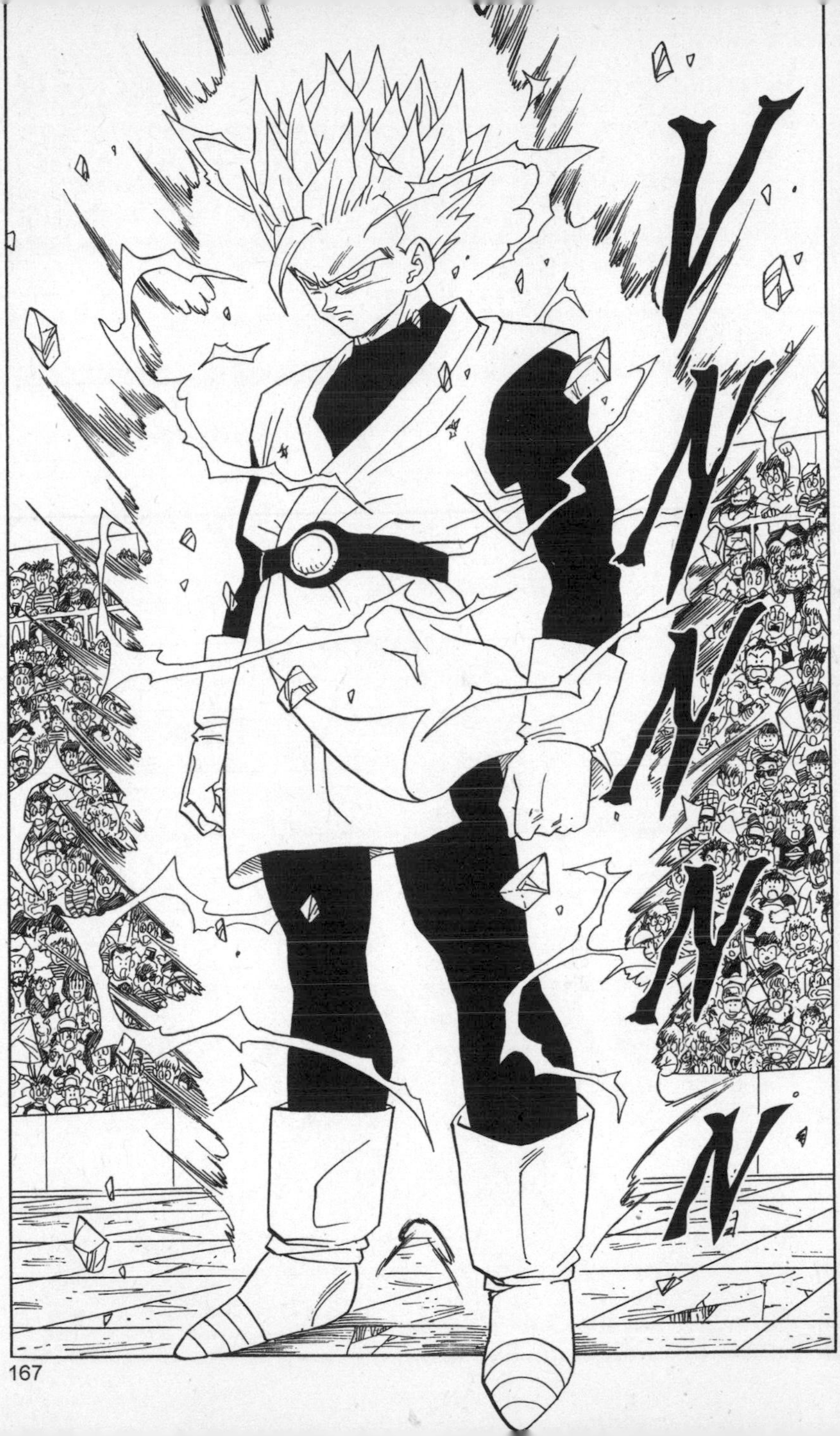
VNNNNNN

READ THIS WAY

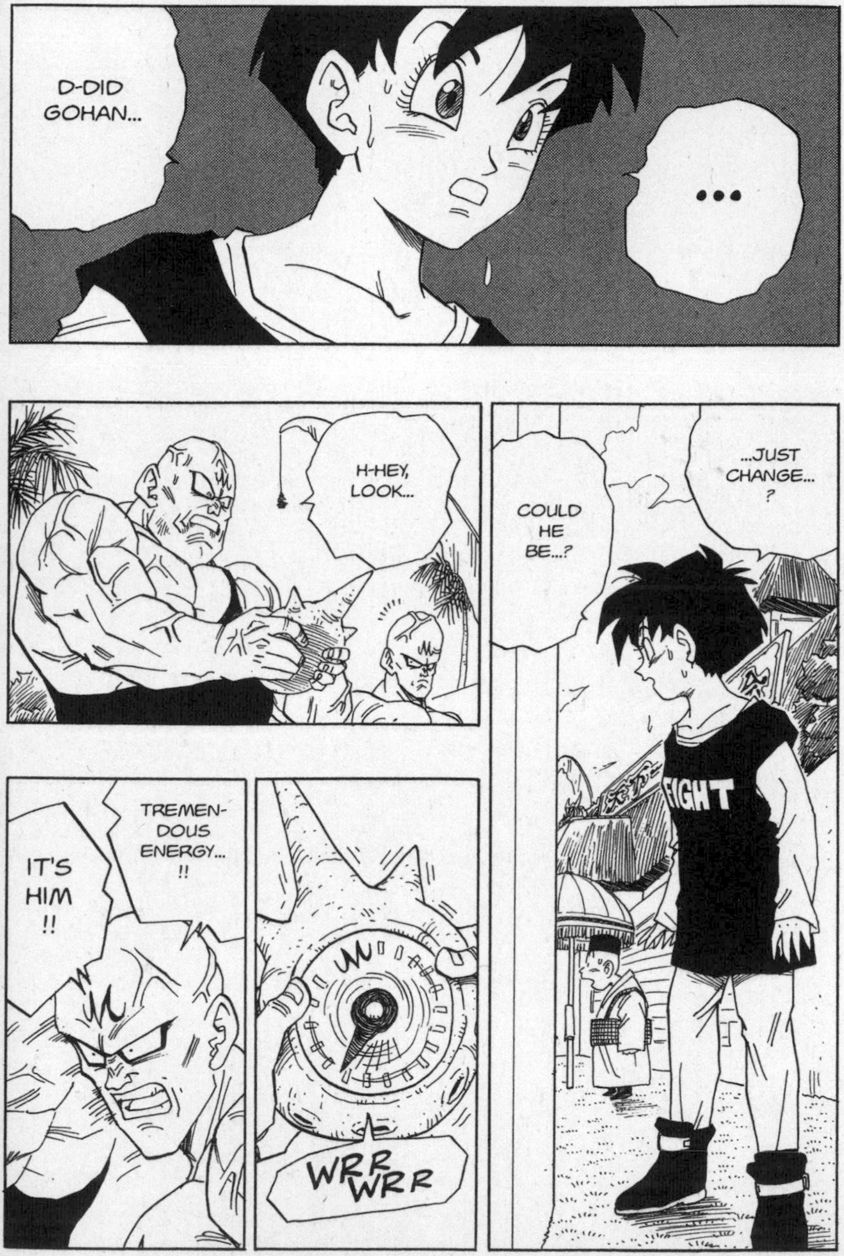

...
D-DID GOHAN...
...JUST CHANGE...?
COULD HE BE...?
H-HEY, LOOK...
WRR WRR
TREMEN-DOUS ENERGY...!!
IT'S HIM!!

READ THIS WAY

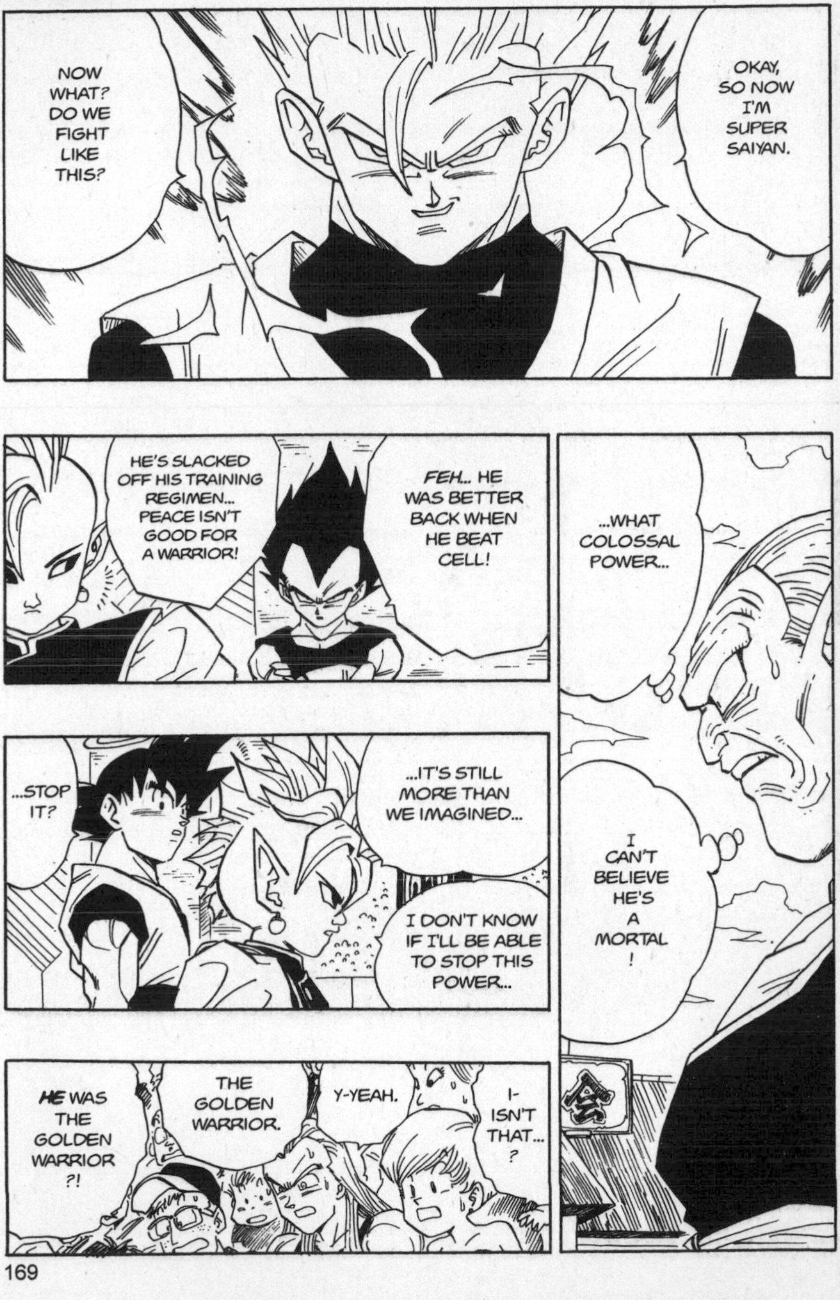

OKAY, SO NOW I'M SUPER SAIYAN.
NOW WHAT? DO WE FIGHT LIKE THIS?
...WHAT COLOSSAL POWER...
I CAN'T BELIEVE HE'S A MORTAL!
FEH... HE WAS BETTER BACK WHEN HE BEAT CELL!
HE'S SLACKED OFF HIS TRAINING REGIMEN... PEACE ISN'T GOOD FOR A WARRIOR!
...IT'S STILL MORE THAN WE IMAGINED...
I DON'T KNOW IF I'LL BE ABLE TO STOP THIS POWER...
...STOP IT?
I-ISN'T THAT...?
Y-YEAH.
THE GOLDEN WARRIOR.
HE WAS THE GOLDEN WARRIOR?!

READ THIS WAY

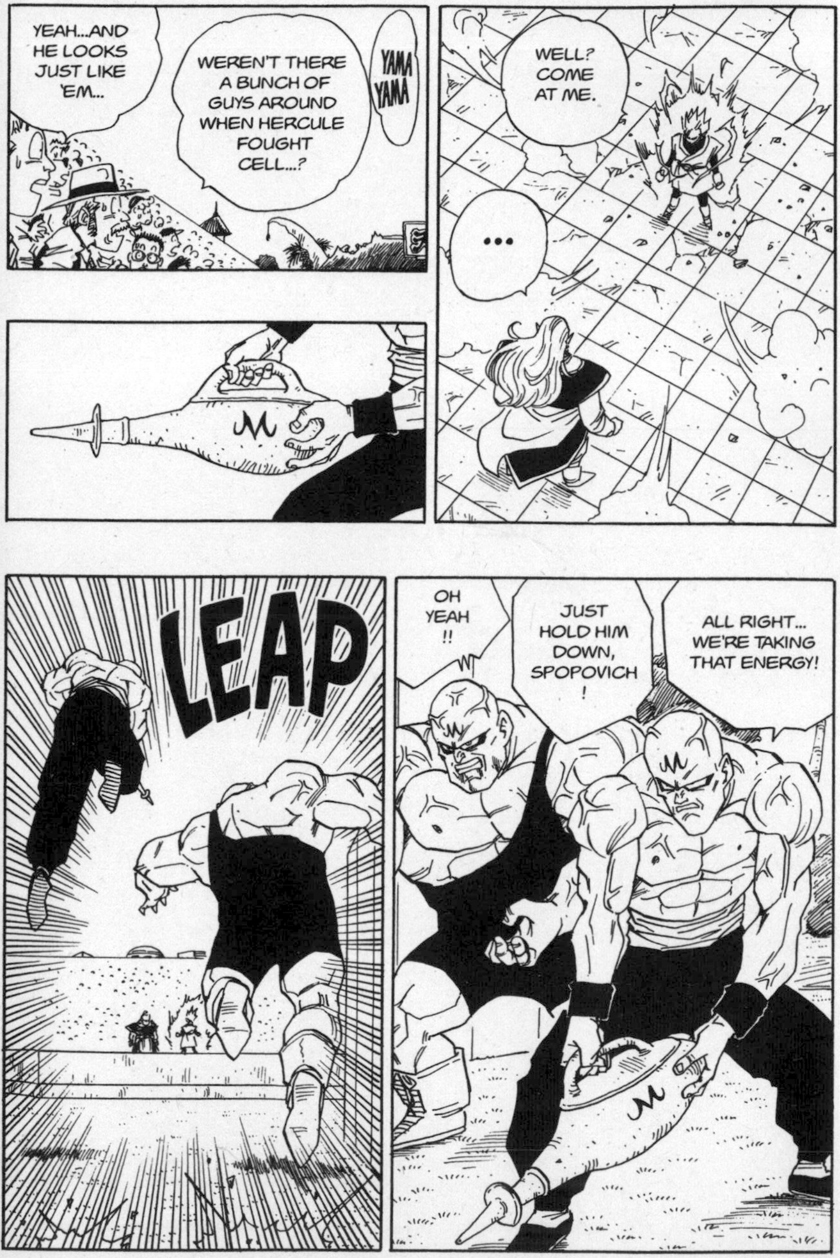
WELL? COME AT ME.
...
YAMA YAMA
WEREN'T THERE A BUNCH OF GUYS AROUND WHEN HERCULE FOUGHT CELL...?
YEAH...AND HE LOOKS JUST LIKE 'EM...
ALL RIGHT... WE'RE TAKING THAT ENERGY!
JUST HOLD HIM DOWN, SPOPOVICH!
OH YEAH!!
LEAP

READ THIS WAY

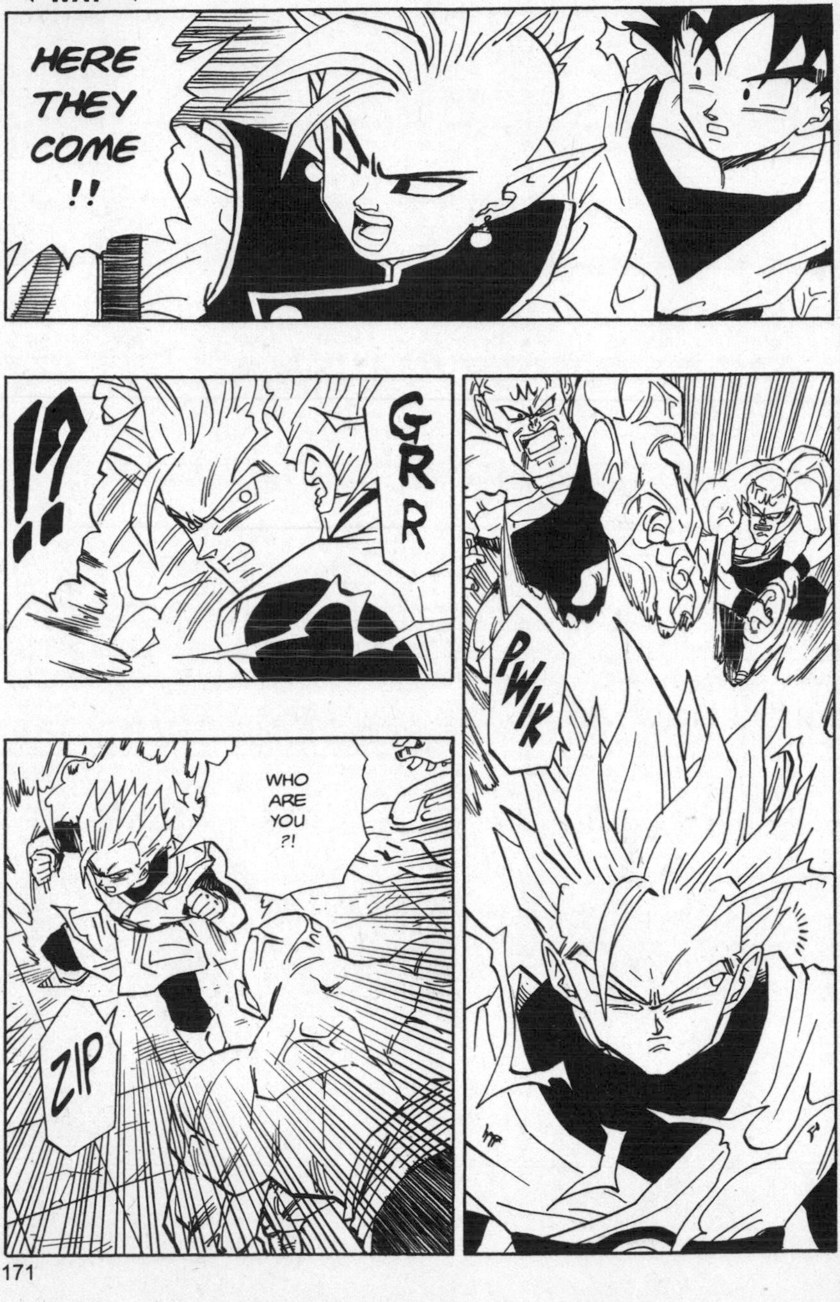
HERE THEY COME !!
PWIK
!?
GRR
WHO ARE YOU ?!
ZIP

READ THIS WAY

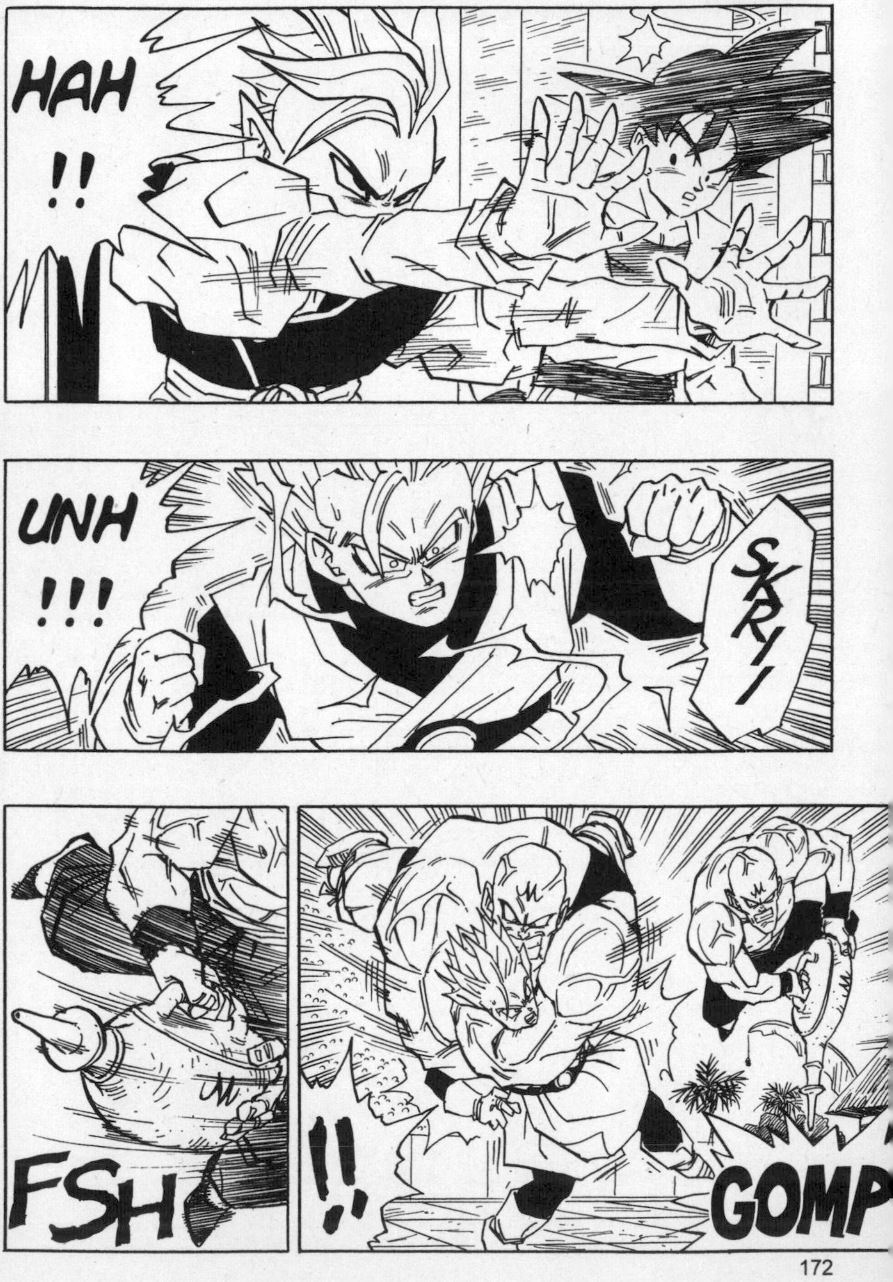

HAH!!
SKRII
UNH!!!
GOMP
!!
FSH

READ THIS WAY

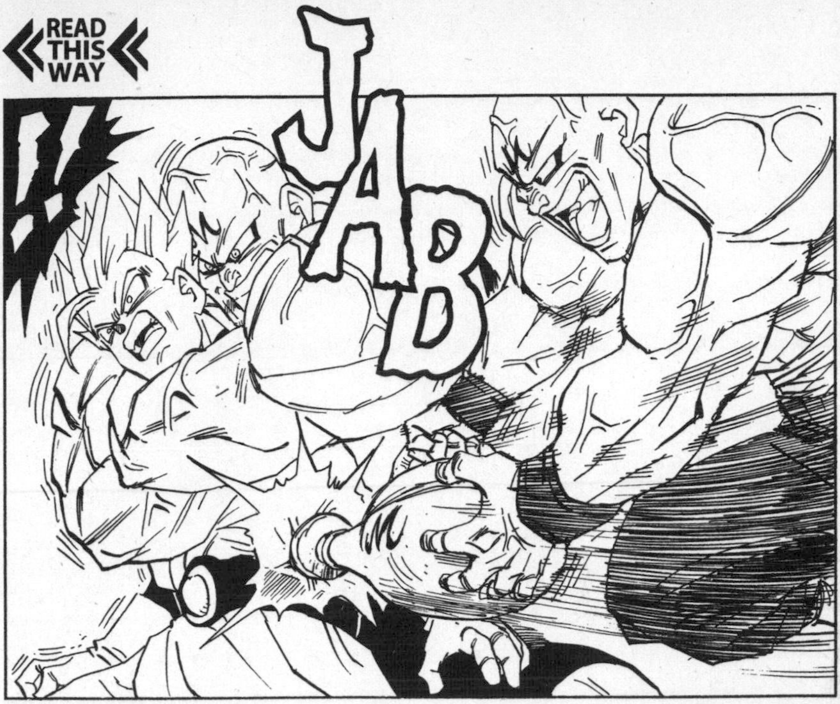
!!
JAB

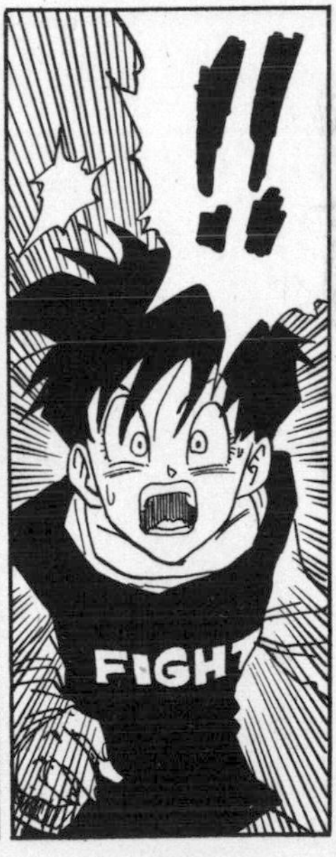
!!
!!

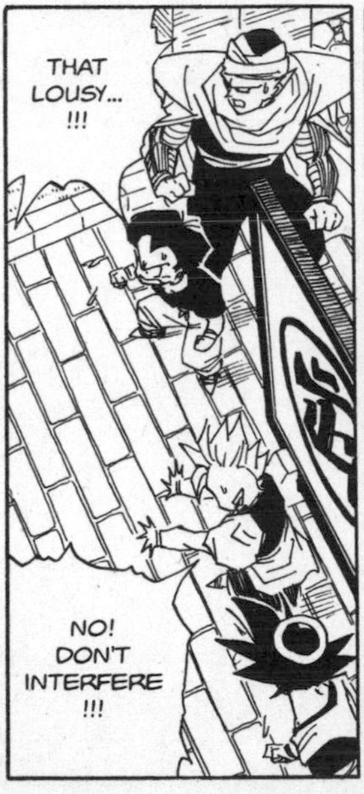
THAT LOUSY... !!!
NO! DON'T INTERFERE !!!

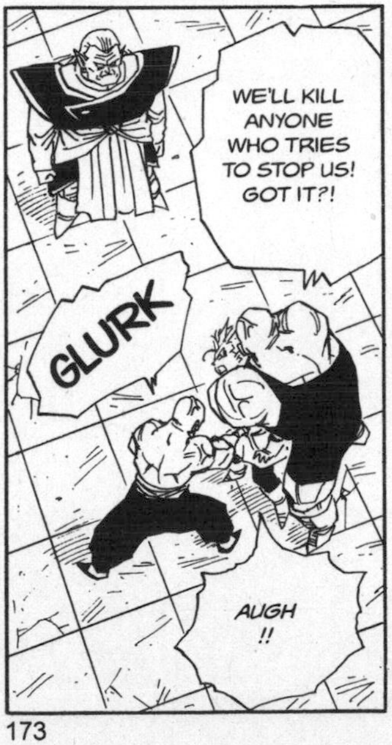
WE'LL KILL ANYONE WHO TRIES TO STOP US! GOT IT?!
GLURK
AUGH !!

READ THIS WAY

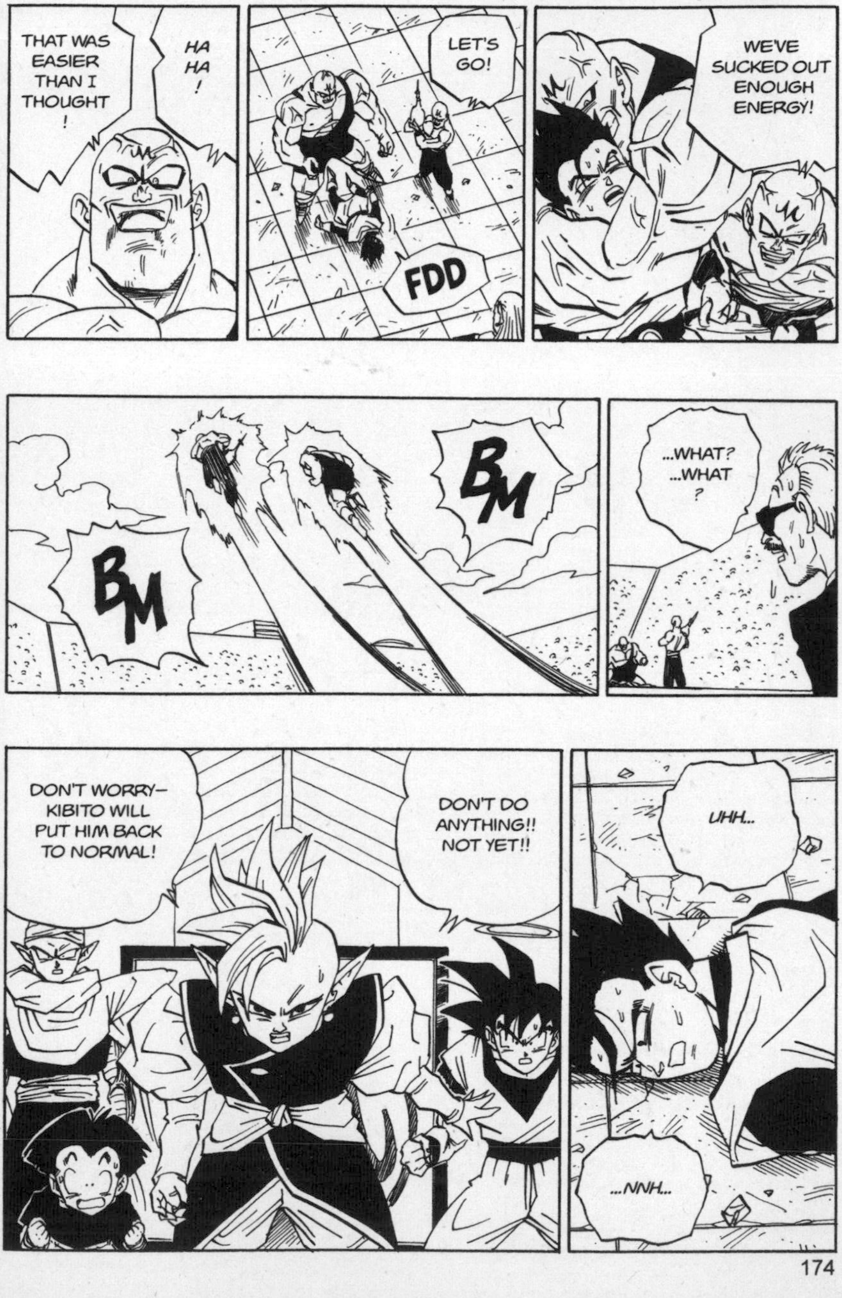
WE'VE SUCKED OUT ENOUGH ENERGY!
LET'S GO!
FDD
HA HA!
THAT WAS EASIER THAN I THOUGHT!
...WHAT? ...WHAT?
BM
BM
UHH...
...NNH...
DON'T DO ANYTHING!! NOT YET!!
DON'T WORRY—KIBITO WILL PUT HIM BACK TO NORMAL!

READ THIS WAY

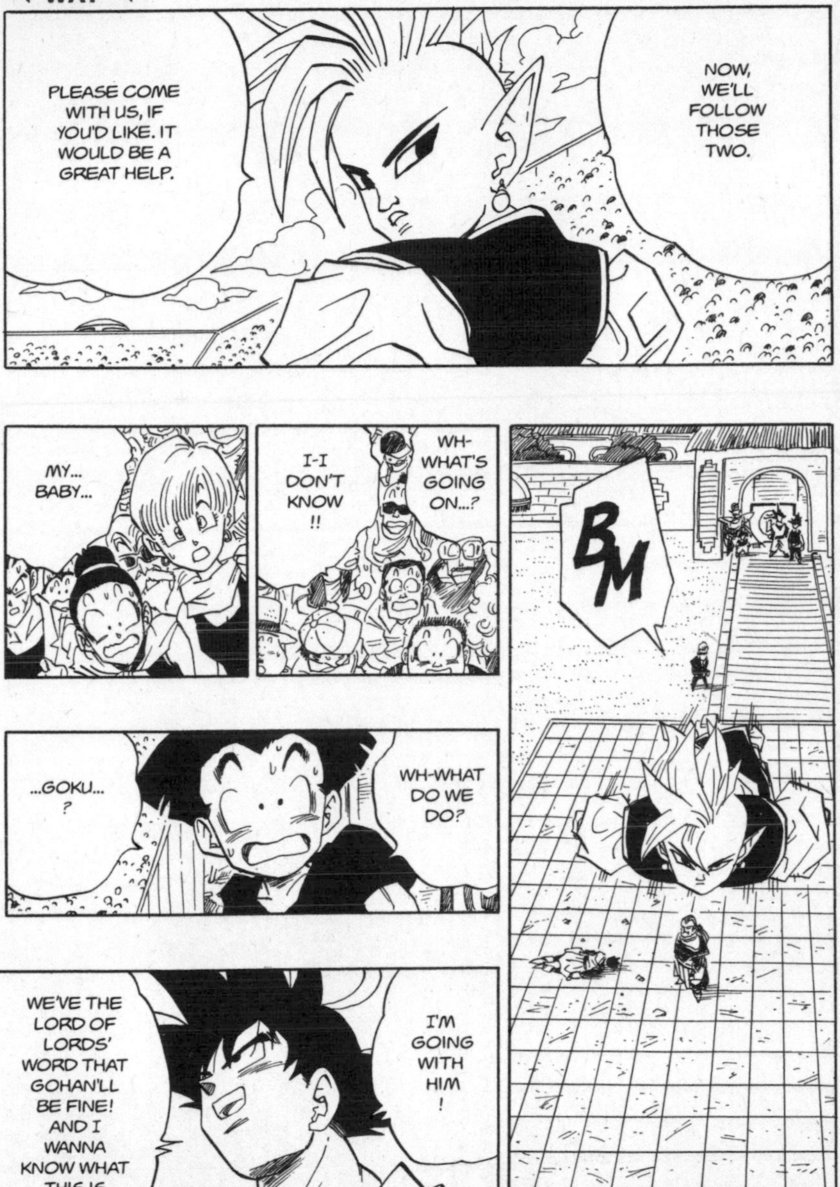
NOW, WE'LL FOLLOW THOSE TWO.
PLEASE COME WITH US, IF YOU'D LIKE. IT WOULD BE A GREAT HELP.
BM
WH-WHAT'S GOING ON...?
I-I DON'T KNOW!!
MY... BABY...
WH-WHAT DO WE DO?
...GOKU...?
I'M GOING WITH HIM!
WE'VE THE LORD OF LORDS' WORD THAT GOHAN'LL BE FINE! AND I WANNA KNOW WHAT THIS IS ABOUT!

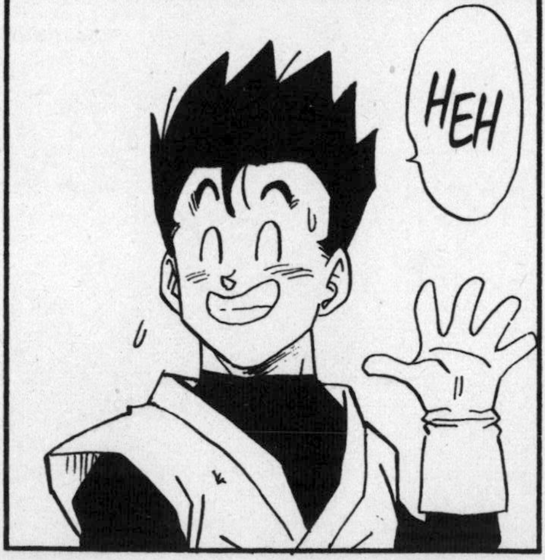
HEH

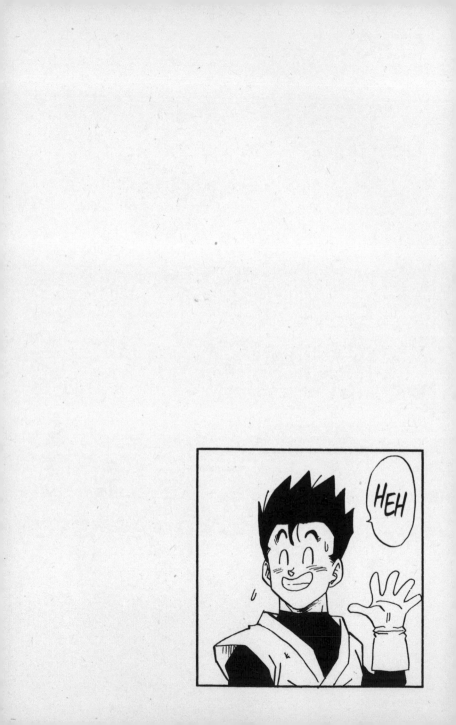

DBZ:251 • The Terrible Mystery

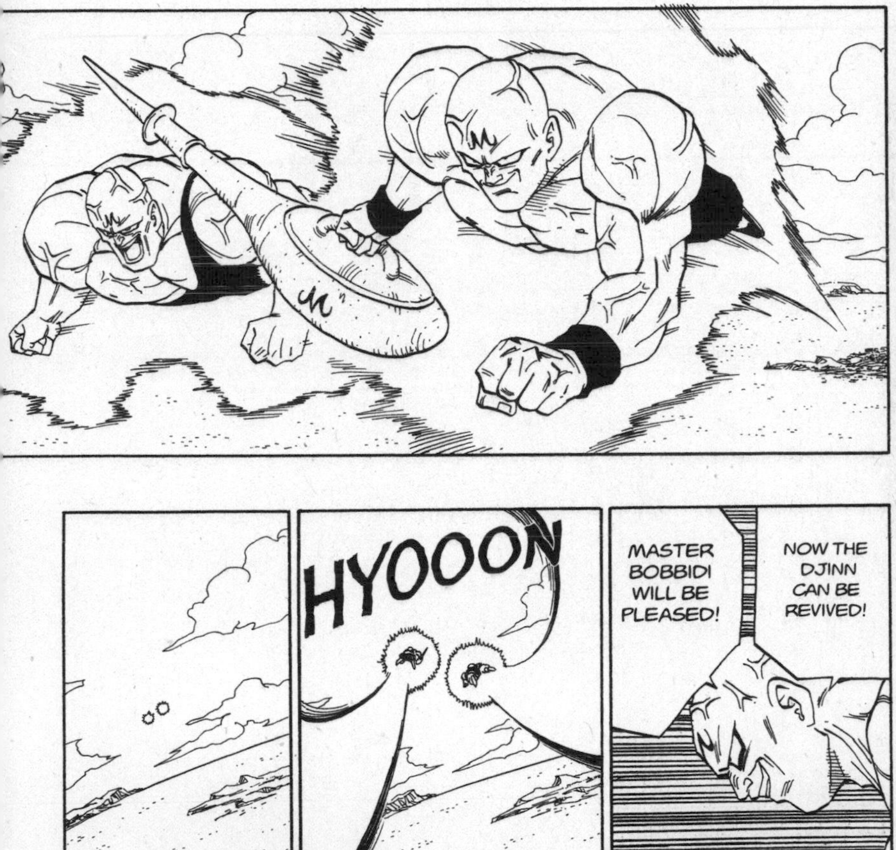
NOW THE DJINN CAN BE REVIVED!
MASTER BOBBIDI WILL BE PLEASED!
HYOOON

READ THIS WAY

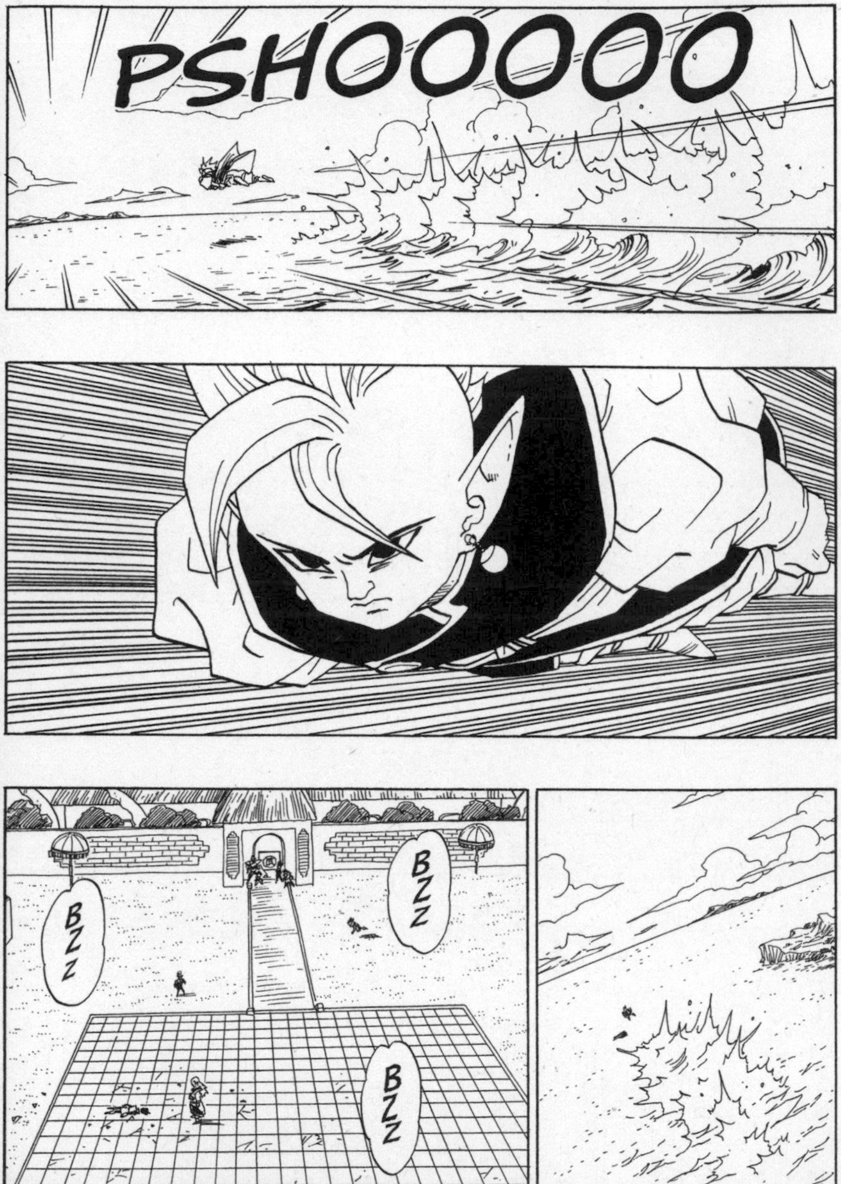
PSHOOOOO
BZZ
BZZ
BZZ

READ THIS WAY

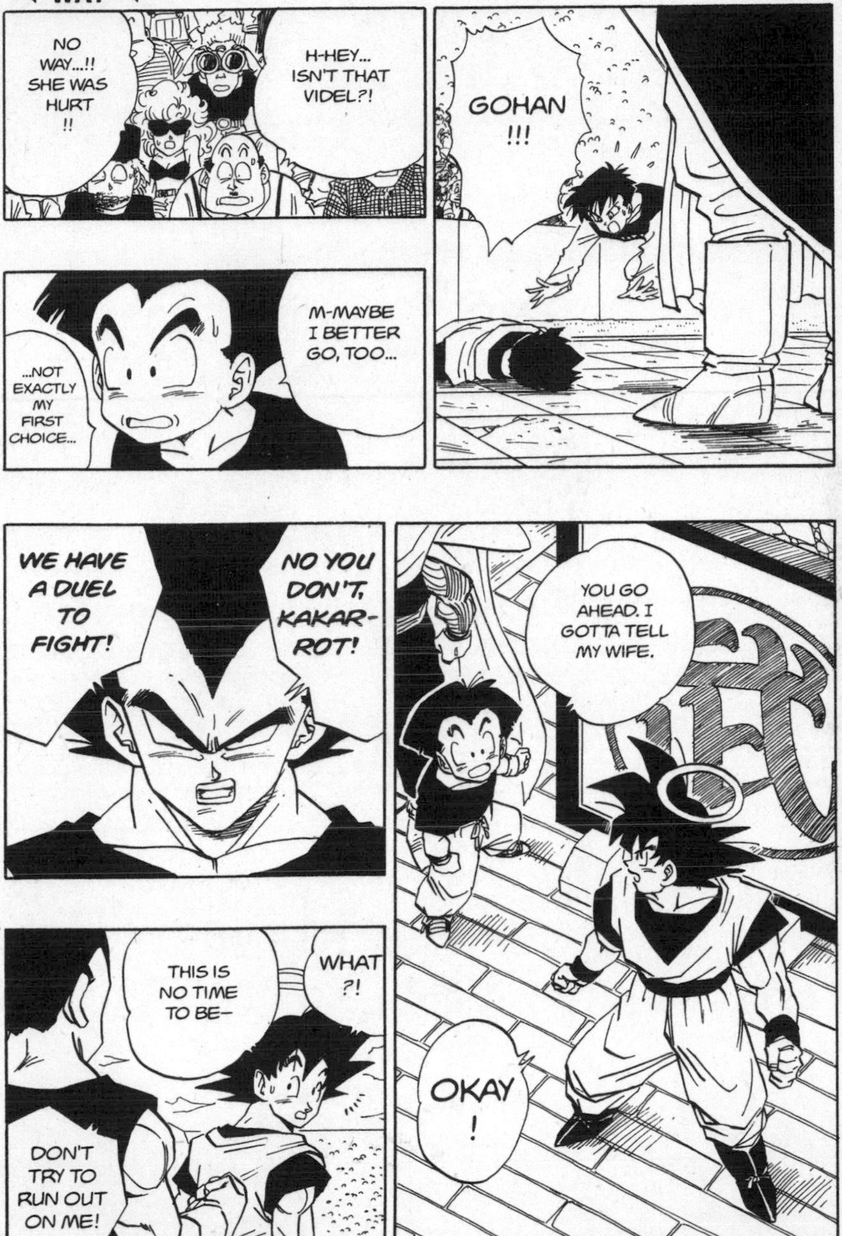
GOHAN!!!
H-HEY... ISN'T THAT VIDEL?!
NO WAY...!! SHE WAS HURT!!
M-MAYBE I BETTER GO, TOO...
...NOT EXACTLY MY FIRST CHOICE...
YOU GO AHEAD. I GOTTA TELL MY WIFE.
OKAY!
NO YOU DON'T, KAKARROT!
WE HAVE A DUEL TO FIGHT!
WHAT?!
THIS IS NO TIME TO BE-
DON'T TRY TO RUN OUT ON ME!

READ THIS WAY

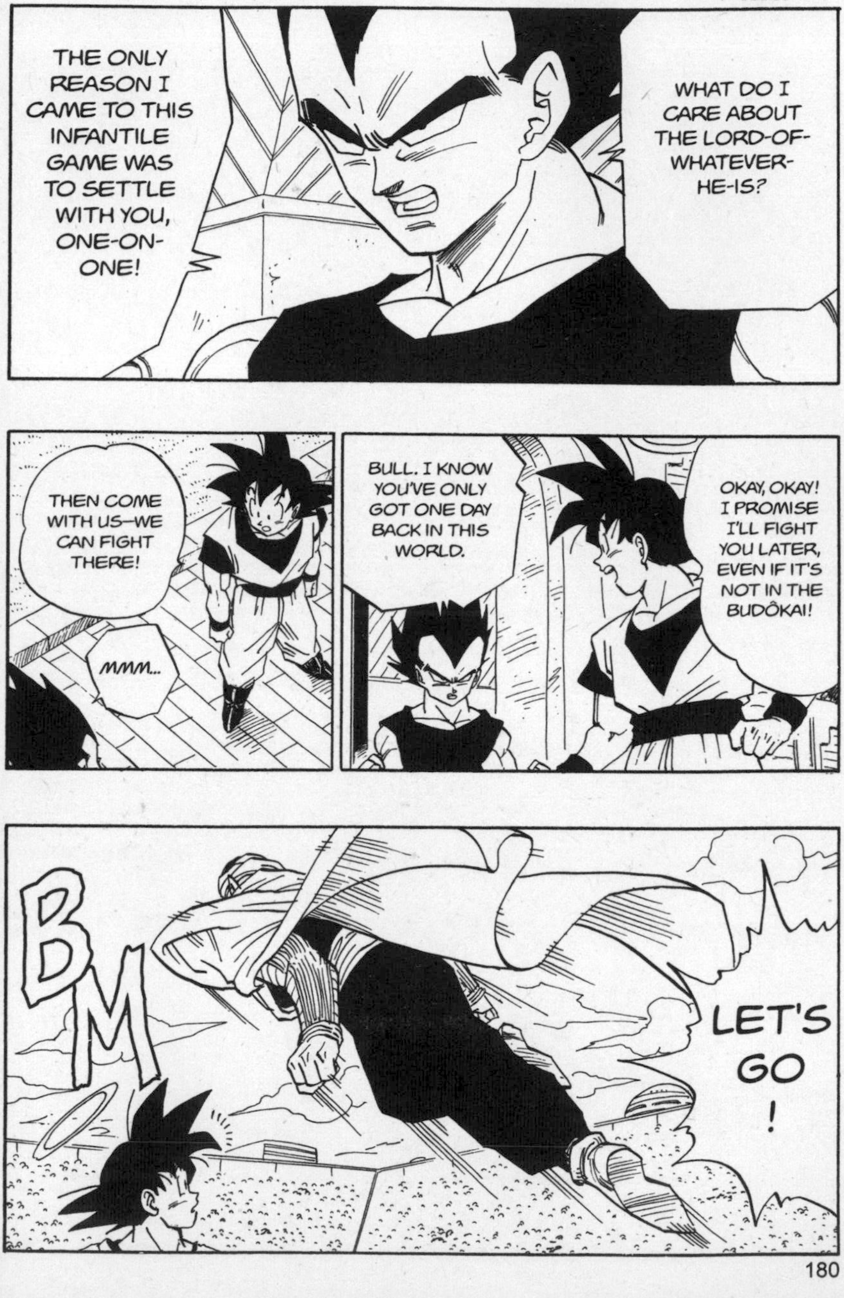
WHAT DO I CARE ABOUT THE LORD-OF-WHATEVER-HE-IS?
THE ONLY REASON I CAME TO THIS INFANTILE GAME WAS TO SETTLE WITH YOU, ONE-ON-ONE!
OKAY, OKAY! I PROMISE I'LL FIGHT YOU LATER, EVEN IF IT'S NOT IN THE BUDÔKAI!
BULL. I KNOW YOU'VE ONLY GOT ONE DAY BACK IN THIS WORLD.
THEN COME WITH US—WE CAN FIGHT THERE!
MMM...
LET'S GO!
BM

READ THIS WAY

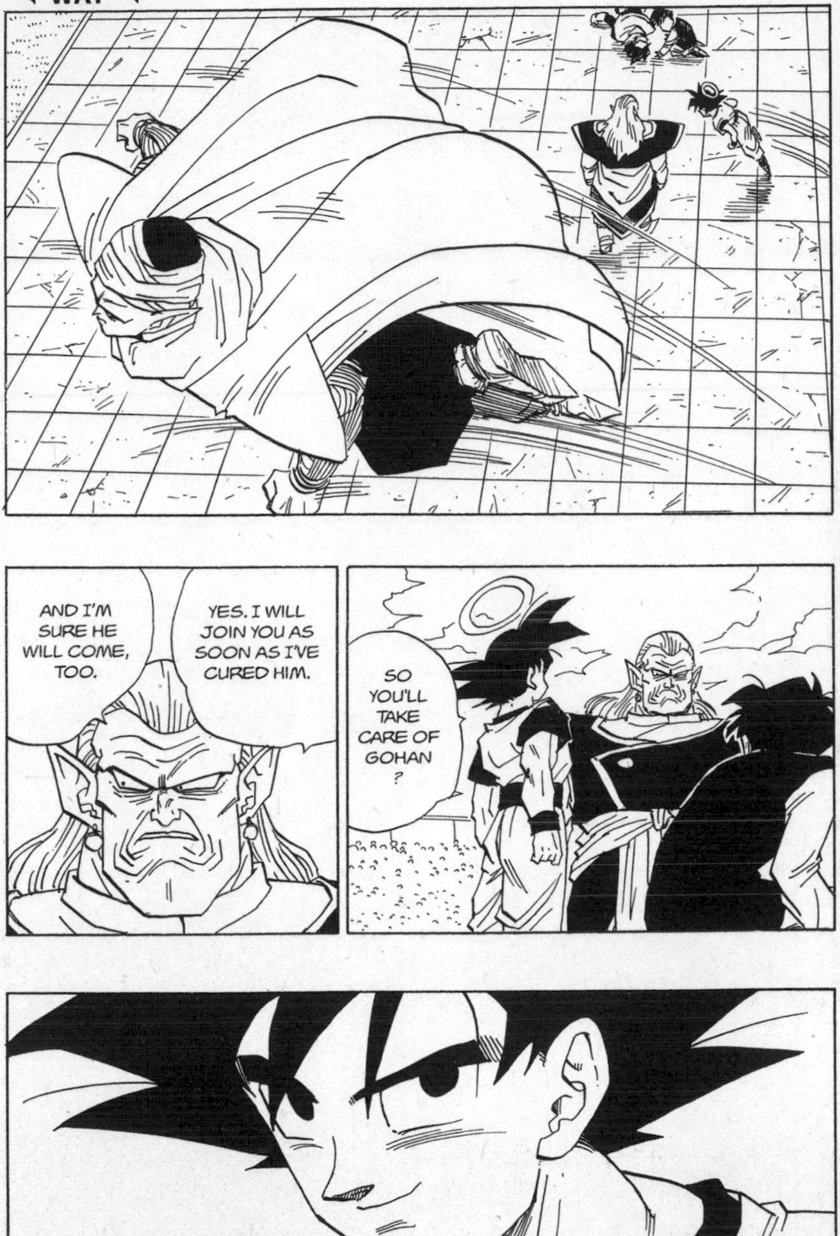
SO YOU'LL TAKE CARE OF GOHAN ?
YES. I WILL JOIN YOU AS SOON AS I'VE CURED HIM.
AND I'M SURE HE WILL COME, TOO.

READ THIS WAY

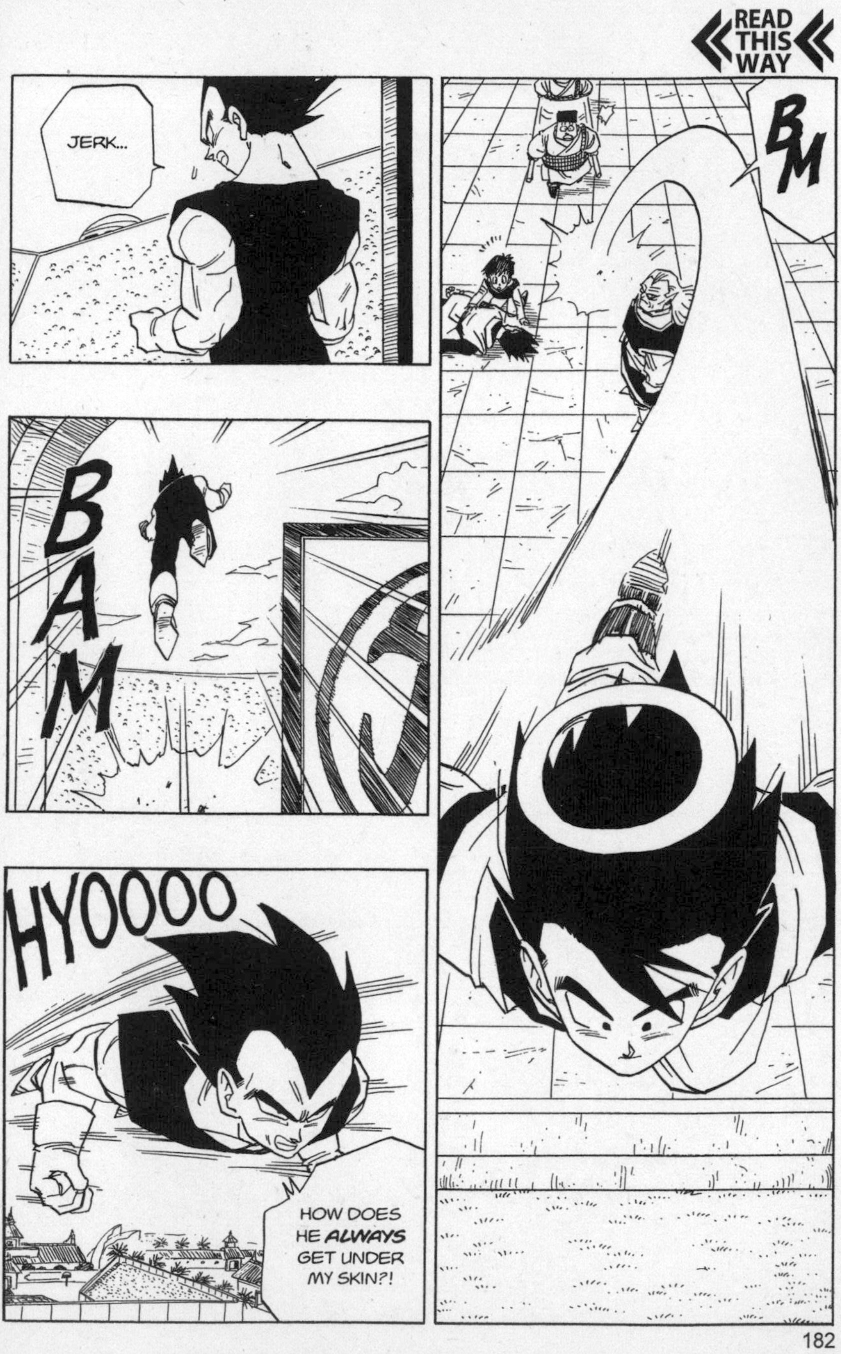
BM
JERK...
BAM
HYOOOO
HOW DOES HE *ALWAYS* GET UNDER MY SKIN?!

READ THIS WAY

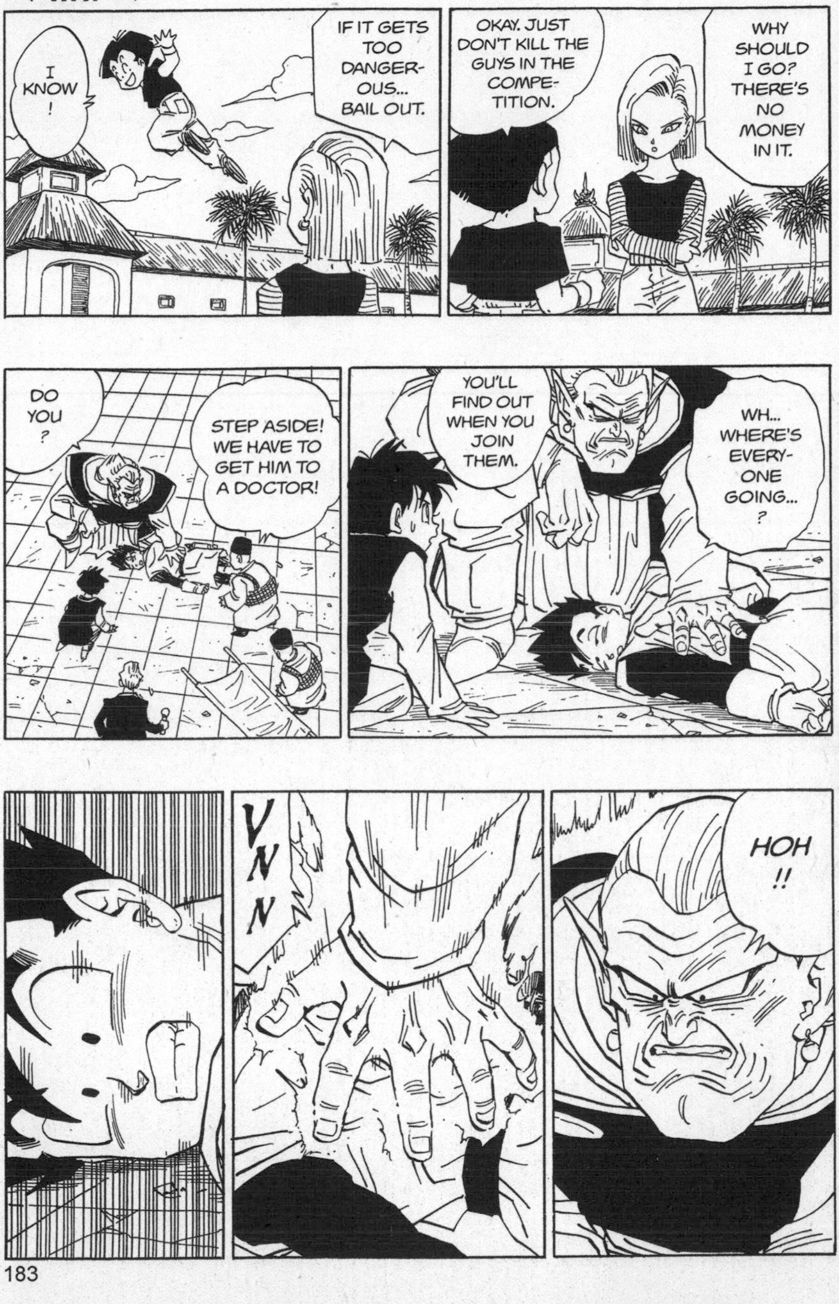
WHY SHOULD I GO? THERE'S NO MONEY IN IT.
OKAY. JUST DON'T KILL THE GUYS IN THE COMPE-TITION.
IF IT GETS TOO DANGER-OUS... BAIL OUT.
I KNOW!
WH... WHERE'S EVERY-ONE GOING...?
YOU'LL FIND OUT WHEN YOU JOIN THEM.
STEP ASIDE! WE HAVE TO GET HIM TO A DOCTOR!
DO YOU?
HOH!!
VNN

READ THIS WAY

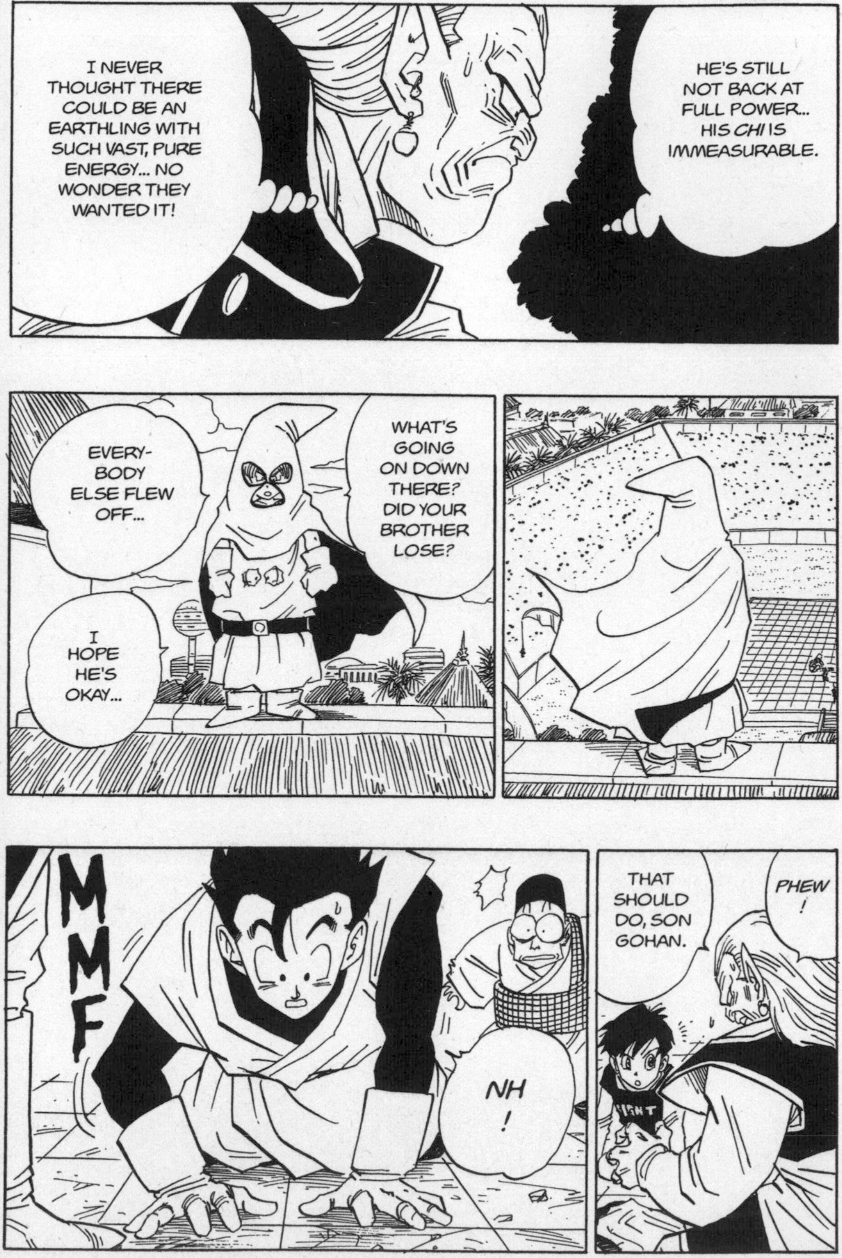
HE'S STILL NOT BACK AT FULL POWER... HIS *CHI* IS IMMEASURABLE.
I NEVER THOUGHT THERE COULD BE AN EARTHLING WITH SUCH VAST, PURE ENERGY... NO WONDER THEY WANTED IT!
WHAT'S GOING ON DOWN THERE? DID YOUR BROTHER LOSE?
EVERY-BODY ELSE FLEW OFF...
I HOPE HE'S OKAY...
PHEW!
THAT SHOULD DO, SON GOHAN.
MMF
NH!

READ THIS WAY

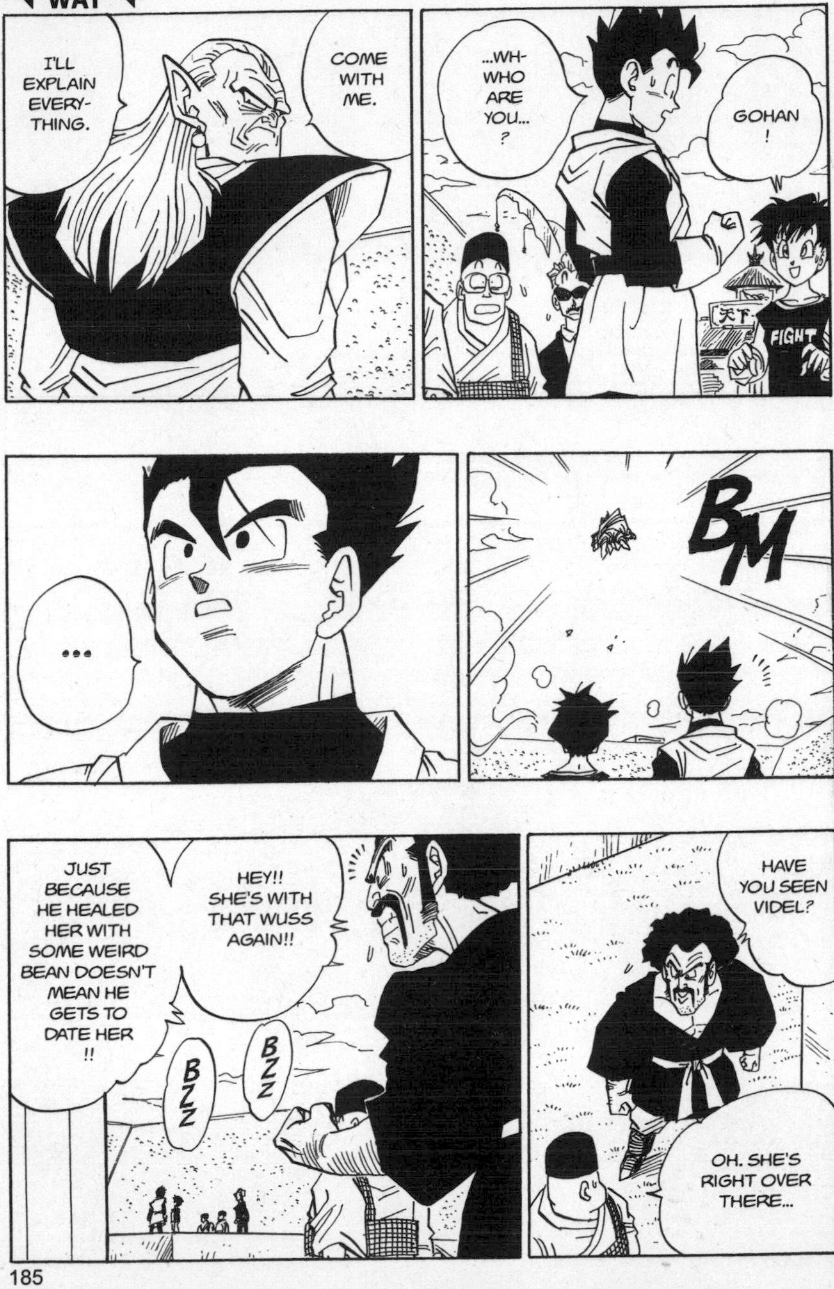
GOHAN!
...WH-WHO ARE YOU...?
COME WITH ME.
I'LL EXPLAIN EVERY-THING.
BM
...
HAVE YOU SEEN VIDEL?
OH. SHE'S RIGHT OVER THERE...
HEY!! SHE'S WITH THAT WUSS AGAIN!!
JUST BECAUSE HE HEALED HER WITH SOME WEIRD BEAN DOESN'T MEAN HE GETS TO DATE HER!!
BZZ
BZZ

READ THIS WAY

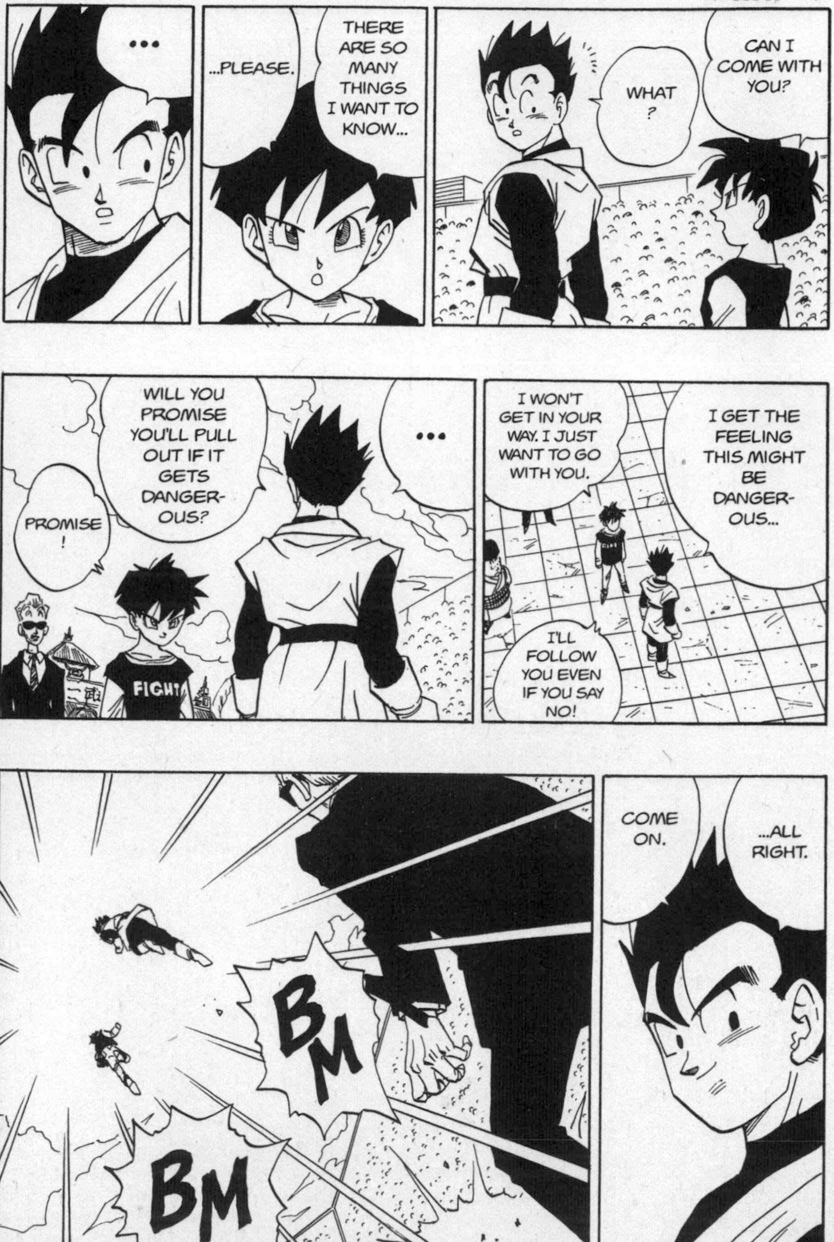
CAN I COME WITH YOU?
WHAT?
THERE ARE SO MANY THINGS I WANT TO KNOW...
...PLEASE.
...
I GET THE FEELING THIS MIGHT BE DANGER-OUS...
I WON'T GET IN YOUR WAY. I JUST WANT TO GO WITH YOU.
I'LL FOLLOW YOU EVEN IF YOU SAY NO!
...
WILL YOU PROMISE YOU'LL PULL OUT IF IT GETS DANGER-OUS?
PROMISE!
FIGHT
...ALL RIGHT.
COME ON.
BM
BM

READ THIS WAY

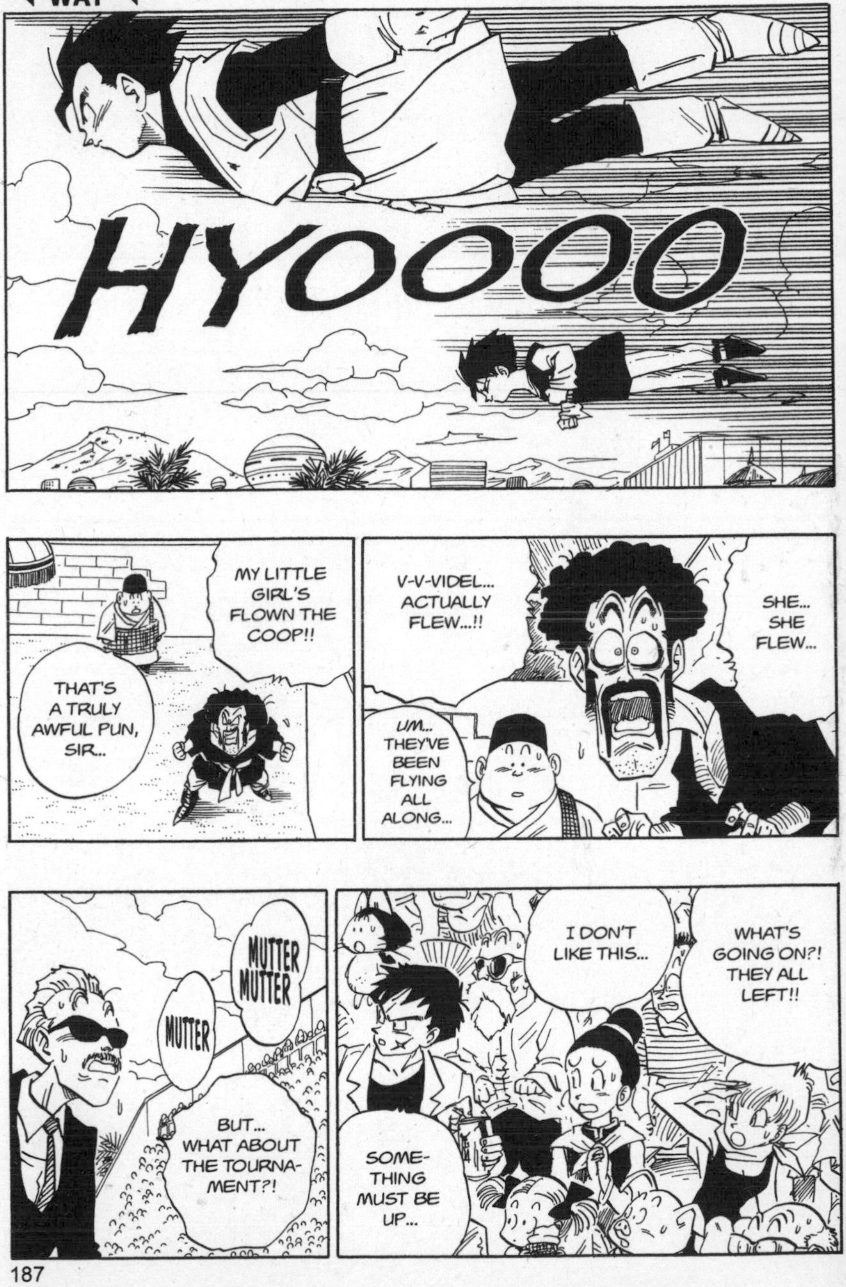
HYOOOO
SHE... SHE FLEW...
V-V-VIDEL... ACTUALLY FLEW...!!
UM... THEY'VE BEEN FLYING ALL ALONG...
MY LITTLE GIRL'S FLOWN THE COOP!!
THAT'S A TRULY AWFUL PUN, SIR...
WHAT'S GOING ON?! THEY ALL LEFT!!
I DON'T LIKE THIS...
SOME-THING MUST BE UP...
MUTTER MUTTER
MUTTER
BUT... WHAT ABOUT THE TOURNA-MENT?!

READ THIS WAY

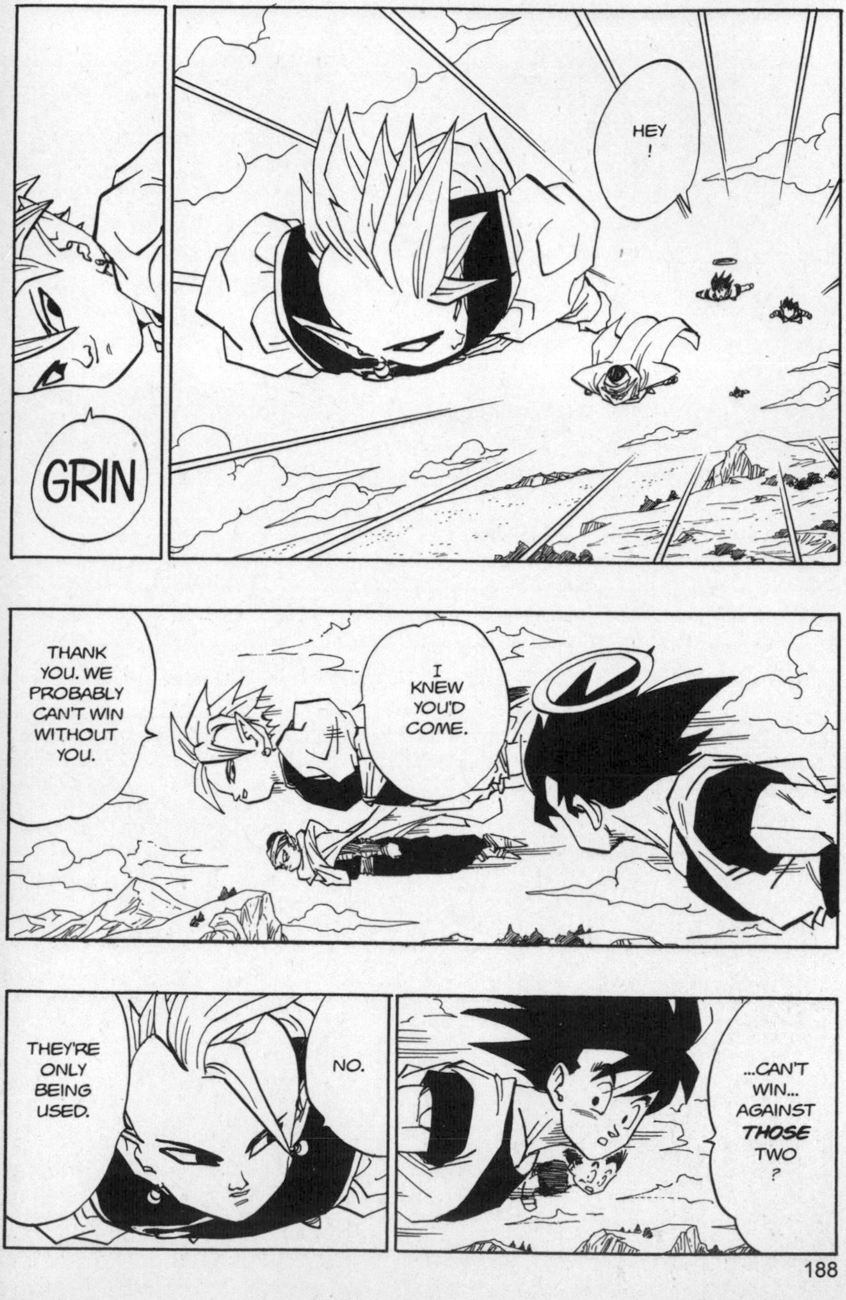
HEY!
GRIN
I KNEW YOU'D COME.
THANK YOU. WE PROBABLY CAN'T WIN WITHOUT YOU.
...CAN'T WIN... AGAINST *THOSE* TWO?
NO.
THEY'RE ONLY BEING USED.

READ THIS WAY

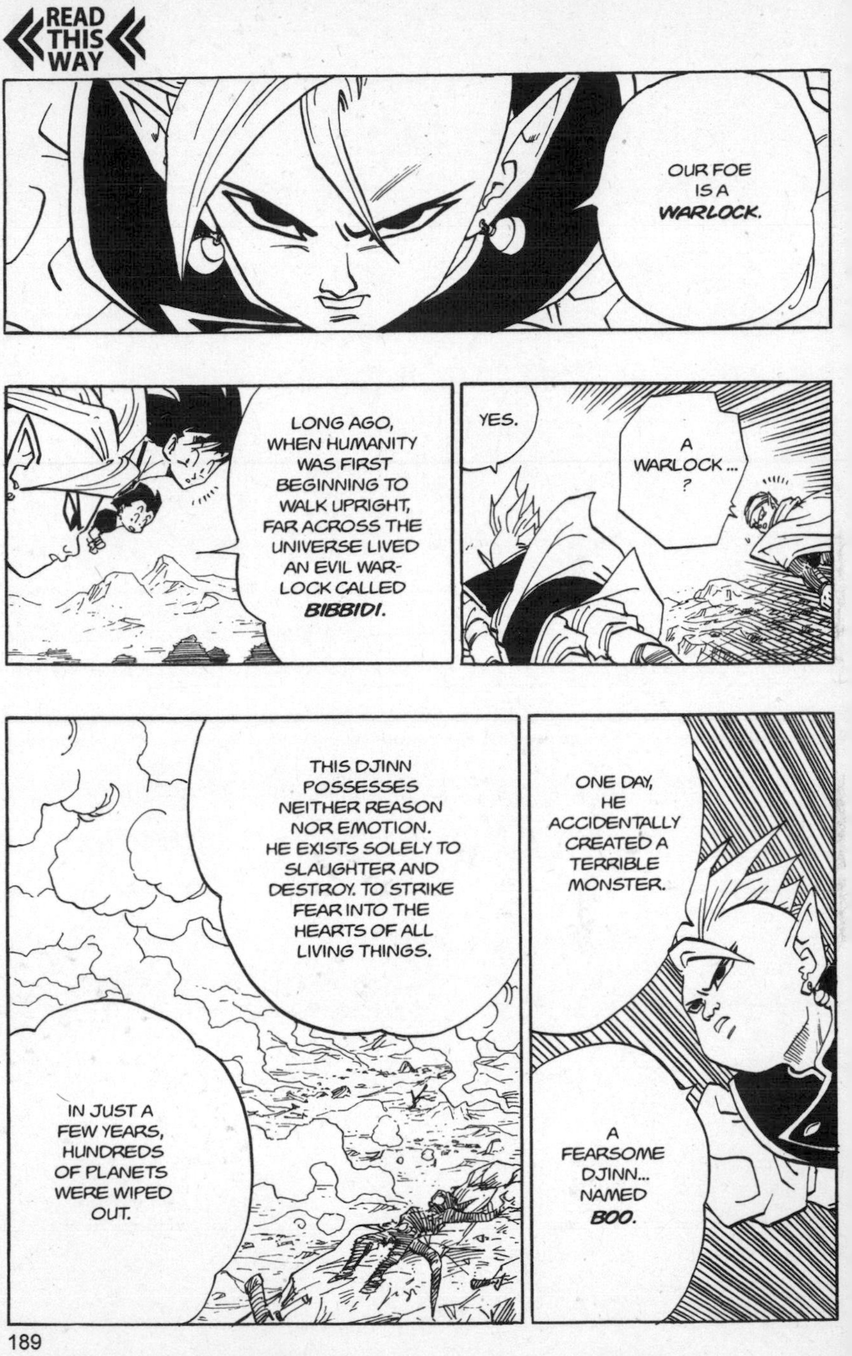

OUR FOE IS A ***WARLOCK***.
A WARLOCK... ?
YES.
LONG AGO, WHEN HUMANITY WAS FIRST BEGINNING TO WALK UPRIGHT, FAR ACROSS THE UNIVERSE LIVED AN EVIL WAR-LOCK CALLED ***BIBBIDI***.
ONE DAY, HE ACCIDENTALLY CREATED A TERRIBLE MONSTER.
A FEARSOME DJINN... NAMED ***BOO***.
THIS DJINN POSSESSES NEITHER REASON NOR EMOTION. HE EXISTS SOLELY TO SLAUGHTER AND DESTROY. TO STRIKE FEAR INTO THE HEARTS OF ALL LIVING THINGS.
IN JUST A FEW YEARS, HUNDREDS OF PLANETS WERE WIPED OUT.

READ THIS WAY

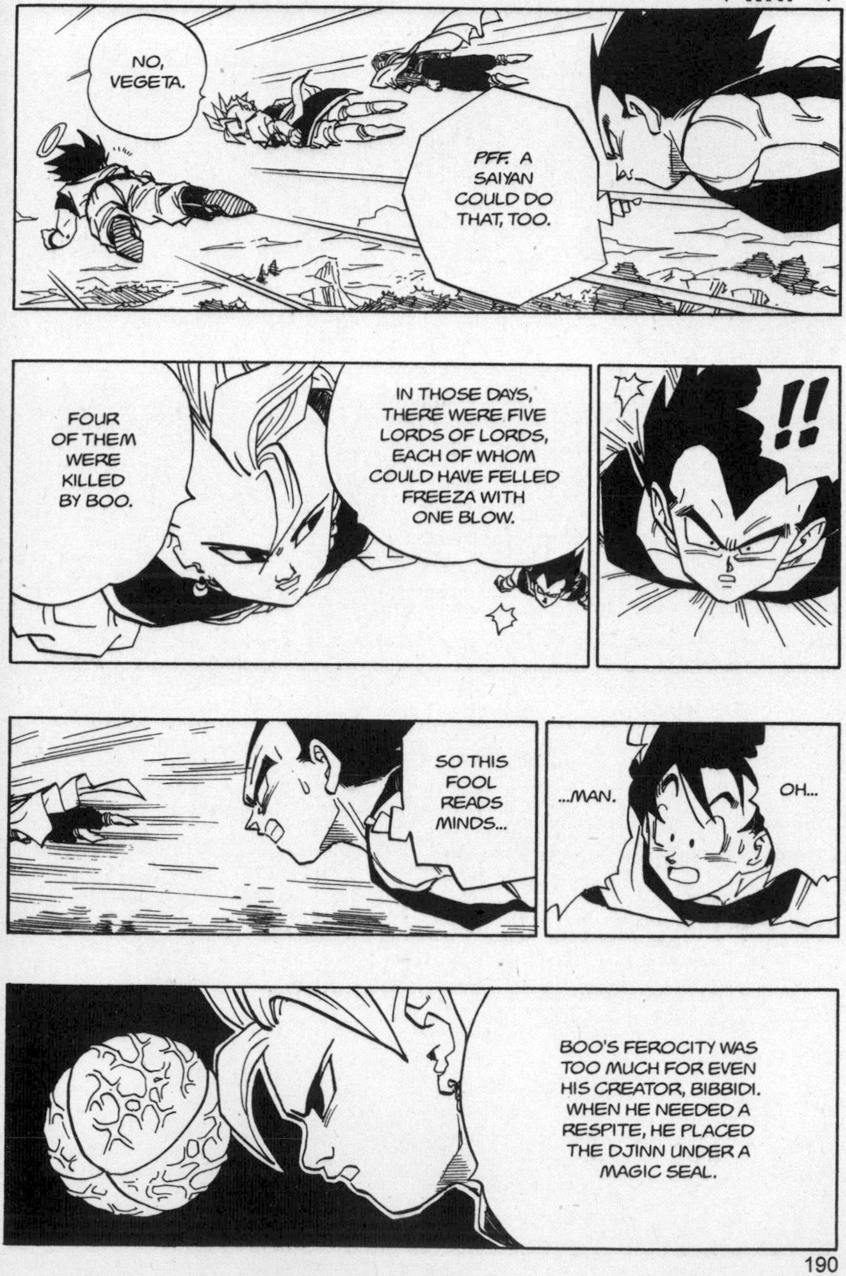

PFF. A SAIYAN COULD DO THAT, TOO.
NO, VEGETA.
!!
IN THOSE DAYS, THERE WERE FIVE LORDS OF LORDS, EACH OF WHOM COULD HAVE FELLED FREEZA WITH ONE BLOW.
FOUR OF THEM WERE KILLED BY BOO.
OH...
...MAN.
SO THIS FOOL READS MINDS...
BOO'S FEROCITY WAS TOO MUCH FOR EVEN HIS CREATOR, BIBBIDI. WHEN HE NEEDED A RESPITE, HE PLACED THE DJINN UNDER A MAGIC SEAL.

READ THIS WAY

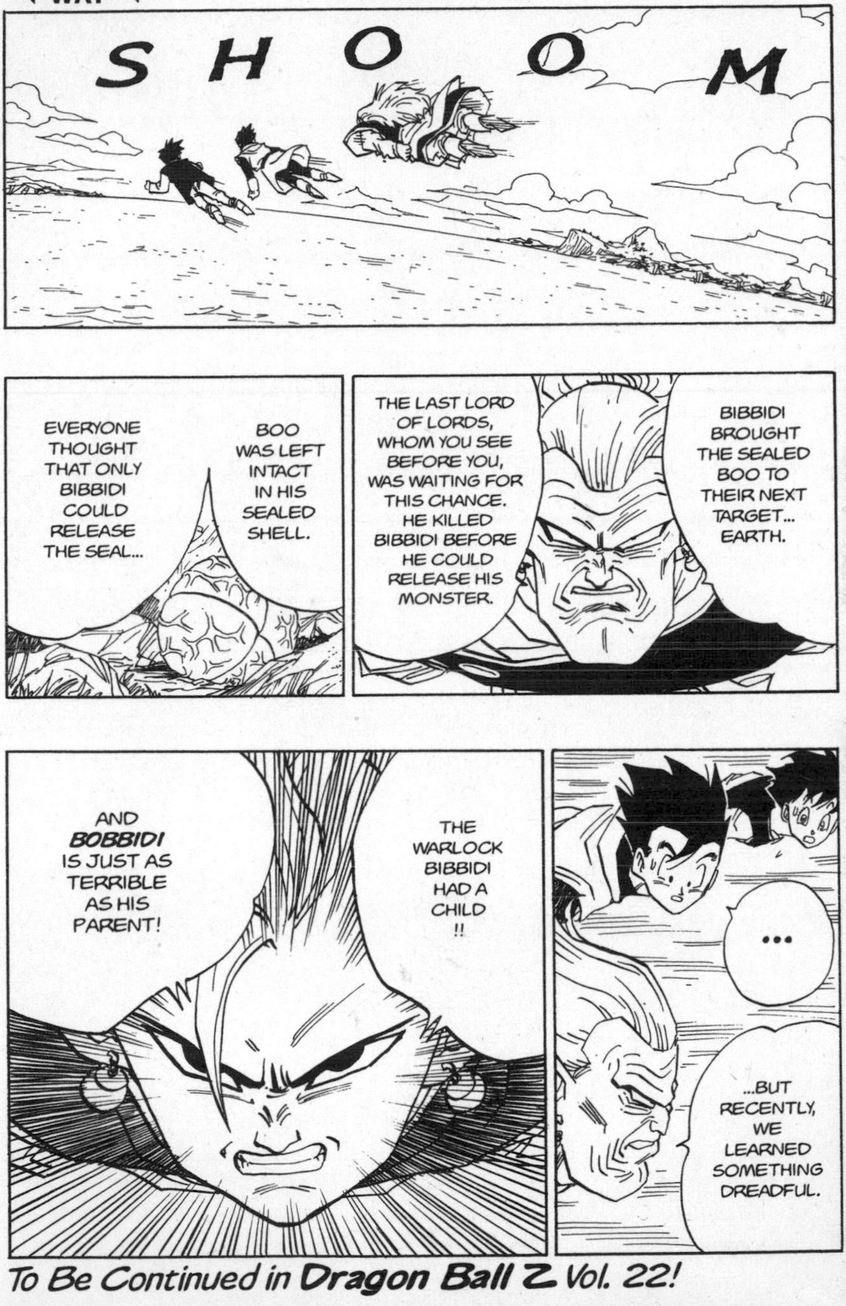
S H O O M
BIBBIDI BROUGHT THE SEALED BOO TO THEIR NEXT TARGET... EARTH.
THE LAST LORD OF LORDS, WHOM YOU SEE BEFORE YOU, WAS WAITING FOR THIS CHANCE. HE KILLED BIBBIDI BEFORE HE COULD RELEASE HIS MONSTER.
BOO WAS LEFT INTACT IN HIS SEALED SHELL.
EVERYONE THOUGHT THAT ONLY BIBBIDI COULD RELEASE THE SEAL...
...
...BUT RECENTLY, WE LEARNED SOMETHING DREADFUL.
THE WARLOCK BIBBIDI HAD A CHILD !!
AND *BOBBIDI* IS JUST AS TERRIBLE AS HIS PARENT!

To Be Continued in **Dragon Ball Z** Vol. 22!

IN THE NEXT VOLUME…
The Lord of Lords, mightiest of the deities, needs the help of Goku, Gohan and Vegeta! From across aeons of time, from across the stars, the evil wizard Bobbidi has returned, gathering *chi* energy to resurrect the imprisoned djinn Boo, the most powerful creature that ever existed. Beneath the ground in a buried spaceship, Bobbidi has assembled a menagerie of vicious beasts from across the galaxy, ready to defeat our heroes and feed their power to the djinn. But the most vicious enemy of all is one our heroes already know…

AVAILABLE NOW!

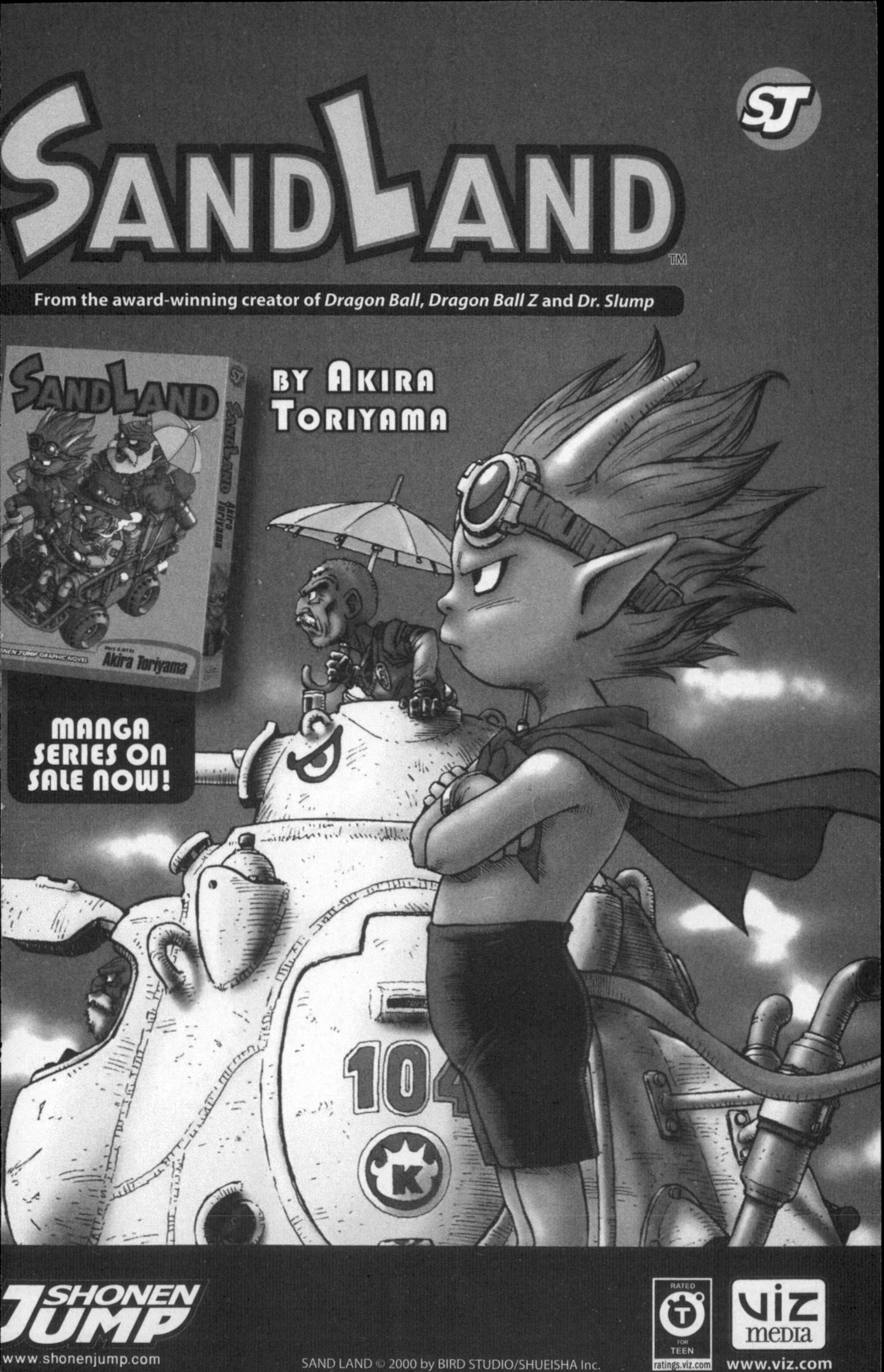
SAND LAND™
SJ
From the award-winning creator of Dragon Ball, Dragon Ball Z and Dr. Slump
BY AKIRA TORIYAMA
MANGA SERIES ON SALE NOW!
Akira Toriyama
SHONEN JUMP
www.shonenjump.com
SAND LAND © 2000 by BIRD STUDIO/SHUEISHA Inc.
RATED T FOR TEEN
ratings.viz.com
VIZ media
www.viz.com

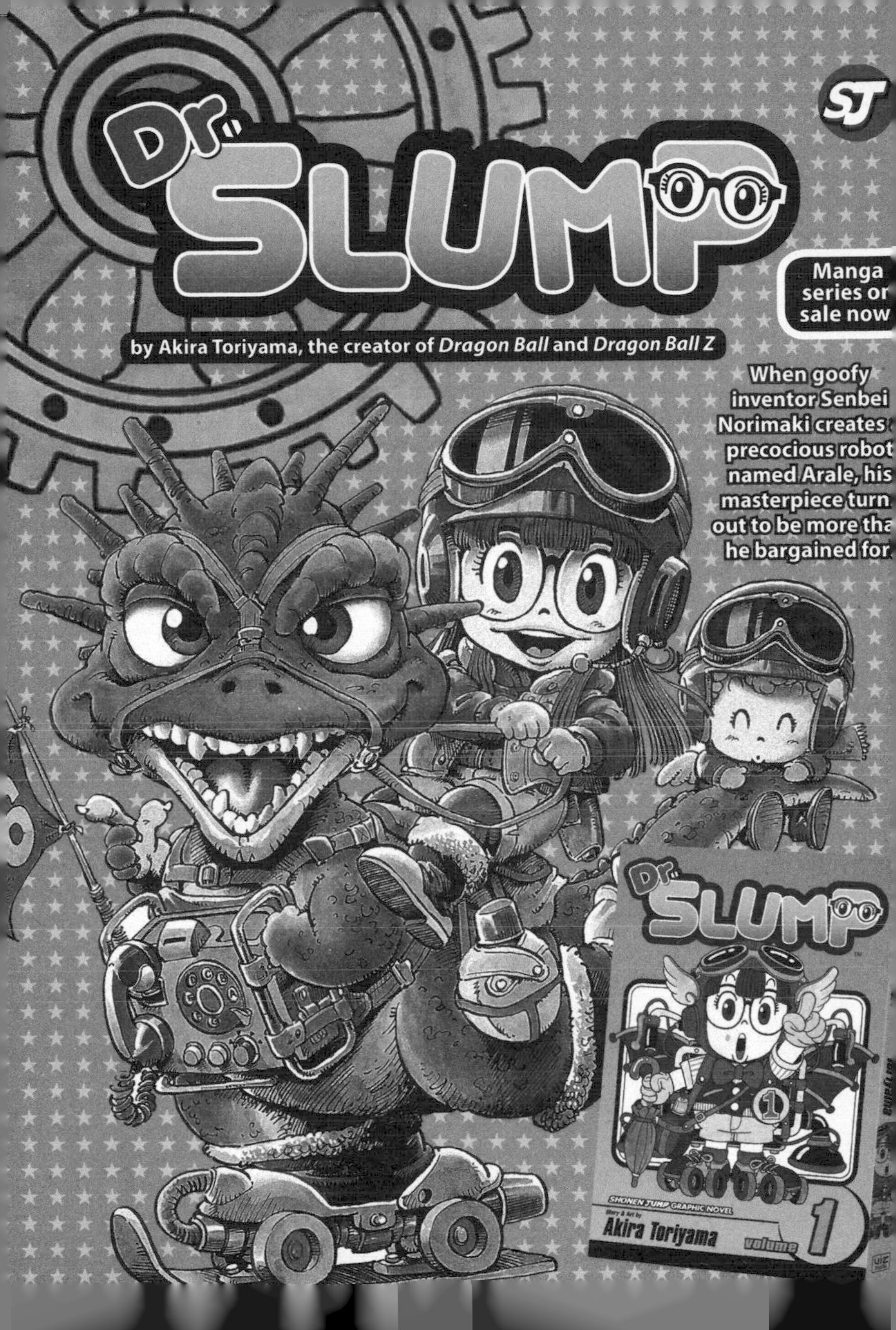

SJ
Dr. SLUMP
Manga
series or
sale now
by Akira Toriyama, the creator of Dragon Ball and Dragon Ball Z
When goofy
inventor Senbei
Norimaki creates
precocious robot
named Arale, his
masterpiece turn
out to be more tha
he bargained for.
Dr. SLUMP
SHONEN JUMP GRAPHIC NOVEL
Akira Toriyama
volume 1

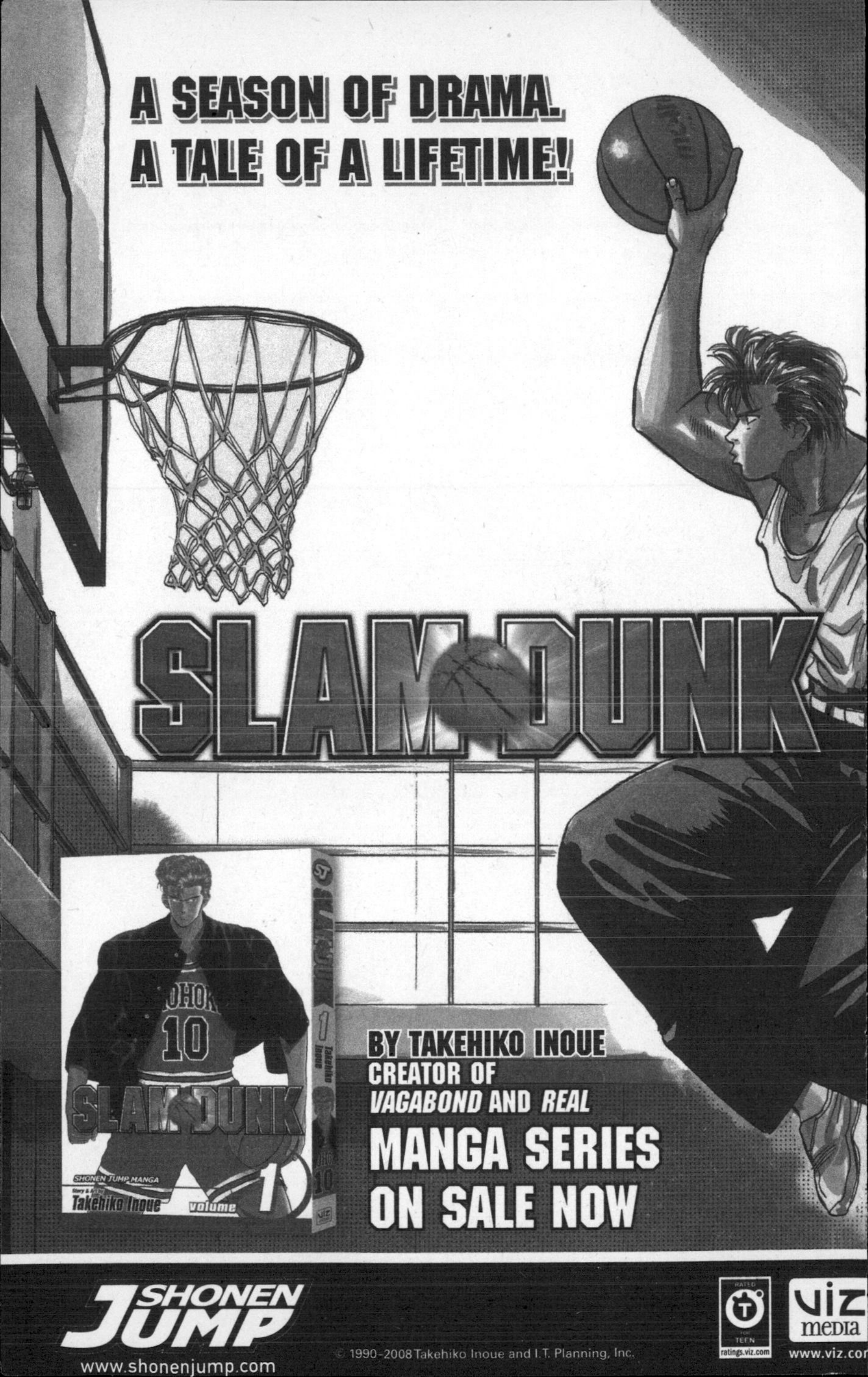
A SEASON OF DRAMA.
A TALE OF A LIFETIME!
SLAM DUNK
SHOHOKU
10
SLAM DUNK
SHONEN JUMP MANGA
Story & Art by
Takehiko Inoue
volume 1
SLAM DUNK 1 Takehiko Inoue
BY TAKEHIKO INOUE
CREATOR OF
VAGABOND AND REAL
MANGA SERIES
ON SALE NOW
SHONEN JUMP
www.shonenjump.com
© 1990-2008 Takehiko Inoue and I.T. Planning, Inc.
RATED T FOR TEEN
ratings.viz.com
VIZ media
www.viz.com

THE BEST SELLING MANGA SERIES IN THE WORLD!

ONE PIECE

Story & Art by EIICHIRO ODA

As a child, **Monkey D. Luffy** was inspired to become a pirate by listening to the tales of the buccaneer "Red-Haired" Shanks. But Luffy's life changed when he accidentally ate the Gum-Gum Devil Fruit and gained the power to stretch like rubber...at the cost of never being able to swim again! Years later, still vowing to become the king of the pirates, Luffy sets out on his adventure in search of the legendary "One Piece," said to be the greatest treasure in the world...

ratings.viz.com   www.shonenjump.com   www.viz.com

A PREMIUM BOX SET OF THE FIRST TWO STORY ARCS OF ONE PIECE!

A PIRATE'S TREASURE FOR ANY MANGA FAN!

STORY AND ART BY EIICHIRO ODA

As a child, Monkey D. Luffy dreamed of becoming King of the Pirates. But his life changed when he accidentally gained the power to stretch like rubber...at the cost of never being able to swim again! Years later, Luffy sets off in search of the "One Piece," said to be the greatest treasure in the world...

This box set includes VOLUMES 1-23, which comprise the EAST BLUE and BAROQUE WORKS story arcs.

EXCLUSIVE PREMIUMS and GREAT SAVINGS
over buying the individual volumes!

You're Reading in the Wrong Direction!!

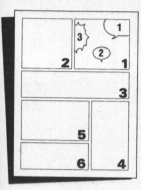

Whoops! Guess what? You're starting at the wrong end of the comic!

...It's true! In keeping with the original Japanese format, Akira Toriyama's world-famous **Dragon Ball Z** series is meant to be read from right to left, starting in the upper-right corner.

Unlike English which is read from left to right, Japanese is read from right to left, meaning that action, sound effects and word-balloon order are completely reversed... something which can make readers unfamiliar with Japanese feel pretty backwards themselves. For this reason, manga or Japanese comics published in the U.S. in English have traditionally been published "flopped"—that is, printed in exact reverse order, as though seen from the other side of a mirror.

By flopping pages, U.S. publishers can avoid confusing readers, but the compromise is not without its downside. For one thing, a character in a flopped manga series who, in the original Japanese version, wore a T-shirt emblazoned with "M A Y" (as in "the merry month of") now wears one which reads "Y A M"! Additionally, many manga creators in Japan are themselves unhappy with the process, as some feel the mirror-imaging of their art skews their original intentions.

In recognition of the importance and popularity of **Dragon Ball Z**, we are proud to bring it to you in the original unflopped format.

For now, though, turn to the other side of the book and let the adventure begin...!

—Editor